# The Gendered Impacts
# of Liberalization

# Routledge/UNRISD Research in Gender and Development

**United Nations Research Institute for Social Development**

UNRISD is an autonomous agency engaging in multidisciplinary research on the social dimensions of contemporary problems affecting development. Its work is guided by the conviction that, for effective development policies to be formulated, an understanding of the social and political context is crucial. The Institute attempts to provide governments, development agencies, grassroots organizations and scholars with a better understanding of how development policies and processes of economic, social and environmental change affect different social groups. Working through an extensive network of national research centres, UNRISD aims to promote original research and strengthen research capacity in developing countries.

Current research programmes include: Civil Society and Social Movements; Democracy, Governance and Well-Being; Gender and Development; Identities, Conflict and Cohesion; Markets, Business and Regulation; and Social Policy and Development. For further information on UNRISD work, visit www.unrisd.org.

# The Gendered Impacts of Liberalization

## Towards "Embedded Liberalism"?

**Edited by Shahra Razavi**

Routledge
Taylor & Francis Group
New York   London

First published 2009
by Routledge
270 Madison Ave, New York, NY 10016

Simultaneously published in the UK
by Routledge
2 Park Square, Milton Park, Abingdon, Oxon OX14 4RN

*Routledge is an imprint of the Taylor & Francis Group, an informa business*

Typeset in Sabon by IBT Global.
Printed and bound in the United States of America on acid-free paper by IBT Global.

*Library of Congress Cataloging in Publication Data*

The gendered impacts of liberalization : towards "embedded liberalism"? / edited by Shahra Razavi.
   p. cm. — (Routledge/UNRISD research in gender and development ; 6)
   Includes bibliographical references and index.
   1. Women—Employment—Cross-cultural studies. 2. Globalization—Economic aspects—Cross-cultural studies. 3. Globalization—Social aspects—Cross-cultural studies. 4. Women in rural development—Cross-cultural studies. 5. Women in development—Cross-cultural studies. 6. Women—Social conditions—Cross-cultural studies. I. Razavi, Shahrashoub.
   HD6053.G4635 2008
   331.4—dc22
   2008029197

ISBN10: 0-415-95650-1 (hbk)
ISBN10: 0-203-88403-5 (ebk)

ISBN13: 978-0-415-95650-5 (hbk)
ISBN13: 978-0-203-88403-4 (ebk)

# Contents

## PART I
## Rural Livelihoods under Liberalization

## PART II
## Informalization and Feminization of Labour

# Figures

# Boxes

# Tables

# Foreword

This volume asks two key questions: How have gender inequalities in access to resources and opportunities been affected by three decades of experimentation with the liberalization of the economy? How, and to what extent, has the (re)discovery of social concerns and social policies made a difference, by either disrupting or entrenching gender inequalities?

The idea that unregulated markets need to be "re-embedded" in society, in a Polanyian sense, for capitalist transformation to be politically and socially sustainable now features prominently in commentaries on market liberalization (and "globalization"). But such analyses rarely draw attention to the *gender dimensions* of both market liberalization and the quest for re-embedding them through social policies. This volume seeks to address this lacuna by providing a gendered account of liberalization policies and their impacts, within agrarian and non-agrarian contexts of sub-Saharan Africa, South Asia and Latin America, followed by an assessment of selected social policies (or anti-poverty programmes, as they are often called) that seek to respond to the inevitable social dislocations.

"Re-embedding" the economy, and doing so in a way that facilitates a more harmonious integration between the twin goals of production and social reproduction, requires the strengthening of publicly accountable systems of mutual assurance against entitlement failure. This means investing in areas that orthodox prescriptions cannot countenance: well-functioning and accessible public health, education and care services; labour standards and rights that protect women's employment and conditions of work; and public provision of a range of complementary services to support the care economy. It is clear that states in many different contexts are putting in place social programmes to address the adverse outcomes of liberalization policies. The full potential of these positive moves, however, is vitiated by the fact that debate over economic development and macroeconomic policy has fallen off the agenda instead of forming an integral part of the current policy rethinking. There is a lack of affinity and complementarity between "social policies" and "economic policies", a failure to rethink "economic" policies through a "social" perspective, so that "economic" policies and "social" policies can work in tandem.

xiv   *Foreword*

Many of the chapters that appear in this volume were commissioned as background papers for the 2005 UNRISD report, *Gender Equality: Striving for Justice in an Unequal World*. UNRISD would like to thank the European Union, the Department for Research Co-operation of the Swedish International Development Cooperation Agency (Sida/SAREC), the International Development Research Centre (IDRC, Ottawa, Canada) and the government of the Netherlands for their financial support for making this work possible.

Thandika Mkandawire<br>
Director, UNRISD

# Acknowledgments

I am indebted to many individuals for making this volume possible. First and foremost are the chapter authors who responded positively to our invitation, who produced high-quality research papers, drawing on their own original research in many cases, and who responded with patience and good humour to several rounds of comments and requests for updates. Many of the authors had been commissioned by UNRISD to produce background papers for the Institute's contribution to the Beijing+10 process, *Gender Equality: Striving for Justice in an Unequal World* (2005). Others were invited subsequently to write chapters on themes and issues that would enrich and shape the arguments of the volume.

I would also like to thank the various individuals who acted as anonymous referees in this process. Some of the chapters were read by friends and colleagues who provided very helpful comments and suggestions for revision. I am particularly grateful to the referee who was asked by UNRISD to review the full volume; the detailed comments provided on individual chapters, as well as more overarching reflections on the volume, were both useful and impressive.

I owe a particular debt to three colleagues at UNRISD: Eleanor Hutchinson who stepped in and provided excellent research assistance, Anita Tombez who provided invaluable support in copy-editing the manuscript and preparing it for publication and Jenifer Freedman who managed a smooth refereeing process (despite my failure to meet her deadline!).

Shahra Razavi
UNRISD, Geneva
30 May 2008

# 1  The Gendered Impacts of Liberalization
## Towards "Embedded Liberalism"?

*Shahra Razavi*

## INTRODUCTION

In the last two decades economic policies have reflected a drive for accelerated global economic integration ("globalization"), which is usually associated with greater economic liberalization, both internationally and within national economies. Components of the liberalization agenda have included trade and financial liberalization, deflationary macroeconomic policies, fiscal restraint, privatization of state-owned enterprises, labour market liberalization and the introduction of market principles ("quasi markets") into public management and the provisioning of public services. While the orthodox prescriptions may have ended hyperinflation, the costs of doing so are now widely perceived to have been unacceptable, in terms of falling wages, rising poverty, sharp declines in employment and rising inequality, not to mention the shifting of the burden of social reproduction onto households and families, in particular women and girls who shoulder a disproportionate share of the unpaid work that is necessary for household reproduction.[1]

In the late 1980s, as a response to mounting criticisms and public protests, global policy pronouncements became less assertive about the imperative of cutting social spending, more apologetic about the imposition of user fees on public services and began to acknowledge that social policy could have a positive role to play in the development process.

The 1990s were marked by financial crises which wreaked havoc with the real economies and livelihoods of people in countries as diverse as Mexico, the Republic of Korea and Russia. The 1997 Asian financial crisis was a defining moment which prompted the Group of Seven (G7) to request the World Bank to formulate "social principles" and "good practice of social policy" as a guide to policymakers worldwide (Holzmann and Jorgensen 2000:2). Some of the subsequent work on social protection within the World Bank was reflected in its *World Development Report: Attacking Poverty* (World Bank 2000), which identified "social risk management" (SRM) as the most sustainable basis for coping with risk and reducing the vulnerability of the poor. In the SRM approach, which was subsequently adopted by other multilateral lending agencies, the state was expected to provide "risk management instruments *where the private sector fails*", in addition to social safety nets for risk-coping for the most vulnerable (Holzmann and Jorgensen 2000:18; my emphasis). The continuities with the earlier generation of residual safety nets were unmistakable, reconfirming that social security should no longer reside solely with the state and shifting a greater share of the responsibility for its provision to the market and to families and individuals who now had to make their own provisions against risk.

The post-Washington consensus thus seemed to embrace some of the concerns that had been hitherto voiced by critics, such as poverty reduction, social protection and "good governance", yet without abandoning the neoliberal basics centred on economic liberalization, fiscal restraint and a nimble state that facilitates the integration of people into the market. Indeed, there seems to be widespread adherence today to the view that if neoliberal globalization (that is, economic liberalization, both domestic and external) is to stay on course, then it must be "tamed" or "embedded" (Ruggie 2003) through social policies and anti-poverty programmes which have mushroomed across a wide range of countries over the past decade or so.

The concept of "embedded liberalism", as we explain later, was initially coined by Ruggie (1982) to refer to the institutional arrangements put in place after the Second World War in many Western capitalist countries, to share the costs of open markets through social protection and other forms of intervention (such as wage restraint by trade unions in return for employment creation on the part of capital). The notion drew on Karl Polanyi's (1957) ground-breaking analysis of the "double movement" in the early years of industrialization in Britain—how the social disruptions brought about by unregulated market forces, or the "disembedding" of markets from society, gave rise to the need for a "counter-movement" to bring markets under societal control. These concepts feature regularly in the writings of those concerned about the social ramifications of deregulated markets in the present era (Standing 1999b; Ruggie 2003), but they are rarely used to draw attention to the *gender dimensions* of liberalized markets and the quest for re-embedding them (Kabeer 2007).

This volume seeks to address this lacuna by providing a gendered account of liberalization policies and their impacts, beginning in Part One with the rural economies of sub-Saharan Africa, Asia and Latin America and moving on to the urban informal economies in Part Two. Part Three provides a detailed account of some of the current efforts being made in a variety of countries to respond to the social dislocations caused by economic liberalization, by putting in place social assistance and anti-poverty measures. Here the chapters pose two cross-cutting questions. First, what assumptions about women's and men's roles and gender relations underpin these efforts? And second, how are these programmes in turn entrenching and/or disrupting existing gender relations and inequalities?

## AGRARIAN RESTRUCTURING

The economic crisis of the early 1980s was diagnosed by the international financial institutions to stem from heavy state involvement in the economy. The agricultural sector, it was argued, was a prime victim of state-directed economic regimes marked by "urban bias": The heavy drainage of agricultural surplus through forced indirect taxation depressed farming incomes and led to the poor performance of the agricultural sector. The "distortions" introduced by state policy were to be corrected by letting market forces determine product and input prices and the terms of trade between agriculture and the rest of the economy, while tenure insecurity was to be tackled through land titling (World Bank 1989). These standard measures, it was argued, would restore agricultural export growth and improve rural incomes and livelihoods. At the same time, cutbacks in public expenditure outlays on agricultural input subsidies, marketing boards and research and extension services were prescribed and justified on the grounds that state expenditure needed to be significantly lowered and that the benefits were, in any case, either being captured by big farmers or squandered by state officials.

There followed two decades of extensive experimentation with the liberalization of the agricultural sector, through the removal of guaranteed prices and export crop controls, the dismantling or cutting back on public provisioning to farmers (marketing, credit, inputs, infrastructure and other services) and the boost given to corporate farming for export. The three chapters in Part One of this volume—chapter 2 on sub-Saharan Africa by Ann Whitehead, chapter 3 on India by Cecile Jackson and Nitya Rao and chapter 4 on Latin America by Carmen Diana Deere—provide an account of liberalization policies shaped by regional and national specificities, an assessment of their outcomes in macro terms (growth, poverty), and a more fine-grained analysis of their gender-differentiated impacts. All three accounts draw attention to the methodological challenges involved in providing a gendered account of liberalization, given the gaps in evidence and data, and the difficulties in interpreting the existing evidence and in attributing causality. Despite the poor evidence base and the challenges of interpretation, there are some important empirical and analytical elements that emerge from their analyses.

### Growth, Poverty and Inequality

In both sub-Saharan Africa and South Asia a high proportion of the economically active population (63 and 57 per cent, respectively) continue to be engaged in agriculture, and agriculture constitutes a significant proportion (27 per cent in 2000) of the gross domestic product (GDP). Latin America, by contrast, is far more urbanized with close to one-fifth (21 per cent) of the economically active population engaged in agriculture and the sector contributing no more than one-tenth of the GDP, although the sector's contribution to export earnings (at 44 per cent) is not far behind sub-Saharan Africa's (at 52 per cent) (see table 1.1 in appendix 1.1).

After two decades of experimentation with liberalization policies, overall growth rates in most African economies remain low (with some fluctuations, and the exception of recent growth spurts due to rising commodity prices), and the impact on poverty at best patchy, if not negligible. Throughout the 1980s and 1990s as liberalization progressed, sub-Saharan Africa witnessed the steady decline of its agricultural exports as a share of world agricultural trade, while the problems surrounding food production and security remained unresolved.

What has liberalization actually involved in countries such as Tanzania and Malawi? In the early stages, guaranteed prices were removed for food crops, and the state marketing boards which governed production and trade in major agricultural products, and provided subsidies, inputs and pan-territorial pricing,[2] were weakened if not dismantled. Later in the liberalization process, the removal of export crop controls exposed farmers to both the fluctuations in world commodity prices and competition with producers in other parts of the world enjoying more favourable production regimes. Adding to this battery of policies for the agricultural sector have been policy incentives for the promotion of high-value horticultural export products (cut flowers, vegetables) often through medium- and large-scale enterprises (in countries like Kenya, Uganda, Zimbabwe, South Africa) and tourism, and the imposition of user fees on public health and education services. All of these policies and responses to them have had gender differentiated features and outcomes to which we turn in the following section.

In many places private traders and private systems of credit provision have not emerged to fill the gap left by state withdrawal, and where they have they do not often reach farmers in remote areas (given the cost), nor do private sources of credit easily reach poor farmers. Deteriorating household food security in Malawi, Zambia and Zimbabwe in the late 1990s was attributed to the loss of subsidies for fertilizers and seeds and of rural credit, and the erosion of agricultural marketing services, especially in remote areas (Abalu and Hassin 1999). The situation of cashew farmers in Tanzania and Mozambique, described in some detail by Whitehead, clearly illustrates how farming households have had to adjust to the fluctuations of world commodity prices over a short period.

The liberalization of the agricultural sector in India, which came later (in 1991) than the reforms in sub-Saharan Africa, entailed some similar policy elements interwoven with national specificities. The Indian reforms have stressed reduced state provision of extension services, institutional credit, irrigation and price support systems. At the same time the removal of quantitative restrictions and the opening up to global trade have exposed some major agricultural products (tea, coffee, cotton and rice) to global prices which were falling steadily between 1995 and 2001 (Patnaik 2003). Millions of food-grain producers too were facing competition from exceptionally low-priced foreign grain (Patnaik 2003).

Agricultural growth rates in the 1990s were sluggish (around 2 per cent per annum), especially when compared with the strong growth record of the Indian economy as a whole. Public investment in agriculture (on irrigation and flood control) has been low and declining, and there is general stagnation in agriculture and in agricultural employment. While the record on poverty remains contested, there is consensus that inequality has increased (across regions, across rural–urban divides and across occupational categories), and that food security is a serious issue for some segments of the rural population. A comparison of food consumption data (for 1993–1994 and 1999–2000) confirms worsening nutritional standards over the decade, in the midst of a highly controversial government effort to reform the Public Distribution System (PDS) which provided subsidized food items to the population. The 1990s saw swift increases in issue prices (price at which government sells grain) to match the rises in the procurement price (price at which government purchases grain); and targeting was introduced which narrowed access to subsidized food items. As a result of these measures, sales from the PDS declined and government food stocks have mounted. Critics fear that targeting has led to the exclusion of a large number of people suffering from food deficits, who are not classified as "poor" according to the criteria introduced for determining eligibility to the PDS.

For much of Latin America, during the 1980s—the first reform decade—the growth rate veered widely; this crisis-ridden period also saw an overall increase in poverty, from 41 to 48 per cent of all households. During the 1990s agricultural growth averaged only 2.2 per cent. Poverty indices improved, but only at a laggardly pace, so that Latin America entered the new millennium with a higher proportion of poor and indigent rural people than in 1980. At the same time, the economic reforms have reinforced the existing inequalities across regions, producers and products. The sectors that have experienced dynamism and growth are the non-traditional export crops (NTEC) (livestock, fruits and vegetables, oil seeds) and those that have stagnated are traditional export crops (coffee, sugar, cotton). The NTECs are produced by agribusiness firms, as well as by the more modern and capital-intensive farmers with links to agro-industry and export markets. These units have been an important source of employment in several countries, including Brazil, Chile and Mexico. Traditional export crops are generally produced by small farmers. As noted earlier in relation to sub-Saharan Africa, the pro-market reforms have effectively meant the dismantling of public support for precisely those regions, products and producers that are less competitive but important for fighting poverty.

Given the poor record of these policies the proponents of reform have increasingly accepted that agriculture's response to liberalization has been disappointing (World Bank 1994). It has also been shown that the notion of "urban bias" has in fact obscured more than it has illuminated the problems in developing country agriculture by reducing the problem to one simple cause outside the sector itself (namely, government policy bias), while ignoring the resource transfers into agriculture (Karshenas 2004). In other words, while agricultural prices may have been artificially depressed due to an overvalued exchange rate and export taxes, this was to varying degrees redressed through positive resource transfers into the sector via public investment, subsidized credit and agricultural services (Spoor 2002).

## The Gendered Impacts of Liberalization

Assessing the gendered impacts of liberalization policies is difficult, especially given the already mentioned gaps and deficiencies in existing surveys and databases. National agricultural statistics, for example, as well as international databases that are constructed by the Food and Agricultue Organization (FAO) (using national sources) provide ample data on crops and production methods. But as Whitehead notes, these are inadequate for a gender analysis because they say very little about the people (women, men) who are growing and producing these crops, and their relationships to each other. This means that information about women who are own-account farmers, but not heads of their households, is particularly sparse—a phenomenon that is widespread in many African rural economies.

National labour force surveys are supposed to cover the population residing in rural areas and to provide data on their economic activities. While efforts have been made over the past three decades to capture more adequately women's economic activities, and while recent surveys provide more accurate estimates of women's work, the nature of women's work—the fact that much of it is seasonal, unpaid ("family labour"), subsistence based and small-scale (tending a garden or small number of animals, processing of crops)—means that it is likely to remain undercounted. Hence, making comparisons of women's economic activity rates *over time* is highly problematic. With respect to Latin American labour force data, for example, Deere questions the evidence emerging from these surveys, which points to rural women's concentration in non-agricultural occupations. Her contention is that women's agricultural activities, both seasonal wage work and own-account farming, continue to be underenumerated in these large-scale surveys.

### Assets, Labour and Social Provisioning: A Gendered Analysis

Understanding the gendered impacts of liberalization in the agrarian economy requires simultaneous attention to at least three sets of interconnected institutions that shape women's and men's capacities to seize opportunities opened up by liberalization policies and to cope with the risks and fall-outs of those same policies. We refer to these three institutional arenas in a stylized fashion as assets, labour and social provisioning, and further suggest that all three are gendered.

*Assets*

The chapter by Whitehead, in particular, elaborates the gender-differentiated constraints to women's and men's access to capital and land, with reference to the rural economies of sub-Saharan Africa. Her analysis questions the rather simplistic view in some policy and advocacy circles that attributes in a blanket fashion rural women's poverty to their lack of access to land. Although in some cases women's smaller land-bases are due to their inferior property rights under customary practices, this is not the case everywhere. She emphasizes the great variation in the claims that women can make to land—as wives, widows and in their own right—and the strength of those claims in many settings, although in some contexts women's strong claims to land have weakened as a result of severe land scarcity and competition (for example, Uganda).[3] In some areas of sub-Saharan Africa marked by severe land scarcity, an inability to access land constitutes a constraint on women's farming; in other areas, women smallholders experience other constraints (inadequate access to labour and other inputs). Although women farm much less land than do men, this is not always because women are prevented from accessing land, but because they lack capital to hire labour, purchase inputs and access marketing channels.

The issue of land scarcity and the constraints it imposes on women's land claims also emerges from Jackson and Rao's chapter on India, where land is increasingly scarce and commoditized and where the average size of per capita land holding has declined over the 1990s (see table 3.3 in chapter 3). In India, they claim, growing land scarcity has intensified male competition and created additional constraints to women's usufruct, trusteeship and ownership rights.[4] Some Indian states, such as Haryana, have seen the rising popularity of widow remarriage to a husband's brother, cousin or other agnatic relative, sometimes under compulsion, in order to keep the land within the family. The pressure to keep land within the community, especially marginalized communities (tribals), has also undermined women's inheritance rights, on the pretext that if women are allowed to inherit, then non-tribal men would marry them in order to acquire the land.

While women's access to land seems to have become more constrained in India, the reverse seems to be happening as far as their access to capital/credit is concerned. The provision of microcredit to women in India (and other countries of South Asia) has been hailed as one of the main advances of the past two decades—one of the demands made in the Beijing Platform for Action that seems to have received a positive response. While the provision of microcredit has not eradicated poverty or produced successful female entrepreneurs across the board, it is generating some positive outcomes. It has, for example, provided some options for women's self-employment and assisted household reproduction. It has also enhanced women's self-assertiveness and thus produced some shifts in conjugal and gender relations. This may, in turn, be one of the reasons for the reported increase in intrahousehold tensions and conflicts among women recipients of microcredit (Goetz and Sengupta 1996). However, at a broader level, the provision of microcredit for women may indeed be paving the way to a two-tier system in which women have excellent credit access but only to small amounts (to help household reproduction), while men access bank loans which are large enough for significant investments, as our authors suggest.

## Labour Markets

Labour markets are understood here very broadly to include both formal and informal *wage* labour markets as well as *quasi* labour markets where workers sell a product or service, but within a set of dependent relationships that limit their authority over the employment arrangement (such as subcontracted production and different forms of self-employment which are essentially disguised forms of wage labour) (Heintz 2008). A cross-cutting argument that emerges from the chapters in Part One is that livelihood strategies in agrarian economies are increasingly diversified to include not only wage labour in agriculture (on both small farms and large-scale corporate units), but also non-farm work. This should not come as a surprise after what was said earlier about land scarcity and falling per capita land availability.

One striking feature of agrarian change and industrialization in contemporary developing societies to which many observers have drawn attention is the growing prevalence of what is sometimes referred to as livelihood diversification, defined as "the process by which rural families construct a diverse portfolio of activities and social support capabilities in their struggle for survival and in order to improve their standard of living" (Ellis 1998:4; Bryceson 1999). Diversification captures several different economic processes and its blanket use to describe all forms of non-farm employment is misleading. It is particularly important, from the point of view of thinking about poverty, to distinguish between diversification as a survival strategy (which it very often is) and diversification that feeds into a process of accumulation. The fact that "poorer countries today confront more formidable barriers to comprehensive industrialization—and *a fortiori* to the generation of comparable levels of industrial employment—than did the advanced industrial countries in the past" (Bernstein 2004:204), is an important part of what drives this process. For vast sections of the population, both female and male, this means a constant search for income through wage work and "self-employment" (often thinly disguised forms of wage work) away from the village. Thus, work on the household plot (if there is one) becomes articulated with other forms of work (paid or unpaid, formal or informal, industrial or services) beyond the agricultural sector and indeed very often beyond the confines of the village (Breman 1996).

Clearly women have become more visible in the agricultural labour force, as casual and seasonal wage workers in some regions and countries. While such work is not adequately captured in labour force surveys to allow detailed analysis of the numbers involved, their wages, and changes in both dimensions over time, the evidence analysed by Deere for Latin America suggests that corporate farming of NTECs has increased absolute employment opportunities for women in agriculture, given the highly labour-intensive nature of production and packing (compared to traditional agricultural exports such as coffee and bananas). The promotion of corporate farming for export has been happening on a much smaller scale in sub-Saharan Africa (although Kenya, South Africa and Zimbabwe may be exceptions) and India, where women's agricultural employment remains largely confined to more traditional farming enterprises and smallholder agriculture where they work as casual and daily labourers (*ganyu* labour in Malawi, seasonal harvest workers across India), often paid on a piece-rate basis and receiving far lower wages than men.

Interestingly though, "traditional" gender stratifications have reproduced themselves within the "modern" corporate farming enterprises, with women largely confined to the more seasonal and repetitive tasks while men assume the few permanent positions. The occupational segregation by gender contributes to lower wages for women. As generations of political economists and sociologists have argued, contrary to the abstract market of neoclassical textbooks, real markets are political (and social) constructs infused with social norms and regulations. This also means that wages and conditions of work can change if workers are able to organize in pursuit of their interests. Deere, for example, reports that by the 1990s conditions of work and wages of workers in the largely female-dominated flower industry in Colombia had improved and the gender wage gap significantly narrowed, largely due to the pressure exerted by workers' organizations and non-governmental organizations (NGOs). It is also worth underlining that, while wages in the horticultural export sector may be unfavourable by international standards, they are often far better than those prevailing elsewhere in the rural economy (for data on Kenya, see Heintz 2008).

The other important issue that arises from our three chapters, especially the one on sub-Saharan Africa, is that women and men are positioned very differently in relation to the changes in economic behaviour, which liberalization both requires and brings about. The entry costs to different kinds of non-farm, income-generating activities are a major fact affecting men's and women's locations in these economies. Women's constrained access to capital and other resources (hired labour or unpaid labour of others), along with gender biases in markets and the social norms and social networks that shape them, have the affect of clustering women in low-entry and low-return off-farm activities, which yield little surplus for investing back in agriculture or the off-farm activity itself. Whitehead also raises a critically important point which may further limit women's access to high-return activities, and this concerns the nature of their skills. In rural areas the skills individuals acquire are largely through "informal education and invisible training" which take place in the household or community and segregate women and men into different activities. These activities are rewarded at different levels—not so much a reflection of the intrinsic complexity of the tasks involved, but rather according to who has them, with women's skills often accruing less reward by virtue of their being female tasks.

## Social Provisioning

In the rural areas of many developing countries, the contribution of the state to social provisioning tends to be much less significant than in urban areas (which have more political visibility), and in any case far from comprehensive. In the rural economies under consideration, providing care for the young, old and sick, attending to the physical and emotional needs of other household members, preparing food, cleaning and mending clothes, utensils and homes, fetching water and firewood, are all time-consuming responsibilities which are overwhelmingly assigned to women and girls. This constitutes the bedrock of social provisioning that sustains and reproduces the household over time. As Jackson and Rao rightly remind us, livelihood research pays lip-service to these activities but there are still too few studies which collect data on this "invisible" part of the rural economy, alongside descriptions and analyses of employment and farm production. Within some strands of mainstream research on employment (Anker et al. 2003; Melkas and Anker 2003) it is now recognized that women's participation in the paid workforce (its duration, continuity and degree of formality), and in rural economies women's ability to respond to market opportunities and incentives (Collier 1989), have much to do with how households and societies arrange the provision of unpaid care.

It is also encouraging that increasing numbers of developing countries are now undertaking time use surveys (sometimes also called time budget surveys). These surveys aim to provide information on what activities people do over a given time period (generally a day or a week) as well as how much time they spend on each of the different specified activities (Budlender 2007). While differing in scope and purpose, one of the common aims of these surveys has been to provide better information on the work done by different categories of people (male and female, in particular), and to highlight the time spent on unpaid activities that are generally either underrecorded in other surveys or not recorded at all (Budlender 2007). Such progress notwithstanding, it is still not feasible to answer the important question often posed in feminist research as to what happens to women's unpaid care burdens under the impact of liberalization policies with rigorous data. There are very few developing countries that have more than one time use survey (with comparable methodologies) to allow comparisons of unpaid care burdens to be made *over time* so as to assess the impacts of liberalization policies. It is often through in-depth case studies and ethnographic research that researchers have been able to tackle this difficult question.

### Feminization of Agriculture?

So to conclude this subsection, has agriculture become feminized over the past two decades as a result of liberalization? Feminization of agriculture, as some of our authors underline, is an ambiguous term and needs to be unpacked. Does it refer to the increasing rates of participation by women in the agricultural labour force (either as own-account farmers or wage labourers)—relative to women's participation in other sectors (industry, services), or relative to men? Or does it refer to a rise in the share of the agricultural labour force that is female (because of higher female activity rates in agriculture, or because men's share is declining)? Or alternatively, does feminization of agriculture refer to the deterioration in the quality of agricultural work in some regards, that is, its casualization?

For Latin America, Deere contends that several overlapping processes over the past 30 years have contributed to changes in the gender division of labour among smallholders, sometimes described as a tendency towards the "feminization of agriculture." The leading cause has been the emergence of a class of impoverished and dispossessed smallholders, a process which gained momentum in the 1960s and 1970s, and is generally associated with men becoming landless or land-poor labourers. Male participation in temporary wage labour, particularly when it involves seasonal migration, has everywhere been associated with higher female participation in agriculture. During the liberalization era, women's participation in agriculture appears to have changed: they are no longer merely "secondary" workers. Women are emerging as farm managers, providing the bulk of family farm labour and taking on extra tasks as men migrate in search of alternative sources of income. By withdrawing direct state support to domestic food production, agricultural reform has galvanized this process. In addition, the export boom associated with NTEC has intensified the demand for female labour in the agricultural wage labour market, both absolutely and relative to men.

The feminization of agriculture in India has taken a different form. Between 1972–1973 and 1999–2000, the proportion of rural workers in agriculture declined from 84 to 76 per cent. This was largely due to male workers moving out of agriculture entirely, while women substantially remained. Since 1987–1988, whatever absorption there was of women into the non-agricultural sector has slowed down, and since the economic reform programme began in 1991, the deceleration has been dramatic. Indeed, rural women's employment at the all-India level has shown remarkable stability over the years. In 1961, nearly 90 per cent of rural women workers were in agriculture; in 1994 the figure was 86 per cent, a marginal drop, and it reached 83.5 per cent in 2005. Women comprise an increasingly important proportion of the casual labour force in rural areas, as men withdraw from agriculture into other occupations. Some analysts therefore claim that rural India has also been witnessing a feminization of agriculture (Agarwal 2003). But feminization of agricultural wage labour—often fieldwork of the most laborious, worst paid and lowest-status kind—is not the same as the feminization of farm management. As far as India is concerned, there is little evidence that farm management is being assumed by women.

## THE INFORMALIZATION OF LABOUR

Industrial growth has historically been the *sine qua non* of massive poverty reduction by absorbing the labour force that is released from agriculture. In developing countries, industrial and manufacturing growth has remained anemic in recent decades, with the exception of East Asia (Byres 2003). Indeed, one of the remarkable features of structural change in contemporary developing countries has been the disproportionate shift of the labour force from agriculture to services (rather than to industry), which is ominous, as much of this can be thinly disguised survival strategies indicative of a desperate effort to turn to anything that might be available (which happens to fall under the "services" rubric) (Byres 2003). Global competition facilitated through trade liberalization and state reluctance, or incapacity, to play a catalytic role in the provision of infrastructure and technical support to domestic firms are partly to blame for the low rates of growth and the lack of structural transformation that many developing countries have been witnessing. At the same time, the informal economy has been growing, composed of various forms of self-employment as well as informal wage work (in formal or informal enterprises), deeply segmented by gender, class, ethnicity and other social markers. Some countries have witnessed significant outmigration of their working-age population, both female and male, to neighbouring countries and further afield in search of paid work. This is, in turn, reshaping care arrangements and social reproduction regimes in communities and countries of origin as well as those of destination.

This is the context within which the four chapters in Part Two of this volume are located. Dzodzi Tsikata in chapter 5 and Jayati Ghosh in chapter 6 explore the changing prospects and conditions of women's paid work within the urban economies of sub-Saharan Africa and Asia, respectively. While liberalization policies have taken hold in different moments, under different political and economic conditions, and entailed very different outcomes in these two (themselves highly heterogeneous) regions, the informalization of labour, the marginalization of employment from the policy agenda and the persistent gender stratifications of paid work and unpaid work are some of the common themes that emerge from their analyses. In chapter 7, Martha Altar Chen elaborates further the informal economy by exposing its heterogeneity, its gendered structures and its significance beyond developing regions, followed by an assessment of the different political and policy responses currently being advocated to deal with the problem of "informality". Paid work, whether formal or informal, does not produce growth and social development on its own. The other essential ingredient, often overseen and taken for granted by policy actors, is the care and reproduction of human beings. In chapter 8, Nicola Yeates draws attention to the regulations and restrictions that govern the flow of people not blessed with elite membership across borders in an age when finance capital has been "freed" from all restrictions. The specific issue she explores is how the cross-border migration of women from the countries of the "periphery" to the "core" is reshaping care regimes in both contexts and in turn reproducing (old) global patterns of inequality more broadly.

## Industrial Development: The Role of Markets and States

Asia, or more accurately northeast Asia, had seen high-capacity developmental states guide the economy, dominated by big business and intermediated by the banking system. "The normative glue that held the system together," as Meredith Jung-En Woo (2007:xii) has put it, "was a social compact peculiar to capitalist Northeast Asia, obligating private corporations, in return for munificent financial and fiscal support from the state, to provide for societal full employment". States in southeast Asia (Malaysia, Indonesia, Thailand), most commentators agree, worked along less interventionist lines, with less impressive outcomes in terms of industrial growth, employment generation and poverty reduction (but were nevertheless touted by the World Bank as models for emulation) (Jomo 2003). In both contexts production of manufactured goods for export, which was highly female-dominated, played an important role in financing industrial and technological imports (in the 1960s and 1970s in northeast Asia, and from the 1980s onwards in southeast Asia). However, as the Malaysian political economist Jomo Sundaram underlines, export promotion has to be distinguished from open economic policies that are being advocated by the international financial and trade institutions (and the affluent developed countries that largely control them) to developing country governments.

> The East Asian miracle is said to have been principally due to export-led growth. But as various studies suggest, while exports tend to rise with trade liberalization in the short term, imports also tend to rise strongly, especially if the domestic currency appreciates in real terms.

Thus, trade liberalization tends to limit or only weakly supplement domestic effective demand. Hence, while increased international trade may enhance growth, the added stimulus tends to be much less than presumed by proponents of trade liberalization. Despite efficiency gains from trade liberalization, increased exports do not necessarily ensure stronger domestic economic growth, that is, export-led growth. The experiences of the SEA3 [Indonesia, Malaysia, Thailand] as well as Hong Kong and Singapore more closely approximate this imagined export-led growth model than those of Japan, South Korea and Taiwan PoC. The latter appear to have promoted exports very actively while also protecting domestic markets, at least temporarily, to develop domestic industrial and technological capabilities in order to compete internationally. This strategy of temporary effective protection conditional upon export promotion . . . can hardly be equated with trade liberalization, (Jomo 2003:19)

This comparison of diverse experiences within Asia reminds us of the difficulties that many developing countries are currently experiencing in nurturing their industrial capabilities without the protection that pioneer and successful countries were able to give to their "infant industries".[5] In sub-Saharan Africa, as in other developing regions, many countries have seen their nascent industries collapse under pressure from cheap manufactured imports. Tsikata refers to the phenomenon of "de-industrialization" in the region (Mkandawire and Soludo 1999), with new primary commodity exports not doing well enough to make up for the loss of those industries.

A recent study of small manufacturing firm clusters in Nigeria documents the crippling competition to which these units are exposed as a result of the country's World Trade Organization undertaking to achieve substantial trade liberalization by 2000, which resulted in the elimination of long-standing bans on textile and footwear imports between 1997 and 2000. This, added to the already mounting problems of over-competition and quality adulteration has been disastrous for the textile clusters, where "masters and weavers alike are hemorrhaging out of the business" (Meagher 2007:493). At the same time, the collapse of regional and federal government services (including policing, education and electricity) has left firms vulnerable to extortion from officials and criminals, unable to attract good quality apprentices, and suffering from technical regression (Meagher 2007). In countries like Ghana, manufacturing employment has fallen, and much of the foreign direct investment (FDI) flows, as Tsikata points out, have been in the area of extractive industries.

While the effects of global integration on workers in the South have been regarded, by trade economists at least, to have been positive for developing countries, the available evidence is ambiguous (Ghosh 2003). For the vast majority of developing countries, manufacturing employment has actually stagnated or declined over the past decade, while the growth in manufacturing activities and employment has been confined to a handful of countries: China, Malaysia, Indonesia, Thailand and Chile. The rapid surge in imports associated with trade liberalization is responsible for manufacturing's poor performance elsewhere, as cheap, newly deregulated imported goods have displaced those made by small-scale, employment-intensive domestic producers unable to compete in international markets. Job losses from import competition have been significant in some developing countries and have not been compensated for by the opening up of export employment (Ghosh 2003).

## Formal and Informal Employment

A very significant change of recent decades in developing countries has been the stagnation in formal employment and a substantial rise in the proportion of people who are engaged in what is often referred to as *informal* work. In much of sub-Saharan Africa (with the exception of South Africa) and South Asia, and in such Latin American countries as Bolivia, Ecuador and Peru only a fraction of the workforce, predominantly male, has ever been engaged in formal employment (often state employees and workers in strategic/protected industries). But in countries such as Argentina and Chile, whose labour markets had come to resemble those of the industrialized world, factories have closed, public sector employment has been cut, real wages have fallen and increasing numbers of households have become dependent on the informal and unregulated economy (Pearson 2004).

This trend was unforeseen. In the 1960s and 1970s, it was assumed that the worldwide development of the modern economy would shrink and absorb informal activity, as had happened historically in the industrialized countries. The subsequent extensive growth of the informal economy has reversed such expectations; instead, the global economy has shown a tendency to encourage precarious forms of work which do not bring in sufficient earnings to meet subsistence. In spite of this deepening phenomenon, work and employment currently receive relatively little attention internationally; this is even the case within the poverty reduction agenda of the last decade. Initially, employment hardly featured in the Millennium Development Goals, and was only later included.

What exactly do we mean by "informal employment"? As the chapters in Part Two explain, over the past decade or so increasing emphasis has been placed on the need to shift definitions of labour informality from the enterprise-based understanding which underpinned the notion of "informal sector" widely used in the 1970s (equating informality with the small size of the enterprise) to one based on *labour relations* (whether workers are socially protected and whether minimum wage legislation applies to them). This pressure was eventually endorsed by the International Labour Organization (ILO 2002), which defined the "informal economy" to include labour relations that are not governed by formal economic regulations and/ or basic legal and social protections.

Moreover, while it was often assumed that informal work was linked to low rates of economic growth, the relation between the two seems to be more complex. Based on data for 20 counties with reliable data, Heintz and Pollin (2003) show that, while there is an overall inverse relationship between labour informalization and economic growth (confirming the countercyclical nature of informal work), informal employment has been growing not only in contexts of low economic growth but also where rates of growth have been modest. The latter suggests that informal forms of paid work are not just "lingering vestiges of backwardness" or a by-product of economic stagnation. In fact, in some contexts the very growth of global production networks made possible by the expansion of FDI has generated informal production processes as multinational firms have sought out "low cost and 'flexible' labour relations in their production-level operations" (Heintz and Pollin 2003:4).

Hence, "informal employment" often captures very *different* kinds of work, some more akin to survivalist strategies with low returns that people resort to when economies stagnate, while other kinds of informal work (piece-rate, wage work) are integrated with and contribute to processes of accumulation on a national or global scale (as is the case with industrial outworkers for example). As Chen's chapter further explains, within informal labour markets, there is a marked segmentation in terms of average earnings across the different employment statuses, and it is difficult to move up these segments due to structural barriers (state, market and social) and/or cumulative disadvantage. Informal employment tends to be a greater source of employment for women than for men in all developing regions, except North Africa (ILO 2002), with women's hourly earnings typically falling below those of men in identical employment categories, especially in the case of own-account workers. Many workers, especially women, remain trapped in the lower earning and more risky segments. Relatively high shares of informal employers are men and relatively high shares of industrial outworkers are women.

A large part of the informal economy in countries of sub-Saharan Africa, covered by Tsikata, is composed of low-return self-employment in the services sector, such as food traders and processors, traders in imported items, and domestic, health and sanitation workers, while employment in manufacturing and construction has shrunk. Under the impact of public sector reforms in several countries of the region, even hitherto well-paid public sector workers have been forced to make regular forays into the informal economy to complement their diminishing real wages, as illustrated by the case study of Cameroon cited in Tsikata's chapter. For many observers of long-term change in the region, the growth of trade in goods and services, very often at the level of self-subsistence, is a sign of economic stagnation and crisis.

While in several Asian countries, especially in South Asia, survivalist strategies are also prevalent, these are nevertheless interlaced with other forms of informal work, notably, subcontracted work that is linked to national and global production systems. Participation in these global production chains raises a range of different issues and concerns. These include, for example, concerns about workers' health related to work intensification (that is, having to complete an unrealistic number of tasks within a limited time-frame which engenders self-exploitation and burn-out), safety of workers and their family members when work is carried out in homes, problems of irregular and delayed payments, low wages that fall below the national minimum wage (if one exists) and the absence of social protection mechanisms (Harriss-White 2000). Besides these issues of *quality*, there are also broader questions about the *quantity* of employment that is being generated even in the more dynamic Asian economies which are often seen as a part of the world that has benefited from liberalization and globalization.

The latter concerns are triggered by evidence showing the deceleration or even absolute declines in manufacturing employment in many countries of Asia despite the modest or even high growth rates (Ghosh 2003). As Ghosh elaborates in her contribution to this volume, in general, employment generation has not kept pace with population increase and has expressed itself in higher rates of unemployment and underemployment, as well as declining labour force participation (not fully accounted for by increasing involvement in education). She further highlights the deterioration in the quality of employment, manifested through the decline in regular work and the rise in either casual contracts or self-employment in adverse conditions. We discuss some of these issues further in the following section, given that they manifest themselves clearly in the case of *female* employment.

## Feminization of Labour

Over the past three decades women's economic activity rates have been rising in most parts of the world. There are exceptions to this general global trend, notably in the transitional economies which are part of Eastern Europe as well as Central and Western Asia, where there have been notable reversals, and in the Middle East and North Africa, where they remain very low. But the general trend is towards increasing female visibility in the economic domain. In some countries women's activity rates are nearing men's.

Women, however, continue to be concentrated in jobs with low pay and authority levels, placing limits on their overall access to income, status and power. Recent research finds that despite some improvements in the 1990s, levels of gender segregation in labour markets remain high throughout the world (Anker 1998; Anker et al. 2003). Women tend to congregate in relatively low-paid and low-status work at the bottom of the occupational hierarchy, and also to have little job security.

The ambivalent nature of women's entry into paid work is perhaps captured most strikingly by the double meaning implied in the phrase, "feminization of the labour force" (Standing 1999a). While women's access to paid work has increased in most countries in the last two decades, and women have gained access to the cash economy, the terms and conditions of much of the work on offer have deteriorated.[6] As was noted earlier, the growth of informal work across the world, along with the casualization of formal sector employment, has allowed employers to lower labour costs and to side-step social security obligations and labour laws. For many workers, both female and male, the outcome has been an increasing precariousness of jobs, and greater insecurity of livelihoods.

Besides gender inequalities in paid work, there is also the related issue of inequalities in the provision of unpaid care work, a disproportionate share of which invariably falls onto women and girls in all societies. While increasing numbers of women have entered the traditionally masculine domain of paid work, there does not seem to be much change in the opposite direction: Men's contribution to the provision of unpaid care is remarkably low across countries, age-groups and income groups (or social class) (Budlender forthcoming). The burden is particularly high in the developing countries where infrastructure (for example, piped water and heating) is less developed, public welfare services often rudimentary and inaccessible and where poorer women cannot afford to purchase market substitutes (such as processed food items) or hire-in labour to substitute for their own time.

This does not mean that women from low-income households in poor countries do not need or want paid forms of work (to support their households and to have a degree of economic independence)—they clearly do and this is most evident from the large numbers who move across regions and even countries in search of paid work. While migrant women may be leaving behind family members and delegating care to others (often other women), they are at the same time providing care to individuals in more affluent societies, often working as undocumented domestic or care workers in people's homes, or as paid employees in a variety of care-related institutions. A parallel process is at work when highly trained nurses and medical staff from low-income countries of Africa and Asia (trained and educated in the best public institutions and with public funding) migrate to affluent countries where their skills are in short supply. Through an analysis of the ways in which these variegated migrant streams are inextricably caught up in the social reorganization of care, the chapter by Yeates explores the ways in which inequalities of class, gender and ethnicity are (re)constituted on a global scale.

For both analytical and policy purposes, women's involvement in paid work cannot be seen in isolation from the social arrangements that are in place for the provision of care. The latter is often a domain marked by intense inequalities between women and men within households and families, across social class and indeed between North and South, as the analysis of "global care chains" (Hochschild 2000) has sought to illustrate (see also Kabeer 2007).

## Defeminization of Labour?

Some advocates of trade liberalization argue that women in the South have emerged as winners in the new manufacturing employment scenario. While there is some truth to this statement, the picture is not straightforward. Where export-oriented manufacturing industries have grown (including in China, Malaysia, Bangladesh, Mexico and Thailand), women have been disproportionately absorbed into their workforces (Razavi et al. 2004). Moreover, while the working conditions and terms of pay in many of these factories are poor by international standards, they are usually better than in the urban and rural informal economy (Kabeer and Mahmud 2004), with largely positive implications for women's economic security and sense of autonomy (Kabeer 1995). However, these positive considerations concerning expanding female employment opportunities need to be qualified.

In the first place, there has been a strong tendency in industries with a largely female workforce, especially garment manufacturing, towards deregulation and subcontracting; this often leads to the extensive use of home-workers, one of the most invisible groups in the informal economy. Moreover, as these industries have upgraded, matured and needed a higher skilled workforce, there has been a widespread "defeminization" of their labour forces (UNDESA 1999). This is now increasingly the case in countries like Mexico, which was one of the pioneers of export manufacturing in Latin America (Brachet-Marquez and de Oliveira 2004), as well as in several Asian economies where the phenomenon has been well documented.

These qualifications, though important, are not meant to underestimate some of the positive spin-offs these jobs may have brought forth, giving women their first discretionary income, new social contacts beyond the confines of kinship and neighbourhood, the chance to postpone marriage at a young age, maybe save for a better future, invest in their children's education, or have a greater say in how household resources are allocated. This may not have ended women's subordination and dependence on male protection, but it has given some women at least the tools with which to whittle away at the pillars of patriarchy. Moreover, as Ghosh points out in this volume, if there is adequate compensation and assistance for retraining and mobility across activities and sectors, then something more durable and valuable would have been gained.

## SOCIAL POLICY RESPONSES

In response to widespread discontent with the liberalization agenda, more attention is now being given to social policies and governance issues that undergird the economy. There is the view in some policy circles that if globalization (often used as a shorthand for liberalization of the economy) is to stay on course, then it must be "tamed" or "embedded" through social policies and political reforms (ILO 2004; Ruggie 2003).

The thesis of "embedded liberalism", first put forward by the American political scientist John Ruggie in 1982, was that after the Second World War the Western capitalist countries struck variations of "a grand social bargain" whereby all sectors of individual states agreed to open markets and to contain and share the social costs of adjustments that open markets inevitably produce, through social protection and other forms of intervention. Recalling Polanyi's notion of the "disembedding" of economic life from social life, "embedded liberalism" underlined the ways in which the liberalism of freer trade was re-embedded in society through a commitment to an interventionist programme of governmental action (Polanyi 1957).[7]

Are we seeing something similar happening today? Have the excesses of the "high neoliberalism" of the 1980s given rise to a wider appreciation of the social underpinnings that are necessary for markets to function? Judging by the policy pronouncements of diverse development actors, if the 1980s were about abstracting "the economic" from "the social", then the 1990s and beyond signal a rediscovery of "the social" (Mkandawire 2004), and a welcome, if belated, engagement with it (Molyneux 2002).

The four chapters in Part Three of this volume provide valuable insights into some of the policy efforts that are being made to respond to the discontent associated with liberalization policies. The chapters cover a diverse set of countries and policy efforts. Chapter 9 by Ching Kwan Lee begins with an analysis of the "un-making" of Chinese labour in the era of market reform and considers the Chinese government's efforts to shore up worker discontent and protests by putting in place contribution-based social insurance programmes for health care, unemployment and pensions. The next two chapters turn to the Latin America region where social assistance conditional cash transfer programmes have mushroomed over the past decade or so, often as an emergency response to financial and economic crisis. In chapter 10, Agustín Escobar Latapí and Mercedes González de la Rocha provide a detailed analysis of the Mexican *Oportunidades* programme based on their five-year in-depth ethnographic research conducted in rural, semi-urban and urban settlements in the country, while in chapter 11, Constanza Tabbush takes a hard look at the Argentine public employment programme *Plan Jefas* and its replacement programme, *Plan Familias*, which closely resembles *Oportunidades*. Public employment programmes have a long history in India, and in chapter 12, Smita Gupta describes the difficult road to getting India's National Rural Employment Guarantee Act on the statute books, and the even more contested efforts of turning the legal guarantee to work into a real right for women and men across the country.

## Social Insurance and Problems of Exclusion

In a recent paper, Townsend (2007) has eloquently defended social insurance as a key component of social security—one that has gradually evolved in the currently institutionalized welfare states, and can be expanded and strengthened in developing countries.[8] Broadly universal social insurance programmes are supposed to collect (flat-rate or proportional) contributions on income from employment of all insured persons and employers in exchange for benefits for those insured and their dependents. This is currently the largest item of social security expenditure in the member states of the European Union, and Townsend provides convincing arguments for building up and strengthening social insurance programmes in developing countries as the most effective way of fighting poverty and realizing meaningful social rights.

Enrolment in social insurance programmes is very often employment based, and a fundamental problem in the traditional design of these programmes is the close link of the provision of health care or pensions to formal employment. Coverage has thus tended to be limited, even in middle-income countries due to the large size of the informal economy and the high rate of evasion of contributions by those in both informal and formal workplaces—problems that have been aggravated in recent decades as informalization of labour has intensified. For these reasons, even though social insurance schemes facilitate resource mobilization via contributions, they may not be the most effective vehicle for extending coverage to the majority of the population who work in largely informalized labour markets. Although some women who are outside the workforce or who work informally may be able to obtain indirect entitlements to health care or a pension, if their husbands are formally employed their rights will be dependent on the marriage contract. In several Latin American countries, for example, wives are covered through their husband's health insurance for maternity but not for sickness (Mesa-Lago forthcoming). Moreover, in cases of divorce, abandonment or death of their spouse, women sometimes lose their coverage.

Social sector reform in China is taking place alongside a fundamental restructuring of the labour force marked by massive unemployment in the state industrial sector and large-scale migration of the rural workforce into industrial cities where export-oriented factories are located. Under the pre-reform system women enjoyed very high employment rates, and hence direct entitlements as workers to some form of health insurance and pension via their enterprises. Additionally, as spouses of workers, they had the right to have 50 per cent of their medical expenses reimbursed. However, as Lee shows, women have constituted a disproportionate share of those laid off from the state enterprises and a disproportionate share of the long-term unemployed.

It is interesting that the Chinese authorities have decided to build up pension and health coverage through contribution-based social insurance.

The Labour Law requires that all enterprises, regardless of ownership category, and all employees, including migrant workers, participate in this contributory system. Moreover, contributions are deposited into two kinds of accounts: a social pooling account and an individual account, the proportions of which are decided by the provincial government. A retiree's pension will therefore have both pay-as-you-go and contributory components. But, understandably, coverage has been limited, especially in the non-state sector, and only a small proportion of migrants seem to be covered. In the case of health care too, the overall drift of the reform is to shift the burden of medical care from the state onto employers and employees.

If coverage in social insurance programmes remains employment based and individualized with little subsidy from the state, then women's labour market disadvantages are likely to feed into their weaker claims on health care and pensions. If, on the other hand, the government steps in with financial subsidies to compensate those with lower contributions and those outside the workforce, then the potential for a more egalitarian welfare system will be enhanced. This is the path taken by the National Health Insurance of the Republic of Korea, which has expanded its coverage since the late 1970s, and which can claim to be universalistic since the latest wave of reforms undertaken in 2000 (Kwon and Tchoe 2005).

## Social Assistance Programmes Making a Difference?

In recent years social assistance programmes in the form of conditional cash transfers have been implemented across Latin America. *Bolsa Familia* in Brazil and *Oportunidades* (*Progresa* before 1997) in Mexico are two of the most cited programmes of their kind, not least because of their extensive coverage of the population living below the poverty line in the two respective countries.

*Oportunidades* is a conditional cash transfer programme that, in return for cash stipends given to female heads of poor households, requires that children attend school, family members go for regular health check-ups and that mothers attend hygiene and nutrition information sessions. While it is a targeted programme that identifies beneficiaries based on a means test, its actual reach is more extensive than the narrow targeting associated with "safety net"–type programmes.

As a human development intervention, the programme has had a number of important achievements which are well documented in the chapter by Escobar Latapí and González de la Rocha: School attendance rates have increased and drop-out rates have declined (especially for girls); gender gaps in educational achievements have narrowed; improvements in child nutrition (height and weight increases) have also been registered. Interestingly from the point of view of this volume, the programme has shown sensitivity to gender issues by making the cash transfers directly to mothers in the selected households (motivated by the literature which finds that resources controlled by women are more likely to be allocated to child health and nutrition than resources allocated to men) and by providing larger education stipends for girls than boys (from grade seven onwards). *Oportunidades* is also widely praised for its openness to external evaluations and reviews, as well as its efforts to shun the political patronage that is so endemic to social programmes (Molyneux 2006).

There are nevertheless elements in the design and implementation of the programme that have received critical appraisal in recent years. First, with respect to targeting, the International Food Policy Research Institute's qualitative research (based on focus group discussions and semi-structured interviews) finds extensive discontent among communities in relation to the beneficiary selection process (Adato 2000). The beneficiaries, the non-beneficiaries, the doctors and the *promotoras* (voluntary workers) describe non-beneficiaries' resentment over their exclusion from the programme as well as their lack of understanding of the basis for the differentiation (questioning its accuracy and fairness), leading to social tensions, occasional direct conflict and social divisions that affect participation in community activities (Adato 2000:vii).

Second, Escobar Latapí and González de la Rocha contend that while school enrolment rates have improved, the quality of public education remains poor in the poor communities and that the reform of the public education system is a most pending issue in Mexico. This raises a broader concern which critics have raised about conditional cash transfers, namely, that while cash stipends may enhance poor people's access to education and health services (by enabling parents to purchase school uniforms and books, for example), they do little to strengthen the supply and quality of public health and education services, especially in poor areas and communities, which are often in a dire situation after years of neglect and underfunding.

The gendered implications, as well as gendered assumptions underpinning the programme, have also received extensive attention in recent years. On the one hand, there is the evidence, cited in the contribution to this volume, which supports the programme's claims of enhancing women's self-esteem and financial security as a result of the cash stipends. Escobar Latapí and González de la Rocha also make the observation that the programme has given women more opportunities to leave the house, to access new public spaces and to communicate with other women, producing positive impacts on personal empowerment—an observation that has been documented by other evaluations as well (Adato et al. 2000).

Others, however, have drawn attention to some of the more contentious aspects of the programme. One issue that is considered problematic is the requirement that mothers contribute a set amount of hours of community work, such as cleaning schools and health centres—which non-beneficiaries are not expected to do—in addition to the commitments they have to make to taking their children for regular health checks and attending workshops on health and hygiene—the "co-responsibilities" (Molyneux 2006; Chant 2008). Escobar Latapí and González de la Rocha agree that some women find these burdens "overbearing" and some poor households are excluded from the programme because they are unable to fulfil the work requirements.

More significantly perhaps, attention has been drawn to the ways in which women in such programmes seem to be "primarily positioned as a means to secure programme objectives; they are a *conduit of policy*, in the sense that resources channelled through them are expected to translate into greater improvements in the well-being of children and the family as a whole" (Molyneux 2006:439). Escobar Latapí and González de la Rocha contend that women may be doing so but as "willing agents furthering their *socially bounded responsibilities* through the programme, even if sometimes at a cost to their own interests, than as reluctant instruments fulfilling programme objectives" (this volume, emphasis mine). It would therefore seem fair to conclude that while *Oportunidades* is assisting women in meeting their "practical interests" (Molyneux 1985), we cannot assume that the programme has been designed to do more than that for women *qua women*, for example by giving them a more secure footing in the labour market, greater economic security, and a stronger fall-back position in case of abandonment, separation or divorce. This, however, does not deny the unintended ways in which some women beneficiaries may be enhancing their own "strategic interests" (Molyneux 1985) as a result of participation in the programme by subverting the programme design to meet their own projects and goals. Indeed, Escobar Latapí and González de la Rocha argue that even if those designing the programme did not intend to use the women's meetings for anything more than giving lessons on how to improve family hygiene, women themselves have "appropriated the spaces" offered by the programme for other purposes, such as getting away from home, meeting other women and sometimes organizing to make demands on state authorities.

The importance of providing opportunities for women to enhance their labour market skills and facilitate their entry into the formal workforce emerges forcefully from Tabbush's analysis of the Argentine public works programme, *Plan Jefas*, and its replacement, *Plan Familias*. The origins of *Plan Jefas* can be traced to the economic crisis of 2001 with its highly adverse employment consequences. The programme targets unemployed heads of households (regardless of gender: *Plan Jefas y Jefes*) who are responsible for a child under 18 years of age or caring for a disabled child or a pregnant spouse, and participation is limited to one person per household. The programme's conditionality is in terms of hours of paid work (rather than ensuring children's schooling and nutrition, as in *Oportunidades*). Ironically though, the work conditionality seems to have been an afterthought to the original design, given the large number of applicants and the budgetary constraints imposed on the programme. Beneficiaries are offered a monthly stipend of 150 pesos in return for 20 hours of paid work per week—a seem-ingly "masculine" requirement. Yet contrary to expectations, close to 71 per cent of programme beneficiaries have been women, from households marked by high dependency ratios, low levels of income and education, and poor housing conditions—perhaps a reflection of the small size of the cash stipend. Interestingly though, while the programme intended to target unemployed heads of households, a significant proportion of both female and male beneficiaries reported being economically inactive before joining the programme. The only factor precluding participation in the *Plan Jefas* is social security contributions attached to formal employment—a condi-tionality that may inadvertently promote informal and precarious forms of work. Tabbush cites the tension that is currently being experienced between the national campaign to register and formalize domestic workers and the willingness of some such workers to remain informally employed in order to continue receiving the *Plan Jefas* stipends.

Evaluations suggest that while the programme's impact on levels of poverty has been ambiguous, it has been successful in reducing indigence (extreme poverty) and unemployment (a person registering under the programme is automatically counted as "employed"). Furthermore, *Plan Jefas* seems to have been effective in reducing social tensions produced by the crisis, not only by providing a safety valve through the provision of work/cash but also by facilitating alliances between different social actors, including the unemployment movement, state officials, NGOs and faith-based organizations.

Turning to the gender aspects of the programme, the evidence analysed by Tabbush clearly suggests that despite women's numerical preponder-ance in the programme, higher numbers of men than women graduated from the programme into formal work opportunities (given their prior labour market skills and experiences, and the fact that recent growth patterns in Argentina have created more work opportunities for men, evident in the dynamism of the construction sector). Yet the picture is more complicated than this single finding would suggest, and since 2005 not only do a larger proportion of female programme beneficiaries appear to find employment, but the paid work that they find seems to be more stable. Significantly, even though women participants have been incorpo-rated into the labour market at a much lower rate than their male coun-terparts, many of those who are entering the workforce had no recent experience of formal sector work and seem to be therefore "slowly culti-vating links with the formal labour market" (Tabbush, this volume). Evi-dence from qualitative research suggests that the acquisition of new skills and the greater probability of finding formal employment is something that female participants in the programme strongly value (Tcherneva and Wray 2007).

Flying in the face of these limited achievements, the government of Argentina, with financial and ideational support from various external agencies, most notably the World Bank and the Inter-American Development Bank, is currently replacing *Plan Jefas* with another conditional cash transfer programme, *Plan Familias*, aimed at enhancing children's welfare by making cash stipends targeted at their mothers dependent on children's school enrolment and nutritional levels. Women beneficiaries of *Plan Jefas* who have two children or more, low levels of education and little prior work experience are considered to be "not employable" and thus encouraged to move to *Plan Familias*, while those *Jefas* beneficiaries who have higher educational levels and some work experience are to move to *Seguro*, which reproduces the *Jefas'* work rationale and continues to prioritize reinsertion into formal paid work. *Plan Familias*, however, has no work options and gives no consideration to educational and childcare facilities for young children under five years of age—an area with weak state provision in Argentina, but which has significant implications for the autonomy and labour market success of women with young children.

There is an unmistakable gender subtext to the two-tier system of social assistance that is being constructed in Argentina, with training/labour market entry largely targeted to men, and the more "assistentialist" family- and child-oriented programmes aimed at women, reminiscent of Fraser and Gordon's (1994) analysis of social insurance and social assistance programmes in the United States. Moreover, while *Oportunidades* was instrumental in expanding health and education coverage in Mexico, the benefits of reproducing the same form of conditionality in a context which has already achieved almost universal health and education coverage, though with marked variations in the quality of that provision, as is the case in Argentina, seems doubtful. Despite donor claims to have learned from past mistakes of using "one-size-fits-all" policy blueprints (World Bank 2003), the current donor enthusiasm for transferring "successful" blueprints, of which *Oportunidades* is a shining example, from one country to another, regardless of context and history, suggests that "one-size-fits-all" solutions are alive and well in international policy circles.

If mass unemployment in the context of the 2001 financial and economic crisis was the stimulus for *Plan Jefas* in Argentina, then extensive rural distress, analysed in the chapter by Jackson and Rao, is what spurred the historic passage of the National Rural Employment Guarantee Act in India in 2004—an employment guarantee as part of a constitutional right to work. Gupta's detailed analysis traces the political obstacles that have stood in the way of turning this act into a real guarantee whereby each and every adult citizen in India—regardless of gender, caste or region—can enjoy access to gainful employment. Perhaps the most disabling feature of the scheme from a gender perspective is the guarantee of 100 days of work *per rural household*. This dilutes adult entitlements regardless of gender; and given the rural power equations and inequalities, it risks putting women at the end of the queue, although reservation of one-third of all work for women may help reverse such gender bias. Benefits are further diluted by the low wages that are on offer, and by linking wages to unrealistically high productivity norms, which in the case of work requiring hard manual labour puts women in a particularly disadvantageous position (not to mention the risks that such intense manual labour places on the labouring poor of both genders who are already nutritionally vulnerable). Moreover, worksites' facilities are highly inadequate, especially in the provision of childcare—a most disabling factor from women workers' point of view.

Clearly, what is on offer falls short of a full-fledged "right to work". At least five basic features of a meaningful "right to work" are missing, which include full coverage of all urban and rural areas; individual entitlements; unlimited days for which work is guaranteed; an assured decent living wage; and the inclusion of non-manual work to address the needs of the elderly, the disabled and, in many instances, women. And yet as Gupta concludes, the act is far more than what the government planned to enact and thus even as it is by no means a full-fledged employment guarantee, it is an indisputable defeat of fiscal orthodoxy.

## CONCLUDING REMARKS: TOWARDS "EMBEDDED LIBERALISM"?

Economic liberalization has never been smooth or uncontested, and there have always been spaces for policy experimentation and heterodoxy, whether with respect to macroeconomic policies or social policies. Where policymakers have followed orthodox prescriptions—whether under pressure from Washington or of their own volition—the outcomes have been disappointing, even in the estimate of their designers. Rural livelihoods have become more insecure (as well as more diversified) in contexts where cutbacks in state support to domestic agriculture have coincided with increasing exposure to competition from large subsidized producers. At a time when global commodity markets have been volatile, large numbers of people have been trapped in poverty, hunger and even famine. Insecurity is also etched into the growth of informal economies across the world, where "flexibility" has come to mean a weakening of labour standards rather than creating a better balance between paid work (production) and unpaid care work (social reproduction). With weak public health and welfare programmes, fragile infrastructure and thin social protection mechanisms, the provision of unpaid care by women and girls has been intensified—to intolerable degrees in sub-Saharan Africa, where the HIV/AIDS epidemic is taking a staggering toll of lives.

At the same time, taking on paid work has become ever more necessary for all household members—whether male or female, young or old—to make ends meet in increasingly commercialized contexts. However it is important to underline that the economic policy agenda that has been so deeply adverse to many women and men around the world has also provided new opportunities to some social groups, including some low-income women. Jobs in export-oriented manufacturing firms and capitalist farms producing "high value" agricultural export crops around the world, no matter how fragile and short-lived, and how low the pay and unfavourable the conditions of work, have benefited some women. For the vast majority of women, however, gender equality will remain a distant dream as long as the market calculus remains the principal arbiter of policy.

"Re-embedding" the economy, and doing so in a way that facilitates a more harmonious integration between the twin goals of production and social reproduction, requires the strengthening of publicly accountable systems of mutual assurance against entitlement failure. This means investing in areas that orthodox prescriptions cannot countenance: well-functioning and accessible public health, education and care services, labour standards and rights that protect women's employment and conditions of work and investment in public provision of a range of complementary services (clean water, sanitation, electricity, paved streets) to support the care economy (UNRISD 2005). To have substantive rights and entitlements implies access to an accountable process where access to a resource is not at the arbitrary discretion of a public official, dependent on the favour of a patron or the goodwill of a husband, or the price-fixing power of a monopoly supplier (Elson 2002). Genuine empowerment is about having meaningful institutional alternatives to dependence on familial and conjugal relations, on markets and employers and on public and non-state actors when the terms of any of these relations become unacceptable. It means decent jobs with employment rights, and fair allowances for life-cycle contingencies such as old age, ill-health, disability and periods of intense care. It also means a more equal sharing of unpaid care between men and women, and thus a redefinition of full-time work.

It is clear that states in many different contexts are putting in place social programmes to address the adverse outcomes of liberalization policies. The full potential of these positive moves, however, is vitiated by the fact that debate over economic development and macroeconomic policy has fallen off the agenda instead of forming an integral part of the current policy rethinking. The social distress and inequalities that are being unleashed by current economic policies are far more extensive than the remedies, however well intentioned and important, that are being suggested and experimented with. Such prescriptions thus risk replicating the by now well-rehearsed limitations of minimal safety nets in the era of structural adjustment. In the context of liberalized trade (which reduces import and export taxes) and the pressures from mobile capital (which reduce corporate taxes, capital gains and income taxes) it is very difficult for governments to raise the kind of revenues needed to finance public services and transfers that can meet the casualties of economic policies. In sum, there is a lack of affinity and complementarity between "social policies" and "economic policies", a failure to rethink "economic" policies through a social perspective (Elson 2004), so that "economic" policies and "social" policies can work in tandem (Mkandawire 2004).

# APPENDIX 1.1

Table 1.1 Economically Active Population in Agriculture, Agricultural Value-Added and Agricultural Exports, Regional Averages and Some Country Examples (1980–2000)

| | Proportion of economically active population in agriculture[1] | | | Agriculture, value added (% of GDP)[2] | | | Agricultural exports (% of merchandise exports)[2] | | |
|---|---|---|---|---|---|---|---|---|---|
| | 1980 | 1990 | 2000 | 1980 | 1990 | 2000 | 1980 | 1990 | 2000 |
| **Africa** | **69** | **64** | **59** | **29** | **29** | **27** | **51** | **45** | **43** |
| *North Africa* | *44* | *32* | *27* | *15* | *16* | *13* | *16* | *15* | *11* |
| Egypt | 57 | 41 | 34 | 18 | 19 | 17 | 22 | 19 | - |
| Tunisia | 39 | 28 | 25 | 14 | 16 | 12 | 8 | 12 | 9 |
| *Sub-Saharan Africa* | *72* | *68* | *63* | *31* | *30* | *28* | *59* | *55* | *52* |
| Cameroon | 73 | 70 | 59 | 31 | 25 | 43 | 64 | 35 | 36 |
| South Africa | 17 | 14 | 10 | 6 | 5 | 3 | 11 | 12 | 12 |
| Tanzania | 86 | 84 | 80 | - | 46 | 45 | 76 | - | - |
| Zimbabwe | 72 | 68 | 63 | 16 | 16 | 18 | 43 | 51 | 60 |
| **Latin America and the Caribbean** | **31** | **25** | **21** | **16** | **14** | **10** | **47** | **47** | **44** |
| *Caribbean* | *26* | *22* | *17* | *14* | *11* | *7* | *38* | *36* | *43* |
| Dominican Rep. | 32 | 25 | 17 | 20 | 13 | 11 | 73 | - | - |
| Jamaica | 31 | 25 | 21 | 8 | 7 | 6 | 14 | 20 | 23 |
| *Central America* | *42* | *34* | *27* | *22* | *19* | *13* | *65* | *68* | *57* |
| Guatemala | 54 | 52 | 46 | 25 | 26 | 23 | 70 | 73 | 60 |
| Mexico | 36 | 28 | 21 | 9 | 8 | 4 | 15 | 13 | 5 |
| Nicaragua | 42 | 34 | 27 | 23 | 31 | - | 83 | 91 | 90 |
| *South America* | *31* | *25* | *21* | *13* | *14* | *12* | *42* | *39* | *36* |
| Argentina | 13 | 12 | 10 | 6 | 8 | 5 | 71 | 61 | 45 |
| Brazil | 37 | 23 | 17 | 11 | 8 | 7 | 50 | 31 | 28 |
| Paraguay | 45 | 39 | 34 | 29 | 28 | 20 | 88 | 90 | 80 |
| **Asia** | **46** | **41** | **36** | **21** | **23** | **23** | **28** | **15** | **11** |
| *East Asia* | *49* | *40* | *33* | *15* | *13* | *13* | *5* | *6* | *3* |
| China | 74 | 72 | 67 | 30 | 27 | 16 | - | 16 | 7 |
| Republic of Korea | 37 | 18 | 10 | 15 | 9 | 5 | 9 | 5 | 3 |
| *Southeast Asia* | *56* | *52* | *48* | *21* | *29* | *25* | *31* | *17* | *9* |
| Indonesia | 58 | 55 | 48 | 24 | 20 | 17 | 22 | 16 | 13 |
| Thailand | 71 | 64 | 56 | 23 | 13 | 10 | 58 | 34 | 18 |
| *South Asia* | *67* | *61* | *57* | *40* | *33* | *27* | *48* | *23* | *19* |
| India | 70 | 64 | 60 | 39 | 31 | 25 | 33 | 20 | 14 |
| Pakistan | 63 | 52 | 47 | 30 | 26 | 27 | 44 | 20 | 13 |
| *Central Asia* | *-* | *-* | *-* | *-* | *33* | *32* | *-* | *-* | *-* |
| Kazakhstan | - | - | 18 | - | - | 9 | - | - | 8 |
| Uzbekistan | - | - | 28 | - | 33 | 34 | - | - | - |
| *West Asia* | *26* | *20* | *15* | *9* | *14* | *17* | *19* | *12* | *12* |
| Jordan | 18 | 15 | 11 | 8 | 8 | 2 | 25 | 11 | 16 |

*(continued)*

*Table 1.1* Economically Active Population in Agriculture, Agricultural Value-Added and Agricultural Exports, Regional Averages and Some Country Examples (1980–2000) (continued)

| | Proportion of economically active population in agriculture[(1)] | | | Agriculture, value added (% of GDP)[(2)] | | | Agricultural exports (% of merchandise exports)[(2)] | | |
|---|---|---|---|---|---|---|---|---|---|
| | 1980 | 1990 | 2000 | 1980 | 1990 | 2000 | 1980 | 1990 | 2000 |
| Syrian Arab Rep. | 39 | 33 | 28 | 20 | 28 | 23 | 13 | 18 | 13 |
| Oceania | 48 | 43 | 37 | 27 | 21 | 19 | 70 | 71 | 43 |
| Developed regions | 15 | 11 | 8 | 8 | 10 | 7 | 23 | 19 | 14 |
| *Eastern Europe* | 28 | 23 | 17 | 20 | 18 | 12 | 17 | 15 | 9 |
| *Western Europe* | 12 | 8 | 5 | 7 | 5 | 3 | 21 | 17 | 13 |
| *Other developed* | 7 | 5 | 4 | 6 | 4 | 2 | 34 | 27 | 22 |
| World | 43 | 38 | 34 | 20 | 20 | 18 | 39 | 32 | 29 |

*Note:* Regional averages for each variable have been calculated from countries with available data for at least two of the periods considered. Agricultural exports comprise exports of food and of agricultural raw materials.

*Sources:* UNRISD 2005. (1) Calculated from FAO 2004; (2) World Bank 2004b.

# NOTES

1. In the 1970s and 1980s "reproduction" was a key concept in feminist scholarship to emphasize that women's unpaid work was decisive in reproducing the labour force and society, and in facilitating capitalist accumulation. While this concept is still used, the emphasis has shifted to "care" which is now seen as the core of domestic activities (Anttonen 2005). While women spend a large number of hours on a variety of household tasks (though the time devoted to such tasks has been falling in the more developed countries), it is caring for others that is the main factor that limits women's participation in activities outside the household, including paid work. For elaboration of these issues, see Razavi (2007).
2. This meant that farmers in remote areas were offered the same prices as those close to urban markets.
3. For further elaboration of this point, see Whitehead and Tsikata (2003) and Razavi (2003).
4. Women's inheritance rights are sanctioned by law in India—at least for Hindu and Muslim women (although, according to the Muslim Shari'a Act, daughters only inherit half the share of their brother's). But women's legal rights are not reflected in on-the-ground realities.
5. See Chang (2002) for an elaboration of this argument.
6. There is some debate as to whether women substituted men in existing jobs, or were recruited to fill in new jobs. Given the persistent gender segmentations (both horizontal and vertical) in labour markets, the latter is probably the dominant trend, while some substitution may have happened in some specific sectors and occupations.
7. Indeed the General Agreement on Tariffs and Trade contained a variety of safeguards, exemptions and restrictions, such as preferential trading agreements, emergency safeguards and others which were designed to facilitate and protect a variety of domestic social policies.

8. It is important to underline, as Townsend does, that social security in most Organisation for Economic Co-operation and Development countries began as fragmented, means-tested social assistance. It evolved into a predominantly social insurance–based system with universal coverage because of mass protests against social assistance, due to the latter's discriminatory selection of beneficiaries, meagre level of benefits and poor coverage of those theoretically entitled to assistance.

## REFERENCES

Abalu, G. and R. Hassin. 1999. "Agricultural productivity and natural resource use in Southern Africa." *Food Policy*, Vol. 23, No. 6, pp. 477–490.
Adato, M. 2000. *The Impact of PROGRESA on Community Social Relationships*. International Food Policy Research Institute (IFPRI), Washington, DC.
Adato, M., B. de la Brière, D. Mindek and A. Quisumbing. 2000. *The Impact of PROGRESA on Women's Status and Intrahousehold Relations*. International Food Policy Research Institute (IFPRI), Washington, DC.
Agarwal, B. 2003. "Gender and land rights revisited: Exploring new prospects via the state, family and market." *Journal of Agrarian Change*, Vol. 3, Nos. 1 and 2, pp. 184–225.
Anker, R. 1998. *Gender and Jobs: Sex Segregation of Occupations in the World*. ILO, Geneva.
Anker, R., H. Melkas and A. Korten. 2003. *Gender-Based Occupational Segregation in the 1990s*. ILO Working Paper, Focus Programme on Promoting the Declaration on Fundamental Principles and Rights at Work. ILO, Geneva.
Anttonen, A. 2005. "Empowering social policy: The role of the social care services in modern welfare states." In O. Kangas and J. Palme (eds.), *Social Policy and Economic Development in the Nordic Countries*. UNRISD/Palgrave Macmillan, Basingstoke.
Bernstein, H. 2004. "'Changing before our very eyes': Agrarian questions and the politics of land in capitalism today." *Journal of Agrarian Change*, Vol. 4, Nos. 1 and 2, pp. 190–225.
Brachet-Marquez, V. and O. de Oliveira. 2004. "Gendering the debate on the welfare state in Mexico: Women's employment and welfare entitlements in the globalized economy." In S. Razavi, R. Pearson and C. Danloy (eds.), *Globalization, Export-Oriented Employment for Women and Social Policy: Gendered Connections*. UNRISD/Palgrave Macmillan, Basingstoke.
Breman, J. 1996. *Footloose Labour: Working in India's Informal Economy*. Cambridge University Press, Cambridge.
Bryceson, D.F. 1999. *Sub-Saharan Africa Betwixt and Between: Rural Livelihood Practices and Policies*. ASC Working Paper 43, Africa-Studiecentrum, Leiden.
Budlender, Debbie. Forthcoming. *The Statistical Evidence on Care and Non-Care Work across Six Countries*. Programme on Gender and Development, Paper No. 4, UNRISD, Geneva.
———. 2007. *A Critical Review of Selected Time Use Surveys*. Programme on Gender and Development, Paper No. 2, UNRISD, Geneva.
Byres, T. 2003. "Structural change, the agrarian question and the possible impact of globalization." In J. Ghosh and C.P. Chandrasekhar (eds.), *Work and Well-Being in the Age of Finance*. Tulika, New Delhi.
Chang, H.J. 2002. *Kicking Away the Ladder: Development Strategy in Historical Perspective*. Anthem Press, London.

Chant, S. 2008. "The 'feminisation of poverty' and the 'feminisation' of anti-poverty programmes: Room for revision?" *Journal of Development Studies*, Vol. 4, No. 2, pp. 165–197.

Collier, P. 1989. *Women and Structural Adjustment*. Unit for the Study of African Economies, Oxford University, Oxford.

Ellis, F. 1998. "Household strategies and rural livelihood diversification." *Journal of Development Studies*, Vol. 35, No. 1, pp. 1–38.

Elson, D. 2004. "Social policy and macroeconomic performance: Integrating 'the economic' and 'the social'." In T. Mkandawire (ed.), *Social Policy in a Development Context*. UNRISD/Palgrave Macmillan, Basingstoke.

———. 2002. "Gender justice, human rights and neo-liberal economic policies." In M. Molyneux and S. Razavi (eds.), *Gender Justice, Development and Rights*. Oxford University Press, Oxford.

Fraser, N. and L. Gordon. 1994. "Civil citizenship against social citizenship? On the ideology of contract-versus-charity." In Bart van Steenbergen (ed.), *The Condition of Citizenship*. Sage, London.

Ghosh, J. 2003. "Where have the manufacturing jobs gone? Production, accumulation and relocation in the world economy." In J. Ghosh and C.P. Chandrasekhar (eds.), *Work and Well-Being in the Age of Finance*. Tulika Books, New Delhi.

Goetz, A.M. and R. Sengupta. 1996. "Who takes the credit? Gender, power and control over loan use in rural credit programmes in Bangladesh." *World Development*, Vol. 24, No. 1, pp. 45–63.

Harriss-White, B. 2000. *Work and Social Policy with Special Reference to Indian Conditions*. Paper presented at UNRISD Conference on Social Policy in a Development Context, Tamsvik, Sweden, 23–24 September.

Heintz, J. 2008. *Employment, Informality and Poverty: An Empirical Overview of Six Countries with a Focus on Gender and Race*. Background paper prepared for the UNRISD report on *Poverty and Policy Regimes*, mimeo, UNRISD, Geneva.

Heintz, J. and R. Pollin. 2003. *Informalization, Economic Growth and the Challenge of Creating Viable Labor Standards in Developing Countries*. Political Economy Research Institute Working Paper 60, University of Massachusetts Amherst, Amherst, MA.

Hochschild, A. R. 2000. "Global care chains and emotional surplus value." In W. Hutton and A. Giddens (eds.), *On the Edge: Living with Global Capitalism*. Jonathan Cape, London.

Holzmann, R. and S. Jorgensen. 2000. *Social Risk Management: A New Conceptual Framework for Social Protection and Beyond*. Social Protection Discussion Paper Series, No. 6, The World Bank, Washington, DC.

International Labour Organization (ILO). 2004. *Report of the World Commission on the Social Dimensions of Globalization*. ILO, Geneva.

———. 2002. *Women and Men in the Informal Economy: A Statistical Picture*. ILO, Geneva.

Jomo, K.S. 2003. *Globalization, Liberalization and Equitable Development: Lessons from East Asia*. Overarching Concerns, Paper No. 3, UNRISD, Geneva.

Kabeer, N. 2007. *Marriage, Motherhood and Masculinity in the Global Economy: Reconfigurations of Personal and Economic Life*. Working Paper 290, Institute of Development Studies, Sussex.

———. 1995. *Necessary, Sufficient or Irrelevant? Women, Wages and Intra-Household Power Relations in Urban Bangladesh*. IDS Working Paper 25, Institute of Development Studies, Brighton.

Kabeer, N. and S. Mahmud. 2004. "Globalization, gender and poverty: Bangladeshi women workers in export and local markets." *Journal of International Development*, Vol. 16, No. 1, pp. 93–109.

Karshenas, M. 2004. "'Urban bias', intersectoral resource flows and the macroeconomic implications of agrarian relations: The historical experience of Japan and Taiwan." *Journal of Agrarian Change*, Vol. 4, Nos. 1 and 2, pp. 170–189.

Kwon, H.J. and B. Tchoe. 2005. "The political economy of national health insurance in Korea." In M. Mackintosh and M. Koivusalo (eds.), *Commercialization of Health Care. Global and Local Dynamics and Policy Responses*. UNRISD/Palgrave Macmillan, Basingstoke.

Meagher, K. 2007. "Manufacturing disorder: Liberalization, informal enterprise and economic 'ungovernance' in African small firm clusters." *Development and Change*, Vol. 38, No. 3, pp. 473–503.

Melkas, H. and R. Anker. 2003. *Towards Gender Equity in Japanese and Nordic Labour Markets: A Tale of Two Paths*. InFocus Programme on Socio-Economic Security, ILO, Geneva.

Mesa-Lago, Carmelo. Forthcoming. "Social insurance (pensions and health), labour markets and coverage in Latin America." In Katja Hujo and Shea McClanahan (eds.), *Financing Social Policy: Mobilizing Resources for Social Development*. UNRISD/Palgrave Macmillan, Basingstoke.

Mkandawire, T. 2004. "Social policy in a development context: Introduction." In T. Mkandawire (ed.), *Social Policy in a Development Context*. UNRISD/Palgrave Macmillan, Basingstoke.

Mkandawire, T. and C.C. Soludo. 1999. *Our Continent, Our Future: African Perspectives on Structural Adjustment*. CODESRIA and Africa World Press, Inc., Dakar and Trenton, NJ.

Molyneux, M. 2006. "Mothers at the service of the new poverty agenda: *Progresa/Oportunidades*, Mexico's Conditional Transfer Programme." *Social Policy and Administration*, Vol. 40, No. 4, pp. 425–449.

———. 2002. "Gender and the silences of social capital: Lessons from Latin America." *Development and Change*, Vol. 33, No. 2, pp. 167–188.

———. 1985. "Mobilization without emancipation? Women's interests, the state, and revolution in Nicaragua." *Feminist Studies*, Vol. 11, Summer, pp. 227–254.

Patnaik, U. 2003. "Global capitalism, deflation and agrarian crisis in developing countries." *Journal of Agrarian Change*, Vol. 3, Nos. 1 and 2, pp. 33–66.

Pearson, R. 2004. "Organizing home-based workers in the global economy: An action-research approach." *Development in Practice*, Vol. 14, Nos. 1 and 2, pp. 136–148.

Polanyi, K. 1957. *The Great Transformation*. Beacon Press, Boston, MA.

Razavi, R. 2007. *The Political and Social Economy of Care in a Development Context. Conceptual Issues, Research Questions and Policy Options*. Programme on Gender and Development, Paper No. 3, UNRISD, Geneva.

———. 2003. "Introduction: Agrarian change, gender and land rights." *Journal of Agrarian Change*, Vol. 3, Nos. 1 and 2, pp. 2–32.

Razavi, S., R. Pearson and C. Danloy (eds.). 2004. *Globalization, Export-Oriented Employment for Women and Social Policy: Gendered Connections*. UNRISD/Palgrave Macmillan, Basingstoke.

Ruggie, J.G. 2003. "Taking embedded liberalism global: The corporate connection." In D. Held and M. Koenig-Archibugi (eds.), *Taming Globalization: Frontiers of Governance*. Polity, Cambridge.

———. 1982. "International regimes, transactions, and change: Embedded liberalism in the postwar economic order." *International Organization*, Vol. 36, No. 2, pp. 379–415.

Spoor, M. 2002. "Policy regimes and performance of the agricultural sector in Latin America and the Caribbean during the last three decades." *Journal of Agrarian Change*, Vol. 2, No. 3, pp. 382–401.

Standing, G. 1999a. "Global feminization through flexible labor: A theme revisited." *World Development*, Vol. 27, No. 3, pp. 583–602.

———. 1999b. *Global Labour Flexibility. Seeking Distributive Justice.* Macmillan and St. Martin's Press, Basingstoke and New York.

Tcherneva, P.R. and L.R. Wray. 2007. *Public Employment and Women: The Impacts of Argentina's Jefes Program on Female Heads of Poor Households.* Working Paper 519, The Levy Economics Institute of Bard College, Annandale-on-Hudson, NY.

Townsend, P. 2007. *The Right to Social Security and National Development: Lessons from OECD Experience for Low-Income Countries.* Issues in Social Protection Discussion Paper No.18, Social Security Department, ILO, Geneva.

United Nations Department of Economic and Social Affairs (UNDESA). 1999. *1999 World Survey on the Role of Women in Development: Globalization, Gender and Work.* United Nations, New York.

United Nations Research Institute for Social Development (UNRISD). 2005. *Gender Equality: Striving for Justice in an Unequal World.* UNRISD, Geneva.

Whitehead, A. and D. Tsikata. 2003. "Policy discourses on women's land rights in sub-Saharan Africa: The implications of the re-turn to the customary." *Journal of Agrarian Change*, Vol. 3, Nos. 1 and 2, pp. 67–112.

Woo, M.J.E. 2007. "After the miracle: Neoliberalism and institutional reform in East Asia." In M.J.E. Woo (ed.), *Neoliberalism and Institutional Reform in East Asia: A Comparative Study.* UNRISD/Palgrave Macmillan, Basingstoke.

World Bank. 2003. *World Development Report 2004: Making Services Work for Poor People.* World Bank, Washington, DC.

———. 2000. *World Development Report 2000/1: Attacking Poverty.* World Bank, Washington, DC.

———. 1994. *Adjustment in Africa: Reforms, Results and the Road Ahead.* World Bank, Washington, DC.

———. 1989. *Sub-Saharan Africa: From Crisis to Sustainable Growth.* World Bank, Washington, DC.

# Part I

# Rural Livelihoods under Liberalization

# 2 The Gendered Impacts of Liberalization Policies on African Agricultural Economies and Rural Livelihoods

*Ann Whitehead*

## INTRODUCTION

In 2006, individual countries in sub-Saharan Africa (SSA) continued the economic liberalization policies first started in the early 1980s.[1] At the same time as they further liberalize their trade regimes, encourage private investment and maintain fiscal discipline, international financial institution (IFI) loans are tied to the adoption of national poverty strategies—a tacit recognition that these measures have not so far brought ordinary people out of poverty. The UK Make Poverty History Campaign, its 2005 Africa Commission and the Gleneagles G8 summit declarations are more overt public recognitions of the huge suffering, misery and lost opportunities for African populations that have accompanied liberalization. After two decades, overall growth rates in African economies have been disappointing and the effects on poverty at best patchy and at worst negligible, or even negative. The intertwining of the effects of macroeconomic policy with climatic cycles, conflicts and the failure of African agriculture to thrive are evident in the continued problems of malnutrition and famines. One example of the negative effects on food security was the crisis in Southern Africa in 2002, when several countries experienced severe food shortages proximately caused by drought and localized flooding, but exacerbated by an environment in which many households are already highly vulnerable to food insecurity (RCSA 2003:1; Wiggins 2003; World Bank 2003).

In all countries, the effects on poverty have not been uniformly felt by all sections of the population: There have been winners and losers. Among those who have been most negatively affected, the rural poor figure prominently.[2] In most SSA countries a high proportion of the population lives in rural areas, is dependent on agriculture for its livelihood and is poor. The welfare effects on rural households of the imposition of user fees in health and education, of the removal of subsidies on agricultural inputs, of the closing down of marketing boards and of the continued poor performance of agriculture have depended in part on whether private market institutions have developed to deliver inputs and knowledge and to purchase crops. It has also depended on whether households had assets of various kinds to respond to new incentives and new markets.[3] Many commentators have pointed out that many rural smallholders continue not to be in a position to respond positively (for example, Killick 2001). The family—or more properly the household—is a key institution within the rural economy and is typically characterized by divisions of labour based on gender and generation and by multiple livelihood strategies. Agricultural production for own use and for income is combined with petty income generation, efforts to accumulate assets to invest in business and often also migration of some household members to areas with better labour markets or income opportunities. Men, women and children work hard to maintain the security of their households and the well-being of its members, often in very adverse circumstances. This chapter seeks to provide an overview of ways in which the relations of gender in rural households and communities may have affected the impact of liberalization, and how relations of gender and generation have been affected by changes in the rural economy brought about by liberalization. These include changes in the macroeconomic environment for agricultural production of both food and export crops; changes in the institutions that deliver agricultural inputs, organize markets and distribute outputs; the imposition of user fees in health and education; and attempts in some cases to promote new internal markets in national economic policy.

## APPROACHES TO GENDER AND ECONOMIC REFORM

Approaches to gender and economic reform have evolved over the structural adjustment decades. Drawing on early evidence that the poorest households were ill-placed to withstand the shocks implied by economic restructuring, early critiques of the process often identified women and children as among the most vulnerable (Cornea et al. 1987). Important as this was, little was said in this literature about why women and children were suffering more, and the analysis implicitly rested on the long-held assumption that gender and age were sources of "vulnerability" in themselves.

Feminist economists such as Elson (1991, 1993, 1994, 1995) and Çagatay, Elson and Grown (1995) and Çagatay (1998) opened up critical inquiry into why women were being so adversely affected, making two major theoretical points: First, that women and men do not come to the market with the same material endowments, and hence women often cannot take advantage of new economic opportunities because they lack assets and resources. Second, that men and women have very different roles and relationships to the unpaid economy or the "reproductive sector", where much of what society deems women's work is not only rendered invisible by mainstream economic theory, but is also regarded as infinitely flexible (Sparr 1994; Palmer 1992). Structural adjustment, Elson pointed out, entails changes in the balance between paid and unpaid sectors, with the intensification and extension of unpaid labour a hidden factor in many episodes of stabilization. Initially, unpaid labour can help absorb some of the shocks of adjustment, but at the cost of extending the hours that women work and increasing work intensity. The increased efficiency as identified by economists rather represents a shift in costs from the paid economy to the unpaid economy (Elson 1991; Sparr 1994; Kanji et al. 1991).

The connections between reproductive and productive spheres of the macroeconomy are concretely manifest in rural households in high work burdens for women and low health indicators. Several studies have found evidence for women's increased work burdens during structural adjustment in different parts of Africa, both due to changes in agricultural production and to the removal of subsidies on social services in education and health (Tsikata and Kerr 2000; Blackden 1997; Dolan 1997; Galli and Funk 1995). Too few studies have looked into health and nutrition indicators, but a study in Zimbabwe found more children born stunted because of dietary stress in their mothers during pregnancy (Bijlmakers et al. 1998), and Kabeer (2003) suggests that there is evidence of a rise in already high maternal and child mortality rates in recent years.

A further development of work on gender relations and liberalization in African agriculture concerned the role of gender in agricultural supply response. Rural farm households in many areas of SSA, especially West Africa, do not organize the distribution of resources and incomes on the basis of norms of sharing and pooling. They thus form a special and extreme example of the more general feminist insight that households are not necessarily sites of sharing and equity—an approach which entails a strong challenge to the neoclassical assumption of household unity in the modelling of household behaviour (Agarwal 1997; Evans 1989; Kabeer 1994; Sen 1990; Whitehead 1981). Several studies brought out how the supply response in African agriculture cannot be explained by conventional models of the household and argued that inefficiency in the allocation of productive resources within households and depressed production arise because the separation of resource streams implies individual, not shared, gender incentives with respect to crop outputs. Udry and others (1995) showed that, within the same household, yields were lower on women's plots than on men's for the same crop in the same year, for all plot sizes.[4] Smith and Chavas (2003) posit a conflict between husbands and wives arising from their different interests in cotton (cash-crop) farming due to their separate income streams and labour demands. Warner and Campbell (2000:1329) suggest that "[b]y resisting production that is converted into cash women can reduce the possibility of losing control of their resources".

Attractive though these findings are for suggesting a synergy between improving gender equality and improving agricultural output and for convincing sceptics about the need to consider gender, Whitehead (2001) argues that the conclusions drawn from them are very overstated. First, these accounts are based on stylized facts which do not capture the variety and complexity of the gender division of labour (GDOL) in different areas in Africa. Who does what work in food or cash-crop production varies significantly between countries and even communities, and all these accounts underplay men's important role in food production. Second is the question of what efficiency means in the context of smallholder households. It may well be appropriate for them to maximize a wide range of utilities and not simply cash income from their crops. These might include capacity for diversification, flexibility in the case of agroclimatic shocks, long-term investments and social reproduction (Whitehead and Kabeer 2001).

The final shortcoming in these approaches is that a concentration on the conflicts of interest between men and women is inadequate. Household relations in African smallholder families are a complex and changing set of dependencies, interdependencies and autonomies (Whitehead 2001; Whitehead and Kabeer 2001; Jackson 2007). These create commonalities as well as conflicts of interest. The simple presence of separate income streams and of labour that is not directly remunerated does not tell us enough about the incentives structures of such households. By themselves, they do not tell us about the welfare outcomes that derive for different members from different income sources.

This chapter takes a close look at the effects of liberalization on agriculture in different parts of the United Republic of Tanzania (hereafter, Tanzania) to draw out some important themes and processes which may apply to Africa more generally. It then takes a broader look at the different impacts these processes have on men and women, using an approach which conceptualizes the economy as gendered, and gender relations as conditioning all the operations of the economy (Elson and McGee 1995) to understand why these differential impacts happen. I pay particular attention to the ways in which institutions such as labour markets or markets for goods are gendered. Finally, the chapter considers the very scattered evidence of changes in gender relations conceived more widely.

The chapter proceeds with the major caveat that, despite more than three decades of research and analysis of the central importance of the GDOL in rural African households to agricultural production, data sources from which to draw evidence of the gender effects of liberalization remain astonishingly thin. Agricultural economics does not set itself the task of "addressing social and development issues of rural populations in their roles as producers and consumers" (Randriamamonjy 2000:9); hence, while agricultural data, such as national agricultural statistics and the Food and Agriculture Organization of the United Nations (FAO) database, is rich on crops and production methods, it tells us little about the people who are growing and producing, or in particular their relationships to each other. Information on women who do own-account farming but are not household heads is especially inadequate. Equally surprisingly, case studies which have something to say about gender are rare, with the result that work on gender sensitive economics in African agriculture repeatedly falls back on a handful of studies containing econometric data. The review in this chapter is singularly affected by this poor evidence base, which is important not just as a comment on the arguments I draw out, but for analysis and policy-making in the field as a whole.

## THE DIFFERENTIAL EFFECTS OF LIBERALIZATION
## ON WOMEN AND MEN IN TANZANIA[5]

Liberalization proceeded in several stages in Tanzania. The early removal of guaranteed prices for food crops and dismantling of public institutions for providing marketing, credit, inputs and other services to farmers was not accompanied by any effective growth in market-based institutions for their delivery. Credit systems collapsed, linkages to input and output markets on the whole failed to develop and input use, including fertilizer use, decreased. Agriculture stagnated with no increases in food crop production (Sen 2002) and the reforms were instead accompanied by widespread and persistent reports that rural households felt that income levels had reduced and livelihoods had become more vulnerable. User fees imposed on education and health services have compounded these effects.

Later in the liberalization process, removal of export crop controls exposed Tanzania to world markets, making rural households more vulnerable to changes in agricultural commodity prices, and making it very difficult for small producers to compete with more favourable production regimes in other parts of the world. This was very noticeable when world prices for coffee and cotton declined drastically, stimulating a decline in production of these historically important crops (Baffes 2002; Gibbon 1998) and a considerable loss of rural income. In agro-ecological areas where they could do so, Tanzania's small farmers responded positively when prices for cashews increased, increasing cashew production for export as raw nuts. A subsequent fall in prices for cashews exposed how vulnerable these households were to market forces. Like other countries, the Tanzanian government has attempted to promote new markets to develop local economies, providing incentives in particular to the tourist and mining industries, but with mixed success.

In the face of these largely adverse conditions rural households have sought a variety of solutions to falling and more insecure agricultural incomes. These have included increasing the main food crops, maize and rice, increasing petty trade, and in some areas diversifying into sesame seeds, tomatoes and vegetables, for example, to replace lost cash income (Ellis and Mdoe 2002). But supply responses such as these depend on a large number of factors which are often very locally specific.

The most widespread and long-term trend in local rural economies in Tanzania in the last 20 years, as elsewhere in rural Africa, has been an increased diversification of income sources into off-farm activities. There is no doubt that diversification of Tanzanian rural incomes is increasing, although in different localities to different extents. In Morogoro District, Ellis and Mdoe (2002) found that 50 per cent of incomes are derived from non-farm sources; the poorest households are more reliant on agriculture for their income than richer households; and that non-farm self-employment is the most significant source of non-farm income. But they also found that the kind of waged work undertaken by rich and poor is different: The poor do intermittent seasonal work on other farms; the better off are more likely to work in non-farm enterprises or government jobs. Although they hardly comment on the gender aspects of these findings, men are much more likely than women to have the necessary financial, human and social capital to access these latter. As their research indicates, "diversification" is not a single economic phenomenon and, while some of these activities can generate considerable returns, these are ones with high entry costs. Many other diversification strategies are in effect "survival" strategies, which for some commentators is a key indicator of the stress on rural incomes. This kind of diversification strategy is unlikely to offer a way out of rural poverty.

Bryceson has undertaken a major study of these post-liberalization processes in southern Tanzania, arguing that they add up to a de-agrarianization of rural African economies, a process which she sees as widespread in the continent (Bryceson 1999a, 1999b). She argues that the diversification in rural incomes into mainly non-agrarian sectors is dominated by petty trading and new forms of migration which lack forward and backward linkages in the agrarian economy. Her research examines rural income sources in villages with different farming systems and opportunities, paying particular attention to differences of gender and generation. In one village, which since independence had become highly specialized in commercial maize production, farmers had faced considerable difficulty in marketing crops after the drop in real prices brought by liberalization. As a result, maize acreage was declining, although there were few local cash-earning opportunities in local small industries or in trade. Both young men and young women had turned to migration for income—the men as wage labourers on distant tea estates; and women mainly as house servants in Dar es Salaam. The village had a history of male migration: During the colonial period, men had migrated to sisal plantations. This time, women were migrating too.

A second village, also until recently dependent on maize, had good road links with a nearby town and a greater level of socioeconomic differentiation: Some big commercial farmers were buying up land sold by smallholders becoming poorer with liberalization. A local labour market existed, providing some prospects of relatively skilled work for young men, partly due to the purchasing power of the commercial farmers. But since there was no overall land shortage, many youths were continuing with subsistence farming.

In a third village where land shortage is increasing, situated on Lake Nyasa across from Malawi, farming had been based on food crops, with rice and cocoa as cash-crops. Rice plots are now too small for viable incomes, and young people do only seasonal subsistence farming; few will inherit sufficient land to be farmers. Instead, young men and women are very active in trading at a weekly market catering primarily to Malawians who cross the lake to purchase cheap imported consumer items and second-hand clothing. Young men also transport and trade sugar from Malawi. Bryceson (1999a) reports that there is a profound sense of discontinuity and unease between the generations because of the very different income-earning opportunities and labour markets that each generation has experienced.

None of these communities is in the main cotton and coffee growing areas, which, as noted earlier, suffered a major decline when world prices tumbled. We might anticipate that they too have tried to expand production for national food crop markets and have also experienced outmigration and diversification. The major export crop expansion with liberalization was initially in cashews. Cashew farmers and district officials in the Lindi and Mtwara regions of southern Tanzania interviewed by ActionAid (2004) made a clear distinction between two periods of liberalization. During the initial "honeymoon" period from the mid-1990s until 2000, small producers benefited a great deal from liberalization. Cashew prices rose, and acreage and yields expanded. By 2001, the "crisis period" had set in, with drastic cuts in both world market and producer prices. Buyers had by then also established cartels, through which they were able to squeeze the small producers by weakening their bargaining power. Producers continued to be taxed heavily by a range of levies at central and district levels which sometimes amounted to as much as 20 per cent of the price received per kilo. This study found that men and women were affected differently by the two periods of liberalization because men mainly own cashew trees and control sales. But the story is not a simple one. On the whole, women shared in rising prosperity—albeit that they depended on "goodwill" from men to access the income—as well as in the fall in real incomes during the crisis period. There is limited evidence of overt gender conflict as cashew production increased—in Lidumbe District women complained that the number of divorces went up as producer prices in the cashew nut sector increased, as men made use of women's labour during the cashew nut season, only to abandon them for new wives when the season was over: "Men take the money and take a new wife and she gets it all". But no complaints of increased workloads were reported, even though hired labour had been replaced by family labour during the crisis period. More important has been the loss of real income to households that liberalization has brought, together with increased vulnerability in the face of powerful traders.

A more in-depth study of the gender impacts of liberalization in the cashew sector carried out in a predominantly matrilineal area in Mozambique (Kanji and Vijfhuizen 2003; Kanji et al. 2004) found slightly different effects. In the 1970s, Mozambique was the world's leading exporter of shelled (that is, processed) cashews, with cashews important in both the agricultural and industrial agro-processing sector. But liberalization of the sector from the mid-1990s caused many processing factories to close and 10,000 jobs were lost. There has been some revival since the government put a strategy in place in the late 1990s, but production and processing remain much lower than peak levels. However, about 40 per cent of the rural population have access to cashew trees, and 95 per cent of production is by smallholder farmers. Kanji and Vijfhuizen's study found that the ownership of cashew trees was not restricted to men—women reported significant control over trees and security of land tenure, and both men and women provided labour on all tasks for their cultivation, except for pruning which is done by men. Women were also directly involved in marketing cashews in three-quarters of households. However, the study reports that men had advantages in liberalized marketing institutions such as farmers' associations and larger trading groups, and that women had lost more jobs than men when factories closed. The newly private processing plants employed more men than women, with men moving into previously "female" tasks such as shelling. Women also earned less in the new plants either because their wages were less or because they were assigned to tasks that are less well paid.

Clear gender differentiated patterns in negative and positive impacts have also been found in a small study of the growth of tourism in Zanzibar. Government policy has been to provide incentives for tourism investors, especially from overseas. Tourism potentially provides jobs for women that can form part of their diversification strategies: Nationally, more women than men work in the informal sector in trade, restaurant and hotel work. There are also potential linkages to agriculture in the new markets for foodstuffs in hotels and restaurants. But an ActionAid study of tourism in Zanzibar found that the local population had not benefited much from direct employment in the industry, despite attempts by the Zanzibar Government to ensure they would. Foreign investors preferred to draw in experienced staff from elsewhere to take on managerial and service tasks and an influx of illegal immigrants from the neighbouring regions had depressed wage levels (ActionAid 2004:16). It has been particularly difficult for local women to get employment, kept out partly through the risk of being slandered as prostitutes within the community. Where they did get jobs, they were often forced to "settle for unfair wages and insecure employment" (ActionAid 2004:22).

Except for fresh fish, food supplies to hotels are mainly bought from commercial farms or imported, so women have not been able to exploit the new market for garden produce, poultry or dairy products. While some local male fishermen had benefited, outsiders had entered the fishing sector with larger boats and better equipment and had pushed many of them out. The locals that stayed no longer needed to use women as traders as they sold directly to hotels; and rising fish prices meant that less was available for domestic consumption.

These are probably not isolated findings. Chachage (1999) estimates that two-thirds of the foreign exchange from tourism is lost to Tanzania, and argues that the growth of tourism is leading to land shortage and land conflicts.[6] Research by Tsikata (2003) suggests that women's weaker claims to land mean that they lose out in situations of land shortages, to which recent land-grabbing and land speculation have contributed. In recent work on the political economy of tourism liberalization globally, Williams (2002) notes the high leakage of tourist receipts abroad, skewed ownership of resources to the North and negative gender equity effects. It is common to find that women lose out in formal employment, although they may benefit from selling handicrafts and the like.

## THE GENDERED RURAL ECONOMY

This brief country-based illustration shows how liberalization both requires and brings about changes in economic behaviour which may be both defensive and entrepreneurial. Changes in the profitability of crops may bring new opportunities but, where incomes decline as crops lose profitability, may also lead to a distress search for new income sources. For those that can afford to invest there may be new forms of business and entrepreneurial activity, and changes in the structure of agricultural enterprise may introduce new sources of employment. Many, many others may be forced by falling incomes to seek out multiple income sources defensively, including own-account trading, petty business and casual labour. The empirical evidence from Tanzania shows how men and women are positioned very differently in relation to these changes. The lack of systematic data collection and gender-focused research means that the empirical evidence in SSA as a whole is very patchy, but it is possible to make much greater sense of findings such as these if we follow through on the work of feminist economists who have conceptualized the economy as a gendered structure (Elson and McGee 1995:1991). Gender influences the division of labour, the distribution of income, the productivity of inputs and the economic behaviour of agents. Economic institutions, such as labour and product markets, are sites of social norms which shape the behaviour of individuals and transmit gender biases (Grown et al. 2000:1148). They are "the bearers of gender" (Elson 1995:1852).

### Gendered Access to Resources

One of the major lessons of the experience of economic reform in SSA is that the resource poverty of African farmers prevents them from taking up new opportunities (for example, Fontana et al. 1998). Women face resource constraints in common with many poor men, but to different degrees, and sometimes by different processes.

Capital constraints are extremely important to both men and women farmers. Even subsistence farming requires capital for seeds and tools, but food or export cash-crop farming requires much more outlay. The sums involved are beyond the reach of many women, through whose hands pitifully little cash may pass and who particularly suffer from what Reardon and Vosti (1995) have termed "investment poverty."[7] Women's investment poverty arises out of a combination of factors: The small scale of her farming enterprises provides little surplus to reinvest and her culturally assigned responsibilities for food production may prevent her from squeezing family welfare as men sometimes do to get farming investment. It is exacerbated by limited access to off-farm incomes, the level of these incomes and by public and private policy regarding credit, input schemes and crop markets.

Female-headed households are particularly affected by these constraints. While not a homogeneous category in terms of poverty levels, livelihoods or the processes which have produced female headship, most female-headed households in rural SSA are assetless and labour-poor and lack other resources to respond to market opportunities—such as patronage networks, knowledge, credit and extension services. A study in Uganda (Morrisey et al. 2003) found female-headed households to be among the categories of households unable to benefit from declining poverty levels due to export coffee production, because they lacked the resources to start growing coffee. In Malawi, a study in Somba District (Uttaro 2002) found more female-headed households unable to afford to use fertilizer on hybrid maize, so planting less despite its potential higher yields.

The significance of capital constraints has been exacerbated by the removal of input credit systems with the demise of marketing boards. In many areas the private sector has failed to replace these systems, and where they have, other forms of credit do not reach poorer farmers and often fail to reach women. The Oxfam-Institute of Development Studies (IDS) study in Zambia (1999b) found that, despite being as productive as male-headed households, female-headed households receive only about half the mean credit. Another study in Zambia found that liberalization resulted in a breakdown of local marketing cooperatives, which women had previously had more access to than other markets, and hence liberalization had affected them more profoundly (Wold 1997). Some of the new private marketing schemes have imposed institutional disadvantages like minimum crop output requirements, which may affect women disproportionately: In Zimbabwe, for example, Cotco requires 400 kg of cotton from its smallholders (Oxfam-IDS 1999a). Issues of scale are not gender neutral, and may be doubly important when combined with time constraints: Where women are only marketing small quantities it may not be worth walking to the nearest market centre. More women may therefore be selling crops at the farmgate to itinerant traders who pay poorer prices, or in kind (Samuels 2001).

Issues of scale have gendered implications because women heads of household and women household members who farm independently typically farm much smaller parcels of land than do male heads of household, or household men.[8] Although in some areas these smaller land-bases are related to women's inferior property rights under customary practices, this is not the case everywhere. There is enormous variation in the strength of wives' claims to land, and kinship systems differ in the extent to which divorced and separated women can make claims on their own kin groups for land and in their treatment of widows. When land competition is fierce, men may find it in their interests to block women's claims to land. In Uganda, where land scarcity has become acute in some areas, what were once quite strong claims for women under patrilineal kinship systems have been eroded (Bosworth 1995). Widows are losing their land and other women complain that they cannot get enough (Dolan 2002). In many other areas, however, women who have the capital and labour to work the land are able to claim access, often in a variety of ways. A wife's right to land from her husband is often backed by strong norms and women's entitlements are often recognized by men, even in situations of modernizing agriculture (Sorensen 1996; Whitehead et al. 2000; World Bank 1994). A woman may get land from her own relatives or even non-relatives and a husband may encourage his wife to get land outside his own, because this increases the total amount of land available to a household. In many places widows too have quite strong claims to land for maintenance, often through their sons (Bosworth 1995; Yngstrom 1999). Where there is not acute land shortage then, the absence of statutory property rights and titling is rarely a main reason why women farm less land than men. This should also be contrasted with the too frequent finding that the introduction of modern forms of property titling may weaken women's claims. Where this is accompanied by individual registered titles, women have often lost whatever land access they had, while male claims have been made stronger (Whitehead and Tsikata 2001).

Although the picture is complex, women's small farm holdings are associated first and foremost with their capital and labour constraints and additionally with their inability to make sufficiently strong legal claims against men, in both formal and customary law, as a result of a combination of customary modes of access, discriminatory registration practices, greater male power in the market and gender-differentiated access to other important resources. Women's land claims should be strengthened not because lack of security prevents them from seizing new opportunities,[9] but because land access is linked in other ways to unequal gender relations (Evers and Walters 2000).

## Gendered Diversification in Own-Account Enterprises and Petty Trading

Falling and/or insecure incomes from farming have pushed many women, and men, into own-account activities in rural economies as part of diversification strategies. However, as we have seen, these informal sector activities cover a wide range of enterprises which effectively bifurcate into a low-entry, low-return sector and a relatively higher entry, higher return sector. While the latter is often the source of savings that can be reinvested, including in higher return agriculture, the former often yields such tiny incomes that they are in essence survival strategies undertaken by the very poor.

The entry costs to different kinds of non-farm income-generating activities are a major factor affecting both men's and women's location in these economies. Limited access to start-up capital and other resources combine with gendered biases in the market to cluster women in low-entry, low-return activities. Many typical women's off-farm activities can be surmised as requiring only very low start-up costs: trading in fresh vegetable produce, which may mean selling home produce; making pots for tourists, as Winters (2001) found in Zimbabwe; or selling cooked food, which requires only the costs of a day's ingredients and fuel, and equipment which a woman may already have. Beer brewing is often a larger scale activity, requiring access to large pots and money for ingredients and fuel, but both Winters (2001) and Dolan (2002) suggest that the very poor are not able to find the start-up costs for even those activities requiring the lowest investment. Ameyaw (1990) found that over 90 per cent of women in Techiman Market, Ghana, have less than 5,000 cedis trading capital and are limited both in type and volume of commodities traded. Incomes are correspondingly low. King (1999), for example, found the majority of women in Kumasi Market in the mid-1990s made insufficient profits to support family needs, and Dolan (2002:6), in a recent study of three villages in Uganda, found that at least 50 per cent of the female-headed households whose livelihood portfolios included self-employment fell into the lowest income tercile.

Off-farm income has historically been a major source of investment for agricultural accumulation in SSA so the very low returns to women's off-farm incomes become a vicious circle. Women's lack of capital confines them to lower return off-farm activities, which in turn provide too little to reinvest in farming.

The informal institutions which regulate market access also position men and women differently in business activity. Elson (1999), in an analysis of relatively formal urban institutions, suggests that trust and social capital play an important role in how market players regulate and mitigate risk. Some studies in rural SSA suggest that these may also be important in informal risk handling institutions which are similarly "the bearers of gender" (Elson 1999:615). Bryceson (1993) noted how building up wholesaling contacts in the Tanzanian cereals trade involved an outgoing lifestyle, often involving drinking and promiscuity, which contributed to keeping women at low-risk intermediary levels.

A further factor contributing to women's apparently limited access to higher return activities may be a complex set of circumstances concerning the nature of their skills. While evidence that education levels influence returns to economic activity is ambiguous, it is stronger in urban areas and in the formal sector (Whitehead and Kabeer 2001). In rural areas, the skills individuals have acquired through informal education and the invisible training to do certain work that takes place in the household and community appear to have a strong influence on segregating the activities that women and men take up. Examples are legion: selling cooked food, dressmaking, brickmaking, carpentry; the vast majority of these build on gender-specific performance of activities in the non-monetized arena. These activities are rewarded at different levels. In different contexts, feminist work has shown how skills tend to be rewarded not so much according to their level of complexity but according to who has them (for example, Phillips and Taylor 1980), with women's skills accruing less reward by virtue of their being women's.

## Gendered Labour Markets

Changes in the profitability of different crops and the opening up of some new markets have influenced the nature of rural labour markets. Some new labour opportunities have arisen, and new versions of older arrangements have evolved. There is some evidence that wage labour may offer better prospects for women than self-employment in the informal economy. Dolan (2002) reports that although less that 10 per cent of female heads of households in two villages studied participate in wage employment (compared to around 40 per cent of male heads of household), this wage employment puts the women in the middle-income tercile—compared with self-employment which puts them in the lowest. Wage rates in new high-value export crops are also reported to be relatively high, but these opportunities are not widespread in most countries and the welfare effects for women entering these labour markets remain at best ambiguous, and often negative.

There are also other areas where long-standing opportunities for casual wage labour are associated with gendered access to, on the whole, very low wages. Both women and men work in agricultural casual wage labour. Scattered evidence suggests that women's participation in this labour force in both commercial and smallholder agriculture is sometimes very high: Evans and Young (1988) found that the casual labour used on hybrid maize in Zambia in the 1980s was largely female; Adams (1991) found that in Zimbabwe, 62 per cent of household members who worked in agriculture for wages were female. We know very little about wage rates and total income to women or men for this kind of work, or about its knock-on effects on their own-account farming, but most studies offering estimates suggest that women are paid from one-third to one-half the male rate for a day's work (for example, Whitehead 1996). The Benin poverty assessment reports rural women being paid about half as much as men "because the work given to them is considered less arduous" (World Bank 1994:64). We also know that women and men rarely work at the same tasks, enabling women's wages to be depressed.

Some casual agricultural labour is a clear survival strategy. In the context of Malawi's particularly negative experience of liberalization (for example, McDonagh 2002), Whiteside (2000) notes that rural female-headed households have been particularly badly affected. The main diversification strategy being taken up is *ganyu* work, a term describing a variety of casual piecework arrangements paid for in cash or in kind. Sometime *ganyu* is a way neighbours or relatives seek to help out those in distress, but it is also an important category of estate labour. Returns are generally low, and wage rates are driven down when labour demand or overall food supplies are poor. In Southern Malawi, many poor households, but especially female household heads, have been increasingly engaged in *ganyu* for longer periods, which has knock-on effects in reducing the time they can put into their own food production. Women's *ganyu* wage rates are less than men's and they also tend to be confined to more poorly rewarded *ganyu* close to home.

Bryceson's (1999a) study in Tanzania suggests that migration to access labour markets may be an option increasingly open to women, but Adams (1991) also found that that the welfare conditions of migrant agricultural labour are often poor, since they lose access to own-account farming, but do not have year-round guaranteed employment. Women casual workers in sugar-cane fields and factories in Zimbabwe were able to work only periodically when required so that they had to find other income sources the rest of the time, which included selling sexual services (Adams 1991).

It is clear, then, that labour markets in rural Africa are gender segregated, as they are in many other areas of the world. These forms of segregation filter the effects of liberalization. Several kinds of processes are at work. Local gender ideologies about appropriate work for women and men intersect with a range of factors which mean that women and men behave differently when seeking work. Manifestly women are willing to accept very low returns to their waged labour; much lower that those men are prepared to accept. The very different positions of men and women in the rural economy as a whole affect the reserve price of their labour. Women's reserve price of labour is likely to be low where the income potential of their own production is low, where off-farm income-generating opportunities are few, or give low returns to labour, and where there is urgent need. Evans (1992) found in Uganda that "women, especially women heads of households, women from households with inadequate land endowment and women known to be 'in distress' do not enter the wage bargaining process on the same terms as men" (para 8.18) and that women's time and income-earning constraints frequently place them in a contractually inferior position. In addition, informal social and cultural institutions may operate in gendered ways to regulate the terms of different people's entry to labour markets (Evans 1992). In Uganda, Evans found that women working for male employers was perceived as a sign of a disorganized home and marital problems, hence constraining married women's opportunities to enter this labour market through socially embedded notions of trust. Women willing to challenge such notions are perceived as distress-selling their labour, further diminishing their contractual power. Men's better farming opportunities give them a stronger fall-back position, and there are also more high-return opportunities for men. There is of course a historical virtuous/vicious circle at work here in which men become associated with work that has better returns and women become associated with low-return work and these begin to form part of gender ideologies.

## Employment in High-Value Intensive Agriculture

The double whammy for women is that many modern agricultural employment practices also use gender stereotypes to create a segmented labour market which enables overall wage costs to be kept down. The heavy competition in the fast-expanding horticulture export sector increases pressure to use more flexible labour under poorer conditions and for lower wages. This sector is often cited as an example of liberalization-driven growth offering new and positive labour opportunities for women, and in some countries in Africa women form a high proportion of this new workforce (Dolan and Sorby 2003). However, there are several factors that undermine the welfare enhancing potential of this new employment: Agribusiness enterprises operate gender-segregated employment with women overwhelmingly employed in more insecure and unskilled forms of work, as seasonal, temporary or casual workers. Barrientos and others (2006), in research on global value chains in South Africa, found fruit-farmers increasingly using contract and seasonal workers, the majority of whom were women. Seasonal and contract workers had low average weekly earnings, with women's much lower than men's. Segregation allows for gender wage differentials and reduces opportunities for women to become skilled. One study in Zimbabwe found pay and working conditions to be so bad that any net welfare gain seemed unlikely (Oxfam-IDS 1999a). Dolan and Sorby (2003) suggest that women migrating to work in horticulture may be particularly badly off, as own-account farming is not open to them when they are not employed. Women's relatively high involvement in it might, then, be a cause more for alarm than for celebration.

## CHANGING GENDER RELATIONS

Unfortunately, we know very little about how the hallmarks of liberalization—changes in the income sources of farm families, in the balance of profitability of various activities and the greater impoverishment of some rural households—have led to renegotiations between men and women or to gender conflicts within households.

That women are disproportionately affected by the shift against food producers, for example, is clear from the fact that many women (but not all) in male-headed households are primarily responsible for food production, and that female-headed households are much more heavily dependent on food farming than any other population sector. But there is a dearth of good case studies that might tell us whether, or when, men's income is used to compensate declining income from women's food production, or what kinds of gender conflicts (or solidarities) might arise in these circumstances.

Some scattered evidence—sometimes indirect—exists that responsibilities are changing in some places, and of reasons for gender conflict. Women have definitely faced much more difficulty than men in growing export crops themselves due to lack of access to factor markets, and though the cashew study in Tanzania (ActionAid 2004) suggests that women have shared in the overall fortunes of the household, it does not show that they shared *equally* in them. Research in a tea-growing area of Kenya which compared baseline data from 1985–1986 with new data in 1995–1996 found that in 1995–1996 tea-growing households relied much more heavily on family labour. Women in male-headed households worked in the tea-fields mainly as unpaid family labour and received no bonus or monthly payments from the Kenya Tea Development Authority. This, together with the fact that they cannot control the income from tea, is likely to have a negative effect on their incentive to work in the tea-fields. Women from male-headed tea households said that they would devote more time to tea production if they received part of the bonus payment (Ongile 1999).[10]

Gender conflicts are expressed somewhat differently in a Gender and Economic Reforms in Africa (GERA) study in Kenya, which found that women had increased their food production to meet family needs because men had reduced their input to family responsibilities. The authors argue that this was due to men's lower incomes arising from increased input costs in agricultural production, which absorbed almost three-quarters of agricultural revenues. The burden falls more on women "by default" (Yego et al. 2002).

Bryceson's work in Tanzania foregrounds how the "scramble for cash has caused an upheaval in age-old gender and generation divisions of labour" (1999a:17). Rural men have generally accepted that their wives and daughters can, and in fact should, work outside the home, and "this change in male attitudes appears to have taken place quite rapidly and under duress" (1999a:19). Opportunities for young women are almost exclusively low-entry low-return, and "rural women often refer to their new income earning role in terms of it having been thrust upon them by worsening economic circumstances" (1999a:19).

Lyimo-Macha and Mdoe's (2002) research in Morogoro, Tanzania, reports that women have full control over the income brought in by their non-farm activities, which they contrast with their farming income. This finding might point to a more significant change in gender relations if the incomes were not so small: Most of the craft and casual farm-work women are doing brings in relatively little.

Processes of diversification are likely to have affected gender relations, with tensions over how new earning opportunities affect existing divisions of economic responsibility between male and female household members. Bryceson finds that while men are willing to acquiesce in women's new cash earning opportunities, they are much less willing to accept a restructuring of household relations, with the result that cash earning is added to women's other productive and reproductive work. She suggests that "coordinated decision-making and income pooling is on the decrease" as the cash and income crisis has forced

> virtually all able-bodied adults as well as many children to seek different forms of income. . . . The individualisation of economic activity and the increasing tendency to engage in non-agricultural income earning have had a dissolving force on long standing agrarian division of labour as well as economic rights and responsibilities within rural households. (Bryceson 1999a:21)

Such tensions may be exacerbated if men cannot find employment or their farming income is going down. A study in rural Kenya (RODI-Kenya 2004/2002), reports considerable shifts in household gender relations: As men's income and employment opportunities have been undermined by liberalization, women have found opportunities for both farm and non-farm incomes. The main earners—maize, pyrethrum, milk and cattle—are no longer marketed and controlled only by men, and there is a greater dependence on women's incomes both from sales which they previously controlled (chickens, eggs, small milk quantities) and diversified products such as groundnuts, pigs, tomatoes and kale. Women's workloads have increased as they take on more cash-production work without being free of food production and household responsibilities.

The women comment graphically on the dilemmas, gender conflicts and renegotiations that have ensued. One woman said: "Instead of my husband respecting and awarding me for enabling the family in a bad situation, he calls me 'a female tycoon'" (RODI-Kenya 2004/2002:35). A key element that plays into these conflicts is not simply that women's economic role has expanded, but that men's has been reduced. Women's increased role in income earning has bolstered their self-respect but damaged that of men. One woman is quoted as saying: "I really sympathize with my husband because of the frustration he has been going through. Before the coming of *soko huru* (free market) he used to fend for the family. Nowadays I have to buy him clothes. This has on the one hand increased my dignity but on the other it has created animosity in the house." Women report that domestic violence has risen as men lose their role as sole breadwinner, and with pressure on scarce resources. Women's time use has also caused conflict as their increased production work leaves less time for household and childcare tasks. The use of and control of income has been contested, and caused men's suspicion and distrust: "If my husband could recognize my role, responsibilities and respect me, I would not complain, but now the opposite/reverse is the reality" (RODI-Kenya 2004/2002:35). "Men also suspect women that they go to the market to look for other men and for prostitution" (RODI-Kenya 2004/2002:37).

This Kenya case and Bryceson's case in Tanzania are neither unique, nor universal, but we simply know too little about the situation in other places to make confident generalizations which could guide new policy initiatives. Good comparative studies over a wide range of circumstances and explicitly concerned with the impacts of liberalization on gender relations are urgently needed. Advocates of policies which could mitigate the negative effects on women continue to be seriously hampered by having to depend on an evidence base which remains piecemeal and thin. Without good comparative studies over a wide range of circumstances we can neither say confidently what the impacts of liberalization have been on gender relations, nor can we begin to establish policy that will mitigate the negative effects on women and on gender relations.

## CONCLUSION

Liberalization and economic reform in SSA has not been as successful as predicted by IFIs, particularly in terms of welfare effects in rural areas. The private sector, especially in marginal areas and for small-scale producers, has failed to compensate for the loss of state input and marketing institutions; exposure to world markets has brought increased vulnerability both to those involved in export crop production—such as cashews—and to those involved in food cash-crops, now subject to increased competition from imported food and suffering increased input prices; and many people, including a majority of rural women, remain simply too poor to enter into welfare-enhancing opportunities, such as there are. This chapter has argued that the gender effects of these processes are specific to particular countries and regions within them, as they depend on a number of factors including the pattern of agriculture (farming systems, crop patterns, agro-ecological constraints) and the potential for new crops; the prevailing gender division of labour (by crop, by task etc.); household structure; access to crop inputs and credit markets; and the actual or potential level of development of the accessible non-farm sector. Nevertheless, there are clear ways in which men and women are affected differently by liberalization because of systematic gender differences. These occur in the control over key resources, in labour inputs to crops, in control over income and in their relationships with labour and product markets. Many women may have lost out in the rearrangement of labour in export crops and they may be unable to take advantage of apparent opportunities in local economies. Emerging trends appear to be that diversification is indeed increasing, but in a differentiated form which includes a majority of "survival"-type diversification strategies. Women are clustered in this group because of a complex set of factors mediating their relationship to labour and product markets and because investment poverty keeps them there.

These systematic interactions make it appropriate to rethink radically the conventional notion that the economy is somehow gender neutral; exploring the effects of liberalization on rural African men and women suggests rather that the economy embodies systematic links with gender hierarchies. These systematic links should not be thought of as lying in the realm of culture and beyond the reach of economic analysis. It is because these connections between gender and economic behaviour are largely unrecognized beyond gender specialists that the empirical evidence to explore trends and implications is so woefully lacking.

**APPENDIX 2.1**

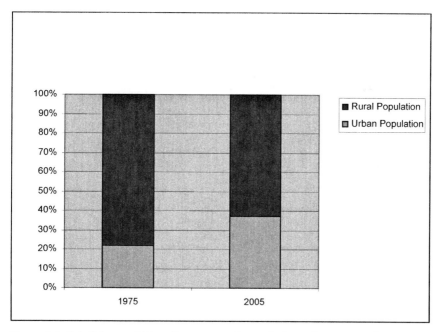

*Figure 2.1* Sub-Saharan Africa: Percentage of population urban vs. rural.
*Source*: UNDP 2007.

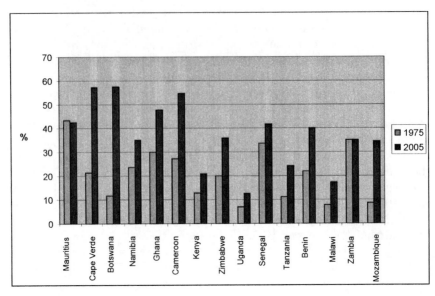

*Figure 2.2* Percentage of population living in urban areas: Selected countries in sub-Saharan Africa.
*Source*: UNDP 2007.

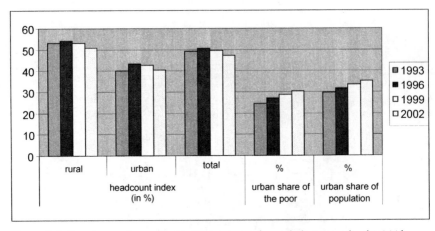

*Figure 2.3* Rural vs. urban poverty: Percentage of people living under $1.00/day.
*Source*: Adapted from M. Ravallion, S. Chen and P. Sangraula (2007).

## NOTES

1. Although structural adjustment conditionality ended in 1999 with the abandonment of the Washington consensus, several forms of conditionality

remain attached to World Bank and International Monetary Fund lending, frequently entailing privatization and liberalization (ActionAid 2006; Norwegian Ministry of Foreign Affairs 2006; Oxfam 2006). A recent report from EURODAD examining 20 poor countries found 18 of them had "privatisation-related conditionalities attached to their development finance" (EURODAD 2006:3). Thirteen of these countries were in Africa. Oxfam (2007) contains a very interesting analysis of the impacts of conditionality, entailing privatization and liberalization, in Mali.

2. Establishing the relative impact on rural and urban populations is not an easy matter. Urban populations in SSA countries have been growing rapidly (see figures 2.1 and 2.2 in appendix 2.1) and there is evidence that rates of urban poverty have lately been increasing more than rural poverty. However, much of the growing urbanization derives from increased rates of rural out-migration, whose causes and dimensions are poorly understood and documented. Such migration needs to be taken into account in evaluating data on rural and urban poverty rates. Most work comparing household survey data on urban and rural household incomes does not identify the contribution that urban to rural remittances make to rural household income. In many countries the high proportion of rural poor (see figure 2.3 in appendix 2.1), together with the depth of rural poverty, mean that the rural poor still figure prominently as households negatively affected by liberalization.

3. See *Journal of Development Studies*, Vol. 42, Issue 2 for a special issue exploring the importance of assets in avoiding persistent poverty (Barrett, Carter and Little 2006).

4. This empirical demonstration is done only for a single crop in the total array of crops in the farming systems.

5. The geographical coverage in this chapter is by no means comprehensive, not least because the author has only used the anglophone literature. There is also a surprising paucity of detailed case study material on the gender dimensions of the impact of liberalization in the rural areas of SSA. Tanzania has been chosen as a main case example because of the variety of different studies that have been done there.

6. Wildlife parks and safari tourism are especially significant here, but so are the effects of tourism in areas where land is already in finite supply—such as the coastal areas, and urban areas such as Dar es Salaam.

7. They distinguish between investment poverty and welfare poverty. Welfare poverty is essentially consumption/income or expenditure poverty, and investment poverty is lacking any resources to put into income generation.

8. Whitehead and Tsikata (2001) discuss gender and land issues in detail.

9. In some places, however, men resist women growing tree crops on their land because it gives them greater "ownership" rights.

10. Some caution needs to be exercised in interpreting the source of increased workloads: In similar circumstances in Zambia, women interpret the pressure as coming from external sources, not men—in this case the lack of traders in anything except labour-intensive cotton (Oxfam-IDS 1999b).

# REFERENCES

ActionAid. 2004. *Gender and Trade Liberalisation in Tanzania.* Internal Research Report, ActionAid, London. Mimeo, January.

ActionAid. 2006. *What Progress? A Shadow Review of World Bank Conditionality.* ActionAid International, Johannesburg.

Adams, J. 1991. "Female wage labour in rural Zimbabwe." *World Development*, Vol. 19, Nos. 2 and 3, pp. 163–177.

Agarwal, B. 1997. "'Bargaining' and gender relations: Within and beyond the household." *Feminist Economics*, Vol. 3, No. 1, pp. 1–51.

Ameyaw, S. 1990. *The Dynamics of Female Entrepreneurship and Indigenous Food Markets: A Case of Techiman Market Women, Ghana*. Office of Women in Development, Michigan State University.

Baffes, J. 2002. *Tanzania's Coffee Sector: Constraints and Challenges in a Global Environment*. World Bank, Washington, DC.

Barrett, C.B., Carter, M.R. and Little, P.D. 2006, (eds) "Understanding and reducing persistent poverty in Africa": *Journal of Development Studies: Special Issue*, Vol. 42, Issue 2.

Barrientos, S., A. Kritzinger, G. Muller, H. Rossouw, P. Termine, N. Tregurtha and N. Vink. 2006. *The Global Value Chain and Changing Employment Relations in South African Fruit: Summary of Findings*. www.gapresearch.org/production/Draft%204%20summary%20of%20report.pdf, accessed on 27 September 2006.

Bijlmakers, L.A., M.T. Bassett and D.M. Sanders. 1998. *Socioeconomic Stress, Health and Child Nutritional Status in Zimbabwe at a Time of Economic Structural Adjustment: A Three Year Longitudinal Study*. Research Report No. 105. Nordic Africa Institute. Uppsala.

Blackden, M. 1997. *All Work and No Time: The Relevance of Gender Differences in Time Allocation for Agricultural Development in Zambia*. World Bank, Washington, DC.

Bosworth, J.L. 1995. *Land Tenure Systems in Sub-Saharan Africa*. PhD thesis, Faculty of Social Studies, University of Oxford, Trinity College, Oxford.

Bryceson, D. 1999a. *African Rural Labour, Income Diversification and Livelihood Approaches: A Long-term Development Perspective*. Working Paper 35, African Studies Centre, Leiden.

———. 1999b. *Sub-Saharan Africa Betwixt and Between: Rural livelihood Practices and Policies*. Working Paper 43, African Studies Centre, Leiden.

———. 1993. *Liberalising Tanzania's Food Trade: Public and Private Faces of Marketing Policy: 1939–1988*. UNRISD, Geneva/James Currey, London.

Çagatay, N. 1998. *Engendering Macroeconomics and Macroeconomic Policies*. United Nations Development Programme, New York.

Çagatay, N., D. Elson and C. Grown (eds.). 1995. "Gender, adjustment and macroeconomics." *World Development Special Issue*, Vol. 23, No. 11, pp. 1827–1836.

Chachage, C.S.L. 1999. *Globalisation and Transitions in Tourism in Tanzania*. Paper presented at the ICSTD Regional Trade and Environment Seminar for Governments and Civil Society, Harare, Zimbabwe, 10–12 February.

Cornea, G.A., R. Jolly and F. Stewart. 1987. *Adjustment with a Human Face: Protecting the Vulnerable and Promoting Growth*. Oxford University Press, New York.

Dolan, C.S. 2002. *Gender and Diverse Livelihoods in Uganda*. LADDER Working Paper 10, mimeo, University of East Anglia, Norwich.

———. 1997. *Tesco is King: Gender and Labour Dynamics in Horticultural Exporting, Meru District, Kenya*. PhD thesis, State University of New York at Binghamton. Available from UMI Dissertation Services, Ann Arbor.

Dolan, C. and K. Sorby. 2003. *Gender and Employment in High-Value Agriculture Industries*. Agriculture and Rural Development Working Paper 7, World Bank, Washington, DC.

Ellis, F. and N. Mdoe. 2002. *Livelihoods and Rural Poverty Reduction in Tanzania*. LADDER Working Paper 11, mimeo, University of East Anglia, Norwich.

Elson, D. 1999. "Labour markets as gendered institutions: Equality, efficiency and empowerment issues." *World Development*, Vol. 27, No. 3, pp. 611–627.

———. 1995. "Gender awareness in modelling structural adjustment." *World Development*, Vol. 23, No. 11, pp. 1851–1868.

————. 1994. "Micro, meso, macro: Gender and economic analysis in the context of policy reforms." In I. Bakker (ed.), *The Strategic Silence: Gender and Economic Policy*. Zed Press, London and North-South Institute, Ottawa.

————. 1993. "Gender-aware analysis and development economics." *Journal of International Development*, Vol. 5, No. 2, pp. 237–247.

————. 1991. "Male bias in macroeconomics: The case of structural adjustment." In D. Elson (ed.), *Male Bias in the Development Process*. Manchester University Press, Manchester.

Elson, D. and R. Mcgee. 1995. "Gender equality, bilateral programme assistance and structural adjustment: Policy and procedures." *World Development*, Vol. 21, No. 11, pp. 1987–1994.

EURODAD. 2006. *World Bank and IMF Conditionality: A Development Injustice*. EURODAD, Brussels.

Evans, A. 1992. *A Review of Rural Labour Markets in Uganda*. Mimeo, World Bank Agricultural Secretariat, Washington, DC.

————. 1989. *Women: Rural Development and Gender Issues in Rural Household Economics*. IDS Discussion Paper No. 254, IDS, University of Sussex, Brighton.

Evans, A. and K. Young. 1988. *Gender Issues in Household Labour Allocation: The Transformation of a Farming System in Northern Province, Zambia. A Report to ODA's Economic and Social Research Committee for Overseas Research*. Overseas Development Administration, London.

Evers, B. and B. Walters. 2000. "Extrahousehold factors and women farmers' supply response in sub-Saharan Africa." *World Development*, Vol. 28, No. 7, pp. 67–78.

Fontana, M., S. Joekes and R. Masika. 1998. *Global Trade Expansion and Liberalisation: Gender Issues and Impacts*. BRIDGE Report No. 42, IDS, University of Sussex, Brighton.

Galli, R. and U. Funk. 1995. "Structural adjustment and gender in Guinea-Bissau." In G. Thomas-Emeagwali (ed.), *Women Pay the Price: Structural Adjustment in Africa and the Caribbean*. Africa World Press, Trenton, NJ.

Gibbon, P. 1998. *Peasant Cotton Cultivation and Marketing Behaviour in Tanzania since Liberalisation*. Working Paper 98.16, Centre for Development Research (CDR), Copenhagen.

Grown, C., D. Elson and N. Çağatay. 2000. "Introduction." In *World Development Special Issue on Growth, Trade, Finance and Gender Inequality*, Vol. 28, No. 7, pp. 1145–1156.

Jackson, C. 2007. "Resolving risk? Marriage and creative conjugality." *Development and Change*, Vol. 38, January, pp. 107–129.

Kabeer, N. 1994. "Benevolent dictators, maternal altruists and patriarchal contracts: Gender and household economics." In N. Kabeer (ed.), *Reversed Realities: Gender Hierarchies in Development Thought*. Verso, London.

————. 2003. *Gender Mainstreaming in Poverty Eradication and the Millennium Development Goals*. Commonwealth Secretariat, London.

Kanji, N., N. Kanji and F. Manji. 1991. "From development to sustained crisis: Structural adjustment, equity and health." *Social Science and Medicine*, Vol. 33, No. 9, pp. 985–993.

Kanji, N. and C. Vijfhuizen. 2003. *Cracking the Cashew Nut Myth? The Dilemmas of Gendered Policy Research in the Cashew Sector in Mozambique*. Paper presented at the Gender Myths and Feminist Fables Workshop, IDS, University of Sussex, Brighton, 2–4 July.

Kanji, N., C. Vijfhuizen, L. Artur and C. Braga. 2004. *Liberalisation, Gender and Livelihoods: The Mozambique Cashew Nut Case—Summary Report*. International Institute for Environment and Development, London.

Killick, T. 2001. "Globalisation and the rural poor." *Development Policy Review*, Vol. 19, No. 2, pp. 155–180.

King, R. 1999. *The Role of Urban Market Women in Local Development Processes and Its Implication for Policy: A Case Study of Kumasi Central Market.* Unpublished PhD dissertation, Sussex University, Brighton.

Lyimo-Macha, J. and N. Mdoe. 2002. *Gender and Rural Poverty in Tanzania: Case of Selected Villages in Morogoro Rural and Kilosa Districts.* LADDER Working Paper 18, University of East Anglia, Norwich.

McDonagh, J. 2002. *Crop-Based Farming Livelihoods and Policies in Malawi.* LADDER Working Paper 23, mimeo, University of East Anglia, Norwich.

Morrisey, O., N. Rudaheranwa and L. Moller. 2003. *Trade Policies, Performance and Poverty in Uganda.* Uganda Trade and Poverty Project (UTPP), ODI, London and Ministry of Tourism, Trade and Industry, Government of Uganda.

Norwegian Ministry of Foreign Affairs. 2006. *The World Bank's and IMF's Use of Conditionality to Encourage Privatisation and Liberalisation: Current Issues.* Ministry of Foreign Affairs, Oslo.

Ongile, G. 1999. *Gender and Agricultural Supply Response to Structural Adjustment Programmes: A Case study of Smallholder Tea Producers in Kericho, Kenya.* Research Report No. 109, Nordic Africa Institute, Uppsala.

Oxfam. 2007. *Pricing Farmers Out of Cotton: The Costs of World Bank Reforms in Mali.* Oxfam Briefing Paper 99, Oxfam International, Oxford.

———. 2006. *Kicking the Habit: How the World Bank and IMF Are Still Addicted to Attaching Economic Policy Conditions to Aid.* Oxfam Briefing Paper 96, Oxfam International, Oxford.

Oxfam-IDS. 1999a. *Liberalisation and Poverty: Zimbabwe Case Study.* Unpublished Report to DFID.

———. 1999b. *Liberalisation and Poverty: Zambia Case Study.* Unpublished Report to DFID.

Palmer, I. 1992. "Gender, equity and economic efficiency in adjustment programmes." In H. Afshar and C. Dennis (eds.), *Women and Adjustment Policies in the Third World.* Macmillan, Basingstoke.

Phillips, A. and B. Taylor. 1980. "Sex and skill: Notes towards a feminist economics." *Feminist Review*, No. 6, pp. 79–88.

Randriamamonjy, M. 2000. *Gender and Statistics: Key Elements for the Advancement of Women.* FAO Women and Population Division. www.fao.org/sd/WPdirect/WPan0045.htm, accessed on 27 September 2006.

Ravallion, M., S. Chen and P. Sangraula. 2007. *New Evidence on the Urbanization of Global Poverty.* World Bank Policy Research Working Paper 4199, April, World Bank, Washington, DC.

Regional Centre for Southern Africa (RCSA)/United States Agency for International Development. 2003. *RCSA Food Security Strategic Option. Synthesis and Analysis of Selected Readings Final Report.* USAID/RCSA, Washington, DC.

Reardon, T. and S.A. Vosti. 1995. "Links between rural poverty and the environment in developing countries: Asset categories and investment poverty." *World Development*, Vol. 23, No. 9, pp. 1495–1506.

Resources Oriented Development Initiatives (RODI)-Kenya, 2004/2002. *Agricultural Trade Liberalisation—Its Effect on Women and Food Security in Kenya.* Gender and Economic Reforms in Africa (GERA) (II), Third World Network, Ghana.

Samuels, F. 2001. *"We Kaonde We Don't Migrate": The Stretching of Contemporary Kaonde Life-Worlds between Rural and Urban.* PhD thesis, University of Sussex, Brighton.

Sen, A. 1990. "Gender and cooperative conflicts." In I. Tinker (ed.), *Persistent Inequalities: Women and World Development.* Oxford University Press, New York.

Sen, K. 2002. *Economic Reforms and Rural Livelihood Diversification in Tanzania*. LADDER Working Paper 12, mimeo, University of East Anglia, Norwich.

Smith, L.C. and J.P. Chavas. 2003. "Supply response of West African agricultural households: Implications of intra-household preference heterogeneity". In A. Quisumbing (ed.), *Household Decisions, Gender and Development: A Synthesis of Recent Research*. IFPRI, Washington, DC/Johns Hopkins University Press, Baltimore, MD.

Sorensen, P. 1996. "Commercialization of food crops in Bugosa, Uganda and the renegotiation of gender." *Gender and Society*, Vol. 10, No. 5, pp. 608–628.

Sparr, P. 1994. *Mortgaging Women's Lives: Feminist Critiques of Structural Adjustment*. Zed Books, London.

Tsikata, D. 2003. "Securing women's interests within land tenure reforms: Recent debates in Tanzania." *Journal of Agrarian Change*, Vol. 3, Nos. 1 and 2, pp. 149–183.

Tsikata, D. and J. Kerr. 2000. *Demanding Dignity: Women Confronting Economic Reforms in Africa*. The North-South Institute, Ottawa/Third World Network-Africa, Accra.

Udry, C., J. Hoddinott, H. Alderman and L. Haddad. 1995. "Gender differentials in farm productivity: Implications for household efficiency and agricultural policy." *Food Policy*, Vol. 20, No. 5, pp. 407–423.

United Nations Development Programme (UNDP). 2007. *Human Development Report 2007*. http://hdrstats.undp.org/buildtables/rc_report.cfm, accessed on 21 May 2008.

Uttaro, R.P. 2002. "Diminishing choices: Gender, small bags of fertilizer, and household food security decisions in Malawi." *African Studies Quarterly*, Vol. 6, Nos. 1 and 2, www.africa.ufl.edu/asq/v6/v6i1a4.htm. Accessed 19 July 2006.

Warner, J.M. and D.A. Campbell. 2000. "Supply response in an agrarian economy with non-symmetric gender relations." *World Development*, Vol. 28, No. 7, pp. 1327–1340.

Whitehead, A. 2001. *Trade, Trade Liberalisation and Rural Poverty in Low-income Africa: A Gendered Account*. Background paper prepared for the Least Developed Countries Report 2002, United Nations Conference on Trade and Development (UNCTAD), Geneva.

———. 1996. *Poverty in North-East Ghana*. Report to ESCOR, Overseas Development Administration (ODA), London.

———. 1981. "I'm hungry mum: The politics of domestic budgeting." In K. Young (ed.), *Of Marriage and the Market*. Routledge and Kegan Paul, London.

Whitehead, A. and N. Kabeer, 2001. *Living with Uncertainty: Gender, Livelihoods and Pro-Poor Growth in Rural Sub-Saharan Africa*. Working Paper 134, IDS, Brighton.

Whitehead, A. and D. Tsikata. 2001. *Policy Discourses about Women's Land Rights in Sub-Saharan Africa*. Mimeo, UNRISD, Geneva.

Whitehead, A., J. Vivian, M. Lockwood and D. Kasente. 2000. *Gender and the Expansion of Non-Traditional Agricultural Exports in Uganda*. Beijing Occasional Paper No. 12, UNRISD, Geneva.

Whiteside, M. 2000. *Ganyu Labour in Malawi and Its Implications for Livelihood Security Interventions: An Analysis of Recent Literature and Implications for Poverty Alleviation*. Network Paper No. 99. ODI Agriocultural Research and Extension Network (AgREN), London.

Wiggins, S. 2003. "Lessons from the current food crisis in Southern Africa." In M. Lafon and S. Drimie (eds.), *Food Security in Southern Africa: Causes and Responses from the Region*, IFAS Working Paper Series, No. 3, pp. 23–34.

Williams, M. 2002. *The Political Economy of Tourism Liberalisation Gender and GATS*. Occasional paper series on Gender, Trade and Development, International Gender and Trade Network (IGTN), Washington, DC.

Winters, L.A. 2001. *Trade Policies for Poverty Alleviation in Developing Countries*. Paper for the Series of Advanced International Policy Seminars (SAIPS) on Trade and Development, Brussels.

Wold, B. 1997. *Supply Response in a Gender Perspective: The Case of Structural Adjustment in Zambia*. Statistics Norway, Oslo/Zambian Central Statistical Office, Lusaka.

World Bank. 2003. *Mitigating the Food Crisis in Southern Africa: From Relief to Development*. World Bank, Washington, DC.

———. 1994. *Benin: Towards a Poverty Reduction Strategy*. World Bank, Washington, DC.

Yego, H., T. Barasa, F.K. Were, E. Ngunjiri, M. Afandi and J. Mwangi. 2002. *Agricultural Trade Liberalization—Its Effect on Women and Food Security in Kenya*. Research Report by Resources Oriented Development Initiatives (RODI)-Kenya for GERA, Ruiru.

Yngstrom, I. 1999. *Gender, Land and Development in Tanzania: Rural Dodoma 1920–1996*. PhD thesis, University of Oxford.

# 3  Gender Inequality and Agrarian Change in Liberalizing India

*Cecile Jackson and Nitya Rao*

## INTRODUCTION[1]

The startling recent Indian growth rates gives added significance to the question of the gendered effects of the liberalization ushered in during the 1990s. Gender relations interact with liberalization as both cause and effect; in other words, gender influences the level and character of growth, and it patterns the distribution of the benefits of growth. Gender inequality in human capital and labour force participation has been shown to significantly inhibit growth through a number of direct and indirect pathways (Verschoor et al. 2006). Our focus here is on the gendered effects of liberalization, which then, over time, recursively become determinants of levels of achieved growth, and on effects in rural India, since, despite urbanization, the majority of the poor remain located in rural locations and the character of rural poverty is especially entrenched[2]; a higher proportion of rural than urban Indians have been poor for many years (Dubey and Palmer-Jones 2005; Deaton and Drèze 2002).

Gender marks a primary form of social differentiation and inequality, and Karin Kapadia has linked liberalization to "an erosion of women's rights and social status . . . and a deterioration in women's position in contemporary India" (Kapadia 2002:33–34). But understanding the effects of liberalization on gender relations is methodologically very difficult. The degree of variation between states and cross-cutting agro-ecological domains in rural India, with their particular histories, makes any analysis of gender relations a complex task. In addition, within these spatial and temporal locations class, caste and ethnicity create distinctive kinship and marriage patterns constitutive of very different gender relations. Despite variations between regions there are, however, trajectories of change which appear to have considerable reach: sanskritization among lower castes and "tribes", the spread of dowry into new social spaces, the deepening of son preference and consequent masculinization of landed rural households, as well as positive changes such as rising age at marriage, closing gender gaps in education and rising life expectancy.

What several studies of well-being indicators across Indian states appear to reveal is a troubling and complex relationship between economic growth and gender inequality, since equality indicators for north Indian states which have seen dramatic agricultural growth are worsening, gender disparities are highest in the wealthiest northern states and a number of studies find sex ratios to be more adverse to women in more agriculturally advanced villages (for example, Nillesen and Harriss-White 2004; Roy 1995:198). This pattern emphasizes the importance of separating poverty/well-being analysis from gender analysis.

The overlapping identities of rural women also may produce identity-specific effects. Successful liberalization may make women more prosperous as persons but more disadvantaged as women, or it may make them better off as members of poor households and as women. Intensive cropping cycles, for instance, can contribute to the prosperity of smallholder households, yet at the same time intensify women's work burdens in terms of cooking for additional labour, post-harvest processing and so on. "Failed" liberalization can leave women less prosperous as persons but not necessarily as women, or indeed a grim lose-lose scenario in which they are worse off both as persons and as women. Added to this are the differential effects on absolute material well-being and on relations of inequality, which offer further analytical challenges.

Trying to understand the effects of liberalization on rural women in India is an important endeavour, but it is not an easy one, being beset by methodological problems, of evidence and information, of procedures, of assumptions and conceptual uncertainties, and the generally difficult business of extracting meaning from empirical data. Given these methodological challenges, we consider it wise to offer this analysis as an appropriately tentative exploration of the gendered effects of liberalization in agrarian India, as a policy turn within a context of shifting degrees of state involvement in development, and changing character of interventions. With a population of over a billion and considerable state-level policy independence, the picture is diverse, and the time-lags and differential implementation of the liberalization agenda create a very uneven landscape of change.

We first consider what liberalization has meant in practice in India, with a focus on agricultural reforms, and then discuss some of the methodological complexities of seeking connections between liberalization and particular gendered outcomes. The main part of the chapter then considers how gendered rural livelihoods are changing and what is happening to forms of social reproduction.

## LIBERALIZATION AND RURAL INDIA

The Indian elections of 2004 saw the ejection of the Bharatiya Janata Party (BJP), in favour of the Congress Party, in what was widely seen as a protest by the rural masses who have not benefited from the liberalization policies introduced in 1991, despite the growth of the Indian economy;

and in an ironic twist it was the architect of the 91 reforms, Dr. Manmohan Singh, who became prime minister. When he unveiled his economic agenda it emphasized agricultural revival, rural investment, a softer line on privatization and labour reform and a declared commitment to boost farm incomes and generate employment. The strong growth of the Indian economy recently (8.1 per cent in 2004), based on information technology (IT) manufacturing and services, compared to the slow growth of agriculture (2 per cent per annum over the last decade)[3], can be explained, however, in several ways: a failure of liberalization policies, insufficient liberalization of agriculture, inadequate public investment in agriculture or the particular difficulties of benefiting from agricultural liberalization in the face of subsidized developed country agriculture. After 1991 India only partially liberalized agriculture, the international agricultural trade regime has remained biased against developing countries due to United States and European Union agricultural subsidies, and notwithstanding a string of "good monsoons", agriculture appears not to have grown as fast as in the previous decade.

The India-wide situation in the 1980s was one of falling poverty, and on the eve of liberalization, Bhalla and Singh (1997) use state-level analysis for the years 1962–1965 to 1992–1995 to show the acceleration of agricultural growth during 1980–1983 to 1992–1995, compared to earlier periods, and the shift from coarse grains into oilseeds in particular. This was largely aided by public spending on the rural sector in the 1970s and 1980s. Male agricultural productivity also rose strongly in the 1980s in many states. The 1980s saw what Bhalla calls "an indigenously sponsored liberalization" (1999:33), in response to the apparently poor economic performance resulting from Indian planning. The evidence, up to the 1990s, shows that Green Revolution (GR) technologies, especially when assisted by public investment in infrastructure and services, in particular irrigation and credit, do stimulate rural growth, though clearly with different implications for different groups. While GR technologies themselves may have boosted production, the benefits of policies, including support prices, subsidies for fertilizers and other inputs and incentives (agricultural credit or power supply), did little to counter class and regional inequities (Agarwal 1985; Rao and Storm 1998:218).

What has liberalization actually involved in India during the 1990s? The reforms lay stress on competition and free trade (dismantling the system of licensing and encouraging foreign equity investment in the Indian economy), modern technology, subsidy reduction, a reduced role for the state and economic stabilization (Sundaram 2003). In practical terms, some of the key fall-outs have been falling extension services, less institutional credit and inadequate price support systems. The reduction in state support to agriculture, particularly in terms of irrigation investments and institutional reforms, and its inability to monitor and control prices effectively, has contributed to the slowing down of agricultural growth including food-grain production across the country during the decade, including a negative growth in few states such as Bihar.

The reforms appear to have prioritized the country's business and trading regime over its "social investment" regime (Corbridge and Harriss 2000:146). The interests of the rural social elites, as indeed urban private capital, continue to be met, while declines in provision of education, health or extension services have adversely affected the poor and assetless. Faced with rising prices and excluded from the "new" regime of accumulation on the one hand, institutions of redress for the poor have also withered away, replaced by local control by the mafia or other dominant groups. In the following section we review the broader changes to poverty and inequality since 1991, before focusing on gendered rural livelihoods.

## LIBERALIZATION, POVERTY AND INEQUALITY

Women have gender identities alongside other identities, and it is therefore important to know how they have fared simply as poor rural citizens. Analytically separating gender and poverty means avoiding the assumption that how women fare *as women* will be the same as how they fare as poor people, and indeed it is the potential for contradictory effects which can militate against collective action by women. For example, if male wages and therefore household incomes are rising, even if women's wages are not, then their experience of poverty is likely to be ameliorated, unless (as must be vanishingly rare) there is absolutely no joint consumption and shared well-being.

Despite competing accounts of the poverty story in India, in a detailed examination of data for 1987–1988, 1993–1994 and 1999–2000 which adjusts for the problems with the 55th Round of the National Sample Survey (NSS), Deaton and Drèze (2002:3735) conclude that poverty declined in the 1990s more or less in line with earlier trends, and the all-India headcount ratio[4] dropped from 29 per cent in 1993–1994 to 23 per cent in 1999–2000. While headcount poverty has continued to decline at a similar rate to the pre-reform period, liberalization has not accelerated the reduction in headcount poverty as was hoped. Further, disaggregating the figure of headcount poverty for India, Dev (2003) finds that poverty incidence for Scheduled Castes was 36.25 per cent, for Scheduled Tribes 45.86 per cent and for agricultural labourers 46.8 per cent, against an average incidence of 27.09 per cent in rural areas.

An important part of the overall picture is the general stagnation in agriculture and agricultural employment. Between 1995 and 2000, global prices for all major crops—food-grains, oilseeds and cotton—have declined (the largest being for edible oils) and are now much lower than domestic prices. The removal of quantitative restrictions on some major agricultural products, such as rice, cotton and skimmed milk, and exposing them to global recessionary trends has, according to Patnaik (2002:120), contributed to a deepening agrarian crisis.[5] The average annual growth rate of the agriculture sector has declined from 4 per cent in the Eighth Plan period (1992–1996) to about 1.4 per cent during the first four years of the Ninth Plan (1997–2002) (Government of India 2002:22).[6]

Furthermore, public investment in agriculture is low and declining. While in the Sixth Five-Year Plan (1980–1985), 10 per cent of outlay was on irrigation and flood control and 6.1 on agriculture and allied activities, by the Ninth Plan (1997–2002) these declined to 7.5 and 4.5 per cent, respectively. The relationship between public expenditure and poverty levels is not straightforward, as the type and scale of public investment made is important (Fan et al. 1999), but agricultural stagnation, and thus growing rural–urban inequalities, is the context within which the changing well-being of rural women is situated.

While poverty figures may be contested, there is consensus over rising inequalities of various kinds. This is also part of a long-standing pattern, as shown in a Tamil Nadu study, of two decades of agricultural growth which was judged modest, unstable and based on extraction of groundwater resources. At the same time, Harris-White and Janakarajan (1997:1473) note that while real incomes have increased substantially between 1973 and 1994, this has been sixfold for the rich producers, 4.5 times for poor producers and 2.8 times for landless labourers. Deaton and Drèze (2002:3739) emphasize the important recent rise in inequalities and show that inequality affected the decline in headcount ratios of poverty by 1.3 per cent, that is, it would have been 21.4 per cent instead of 22.7 per cent in the absence of the increase in inequality. Three important aspects of inequality are identified: already better-off western and southern states have grown more strongly than poorer northern and eastern ones; rural–urban expenditure disparities have risen; and there has been a widening of the gap between wages to occupational groups, with agricultural wages increasing more slowly than public sector salaries, indicating occupational inequalities. They note a decline in cereal consumption, in real agricultural wages, in the rate of decline of infant mortality, though an improvement in literacy over this period. Among the pervasive evidence for continuity in pre-reform trends, it is the rise in inequalities which seems to be a new development. Dev (2000:825) finds Gini coefficients showing increased inequalities in consumption in the post-reform era (from 27.98 per cent in 1989–1990 to 29.50 per cent in 1995–1997).

The implications for rural women are that their experience of household poverty reduction will have been dependent on regional locations, rural–urban migration may be accelerated by widening well-being gaps, transfers from men in poor households may have become more uncertain, employment may have become more imperative than ever and social mobility via marriage transactions increasingly urgent as differentiation proceeds.

What do the poverty figures mean for consumption? Over the long term there has been considerable improvement in nutrition; Harriss-White and Janakarajan note that in their Tamil Nadu study between 1973 and 1994, the proportion of households in nutritional stress has halved (1997:1473). Few commentators on long-term change in rural India fail to point out the obvious changes in consumption behaviour signalled by the proliferation of tea-shops, bakeries and grocery stores in even small villages (for example, Gough 1989). Yet, during the 1990s food-grain output per capita fell (Patnaik 2003:32), and Meenakshi and Vishwanathan (2003:369) note that "there has been a secular decline in calorie intake in rural areas, amounting to approximately 70 calories per capita over the period 1983 to 1999–2000." A comparison of food consumption data from the National sample Survey Organization (NSSO) 50th Round in 1993–1994 and the 55th Round in 1999–2000 seems to confirm fears of worsening nutrition (NSSO 1997, 2001). The proportion of rural people consuming less than 2,400 kcal per day increased from 42 to 45.2 per cent, while those consuming less than 1,890 kcal increased from 13.40 to 15.10 per cent over this period.

Food intakes are notoriously imprecise and difficult to interpret (Harriss 1990), while nutritional outcomes, such as body mass indices[7] (BMIs) are much less ambiguous, and we know that BMIs indicate vulnerability for landless working men as well as some women. Swaminathan, using the BMI criterion on the 1993 National Nutrition Monitoring Bureau (NNMB) data, shows that a fairly similar proportion of adult men and women faced chronic energy deficiency (46.02 per cent and 45.84, respectively) for nine Indian states, though there were some variations across states. Malnutrition among boys one to five years at 57.2 per cent was in fact marginally more than for girls of the same age-group at 55.1 per cent (2000:27–28). The NNMB rural survey data from 2001 reveals a worrying trend from a gendered viewpoint. While chronic energy deficiency declined from the previous 46 per cent to 37 per cent for men and 39 per cent for women, the male–female gaps have widened. In the case of one- to five-year-old children, while the gender gap in malnutrition levels is small, the proportion of underweight children has increased to 59.7 and 60.5 per cent, respectively, for boys and girls (NNMB 2002:88–93).[8] Outcomes in both periods indicate that the overall calorie adequacy as indicated by BMIs of adult women is less of a problem than the quality of those calories, since anaemia and micronutrient deficiencies continue to be pervasive and intakes of iron and vitamin A are grossly deficient among poor rural women in South Asia (NNMB 2002:48). What is worrying from this data is that, while both boys and girls suffer from nutritional inadequacy in their early years, girls seem to lose out as they grow up, as evident from the widening gender gap among adults in the 1990s.

One of the most debated moves since the reforms has been the changes to the Public Distribution System (PDS). Sales from ration shops had declined by the early 1990s associated with increasing issue prices. Government in

1997 therefore introduced a more rigidly targeted food subsidy programme to replace the previous universal access to PDS, and ignored calls for large-scale food-for-work programmes in rural areas. The universal PDS had also been severely criticized for being inefficient and corrupt with "leakage" of a third of wheat, rice and sugar and half of oils onto the open market, poor quality of food, uneven spread among states and a distribution not consistent with locations of high poverty, and particularly bad rural distribution with an estimated 10 per cent of PDS food going to 50 per cent of the poor (Randhawa 1994:369).

Swaminathan (2000), however, has argued that using income criteria for targeting households has led to the exclusion of a large number of people suffering from calorie and micronutrient deficits, who are no longer technically classified as poor. She also notes that offtake from the PDS is not related to poverty per se, but state-level political commitment to food security. So, while in Kerala, 87 per cent of the population purchased from the PDS in 1994–1995, it was only 2 per cent in Bihar. At the same time, the extent of severe malnutrition was lowest in Kerala and highest in Bihar (Swaminathan 2000:29); Kerala also being one in three states that has shown improvements in calorie intakes across both the 1,800 and 2,400 kcal norms. This has raised fears that the confident predictions that sustained increase in food prices are not a threat to India's poor in the longer run (Gulati and Kelly 1999), and adverse effects merely short term (Ravallion 1998), may be incorrect.

Infant mortality rates (IMR) are a commonly used well-being indicator; hence, it is important to note the slackening of the rate of decline in the IMR over the last decade: It fell by 17.7 per cent between 1971 and 1981 and by 27.3 per cent between 1981 and 1991, but stagnated at 10 per cent between 1991 and 1999. The decline in the under-five mortality rate shows similar slowing down (Rao 2005). Of critical importance are the gender differentials in infant and child mortality. The child sex ratio[9] in India has deteriorated from 945 girls to 1,000 boys in 1991, to 927 in 2001, most notably in Himachal Pradesh (897), Punjab (793), Chandigarh (845), Haryana (820) and Delhi (865). Furthermore, the sex ratio at birth deviates increasingly from the normal 952 females for 1,000 males [10] to an all-India figure of 900 females per 1,000 males, indicating massive sex-selective abortion of female fœtuses with a similar line-up of states with the worst figures: Haryana, Punjab, Uttar Pradesh, Rajasthan and Gujarat (Rao 2005:123).

Alongside this is the substantial increase in private health-care provision in the 1990s at the cost of public health care. Rama Baru (2003:4436) notes a jump in the share of private hospital beds in India from 28.8 per cent in 1973 to 40.7 per cent in 1983 and to 61 per cent in 1996. This could conceivably lead to a regression in women's mortality if private health services are not affordable. The rate of untreated ailments rose by 40 per cent in the poorest decile, those not accessing health care for financial reasons rose from 10 to 20 per cent (Rao 2005) and health expenditure is emerging as one of the main reasons for indebtedness (Krishnan 1999). In addition to cost, private health facilities are concentrated in urban areas, and Krishnaji and James, based on an analysis of Sample Registration System (SRS) data from 1971 to 1997, note that, while there has been a general improvement in mortality rates and a reduction in the female–male mortality gap in urban areas, rural females in the age-group of 15 to 29 years continue to be the most disadvantaged (2002:4634). Mortality rates for them are 27 per cent higher than for rural males and 67 per cent more than for urban men. This seems to be on account of lack of health-care provision in rural areas combined with discrimination against women and their lack of control over cash incomes. As we discuss in this chapter, women are increasingly confined to family farming and low-paid non-farm work, as not many well-paid options in terms of off-farm employment are available to them. With enhanced competition, commodity markets too are getting more masculinized and inaccessible for women (see Harriss-White 2003), thus implying reduced access to cash.

A major shift, however, is that gender disadvantage lasts for a shorter period of time. Women having completed the main reproductive period tend to be stronger in terms of survival, while many male jobs may involve greater risk during their peak productive years, and in the 30–44 age-group, it is rural men who are most disadvantaged in mortality statistics. Krishnaji and James also show that male deaths—unlike women's—are not well correlated to health-care supply, and there seems to be a stagnation in male mortality (2002:14). This may be because women's mortality is connected to areas of health care which have been prioritized (reproductive health for fertility control) and are more tractable for basic services, while the primary causes of male mortality have not been population policy priorities.

Interestingly, a recent investigation of sex ratios has shown that between 1991 and 2001 the *overall* sex ratio became much less adverse to women, and for only the second time in census history the growth rate of males was exceeded by the growth rate of females (Gajalakshmi et al. 2003; Nair 2004). This shift would have been even greater if not for the mass female foeticide which is responsible for the great deterioration in the child sex ratio between 1991 and 2001. A pattern of excess male mortality is now showing up in statistics—related to smoking, alcohol and occupational hazards—which reinforces our argument that male gendered vulnerabilities deserve attention.

What seems to emerge from this analysis is a widening of inequalities between rural and urban areas, between different states and between different caste groups, rather than gender differences per se. Improvements in reproductive health facilities and public investment have produced better maternal health, and stable or declining fertility rates mean fewer pregnancies and lower exposure to risk of maternal mortality.[11] But other aspects of health are neglected and contribute to mortality for both men and women who are unable to access health care on time and at affordable prices, and gender ideologies work against women's health-seeking behaviour, as reported in the case of Andhra Pradesh. For better health outcomes for rural women it is important to improve rural health infrastructure and its efficiency (Sankar and Kathuria 2004).

One approach to the sex ratio problem has been to attempt to compensate parents of girls to discourage fœticide and infanticide. In the early 1990s Tamil Nadu launched a cradle scheme where unwanted girl babies could be left at health facilities, and a payment scheme to offset the costs of girl babies. Unfortunately, a high proportion of girl babies left in the cradles died (70 out of 143 in one instance) due to lack of adequate care (Krishnakumar 2002) and the payment system is hopelessly inadequately resourced. Overall, the impact on the sex ratio has not been noticeable, and for Tamil Nadu the child sex ratio has actually declined between 1991 and 2001. The payment policy has been relaunched recently (Ramesh 2008) but since we know that poverty is not what drives the aversion to girls, paying families to let girls live may be more complicated than getting the price right.

One favourable gender change is the rising level of education of girls and the narrowing gender education gap, which might reflect expectations of girls joining the paid workforce and hence increasing intergenerational investment in daughters. This is possibly the case, but long-term studies of change suggest that education, and the level aspired to, for girls is not for employment but in order to allow them to write home if mistreated in marital homes and to arrange marriage to a boy with university education who would not want an illiterate wife. Both Harriss-White (2003) and Heyer (1992) find in south Indian studies that marriage alliance is the main reason for education for girls. Education for a girl does drive dowry costs up. Further, education appears to lead to a refusal to work on family lands, and many boys end up sitting idle if they cannot get work suited to their aspirations (Wadley 2002:387).

Whatever the motives of parents in educating girls, the progressive impacts in the long run and the expansion of women's aspirations and agency are good reasons for states to continue to invest intensively in education of girls and women. The failure to accelerate investment in rural education when so much remains to be achieved for women is worrying, since education is implicated in both employment prospects and those ideational changes which are difficult to pin down but clearly contribute to more equitable gender relations. A key requirement for better quality employment or self-employment is educational status. Literacy has often been used as an indicator of educational levels; however, in order to get a higher quality of employment, minimum literacy is often not enough. Table 3.1 shows that while literacy rates have been consistently improving, even in 1999–2000, 68 per cent of rural males and 91 per cent of rural females are either illiterate or educated only up to primary level. Less than 10 per cent of female workers have education of middle school level or above; a real constraint in terms of their economic mobility.

*Table 3.1* Distribution of Workers by Education Category

| Category | Rural male(per cent) | | Rural female(per cent) | |
|---|---|---|---|---|
| | 1977–1978 | 1999–2000 | 1977–1978 | 1999–2000 |
| Not literate | 55.0 | 40.3 | 88.1 | 74.9 |
| Literate up to primary | 30.8 | 27.7 | 9.1 | 15.7 |
| Middle school | 8.5 | 15.9 | 1.6 | 5.6 |
| Secondary and higher secondary | 4.7 | 13.0 | 1.0 | 3.0 |
| Graduate and above | 1.0 | 3.1 | 0.2 | 0.7 |

*Source*: NSS Rounds on Employment and Unemployment from Dev (2003).

Present government policies have focused almost entirely on universalizing primary education. Beyond this lies a vast gap in numbers of secondary schools and high schools. Due to constraints in relation to distance from the home, issues of security and violence, especially in the absence of female teachers at higher levels, girls tend to drop out of school after primary education. So while India will probably meet the Millennium Goal of gender parity in primary education, the gaps persist at secondary and higher levels.

Further, to meet the goals and targets, there has been a rapid expansion of the education system with no reference to the quality of education imparted. Thus the middle classes have completely moved away from public education, as from public health (Baru 2003), and even the poor, where possible, send their children to private schools. The government, especially in states such as Andhra Pradesh, has actively encouraged these schools, but since parents often have to choose which child to educate, girls tend to lose out to their brothers. As the Probe Report notes, "parents are not generally opposed to female education, but they are reluctant to pay for it" (PROBE Team 1999:97). Ramachandran and Saihjee (2002) argue that soon one will find a new segregation in basic education—with Scheduled Castes, Scheduled Tribes and girls going to poorly run and ill-equipped government schools, and all the others attending private schools. With an increasing privatization of education, there is evidence of polarization—those with resources are likely to benefit, and those without are further marginalized in relative terms.

Though inequalities in class relationships seem to have weakened, the picture for asset ownership patterns is complex. Reproduction of agrarian class structures depends to a great degree on patterns of landholding, and Drèze finds in his long-term study of Palanpur in Western Uttar Pradesh that land-based inequalities have remained very stable, and that by examining landholding dynasties, the distribution of land is seen to have remained remarkably constant over time, although there are now smaller holdings and more landless households, the latter particularly since 1974 (Drèze 2002:211–213). Interestingly, the increased landlessness is not driven by land sales but by in-migration of landless households and thus cannot be seen as impoverishment of marginal farmers or signifying economic distress. Declining size of landholdings is also found elsewhere, for example, Harris-White and Janakarajan (1997) report that in 1993–1994, 64 per cent of households cultivated less than one hectare.

One element of inequality which may be said to have improved, however, is in the nature of labour contracts, which have shifted from attached[12] and bonded labour contracts to more casual ones. Brass (1999) is critical of the permanent or attached labour contracts, because these tend to provide poorly paid employment. The casualization of labour is a long-standing pattern in rural India, and Pal (1997) uses International Crops Research Institute for the Semi-Arid Tropics (ICRISAT) data from 1980–1984 and resurvey 1992 to show that economic development in India goes hand in hand with the expansion of alternative employment opportunities for agricultural labour and also an expanded access to credit, both of which lead to a decline in attached labour contracts and a gradual casualization of agricultural labour. The downside is that while earnings from attached contracts are usually lower than from daily casual labour, they do provide comparative security. The diversification of opportunities, however, has also contributed to a desire for greater economic independence among labourers, hence a preference for casual contracts.

Gender-based inequality has proven more intractable in many ways than class. What Rustagi (2000:45), in her district-level analysis of gendered well-being, identifies as Gender Backward Districts (GBD) are also prosperous districts—none of her GBDs are listed in the Relative Index of Development calculated by the Centre for Monitoring Indian Economy to identify districts with low levels of development. This association of rural prosperity with deepening gender discrimination is important to recognize. The next section deals with processes of livelihood diversification and the opportunities this has offered women as well as constraints it has enhanced in terms of divisions of labour.

To summarize, levels of headcount poverty have continued to decline in line with pre-reform trends, paddy yields remain static, average landholding size has declined, agricultural labour has become more casualized and somewhat better paid, but agricultural employment has stagnated along with the agricultural sector in general. This last point is explored further in the next section. Consumption patterns reflect declining cereal and total calorie intake and increasing expenditure on household goods largely oriented to status and male leisure. There is clear evidence of widening regional disparities, with already more prosperous states benefiting more than poorer ones, rural–urban disparities increasing and income inequalities between occupational groups widening. Despite improvements in basic education, broader indicators of well-being show deterioration—slowing down of infant mortality decline, and deepening well-being crises for particular groups—among which female fœtuses, infants and girls are most salient. Women as members of poor rural households are therefore not obviously enjoying shared improvements in household well-being. Drèze's study of 35 years of change does not show growing class-based inequality, but does signal continuing gender discrimination even where poverty has fallen, and thus emphasizes the importance of a specifically gendered analysis of liberalization. After reviewing the grim situation that makes western Uttar Pradesh "a region of exceptional gender inequality" (Drèze 2002:216), he observes that over the period 1957–1993, "[t]here are few signs of any profound change in gender relations having taken place during the survey period" (2002:218). Women themselves mentioned the displacement of hand grinding by mechanized mills, a rising age at marriage, the tendency to form nuclear families, a decline in wife-beating and stronger bonds between husbands and wives as areas of improvement. The baseline inequalities remain as deep as ever in terms of son preference and sex ratios, constrained mobility of women and absence from public life. No gender change has occurred which is remotely comparable to the change in caste relations. Drèze ascribes this stasis to the absence of change in the economic institutions of patrilineal inheritance, patrilocal exogamy and the organization of agricultural production to drive gender change. Liberalization will not necessarily challenge these institutions towards more progressive gender relations.

## GENDERED LIVELIHOODS UNDER LIBERALIZATION

Livelihood diversification in rural areas is not new, but related to positive factors (agricultural growth, increased public expenditure) and negative ones (unemployment, urbanization and stagnation in real wages in agriculture).[13] Migration for employment to diversify household portfolios and add extra income streams may be "voluntary" and lead to an improvement in the quality of life of the migrant workers and their families (Breman 1996; Mosse et al. 2002), or reflect poverty and food insecurity and the absence of choice. There is still little analysis available in terms of the impact of the broader phenomena of diversification on women's lives.

NSSO data in table 3.2 on the sectoral distribution of rural workers between 1977–1978 and 1999–2000 reveals considerable diversification, which slowed considerably in the 1990s but has mostly been confined to male workers.

While male participation in the rural non-agricultural sector has increased by 9.4 per cent, female employment has more or less remained stable and

*Table 3.2* Broad Sectoral Distribution of Workers in Rural India, 1977–1978 to 1999–2000

| Year | Primary | Secondary (1) | Tertiary (2) | Rural non-agricultural (1+2) |
|---|---|---|---|---|
| *Rural males* | | | | |
| 1977–1978 | 80.7 | 8.8 | 10.5 | 19.3 |
| 1983 | 77.5 | 10.2 | 12.2 | 22.4 |
| 1987–1988 | 74.5 | 12.3 | 13.4 | 25.7 |
| 1993–1994 | 74.1 | 11.3 | 14.7 | 26.0 |
| 1999–2000 | 71.4 | 12.7 | 16.0 | 28.7 |
| 2004–2005 | 65.51 | 0.76 | 33.74 | 34.5 |
| *Rural females* | | | | |
| 1977–1978 | 88.2 | 6.7 | 5.1 | 11.8 |
| 1983 | 87.5 | 7.4 | 4.8 | 12.2 |
| 1987–1988 | 84.7 | 10.0 | 5.3 | 15.3 |
| 1993–1994 | 86.2 | 8.3 | 5.6 | 13.9 |
| 1999–2000 | 85.4 | 8.9 | 5.7 | 14.6 |
| 2004–2005 | 80.65 | 0.58 | 18.77 | 19.35 |

*Source*: Various rounds of NSS Employment and Unemployment Surveys from Dev (2003).

confined to agriculture. The main sectors of growth in the non-farm sector appear to be construction, trade, hotels and restaurants, transport and storage,[14] all of which have shown a preference for men. Construction, manufacturing and services have been the sectors where women's employment too has increased marginally (Bhaumik 2002). Livelihood diversification in rural areas seems therefore to be offering opportunities to men—as small businessmen and as employees in better paid jobs, while for women it involves extremely lowly paid work as a last resort when agricultural wage work is absent. This is linked to the control over assets and resources, but also the gendered divisions of labour, as discussed in the following sections.

## Livelihood Resources: Land and Credit

Land is increasingly scarce and commoditized in India, with implications for both livelihoods and gender relations. Over the 1990s, the average size of per capita landholding has declined, in line with earlier trends as reflected in table 3.3.

Table 3.3 Average Area of Land Possessed and Average Household Size by Size Class of Land and Sex of the Head of Household (Rural Areas Only), 1993–1994 and 1999–2000

| Size class of land | Male-headed households | | | | | | Female-headed households | | | | | |
| --- | --- | --- | --- | --- | --- | --- | --- | --- | --- | --- | --- | --- |
| | Per 000 distribution of household | | Average area of land possessed (0.00 ha) | | Average household size (0.0) | | Per 000 distribution of household | | Average area of land possessed (0.00 ha) | | Average household size (0.0) | |
| | 1993–1994 | 1999–2000 | 1993–1994 | 1999–2000 | 1993–1994 | 1999–2000 | 1993–1994 | 1999–2000 | 1993–1994 | 1999–2000 | 1993–1994 | 1999–2000 |
| 0.00 | 122 | 70 | 0.00 | 0.00 | 4.1 | 4.1 | 190 | 83 | 0.00 | 0.00 | 2.4 | 2.5 |
| 0.01–0.40 | 391 | 492 | 0.11 | 0.09 | 4.6 | 4.8 | 527 | 668 | 0.09 | 0.07 | 3.1 | 3.3 |
| 0.41–1.00 | 192 | 197 | 0.69 | 0.67 | 5.1 | 5.3 | 143 | 137 | 0.66 | 0.63 | 3.8 | 4.0 |
| 1.01–2.00 | 146 | 121 | 1.43 | 1.39 | 5.6 | 5.7 | 81 | 62 | 1.41 | 1.4 | 4.0 | 4.1 |
| 2.01–4.00 | 94 | 77 | 2.72 | 2.64 | 6.0 | 6.2 | 36 | 34 | 2.68 | 2.64 | 4.2 | 4.4 |
| Above 4.01 | 55 | 42 | 7.49 | 7.23 | 6.8 | 7.0 | 21 | 16 | 6.92 | 6.78 | 4.7 | 4.8 |
| Total | 1,000 | 1,000 | 1.05 | 0.85 | 5.0 | 5.2 | 1,000 | 1,000 | 0.50 | 0.42 | 3.2 | 3.5 |
| Estimated Households (00) | 1,078,893 | 1,227,336 | - | - | - | - | 116,403 | 143,461 | - | - | - | - |

Source: Table compiled from NSSO 1997 and NSSO 2001.

Several interesting points emerge from the table 3.3. First, for both male- and female-headed households there is a decline in average area of land possessed, revealing in a sense that, with growth of population and a larger number of people demanding land, the average size of holding is declining. This also points towards the growing wage dependence of small farmers and raises questions about how much land can actually contribute to household livelihoods (Krishnaji 2001). With larger numbers seeking agricultural work, it also provides corroboration for stagnation in growth rates of agricultural wages. Secondly, while 94.3 per cent of female-headed households were small/marginal landowners (less than two hectares) in 1993–1994, this increased to 95 per cent by 1999–2000 (the number of marginal farmers increased from 88.5 per cent to 91 per cent during this period). In the case of male-headed households, there was in fact a sharper decline from 14.9 per cent being medium/large farmers to only 11.9 per cent. Thus, average size of landholding has declined for both male- and female-headed households, though the quantum of land owned by women is about half that of men (Rao 2006). Srinivasan (2004) also shows that, from 1973 to 1982 and then 1993, the percentage of big farmers decreased from 48 per cent, to 42 per cent, to 35.98 per cent, and small farmers increased from 52 per cent, to 58 per cent, to 64.02 per cent. This is based on data for 11 villages. While the pattern across these villages is uneven, with four villages showing a reduction in landlessness over time, in the rest there is almost a doubling of landlessness from between 16 to 24 per cent in different villages to 37 per cent over this period (Srinivasan 2004:87–89).

Growing land scarcity has led to deepening male competition, in which women's usufruct, trusteeship and ownership rights are challenged, denied and overridden through a number of strategies: intimidation, collective action by male kin, court cases and the reinvention of cultural forms. An example of the latter is the increasing popularity of widow remarriage in Haryana, where it is essentially a levirate in which the wife is married by a brother or agnatic cousin of the husband, frequently with the compulsion of the widow. Its growing popularity is based on the desire to control land and keep it within family since, in the absence of male heirs, the wife inherits the estate for the duration of her life (Chowdhry 1994:74).

Legally in India, most women have inheritance rights—the Hindu Succession Act 1956 (with its amendment in 2005) entitles Hindu women to an equal share of family property, and the Shariat Act 1937 entitles Muslim women to inherit half the share as their brothers (see Agarwal 1994). Yet, in practice, few women claim their rights, as the relationship with their natal kin, especially brothers, is seen as more important to their well-being than the potential material benefits from land. Pushed by feminist advocacy since the mid-1970s, both in India and internationally in the context of the United Nations Women's Decade (1975–1985), the Indian state has increasingly sought to recognize and support women's land claims. The legislation mentioned earlier sought to make land inheritance more gender equitable, and affirmative action was put in place in state-led land reform and land redistribution programmes, even though these cover only three million hectares, or 1.6 per cent of arable land (Agarwal 1998).

Further, despite the existence of such policy statements, as described, the reality appears far removed. In the case of women, Thakur (2001) points out that, as implementation of central policy statements are based on state enactments, women's rights continue to be largely ignored both in land reform and rehabilitation policies, with the exception of Kerala, Andhra Pradesh and West Bengal. Even in West Bengal, which has had a major land reform programme under the Left Front government, women were almost totally excluded from gaining a land title, on the plea that since they did not plough the land; they were not "tillers" (Gupta 1997). This viewpoint was modified only in 1991, after intense lobbying by the women's movement in West Bengal.

In the case of tribals, in Kerala, each landless tribal household was promised between 0.40 and two hectares of land, depending on availability, by the state government in October 2001. In February 2002, a total of 575 families were given land, yet another 22,780 remained landless (Kaul 2003). When it was clear that the government was backing down on its commitment, the tribals protested. This led to police firing in Muthanga in Wynaad district in February 2003 and arrest of the leaders (Damodaran 2003). Similar examples of the use of state force against tribals are available from other parts of the country. What this double-speak has led to is in fact a rigidification of marriage and kinship norms, as households and kin groups come closer together to face the growing competition for land—from the state for industrial and mineral development, and from Hindu and Muslim traders and moneylenders seeking to extend their base in villages and gain status as cultivators. The competition intensifies due to the protective tenancy legislation in most Scheduled Areas of the country that prohibits the sale or transfer of tribal lands to non-tribals.[15] While the state has thus used the Land Acquisition Act of 1894 to acquire tribal land, other private parties look for more informal ways of acquiring land, including marriage to tribal women. In a context of economic and social marginalization of the entire group vis-à-vis other ethnic and caste groups,[16] not only is there now a heightened emphasis on customary principles and norms, in line also with this debate in the international arena in recent years, but this emphasis has also meant shrinkage of women's rights. The reason given is that if women are allowed to inherit, "non-tribal" men would marry them and thus acquire the land. Once in non-tribal hands, it is much easier to dispose of or exchange this land. While not yet a major threat, there have been such instances, especially close to urban areas. Tribal leaders are therefore willing to allow women to inherit land only on condition that they marry within the tribe. While customary principles are flexible and do have social sanction, they too are socially embedded. Hence, in a context of growing competition over land, gender identities and a concern for gender justice tend to get submerged under issues of ethnic identity and the right to survival, inheritance rights being circumscribed by the control over marital choice (Rao 2002).

While women's claims to land are increasingly limited, the reverse seems to be the trend in the case of small credit. The banking sector reforms in 1991 led to a decline in the bank credit given to rural areas from 15 per cent during the 1980s (1980–1991) to 10 per cent in 2001–2002 (Ramachandran and Swaminathan 2004), and the government has sought to fill the gap in rural credit demand through a rapid expansion in microcredit through the formation of Self-Help Groups (SHG), especially of women. These are meant to overcome the problems of inaccessibility, high transaction costs and poor repayments that were encountered by the formal credit institutions. The SHG-linkage programme has grown from support to 500 SHGs in 1992 to 500,000 in 2002, covering over 40 million poor people, 90 per cent women (NABARD 2007b).[17]

The impact of such microcredit interventions on gender relations has been found to be contradictory in other South Asian studies (Goetz and Sengupta 1996; Hashemi et al. 1996). In the Indian context,[18] a study of women's SHGs in Andhra Pradesh points to significant gains for women from credit at the individual level, but when women's incomes increase, domestic work burdens also do, there are more frequent instances of domestic violence and tensions in general are accentuated within households (Deshmukh-Ranadive 2003; Nirantar 2007). Credit access may then well have both positive and negative effects simultaneously and expanded microcredit availability since the 1990s is unlikely to have produced significant change in gender relations.

Changes during the 1990s to livelihood resource access by rural women have then involved deepening struggles over land in which the agencies of the state have a crucial role to play in upholding women's inheritance claims against depredations of male kin, and an enormous expansion of credit oriented to women in groups rather than household production groups. This is potentially beneficial but as such programmes disburse small loans, this could possibly become a two-tier system in which women have excellent credit access but only for small amounts, while men access bank loans which are large enough for significant investments. Women-focused credit also risks increased gender conflict in the short term.

## Labour in Livelihoods

Long-term studies and restudies published in recent years, such as that of Palanpur by Deaton and Drèze (2002), have taken a reasonably positive view of social change in the last half of the twentieth century. Scarlett Epstein, for Karnataka, reflecting on her original 1950s analysis and the futures she envisaged, finds less population growth than she predicted and that she underestimated the importance of education to social change, the value of agricultural technical change to sustainable livelihoods and the importance of party politics in increasing the clout of rural areas (Epstein et al. 1998:200–201).

However, much of the positive change noted by Deaton and Drèze and by Epstein seems to have appeared in the 1980s in particular, as Kathleen Gough's earlier restudy in 1976 of her 1952 research produces a considerably more negative account of social change (1989). By 1976 the new capital-intensive industries had not compensated in terms of employment for the decline in artisan industries, agricultural workers were worse off, the GR had made limited inroads and livestock products were consumed less. Thus it is important to periodize any generalizations, and to note that the methodological importance of the base year for comparisons holds for qualitative as well as quantitative research.

All rural livelihoods involve domestic labour to maintain and reproduce the household over time, and women are central to these services: childcare, food preparation, fuel-wood and water collection, care of the ill and elderly, and a range of activities that grade seamlessly into food production and income-generating work, such as livestock care, homestead gardening, crop production and so on. Livelihood research pays lip-service to these activities, but there are still too few studies which routinely collect data on domestic work alongside descriptions and analysis of occupations, employment and farm production, and, as a result, information remains scarce and it is difficult to answer the question of what happens to women's domestic burdens under liberalization-induced changes in livelihoods.

The utilization of women's labour in domestic production as a part of livelihood strategies is affected by a range of factors: shifts in cropping patterns, technical change, availability of alternative opportunities and broader changes in the social organization of agricultural production such as contract farming. These could imply increased demand for women's agricultural labour, since irrigation involves double cropping and intensification, and horticulture is also labour intensive, but much depends on the manner of crop production. Studies from Tamil Nadu by Ramachandran and others (2001) and Nakkeeran (2003) find that shifts in cropping patterns from paddy, coarse grains and vegetables to plantation-grown crops, apart from not being labour-absorbent in general, particularly displace female labour. The effects of displacement of women's labour take a number of years to evaluate, as was seen in the case of rice-milling technologies in Bangladesh, where short-term negative impacts were ultimately compensated for (White 1992), but a beneficial outcome depends on the overall employment demand, the quality of the new jobs relative to those displaced from, and any changes to forms of wage control.

Contract farming appears to have the opposite effect. In Punjab, contract farming started in 1989 with Pepsi Foods Ltd. (PepsiCo) setting up a tomato-processing plant followed by contract farming agreements, and within a decade more than 90,000 acres were contract farmed. In terms of employment, however, vegetable production particularly has led to a boom, especially for women workers.[19] Gill (2001) found that female labour accounted for 60 per cent of total labour used in tomato production, although women's wages were only 60–75 per cent of male wages. Yet, interestingly, compared to other Indian states, while there was no substantial increase in real wages in Punjab during the 1990s (primarily due to in-migration of male labour), the male–female gap in earnings was in fact the lowest in Punjab in 1999 (Chavan and Bedamatta 2006).

In other states such as Andhra Pradesh, contract farming has led to a virtual alienation of the land of small and marginal farmers and a growing casualization of labour as well as the greater use of female and child labour.[20] A study by Venkateshwarlu and Da Corta (2001) of hybrid cottonseed production in Andhra Pradesh found large-scale use of the labour of young girls, male withdrawal from work, dependence on women and girls to earn incomes, work-related health problems for women and girls being withdrawn from schools.

The corporatization of agriculture thus appears to have quite different labour implications compared to the mechanization of family farming. While the latter has tended to displace female labour, corporate farming seeks it out. While these case studies are not conclusive, they indicate that contract farming may provide employment to women, but also a decline in women's status from growing work burdens, as there is little evidence of men taking on a larger share of reproductive work.

So what happened in the 1990s across India? According to official statistics, the growth rate of rural employment slowed down considerably in the decade of the 1990s to 0.5 per cent per annum from 1.7 per cent per annum in the 1980s.[21] The daily status unemployment rate in rural areas increased from 5.63 per cent in 1993–1994 to 7.21 per cent in 1999–2000 (Dev 2003). This is a matter of concern especially in the context of a high gross domestic product (GDP) growth rate overall (7 per cent) and a claim by the government that all sectors of the economy were doing equally well. In terms of crude work participation rates, one finds from NSS data that while male participation rates have remained more or less stable between 1987–1988 (53.9 per cent) and 1999–2000 (53.1 per cent), even till 2004–2005, female participation rates declined from 32.3 per cent to 29.9 per cent during this decade,[22] but picked up thereafter. This decline can primarily be explained by a lack of growth in the agricultural sector that is still the largest employer of women—in 1961 nearly 90 per cent of women workers were in agriculture, in 1994 this was 86 per cent (Banerjee 1999:303)—and at the same time a diversion of land for other uses such as mining and industrial development. The disturbing feature of the growth of female employment between the NSS round of 1999–2000 and 2004–2005 is that a bulk of growth is in the category of subsidiary workers. This represents an erosion of full-time work and an increase in informal, part-time, casual, low-paid work, both in the urban and rural areas (Unni and Raveendran 2007:196).

Some authors have therefore claimed that rural India has been witnessing a "feminization of agriculture" (da Corta and Venkateshwarlu 1999) as well as a process of casualization. It is true that with the slowing down of agricultural growth rates in general and a decline in investment in agriculture, non-farm employment does in fact provide better returns to labour than agriculture; hence, whether to repay debts or to accumulate capital, some member of the household, usually the man, does seem to diversify into non-farm work. If this is the case we may indeed see agricultural labour becoming a low-wage "sink" for women, and a relative feminization take place, despite declining days work in farm labour.

The feminization of agriculture is nevertheless a term that needs unpacking, since it does not obviously fit with either the all-India NSS data referred to earlier, or the statewise data for areas such as Kerala or West Bengal. It is necessary to distinguish three distinct elements in the changing position of women's agricultural employment: the feminization in terms of *relative share* of the employment available to women as compared to men; the changes in the *absolute amount* of agricultural employment available to women; and the *quality of the employment* engaged in by rural women.

In their study, Ramachandran and others (2001:10) remind us that *feminization* of agricultural work is indicated by a rise in the proportion of female agricultural workers in the female workforce, a rise in the ratio of female to male agricultural workers, and a rise in the proportion of female workforce in the female population (Duvvury 1989). Such feminization has been taking place in Tamil Nadu over the 1960s, 1970s and 1980s and is therefore not readily linked to liberalization, but all-India data suggests this pattern has continued, even if not initiated by liberalization; since pre-reforms in rural India 17 per cent of workers over 15 years old were women, after liberalization it rose to 21 per cent (Deshpande and Deshpande 1998:L36).

In terms of the absolute *quantity* of work undertaken by women, these authors also point to a decline in the number of days of agricultural work available to women and an increase in other low-paid forms of work, such as tamarind processing. Gough (1989) too reports a decline from women working 90–240 days in 1951–1953, to a 1976 situation in which average days worked by casual labour declined to 90–180 days for both sexes (Bouton 1985; cited in Gough 1989). Rajuladevi (2000:477) updates this to the 1995 levels, where it has fallen to 62 days in rice agriculture.

These and other studies show that the *quality* of women's labour after liberalization was increasingly casual, intermittent and part-time (Deshpande and Deshpande 1998:L31). Casualization per se is not a problem. However, poverty data reveal that those having the principal employment status of casual labour have the highest ratio of poverty in 1999–2000 (around 42 per cent). For those who were self-employed and occasionally engaged in casual labour, or for those with regular employment and occasional labour, poverty was considerably lower at 37.22 and 30.66 per cent, respectively (Dev 2003). Others point out that, in agriculture, casual is considerably better paid than attached labour. Real wages for casual labourers, especially women, increased faster than for attached workers, but made slow growth in the 1990s (Deshpande and Deshpande 1998:L37).

Thus, agricultural wage labour may have become relatively feminized, but the absolute quantity of work in agriculture has fallen, and the quality of that work deteriorated in some regards.

Next we need to focus on the question of the changing quality of employment, particularly in wage terms, in agriculture and elsewhere in the rural economy for women. An analysis of Agricultural Wages in India (AWI) data from 1964–1970 to 1990–1997 for male and female agricultural labourers reveals an absolute rise in real wages across all districts under consideration (46 districts across 17 states) during this period (Chavan and Bedamatta 2006). Despite this absolute rise, there is a slowing down in the rate of growth in the 1990s in 22 districts (73 per cent of total on which data is available) for women labourers. For the majority of districts, the "decade of the 1980s was the period of highest growth in real wages for both male and female labourers" (Chavan and Bedamatta 2006:4046).

A statewise analysis of male–female daily earnings ratio based on the Rural Labour Enquiry (of the NSSO) points towards a halt to increasing male–female wage differentials in the late 1990s in a large number of states. The exceptions, however, were the more progressive states of Tamil Nadu, Kerala, Andhra Pradesh, Karnataka and Maharashtra, where the male–female earning gap not only continued to increase, but the ratio was more than 1.5 (Chavan and Bedammata 2006).[23] The restricted access for women to non-agricultural employment, as well as the higher degrees of mechanization leading to an overall decline in labour requirements in agriculture in these states could be contributory factors.

There is clearly a need to periodize changing labour market conditions carefully; since the 1980s, studies show increased demand for women's labour as a consequence of irrigation and technical change, and overburdening was a concern, while the post-reform period has seen general stagnation, but a continuing relative rise in women's casual labour. It is also the specific forms of production organization that importantly mediate effects of particular cropping pattern changes, thus horticulture can either intensify demand or displace it in relation to women's employment. Overburdening also is not only related to combining wage work with domestic labour, since in the absence of wage-based income, women may have to buy cheaper unprocessed staples, and engage in foraging and other labour-intensive means of survival.

We may then be able to anticipate effects of liberalization on women by considering what factors explain the variations in women's involvement in agricultural labour—growth in the agricultural economy, changing cropping patterns since different crops have different requirements for women's labour, the expansion or contraction of other labour markets and wage differentials in those competing markets, as well as factors deeply embedded in gender relations within households, such as the incomes earned by spouses which affect the need for women to work, the variable desire by women for employment, the attitudes of spouses and in-laws to women working and the practical constraints of childcare. Rising education levels can also affect engagement in agricultural work.

## Migration

Migration within rural areas and between rural and urban locations is an important element of changing gender relations because it entails new conjugal arrangements, new working lives and new social contexts, whether these are in urban areas, unfamiliar rural ones or indeed "simply" in marital homes.

The expansion of seasonal rural–rural labour migration, and non-farm employment, such as the brick industry in rural areas of Uttar Pradesh is very much associated with the GR (Karlekar 1995:53). As regional disparities seem to be widening under the post-1991 reforms, the level of rural–rural labour movement is likely to increase, and as employment stagnates in rural areas, rural–urban migration is also likely to increase. Connections between migration patterns and liberalization are fairly speculative however, since the patterns are complex, the consequence for gender relations both negative and positive and the attribution of causality uncertain. What evidence is there of change and what might it mean for gender relations?

Recent migration research reflects ongoing debates in relation to push-and-pull factors and the degree to which migration is a negative or positive experience. Much depends on the type of migration, nature of areas of origin and destination, as well as the social standing of the individual or household in the village and their networks in the destination. Mosse and others (2002), based on their study of migration among the Bhils in Western India, note that wealth and social standing both influence outcomes, with the better-off appearing to gain more from migration than the poorest. While class ideologies have been more fully considered by recent research in shaping migration decisions and outcomes, gender ideologies and cultural categorizations of appropriate work roles, divisions of labour and responsibilities within households are still largely unexplored.

Women dominate migrant streams, constituting 77 per cent (Government of India 2001:i) of all migrants in India, but much of this is marriage migration (89 per cent) and largely overlooked in migration research, which focuses on migration for employment. Only 1 per cent of rural women migrants are recorded as migrating for employment, itself an underestimate which partly derives from the view that women who are migrating with husbands are "associational" migrants, simply there to accompany their husbands. However this is mistaken, for wives who fail to find work in areas of destination often return home, and the many who stay are migrants in their own right.

Women's rural–rural seasonal migration is not recent. Breman's (1985) classic studies of migration in Gujarat concluded that intra-rural migrants accounted for at least a fifth of the labour force, and in areas of intense capitalist agriculture this may rise to 30–40 per cent. Further, he found that 58 per cent of migrants in his study were women (see also Teerink 1995). In 1999–2000 nearly three million women were recorded as short duration migrants, amounting to nearly a third of the total short duration migrants (Kak 2003), and, as noted earlier, this is likely to be an underestimate. Most are landless, young and illiterate, work in unskilled work like brick kilns and construction, fish processing and, in some instances, agriculture. While the big cities see a large influx of rural women for construction work (Shah 2006), irrigated areas in other parts of the country also see an influx of migrant labour during peak cultivation seasons (Rogaly et al. 2001). Women migrant workers are generally paid less than local women and work on piece-rate contracts. Karlekar (1995:23–78) points to the surprising degree (given the sensitivity of the topic) to which sexual harassment and exploitation is mentioned in relation to women's migration. Tobacco graders in Andhra Pradesh are perceived to be selected (in line-ups) on the basis of their beauty, and Breman reports expectations that groups of migrant women travelling without men in search of work will provide sexual services to farmers.

Joint migration is favoured in some areas and it reproduces accepted gender relations in the destination areas. After a whole day's labour, women would still be carrying out domestic chores (Teerink 1995), and control over the income is likely to be with men as heads of the household unit (Gupta 2003). These researchers conclude, like Karlekar (1995), that seasonal migration by women does not necessarily enhance status, emancipate or lead to long-term poverty reduction.

Seasonal labour migration has declined over the last 10 years according to NSS data (Kak 2003), which is surprising given the growing regional inequalities. However the drop in the numbers may also reflect a phenomenon commented on by Narayan Banerjee (personal communication), who says that in Bankura district (West Bengal) there is now a reduction in migration duration—people used to go for four–six week spells but now go for half that time—and work 16–20 hour days on piece-rates, to earn the same amount of money in much shorter periods. They return exhausted and fearful of illness after migration. In-depth studies in Jharkhand found that a large proportion of earnings from migration was spent on health care, and, given the lack of public health-care services, this also resulted in high levels of indebtedness (Rao and Rana 1997). Wages are therefore maintained but at the cost of enormous pressure on bodies and minds. If this is the case, then the decline in the extent of seasonal migration may be more apparent than real, and the changing intensities of work a matter of concern for the nutritionally vulnerable labouring poor of both genders.

Rural–urban migration finds more positive gender analysis, both in relation to the emancipating effects of exposure to less restrictive urban cultures and the greater opportunities for economic mobility in urban settings. Some areas of employment for women are expanding in urban areas, for example, domestic work is increasingly feminized, and 89 per cent are now women (Kaur 2003). Men have better paid work available, but employers consider women more trustworthy and are increasingly reluctant to leave female children with male servants. Migrant women with access to salaried employment in cities, whether in manufacturing or in services (Gulati 1993), appear better able to renegotiate existing gender relations. Unnithan-Kumar (2003) shows how in many ways they are not just escaping the burden of indebtedness but also the restrictive demands of extended families. City life has distinctive gender cultures which seem to be more progressive. In a comparative study of attitudes, Jain and others (1997:110) found that while 34 per cent of rural women said they were often beaten by husbands, only 14.5 per cent of urban women did. However, not everything about urban gender cultures is progressive for they also found (1997:83) that, while 35 per cent of rural Scheduled Caste women did not want daughters to seek paid employment, 56 per cent took this view in urban areas.

The sex-working underbelly of rural–urban migration by women is also an area of concern, given the rising risks of HIV/AIDS. In a study of sex workers in Orissa, Gangoli (2003) found that most had transgressed in some way before migrating for sex work, and that there was a phenomenon of "flying sex workers", that is, married women with children who come into towns in the evenings to earn extra money, especially before festivals. Svati Shah (2003), in an ethnographic study in Mumbai, found that at hiring points women will seek construction work in the mornings and, if they fail, after 11 AM, will ply for sex work. When asked which work they prefer, they say construction work because "yes, that is physical work. This? [that is, sex work] What is this?" In particular, they disliked the police harassment and the men refusing to wear condoms. These are examples of sex work as a livelihood element in a portfolio of activities rather than, as often assumed, a specialized occupation. Clearly the implications for HIV/AIDS prevention are important.

In the longer term, however, the consequences of migration and the exposure to new ideas, new technologies and new information, for cultural and ideological change in rural areas can be profound, especially if combined with political mobilization to claim their rights.[24] What seems clear then is that migration decisions, experiences and outcomes, just as other livelihood strategies, are mediated by ideologies of caste, ethnicity and gender, of power, status and the relative valuations of different types of work in society. The access to resources, particularly land and credit, do also influence the types of choices available to individuals and groups. Migrant labour markets are highly segmented, but also gendered with implications for access to particular jobs, the capacity to earn and the conditions of work. Engagements in these then have different implications for men and women of different groups.

## Changing Divisions of Labour

One point which is clear from the earlier discussions is that the degree of gender flexibility in labour is important to changing scenarios, since gender wage gaps depend on certain tasks being reserved for one or the other gender. This can have perverse effects for women, as for example when their tasks are labelled "light" by comparison to male "heavy" work to justify high male wages. But it can also have potentially beneficial effects where it limits competition from male labourers for some work. In Haryana, gender wage gaps have been narrowing and although real male wages stagnated in the 1980s, women's rose by 30 per cent, because male immigration depressed male wages and a strict gender division of labour protected demand for their labour (Chowdhry 1994:184–185). And where this is combined with increasingly narrow time windows for the completion of operations such as weeding or transplanting (where double or triple cropping schedules have to be accommodated), it can offer bargaining opportunities to women workers. Finally, where some tasks are indeed particularly heavy, risky or dangerous, then a division of labour which types these as suited to males might be beneficial to poor women.

The question of women's agency and their work preferences, and how this affects changing divisions of labour, matters. Rural women are not persons existing outside of broader cultural changes, but will change their desires, aspirations and consequent actions in relation to these shifts. For example, the rising levels of rural women's literacy and education in recent decades will change ideas of personhood and aspirations for the future, and the negative impact of education on women's interest in agricultural labour is evident, a good example being Kerala where women would rather migrate for service-sector jobs than engage in agricultural wage work at home. Of course, without opportunities to exercise these preferences, that is, without alternative employment, such desires will only be frustrated ones, but where alternatives do arise they may be pursued with some determination. Furthermore, a generalized denigration of manual labour may lead women with education (and their spouses) to prefer poorer paid but "cleaner" work.

Drèze comments on how educated youth, with expectations of higher living standards, shun manual work, a pattern which is likely to be predominantly found among male youth (Drèze 2002:209).[25] Masculinities may be shifting, among groups that have in the past valorized strength and hard physical labour as ideal forms of manliness, in directions which increasingly emphasize the value of non-manual work. The impact of this on younger women may be that their own options in relation to labour are constrained by male unwillingness to engage in agricultural labour.

One of the puzzles indicated in earlier sections is how we should, as gender analysts, understand what exactly labour force participation signals about gender relations and well-being, for example, the low female participation rate in the paid workforce in West Bengal goes along with considerably less patriarchal cultures than those of other regions with higher participation rates. Similar to Agarwal's (1985) analysis of the impact of GR on women, a study by Nakkeeran (2003) in a Tamil Nadu village indicates that the move away from paddy cultivation has different outcomes on different categories of women. The higher caste women are being withdrawn from agricultural labour on account of higher incomes from the plantation crops. While perhaps lacking autonomy, they are better off in terms of health, nutrition, food security, literacy and leisure. Landless women, however, are increasingly taking on more hazardous as well as lower paid employment to make ends meet. He therefore emphasizes the need to take care in interpreting higher work participation rates as contributing to enhanced autonomy and well-being.

## CONCLUSIONS

This chapter sought to examine the gendered experience of liberalization in rural India, officially launched with the fiscal, monetary and trade reforms in 1991. We are tentative in claiming causality in relation to liberalization, given the methodological challenges this entails in terms of periodization of interventions and the attribution of effects. Further, the complexity of central/state-level policy implementation in a country of a billion people, and the growing competition between states for attracting investments, particularly of foreign capital, work against any generalization for India as a whole. Interstate competition has often led to perverse effects on labour in terms of withdrawal of protection, leading to a deepening of inequalities between states, between rural and urban areas within a state and between those with access to economic and political resources and those without (Corbridge and Harriss 2000). We therefore rather look at the gendered effects of liberalization in agrarian India, as a policy turn within a context of shifting degrees of state involvement in development, and which has considerable continuities with existing patterns of social change.

In theory, the impact of liberalization on the rural sector was expected to operate through removing discrimination in "terms of trade" against agriculture, thereby leading to a rise in agricultural production (and related non-farm rural employment) which would benefit rural people including women. These ideas follow what appear to be robust empirical relations between agricultural growth and poverty reduction and between public spending and well-being. This set of expectations did not address the gender critique of market-oriented approaches to development, which might predict dire consequences for women of reduced expenditure on social services in the short run, increased labour burdens from intensified agriculture without commensurate increases in consumption due to intrahousehold inequalities, and greater poverty of women due to their constrained access to cash and ability to compete in labour and commodity markets.

Moving to the finer grain of women's livelihood activities under liberalization, we find that while non-agricultural employment and incomes have been rising for some years in rural India, and household livelihoods diversifying, women have not managed to retain their share of non-farm employment and appear to be congregating in the poorer paid segments of this sector. Their access to resources, both land and credit, has achieved considerable policy prominence, even though state enactments of national policy are patchy. The stagnation in the rates of growth of agriculture in the 1990s, partly due to the decline in public investment, especially in irrigation, as well as the competition for land by corporate houses and industries in recent years, alongside shrinking landholdings and lack of credit access to men for investment in non-farm work, has led to the growing importance of ethnic and caste identities in resource claims, leaving women's land claims increasingly contested.

The growth in rural employment slowed considerably in the 1990s and overall women's workforce participation rate declined somewhat. However, demand for women's casual labour increased after liberalization, although gender wage gaps remain. While casualization per se may not be a negative development for women, it is the days of labour and gender pay gaps which are most significant here. Being at the lowest end of employment, both on-farm and off-farm, women's relative access to cash incomes may be declining. While detailed studies on intrahousehold control over income and expenditure are not available for the 1990s, since it is likely that women's contribution to total household income is declining, this may well, following Sen's (1990) intrahousehold bargaining model, lead to declining control over household expenditures by women. And if this be the case, their needs are not likely to be prioritized as indicated in patterns of consumption (as in Haryana), widening nutritional gaps as well as producing a new segregation in fee-paying services, especially education and health.

Employment for women is increasingly spatially dispersed as migration to seasonal work opportunities in other rural areas or to towns increases. Migration produces diverse material and cultural effects on gender relations but much depends on the duration of the migration, the presence of spouses, the nature of the work in destination areas and the degree to which control over incomes is reconfigured in new settings. What is clear is that migration involves cultural exposures which can unsettle the taken-for-granted nature of the agrarian gender order and insinuate new ideas.

The troubled relationship between poverty reduction and gender equity, which is apparent in a number of areas of our analysis, for example, in relation to excess girl child mortality, also becomes evident through the consideration of gender divisions of labour. Exactly how divisions of labour relate to women's well-being and gender equity is a difficult question, and requires a consideration of labour as more than a means of survival but also as a cultural phenomenon which is implicated in identities and everyday power relations. We have therefore examined degrees of flexibility in gender divisions of labour, agency and preferences in relation to work, the potentially perverse effects of education and rising household incomes on labour force participation, and the complex relationship between this and other indicators of women's status. The ways these elements are changing in an era of liberalization is by no means clear, beyond the broad prediction that rising incomes, falling headcount poverty and growing class disparities could possibly produce perverse effects on gender relations in some states. However, we signal them as part of our argument for a properly gendered consideration of social change which requires more than sex disaggregated data to answer the important questions about gender justice. It is not possible to make a summary judgment of whether rising household incomes benefit women more than it disadvantages them, but what we can say is that women's gender identities can "discount" their benefits from rising household prosperity, relative to men.

While income inequality appears to have increased in India, this has been accompanied by an advance in legal equality for women, whether in terms of rights to land, protection from violence or indeed representation in local government. Early female panchayat members have been criticized as stooges, and faced considerable resentment and exclusions by male members, but as time passes they have found voice and effectiveness to varying degrees, and women's political participation in local panchayat institutions in 2000 is held to be of better quality than 1993 (Manasa 2000; Chathukulam and John 2000). In the long run it is difficult not to view the reservation system as beneficial to women, and to the degree that the 73rd Amendment was a gift from government, rather than a concession to agitation from below, acting in line with liberal perceptions of democratic representation it might be judged a boon of liberalization in the broader sense, beyond the reform of the economy. These rights can in some ways seek to keep in check the inequalities resulting from gendered land and labour markets, as visible in the case of the high male–female earning gaps, especially in the more progressive states of the country. The continued need for state intervention in certain key sectors, such as education, health and public distribution of food, as well as in functional institutions for redress, seems imperative to sustain progressive gender change. The capture of informal power at the local level by elites would otherwise further accentuate the inequalities between urban and rural, rich and poor, and men and women.

## NOTES

1. We would like to thank the following for useful comments on this chapter: Kunal Sen, Madhura Swaminathan, Richard Palmer-Jones and the UNRISD reviewer. Errors and interpretations, however, remain our responsibility.

2. In 1981, the Indian population was 523,866,550 rural and 159,462,547 urban; in 1991, it was 628,691,676 rural and 217,611,012 urban; and in 2001, 742,490,639 rural and 286,119,689 urban (http://www.censusindia.gov.in).
3. See Government of India (2006).
4. The *poverty headcount ratio* is the proportion of the national population whose incomes are below the official threshold (or thresholds) set by the national government (or, the percentage of population below the national poverty line). National poverty lines are usually set for households of various compositions to allow for different family sizes. Where there are no official poverty lines, they may be defined as the level of income required to have only sufficient food or food plus other necessities for survival. In India, the price-adjusted poverty line based on the monthly per capita total expenditure (MPCTE) was calculated as Rs.335.05 (rural) and Rs.451.09 (urban) for 1999–2000 (Sundaram and Tendulkar 2005).
5. While the overall gross domestic product (GDP) of the Indian economy is estimated to have grown at 3.7 per cent in 2002–2003, the GDP from the agriculture sector declined at the rate of 4.4 per cent during the same year (NABARD 2007a).
6. The growth rate for agriculture declined in 12 out of 15 states in the 1990s as compared to the 1980s, and three states, namely, Bihar, Orissa and Gujarat, showed negative growth rates.
7. Body mass index (BMI) is a statistical measure of the weight of a person scaled according to height. It is used to categorize people as underweight, normal weight, overweight, obese and morbidly obese. A BMI of less than 18.5 denotes chronic energy deficiency.
8. A note of caution in terms of child BMIs—there is substantial age misreporting, especially for girls, which makes the age/height/weight figures unreliable, especially as Western norms tend to be used (personal communication from Richard Palmer-Jones).
9. In India the sex ratio is generally expressed in terms of numbers of women per 1,000 men, and the child sex ratio is used rather than the adult one because it controls the effects of migration. The lower the numbers of girls, the worst the discrimination against them. The normal sex ratio, without distortion, is about 105 women per 100 men because women have biological advantages in life expectancy.
10. More boys are born than girls and thus the natural sex ratio at birth is expected to favour boys, but not to the extent that the recent India data shows.
11. For a fuller discussion of this point, see Jackson and Rao (2004).
12. Attached labour is the term used to refer to labour contracts where the labourer has an ongoing long-term relationship with the employer, which may not amount to bonded labour but nevertheless is characterized by obligation and patronage. It refers to tied or permanent agricultural workers, often belonging to landless or near-landless households. The idea has been linked to that of unfree labour relations based on tied and low wages, and informally defined and open-ended obligations (Byres 1999).
13. On this point, see, for instance, Lanjouw and Shariff (2000), Sen (1998) and Unni (1996).
14. There was little growth in mining, electricity and services during the 1990s.
15. Most of these acts were passed during the colonial period in response to tribal rebellions protesting land alienation and usurious practices of moneylenders.
16. We have noted in the last section the higher incidence of poverty of tribal people.
17. This is perhaps the largest microfinance programme in the world, operating through 444 banks (44 commercial banks, 191 regional rural banks and 209

cooperative banks) in all districts of the country. The cumulative bank loan in March 2003 was Rs.10,263 million and refinance was Rs.7,965 million. Ninety-one per cent of this was given directly to SHGs and only 9 per cent to non-governmental organizations or other facilitating agencies.

18. Collective action was a key strategy for the empowerment of Third World women emphasized by the Development Alternatives with Women for a New Era (DAWN) collective (Sen and Grown 1987), reiterated in later documents, such as Shramshakti (1988). But even earlier in India, soon after independence, the strategy of *mahila mandals* (women's empowerment groups) was adopted, though the language used was one of welfare rather than empowerment.

19. Gill (2001) notes a labour intensity of 3,600–4,000 hours per hectare for tomatoes, compared with only 740 hours per hectare for paddy.

20. Sukhpal Singh (2003) notes that in 1999–2000, Andhra Pradesh had the highest incidence of child labour in the country (25 per cent as compared to 9 per cent for India), higher rates of casualization (47 per cent of rural employment against 36 per cent for rural India) and higher rates of casual employment for female labour at 53 per cent, compared with 43 per cent for male labour.

21. The overall growth rate of employment also declined from 2.04 to 0.98 per cent per annum during this period.

22. For men, the change was from 155 to 152 per 1,000 persons, while for women it fell from 60 to 45 per 1,000 persons (Sen 2002).

23. They also note that the rate of growth in real daily earnings of male and female agricultural labourers that showed a significant rise in the period 1983–1984 to 1987–1988, slowed down considerably thereafter across a majority of Indian states.

24. Anurekha Chari (2003) writes about the organization of rural women in Maharashtra by the left-oriented Lal Nishan Party to claim their rights.

25. A similar finding emerges from the long-term study of Karimpur (Wiser and Wiser 2000), although other work referred to earlier indicates the negative effect of education on employment seems to be greater for women than men.

## REFERENCES

Agarwal, B. 1998. "Disinherited peasants, disadvantaged workers: A gender perspective on land and livelihood." *Economic and Political Weekly*, Vol. 33, No. 13, pp. A2–14.

———. 1994. *A Field of One's Own: Gender and Land Rights in South Asia*. Cambridge University Press, Cambridge.

———. 1985. "Rural women and HYV rice technology." *Economic and Political Weekly*, Vol. 19, No. 13, pp. A39–52.

Banerjee, N. 1999. "How real is the bogey of feminisation?" In T.S. Papola and A.N. Sharma (eds.), *Gender and Employment in India*. Vikas Publishing House, New Delhi.

Baru, R.V. 2003. "Privatisation of health services: A South Asian perspective." *Economic and Political Weekly*, Vol. 38, No. 42, pp. 4433–4437.

Bhalla, S. 1999. "Liberalisation, rural labour markets and the mobilisation of farm workers: The Haryana story in an all-Indian context." In T.J. Byres, K. Kapadia and J. Lerche (eds.), *Rural Labour Relations in India*. Frank Cass, London.

Bhalla, G.S. and S. Singh. 1997. "Recent developments in Indian agriculture: A state level analysis." *Economic and Political Weekly*, Vol. 32, No. 13, pp. A2–18.

Bhaumik, S.K. 2002. "Employment diversification in rural India: A state level analysis." *India Journal of Labour Economics*, Vol. 45, No. 4, pp. 619–744.

Bouton, M. 1985. *Agrarian Radicalism in South India*. Princeton University Press, Princeton, NJ.

Brass, T. 1999. *Towards a Comparative Political Economy of Unfree Labour*. Frank Cass, London.

Breman, J. 1996. *Footloose Labour*. Cambridge University Press, Cambridge.

———. 1985. *Of Peasants, Migrants and Paupers: Rural Labour Circulation and Capitalist Production in West India*. Oxford University Press, Oxford.

Byres, T. 1999. "Rural labour relations in India: Persistent themes, common processes and differential outcomes." In T.J. Byres, K. Kapadia and J. Lerche (eds.), *Rural Labour Relations in India*. Frank Cass, London.

Chari, A. 2003. *Linking Migration, Women and Women's Movement in Maharashtra*. Paper presented at the International Conference on Women and Migration in Asia, New Delhi, 10–13 December.

Chathukulam, J. and M.S. John. 2000. "Empowerment of women panchayat members: Learning from Kerala." *Asian Journal of Women's Studies*, Vol. 6, No. 4, pp. 66–101.

Chavan, P. and R. Bedamatta. 2006. "Trends in agricultural wages in India: 1964–65 to 1999–2000." *Economic and Political Weekly*, Vol. 41, No. 38, pp. 4041–4051.

Chowdhry, P. 1994. *The Veiled Women: Shifting Gender Equations in Rural Haryana 1880–1990*. Oxford University Press, Delhi.

Corbridge, S. and J. Harriss. 2000. *Reinventing India*. Polity Press, Cambridge.

da Corta, L. and D. Venkateshwarlu. 1999. "Unfree relations and the feminisation of agricultural labour in Andhra Pradesh, 1970–95." In T.J. Byres, K. Kapadia and J. Lerche (eds.), *Rural Labour Relations in India*. Frank Cass, London.

Damodaran, A. 2003. "What happened in Wayanad." *Down to Earth*, Vol. 11, No. 23, p. 53.

Deaton, A. and J. Drèze. 2002. "Poverty and inequality in India: A re-examination." *Economic and Political Weekly*, Vol. 37, No. 36, pp. 3729–3748.

Deshmukh-Ranadive, J. 2003. "Placing gender equity in the family centre stage: Use of 'Kala Jatha' Theatre." *Economic and Political Weekly*, Vol. 38, No. 17, pp. 1674–1679.

Deshpande, S. and L. Deshpande. 1998. "Impact of liberalisation on the labour market in India: What do the facts from NSSOs 50th round show?" *Economic and Political Weekly*, Vol. 33, No. 22, pp. L31–L39.

Dev, M. 2003. *Rural Employment: Trends and Policies*. Paper presented at the All India Conference on Agriculture and Rural Society in Contemporary India, Bardhaman, West Bengal, 17–20 December.

———. 2000. "Economic reforms, poverty, income distribution and employment." *Economic and Political Weekly*, Vol. 35, No. 10, pp. 823–835.

Drèze, J. 2002. "Palanpur 1957 December 93: Occupational change, land ownership and social inequality." In V. Madan (ed.), *The Village in India*. Oxford University Press, New Delhi.

Dubey, A. and R. Palmer-Jones. 2005. "Poverty in India since 1983: New poverty counts and robust poverty comparisons." *Economic and Political Weekly*, Vol. XLVII, Nos. 3–4, September–December, pp. 287–328.

Duvvury, N. 1989. "Work participation of women in India: A study with special reference to female agricultural labourers, 1961 to 1981." In A.V. Jose (ed.), *Limited Options: Women Workers in Rural India*. ILO, New Delhi.

Epstein, T.S., A.P. Suryanarayana and T. Thimmegowda. 1998. *Village Voices: Forty Years of Rural Transformation in South India*. Sage, New Delhi.

Fan, S., P. Hazell and S. Thorat. 1999. *Linkages between Government Spending, Growth and Poverty in Rural India*. Research Report 110, International Food Policy Research Institute, Washington, DC.

Gajalakshmi, V., R. Peto, T. Kanaka and P. Jha. 2003. "Smoking and mortality from tuberculosis and other diseases in India: Retrospective study of 43,000 adult male deaths and 3,500 controls." *The Lancet*, Vol. 362, pp. 507–515.

Gangoli, G. 2003. *Sex Work, Poverty and Migration in Eastern India*. Paper presented at the International Conference on Women and Migration in Asia, New Delhi, 10–13 December.

Gill, K.K. 2001. "Diversification of agriculture and women's employment in Punjab." *The Indian Journal of Labour Economics*, Vol. 44, No. 2, pp. 259–267.

Goetz, A.M. and R. Sengupta. 1996. "Who takes the credit? Gender, power and control over loan use in rural credit programmes in Bangladesh." *World Development*, Vol. 24, No. 1, pp. 45–63.

Government of India. 2006. *Towards Faster and More Inclusive Growth: An Approach to the 11th Five Year Plan*. Planning Commission, Government of India, New Delhi.

———. 2002. *Report of the Steering Committee on Agriculture and Allied Sectors for the Tenth Five Year Plan (2002–2007)*. Planning Commission, Government of India, New Delhi.

———. 2001. *Migration in India, NSSO 55th Round*. National Sample Survey Organisation, New Delhi.

———. 2000. *Employment and Unemployment in India 1999–2000: Key Results, NSS 55th Round*. Ministry of Statistics and Programme Implementation, New Delhi.

Gough, K. 1989. *Rural Change in Southeast India*. Oxford University Press, Delhi.

Gulati, A. and T. Kelly. 1999. *Trade Liberalization and Indian Agriculture*. Oxford University Press, New Delhi.

Gulati, L. 1993. *In the Absence of Their Men*. Sage, New Delhi.

Gupta, J. 2003. "Informal labour in brick kilns: Need for regulation." *Economic and Political Weekly*, Vol. 38, No. 31, pp. 3282–3292.

———. 1997. "Voices break the silence." In N. Rao and L. Rurup (eds.), *A Just Right: Women's Ownership of Natural Resources and Livelihood Security*. Freidrich Ebert Stiftung, New Delhi.

Harriss, B. 1990. "The intra-family distribution of hunger in south Asia." In J. Drèze and A. Sen (eds.), *The Political Economy of Hunger, Vol. 1*. Clarendon Press, Oxford.

Harriss-White, B. 2003. *India Working: Essays on Society and Economy*. Cambridge University Press, Cambridge.

Harriss-White, B. and S. Janakarajan. 1997. "From green revolution to rural industrial revolution in south India." *Economic and Political Weekly*, Vol. 32, No. 25, pp. 1469–1477.

Hashemi, S.M., S.R. Schuler and A.P. Riley. 1996. "Rural credit programs and women's empowerment in Bangladesh." *World Development*, Vol. 24, No. 4, pp. 635–653.

Heyer, J. 1992. "The role of dowries and daughters' marriages in the accumulation and distribution of capital in a south Indian community." *Journal of International Development*, Vol. 4, No. 4, pp. 419–436.

Jackson, C. and N. Rao. 2004. *Understanding Gender and Agrarian Change under Liberalisation: The Case of India*. Background Paper for UNRISD Report on Gender Equality: Striving for Justice in an Unequal World, UNRISD, Geneva.

Jain, P., S. Jain and S. Bhatnagar. 1997. *Scheduled Caste Women*. Rawat Publications, New Delhi.

Kak, S. 2003. *Survival Strategies and Migration—The Importance of Being a Woman*. Paper presented at the International Conference on Women and Migration in Asia, New Delhi, 10–13 December.

Kapadia, K. 2002. "The politics of identity, social inequalities and economic growth." In K. Kapadia (ed.), *The Violence of Development: The Politics of Identity, Gender and Social Inequalities in India*. Kali for Women, New Delhi.

Karlekar, M. 1995. "Gender dimensions in labour migration: An overview." In L. Schenk-Sandbergen (ed.), *Women and Seasonal Labour Migration*. Sage, New Delhi.

Kaul, S.K. 2003. "Land is not less: Thanks to state apathy, tribals of Kerala are landless." *Down to Earth*, Vol. 11, No. 23, p. 56.

Kaur, R. 2003. *Negotiating the City: The Social Construction of Poor Women Migrants*. Paper presented at the International Conference on Women and Migration in Asia, New Delhi, 10–13 December.

Krishnaji, N. 2001. "Land and labour in India: The demographic factor." In A. Thorner (ed.), *Land, Labour and Rights*. Anthem Press, London.

Krishnaji, N. and K.S. James. 2002. "Gender differentials in adult mortality." *Economic and Political Weekly*, Vol. 37, No. 46, pp. 4633–4637.

Krishnakumar A. 2002. "A programme without a plan." *Frontline*, Vol. 19, No. 3. Access available at http://www.frontlineonnet.com/fl1903/19030410.htm, accessed 15 Sept 2008.

Krishnan, T.N. 1999. "Access to health and the burden of treatment in India: An inter-state comparison." In M. Rao (ed.), *Disinvesting in Health: The World Bank's Prescriptions for Health*. Sage, New Delhi.

Lanjouw, P. and A. Shariff. 2000. *Rural Nonfarm Employment in India: Access, Incomes and Poverty Impact*. National Council of Applied Economic Research, New Delhi.

Manasa. 2000. "Karnataka and the Women's Reservation Bill." *Economic and Political Weekly*, Vol. 35, Nos. 43/44, pp. WS 49–54.

Meenakshi, J.V and B. Vishwanathan. 2003. "Calorie deprivation in rural India, 1983–1999/2000." *Economic and Political Weekly*, Vol. 38, No. 4, pp. 369–375.

Mosse, D., S. Gupta, M. Mehta, V. Shah and J. Rees. 2002. "Brokered livelihoods: Debt, labour migration and development in tribal western India." In A. de Haan and B. Rogaly (eds.), *Labour Mobility and Rural Society*. Frank Cass, London.

National Bank for Agriculture and Rural Development (NABARD). 2007a. *Rural Economic Environment*. www.nabard.org/ruraleconomy/ruraleconomicenvironment.asp, accessed on 20 December 2007.

———. 2007b. *SHG-Bank Linkage Progress 2006–07*. www.nabard.org/microfinance/shglinkageprogress.asp, accessed on 20 December 2007.

Nair, P. 2004. "Sex ratio: The hidden horrors." *India Together*, 20 April. http://www.indiatogether.org/2004/apr/hlt-csratio.htm, accessed September 15, 2008.

Nakkeeran, N. 2003. "Women's work, status and fertility: Land, caste and gender in a south Indian village." *Economic and Political Weekly*, Vol. 38, No. 37, pp. 3931–3939.

National Nutrition Monitoring Bureau (NNMB). 2002. *Diet and Nutritional Status of Rural Population*. NNMB Technical Report No. 21, National Institute of Nutrition, Indian Council of Medical Research, Hyderabad.

National Sample Survey Organisation (NSSO). 2001. *Report No. 458: Employment and Unemployment Situation in India, 1999–2000 (Part I), NSSO 55th Round, July 1999–June 2000*. NSSO, Ministry of Statistics and Programme Implementation, Government of India, New Delhi.

———. 1997. *Report No. 409: Employment and Unemployment in India, 1993–94; Fifth Quinquennial Survey. NSSO 50th Round (July 1993–June 1994)*. NSSO, Department of Statistics, Government of India, New Delhi.

Nillesan, P. and B. Harriss-White. 2004. "Life chances: Development and female disadvantage." In B. Harriss-White and S. Janakarajan (eds.), *Rural India Facing the 21st Century*. Anthem Press, London.

Nirantar. 2007. *Examining Self Help Groups: A Qualitative Study*. Nirantar, New Delhi.

Pal, S. 1997. "An analysis of declining incidence of regular labour contracts in rural India." *Journal of Development Studies*, Vol. 34, No. 2, pp. 133–155.

Patnaik, U. 2003. *Global Capitalism, Deflation and Agrarian Crisis in Developing Countries*. Programme on Social Policy and Development, Paper No. 15, UNRISD, Geneva.

———. 2002. "Deflation and *deja vu*: Indian agriculture in the world economy." In V.K. Ramachandran and M. Swaminathan (eds.), *Agrarian Studies: Essays on Agrarian Relations in Less-Developed Countries*. Tulika, New Delhi.

PROBE Team. 1999. *Public Report on Basic Education in India*. Oxford University Press, Oxford.

Rajuladevi, A.K. 2000. "Profiles in poverty: Female landless agricultural labour households." *Economic and Political Weekly*, Vol. 35, No. 6, pp. 474–484.

Ramachandran, V. and A. Saihjee. 2002. "The new segregation: Reflections on gender and equity in primary education." *Economic and Political Weekly*, Vol. 37, No. 17, pp. 1600–1613.

Ramachandran, V.K. and M. Swaminathan. 2004. "Institutional reform and rural credit in India, 1969–2003." In V.K. Ramachandran and M. Swaminathan (eds.), *Institutional Reform and Rural Credit in India*. Tulika, New Delhi.

Ramachandran, V.K, M. Swaminathan and V. Rawal. 2001. *How Have Hired Workers Fared? A Case Study of Women Workers from an Indian Village, 1977–1999*. Centre for Development Studies, Trivandrum, Kerala.

Ramesh, R. 2008. "India will pay families to have girls to end fœticide." *The Guardian*, 4 March, p. 14.

Randhawa, N.S. 1994. "Liberalisation and implications for agricultural policy: An overview." In G.S. Bhalla (ed.), *Economic Liberalisation and Indian Agriculture*. Institute for Industrial Studies, New Delhi.

Rao, J.M. and S. Storm. 1998. "Distribution and growth in Indian agriculture." In T.J. Byres (ed.), *The Indian Economy: Major Debates since Independence*. Oxford University Press, Delhi.

Rao, M. 2005. "Looking back in despair: Ten years after Cairo." *Indian Journal of Gender Studies*, Vol. 12, No. 1, pp. 115–125.

Rao, N. 2006. *Women's Rights to Land and Other Productive Assets: Its Impact on Gender Relations and Increased Productivity*. Working Paper 4, UNIFEM, New Delhi.

———. 2002. *Standing One's Ground: Gender, Land and Livelihoods in the Santal Parganas, Jharkhand, India*. PhD thesis, University of East Anglia, Norwich.

Rao, N. and K. Rana. 1997. "Women's labour and migration: Case of Santhals." *Economic and Political Weekly*, Vol. 32, No. 23, pp 1307–1309.

Ravallion, M. 1998. "Reform, food prices and poverty in India." *Economic and Political Weekly*, Vol. 33, Nos.1 and 2, pp. 29–36.

Rogaly, B., J. Biswas, D. Coppard, A. Rafique, K. Rana and A. Sengupta. 2001. *Seasonal Migration for Rural Manual Work in Eastern India*. Research Report submitted to DFID, School of Development Studies, University of East Anglia, Norwich.

Roy, D. 1995. *Women, New Technology and Development: Changing Nature of Gender Relations in Rural India*. Manohar, Delhi.

Rustagi, P. 2000. *Gender Development Indicators: Issues, Debates and Ranking of Districts*. Centre for Women's Development Studies, New Delhi.

Sankar, D. and V. Kathuria. 2004. "Health system performance in rural India: Efficiency estimates across states." *Economic and Political Weekly*, Vol. 39, No. 13, pp. 1427–1433.

Sen, A. 2002. "Agriculture, employment and poverty: Recent trends in rural India." In V.K. Ramachandran and M. Swaminathan (eds.), *Agrarian Studies: Essays on Agrarian Relations in Less-Developed Countries*. Tulika, New Delhi.

———. 1998. "Rural labour markets and poverty." In R.S. Radhakrishna and A.N. Sharma (eds.), *Empowering Rural Labour in India*. Institute for Human Development, New Delhi.

———. 1990. "Gender and cooperative conflicts." In Irene Tinker (ed.), *Persistent Inequalities*. Oxford University Press, Oxford.

Sen, G. and C. Grown. 1987. *Development, Crises and Alternative Visions: Third World Women's Perspectives*. Monthly Review Press, New York.

Shah, A. 2006. "The labour of love: Seasonal migration from Jharkhand to the brick kilns of other states in India." *Contributions to Indian Sociology*, Vol. 40, No. 1, pp. 91–118.

Shah, S. 2003. *Migration, Sex and Work: Gender and Daily Wage Labour in Mumbai*. Paper presented at the International Conference on Women and Migration in Asia, New Delhi, 10–13 December.

Shramshakti. 1988. *Report of the National Commission on Self Employed Women and Women in the Informal Sector*. Government of India, New Delhi, June.

Singh, S. 2003. *Contract Farming in India: Impacts on Women and Child Workers*. Gatekeeper Series No. 111, International Institute for Environment and Development, London.

Srinivasan, M.V. 2004. "Time and space: Intervillage variation in the North Arcot region and its dynamics, 1973–95." In B. Harriss-White and S. Janakarajan (eds.), *Rural India Facing the 21st Century: Essays on Long-Term Village Change and Recent Development Policy*. Anthem Press, London.

Sundaram, I.S. 2003. "India's economy and rural women workers." *Social Welfare*, Vol. 50, Nos. 5 and 6, pp. 67–70.

Sundaram, K. and S.D. Tendulkar. 2005. "NAS/NSS estimates of private consumption for poverty estimation: A further comparative examination." In A. Deaton and V. Kozel (eds.), *The Great Indian Poverty Debate*. Macmillan, Delhi.

Swaminathan, M. 2000. *Weakening Welfare: The Public Distribution of Food in India*. Leftword Books, New Delhi.

Teerink, R. 1995. "Migration and its impact on Khandeshi women." In L. Schenk-Sandbergen (ed.), *Women and Seasonal Labour Migration*. Sage, New Delhi.

Thakur, S.G. 2001. *Women and Land Rights: Policy and Practice*. The Planning Commission, Overseas Development Group (ODG) and Department for International Development–UK (DFID), New Delhi.

Unni, J. 1996. "Diversification of economic activities and non-agricultural employment in Gujarat." *Economic and Political Weekly*, Vol. 31, No. 33, pp. 2243–2251.

Unni, J. and G. Raveendran. 2007. "Growth of employment (1993–94 to 2004–05): Illusion of inclusiveness?" *Economic and Political Weekly*, Vol. 42, No. 3, pp. 196–199.

Unnithan-Kumar, M. 2003. "Spirits of the womb: Migration, reproductive choice and healing in Rajasthan." *Contributions to Indian Sociology*, Vol. 37, Nos. 1 and 2, pp. 163–188.

Venkateshwarlu, D. and L. Da Corta. 2001. "Transformations in the age and gender of unfree workers on hybrid cottonseed farms in Andhra Pradesh." *The Journal of Peasant Studies*, Vol. 28, No. 3, pp. 1–36.

Verschoor, A., A. Covarrubias and C. Locke. 2006. *Women's Economic Empowerment: Gender and Growth. Literature Review and Synthesis*. Report to DFID, Overseas Development Group, Norwich.

Wadley, S. 2002. "The domination of Indira." In V. Madan (ed.), *The Village in India*. Oxford University Press, New Delhi.

White, S.C. 1992. *Arguing with the Crocodile: Gender and Class in Bangladesh*. Zed Books, London.

Wiser, W. and C. Wiser. 2000. *Behind Mud Walls: Seventy-five Years in a North Indian Village*. University of California Press, Berkeley.

# 4  The Feminization of Agriculture?

## The Impact of Economic Restructuring in Rural Latin America[1]

*Carmen Diana Deere*

## INTRODUCTION

The dominant trends in rural Latin America since the 1970s include the continued diversification of rural household livelihood strategies; a notable increase in rural women's measured economic participation rates; a reported concentration of active rural women in non-agricultural activities; and the growing visibility of women, both rural and urban, in agricultural production. This chapter considers whether the process of economic restructuring, induced by the combined effect of economic crises, neoliberal policies and globalization over the past several decades, has led to a process of feminization of agriculture. Further, is the feminization of the agricultural sector consistent with the reported concentration of active rural women in non-agricultural activities?

In this chapter I argue that there is abundant evidence of an increase in women's participation as agricultural wage workers. This growth has been concentrated in the non-traditional agro-export sector favoured under neoliberalism, specifically, in the production and packing of fresh vegetables, fruits and flowers for Northern markets, what now constitutes Latin America's leading agricultural export rubric. In many countries women make up at least half of the field labour for these crops, while they constitute the vast majority of the workers in the packing houses geared to the export market. Nonetheless, the characteristics of this employment, principally its temporary, seasonal and precarious nature, have made it difficult to capture quantitatively in national censuses and household surveys.

There is also evidence, stronger for some countries than others, of a feminization of smallholder or peasant production, as growing numbers of rural women become the principal farmers, that is, own-account workers in agriculture. This phenomenon is associated with an increase in the share of rural female household heads as well as male absence from the farm, in turn related to growing male migration and/or employment in off-farm pursuits.

There is little question that the principal factor driving these trends is the need for rural households to diversify their livelihoods. The combination of growing land shortage (itself a product of the extreme concentration of land in region and population growth), economic crises and unfavourable policies for domestic agriculture under neoliberalism has meant that peasant households can no longer sustain themselves on the basis of agricultural production alone. Moreover, rural poverty rates remain grossly high. In many regions the response to the crisis of peasant agriculture has been an increase in the number of rural household members pursuing off-farm activities. Whether these are male, female, or include both sexes, depends on a myriad of factors, with household composition and the stage of the domestic cycle and the dynamism and gendered nature of local, regional and international labour markets being among the most important.

The chapter is organized as follows. The main trends in Latin America with respect to the content and impact of neoliberal economic policies are summarized in broad strokes in the next section, highlighting the increase in poverty rates and their gendered impact with respect to rural economic activity rates and household headship. The third section focuses on rural livelihoods and summarizes the available survey data on the diversification of household incomes. The fourth considers the methodological problems in analysing changes in rural women's work over time and tackles the puzzle of whether the trend towards feminization of agriculture is compatible with the reported concentration of rural women in non-agricultural activities. The fifth section focuses on agricultural labour markets as gendered institutions, and attempts to establish what exactly is new about women's participation in the labour market for non-traditional agro-export production. The sixth turns to the viability of peasant farming under neoliberalism and the processes that have contributed to the feminization of peasant agriculture. The final section offers some tentative conclusions.

## NEOLIBERALISM AND POVERTY

During the 1980s Latin American governments and the international financial institutions reached an extraordinary consensus around the virtues of neoliberalism. The state-driven policies associated with import substitution industrialization (ISI) were abandoned in favour of free markets and open economies. Facing daunting debt service payments and large current account deficits, Latin American countries adopted stabilization programmes in order to bring about macroeconomic balance. These aimed to reduce the domestic fiscal deficit, establish equilibrium in the balance of payments and reduce inflation while allowing for debt repayment. Structural adjustment was to establish the conditions for long-run growth by moving toward a free market economy that favoured tradables at the expense of nontradables combined with a reduction in the size of the state. The specific timing and manner by which reform and institutional change were fostered varied considerably across the region (Weeks 1995; Tejo 2001; Spoor 2002).

In terms of outcomes, it was not until the first half of the 1990s that the Latin American agricultural sector achieved an average annual rate of growth even approximating that of the ISI period. The annual average growth rate for 1990–1998 was only 2.6 per cent, much below the 1970s average of 3.5 per cent (David et al. 2001:table 1). Neoliberal policies have contributed to increased labour productivity and generated a positive agricultural trade balance (Spoor 2002; García Pascual 2003). Yet, as a result of increasing globalization, between 1979 and 2001 the growth rate of the value of Latin America's agricultural imports was almost twice that of exports, leading to a dwindling positive trade balance by 2001 (David et al. 2001:table 1). Among the main items in which the region experienced a trade deficit in 2001 were those crucial to food sovereignty—beans, rice, cereals, milk and dairy products—and textile fibres.

Neoliberal agricultural policies were expected to have differential effects on different groups of agricultural producers, depending on whether they produced export crops or domestic foodstuffs, the degree of international competition that they faced and the extent to which they had previously relied on government subsidies and services (Carter and Barham 1996). The Economic Commission for Latin America and the Caribbean (ECLAC) emphasizes how the reforms have accentuated the already strong differentiation that existed in Latin America between regions, producers and dynamic and traditional products (David et al. 2001). The most dynamic growth sectors have been non-traditional exports such as oilseeds, livestock, vegetables and fruit. These are largely produced by the most modern and capitalized farmers with links to agro-industry and export markets and by international agribusiness. Those in decline include traditional exports such as coffee, sugar and cotton, as well as roots and tubers. The latter as well as coffee are generally produced by small farmers. The substitution of the market for the institutions of the state has also meant the elimination of state support for precisely those regions, products and producers that are less competitive but crucial to fighting rural poverty (David et al. 2001).

The implementation of neoliberal policies has thus come at a very high cost, exacerbating social and economic inequalities while increasing the vulnerability of the agricultural sector and of Latin American economies. During the Lost Decade of the 1980s the incidence of rural poverty increased from 60 to 65 per cent (see table 4.1). During the 1990s the incidence of poverty declined and finally fell in 2004 below the level of 1980. While the incidence of rural poverty continues to significantly exceed that of urban poverty, the latter in 2005 is still above the pre-crisis level.

Among the factors accounting for the high incidence of rural poverty in Latin America is the extremely unequal distribution of land. Over the 1990s land may have become even more unequally distributed as the number of small farms in existence decreased in countries such as Brazil, Chile, Uruguay, Argentina, Bolivia, Colombia and Mexico. The incidence of rural poverty in the 1990s was concentrated among own-account and unpaid family workers

*Table 4.1* Incidence of Poverty and Indigence, Latin America, 1980–2005
(in Percentages of Population)

| | Poor | | | Indigent | | |
|---|---|---|---|---|---|---|
| Year | Total | Urban | Rural | Total | Urban | Rural |
| 1980 | 40.5 | 29.8 | 59.9 | 18.6 | 10.6 | 32.7 |
| 1990 | 48.3 | 41.4 | 65.4 | 22.5 | 15.3 | 40.4 |
| 1999 | 43.8 | 37.1 | 63.7 | 18.5 | 11.9 | 38.3 |
| 2002 | 44.0 | 38.4 | 61.8 | 19.4 | 13.5 | 37.9 |
| 2004 | 42.0 | 36.9 | 58.7 | 16.9 | 12.0 | 33.1 |
| 2005 | 39.8 | 34.1 | 58.8 | 15.4 | 10.3 | 32.5 |

*Source*: ECLAC (2007:table 1.3).

in agriculture, linked to the distress of agricultural production for the internal market under neoliberalism, among other factors (David et al. 2001).

It is now well established that stabilization and structural adjustment policies are not gender neutral. One of the main consequences of neoliberal policies has been to transfer the costs of reproduction of the labour force from the state to households, and often to the women within them, both because of their primary responsibility for domestic labour and because the crisis has required their growing participation in the labour force (Deere et al. 1990; Elson 1991; Razavi 2002). Reductions in state spending on health, education, transportation, utilities and food subsidies have all increased the burden of domestic labour principally by increasing the time that women must dedicate to caring and providing for their families. At the same time, the higher cost of basic reproduction brought about by the withdrawal of the state, combined with higher male unemployment rates, the informalization of labour and declining real wages, have provided powerful incentives for women, both urban and rural, to increase their labour force participation.

One of the most striking differences by gender is with respect to the trend in measured, rural economic activity rates (see table 4.2). While for men the rural economic activity rate for Latin America (unweighted average) stagnated at around 76 per cent between 1980 and 2000, for rural women it increased from 16 to 25 per cent. Every country but Paraguay reported an increase in the rural female activity rate, and in five countries (Argentina, Chile, Ecuador, Guatemala and Honduras) this rate more than doubled. The share of the rural economically active population that is female in Latin America thus reached 26 per cent in 2000, up from 21 per cent in 1980 (Katz 2003:table 3). These figures lend support to the argument that one of the principal consequences of neoliberal policies has been the growing labour force participation of rural women, linked to the need for rural households to increasingly augment and diversify their sources of livelihood.[2]

*Table 4.2* Rural Economic Activity Rates by Sex, Latin America 1980–2000

| Country | | 1980 *(per cent)* | 1990 *(per cent)* | 2000 *(per cent)* |
|---|---|---|---|---|
| Argentina | Male | 77.5 | 70.1 | 70.4 |
| | Female | 14.1 | 32.4 | 33.9 |
| Bolivia | Male | 78.4 | 77.4 | 77.0 |
| | Female | 20.9 | 29.2 | 32.3 |
| Brazil | Male | 83.8 | 83.5 | 82.3 |
| | Female | 31.3 | 36.1 | 39.4 |
| Chile | Male | 69.0 | 75.9 | 75.2 |
| | Female | 8.9 | 13.6 | 18.4 |
| Colombia | Male | 70.5 | 69.3 | 69.2 |
| | Female | 21.4 | 28.9 | 32.4 |
| Costa Rica | Male | 77.8 | 78.6 | 77.7 |
| | Female | 12.5 | 16.5 | 21.1 |
| Dominican Republic | Male | 74.8 | 76.1 | 76.4 |
| | Female | 21.4 | 25.7 | 29.7 |
| Ecuador | Male | 73.3 | 74.6 | 76.2 |
| | Female | 10.4 | 18.1 | 22.7 |
| El Salvador | Male | 78.8 | 73.4 | 75.6 |
| | Female | 13.5 | 14.1 | 19.7 |
| Guatemala | Male | 74.0 | 72.8 | 72.9 |
| | Female | 6.2 | 11.2 | 16.5 |
| Honduras | Male | 81.4 | 82.3 | 80.7 |
| | Female | 8.0 | 11.0 | 16.3 |
| Mexico | Male | 75.6 | 76.1 | 76.6 |
| | Female | 16.1 | 20.2 | 24.2 |
| Nicaragua | Male | 77.5 | 78.3 | 79.4 |
| | Female | 18.5 | 24.0 | 27.0 |
| Panama | Male | 66.4 | 71.3 | 71.8 |
| | Female | 12.6 | 16.6 | 21.5 |
| Paraguay | Male | 78.7 | 77.4 | 76.3 |
| | Female | 10.9 | 8.4 | 8.2 |
| Peru | Male | 74.0 | 76.2 | 77.3 |
| | Female | 30.8 | 34.9 | 38.1 |
| Uruguay | Male | 76.7 | 77.1 | 75.5 |
| | Female | 24.8 | 33.3 | 35.9 |
| Venezuela | Male | 68.6 | 69.0 | 68.7 |
| | Female | 9.9 | 11.7 | 16.7 |
| Latin America | Male | 75.4 | 75.5 | 75.5 |
| | Female | 16.2 | 21.4 | 25.2 |

*Note*: Refers to population 10 years and over.
*Source*: CELADE/CEPAL (2002:table 5a).

*Table 4.3* Female Household Headship in Latin America, 1994–2005 (by Percentage of Households)

| Country | | 1994 | 1999 | 2002 | 2005 |
|---|---|---|---|---|---|
| Argentina | Urban | 23.8 | 27.6 | 28.6 | 32.5 |
| | Rural | na | na | na | Na |
| Bolivia | Urban | na | na | na | 25.5 |
| | Rural | na | na | na | 21.1 |
| Brazil | Urban | na | na | na | 30.4 |
| | Rural | na | na | na | na |
| Chile | Urban | 22.4 | 24.0 | 24.3 | 27.1 |
| | Rural | 15.6 | 15.3 | 16.0 | 18.3 |
| Colombia | Urban | 24.2 | 28.8 | 30.3 | 32.7 |
| | Rural | 18.7 | 18.7 | 19.7 | 19.6 |
| Costa Rica | Urban | 24.0 | 27.9 | 28.4 | 31.0 |
| | Rural | 16.0 | 18.6 | 19.7 | 19.6 |
| Dominican Republic | Urban | na | na | 34.2 | 35.0 |
| | Rural | na | na | 23.3 | 24.0 |
| Ecuador | Urban | 18.7 | 20.1 | 21.4 | 23.3 |
| | Rural | na | na | na | 17.1 |
| El Salvador | Urban | 30.8 | 31.4 | 35.3 | 35.3 |
| | Rural | 23.4 | 24.5 | 27.3 | 26.9 |
| Guatemala | Urban | 24.3 | na | na | 22.5 |
| | Rural | na | 17.7 | na | 15.9 |
| Honduras | Urban | 25.0 | 30.3 | 31.4 | 31.0 |
| | Rural | 18.7 | 20.7 | 19.2 | 20.6 |
| Mexico | Urban | 17.0 | 19.4 | 21.4 | 25.1 |
| | Rural | 11.2 | 15.8 | 17.6 | 20.1 |
| Nicaragua | Urban | 34.9 | 34.5 | 34.2 | 39.1 |
| | Rural | 18.9 | 18.5 | 18.9 | 21.3 |
| Panama | Urban | 27.0 | 27.4 | 28.9 | 30.2 |
| | Rural | na | na | 15.9 | 19.0 |
| Paraguay | Urban | 23.7 | 27.3 | 29.6 | 32.2 |
| | Rural | na | 20.1 | 19.6 | 20.7 |
| Peru | Urban | na | na | 22.1 | 23.9 |
| | Rural | na | na | 17.1 | 16.0 |
| Uruguay | Urban | 27.1 | 30.5 | 32.3 | 34.3 |
| | Rural | na | na | na | na |
| Venezuela | Urban | 24.6 | 27.2 | 28.8 | 31.8 |
| | Rural | 17.6 | na | na | na |

*Note:* Based on survey series for share of households with female heads by type of household. Precise year of actual survey differs among countries. Na = not available.

*Source:* ECLAC Women's Unit, *Estadísticas de Género*. www.eclac.org/mujer.

Another important trend of the past several decades has been an increase in self-declared female-headed households in both rural and urban areas in almost every Latin American country (see table 4.3). The share of rural female-headed households in 2005 ranges from a low of 15.9 per cent in Guatemala to a high of 26.9 per cent in El Salvador, but these figures may underestimate the share of de facto female headship. Among the sources of underenumeration is the phenomenon of "nesting", whereby female-headed or maintained families reside within larger households (such as a mother's parental home). Another is that, given the high prevalence of consensual unions in regions such as Central America, the most stable unit is often that of a mother and her children, irrespective of whether a man resides in the household (Katz 2003). The cultural tendency to declare a man as the head if he is present would thus tend to understate the "true" share of female household heads and partly account for the higher share of households that are reported to be female-maintained as compared to female-headed (Katz 2003).

There is little question that the growing share of rural female-headed households reported for most countries is linked to the growing distress of the peasant economy. The need to seek off-farm sources of income has spurred temporary as well as long-distance migration among men, leaving married women as the de facto household heads during their absence. Many rural women become de jure household heads as a result of abandonment—another factor on the rise—as when their partner's temporary migration becomes permanent. At the same time there is some evidence that a rising share of rural women are choosing to either remain single (or delaying marriage and child-bearing) as well as opting for separation or divorce, related to a growth in their potential income-generating opportunities.

## RURAL LIVELIHOODS AND THE DIVERSIFICATION OF HOUSEHOLD INCOMES

One of the main discoveries in the heyday of agrarian studies in Latin America in the 1970s was that rural households relied on multiple income-generating activities (Deere 1991). Little attention was paid to whether wage employment was attained in the agricultural or non-agricultural sector, presumably because the majority of wage work was still concentrated in the former. But important transformations were already taking place in the agricultural labour market, primarily the decline of permanent, relative to temporary, employment opportunities (de Janvry et al. 1989).

By the 1990s attention shifted in the literature to the important role of non-agricultural activities in rural household income generation, specifically, income from non-agricultural wage employment and self-employment. Thomas Reardon and colleagues (2001:399) reported that in 12 national surveys conducted in the 1990s rural non-agricultural income represented 46 per cent of total household income or a weighted (by rural population) 40 per cent. The main conclusion reached from these national surveys with respect to gender was that in contrast to rural men, who continue to be concentrated in agriculture, economically active rural women are concentrated in non-agricultural activities.

*Table 4.4* Distribution of the Economically Active Rural Population, by Sex and
Sector of Activity, Latin America[a]

| Country | Sex | Year | Sector of activity (per cent) | | |
| | | | Agriculture | Non-agriculture | Total |
| --- | --- | --- | --- | --- | --- |
| Bolivia | Female | 1999 | 85.7 | 14.3 | 100 |
| | | 2002 | 85.2 | 14.8 | 100 |
| | Male | 1999 | 85.6 | 14.4 | 100 |
| | | 2002 | 86.0 | 14.0 | 100 |
| Brazil | Female | 1995 | 72.1 | 27.9 | 100 |
| | | 2003 | 70.0 | 30.0 | 100 |
| | Male | 1995 | 78.1 | 21.9 | 100 |
| | | 2003 | 79.2 | 20.8 | 100 |
| Chile | Female | 1994 | 29.4 | 70.6 | 100 |
| | | 2002 | 24.7 | 75.3 | 100 |
| | Male | 1994 | 44.9 | 55.1 | 100 |
| | | 2004 | 41.5 | 58.5 | 100 |
| Dominican Republic | Female | 1997 | 7.6 | 92.4 | 100 |
| | | 2004 | 6.6 | 93.4 | 100 |
| | Male | 1997 | 46.6 | 53.4 | 100 |
| | | 2004 | 43.6 | 56.4 | 100 |
| El Salvador | Female | 1995 | 21.6 | 78.4 | 100 |
| | | 2004 | 10.2 | 89.8 | 100 |
| | Male | 1995 | 67.0 | 33.0 | 100 |
| | | 2004 | 56.9 | 43.1 | 100 |
| Guatemala | Female | 1995 | 21.6 | 78.4 | 100 |
| | | 2004 | 10.2 | 89.8 | 100 |
| | Male | 1995 | 67.0 | 33.0 | 100 |
| | | 2004 | 56.9 | 43.1 | 100 |
| Honduras | Female | 1994 | 13.0 | 87.0 | 100 |
| | | 2003 | 20.6 | 79.4 | 100 |
| | Male | 1994 | 75.3 | 24.7 | 100 |
| | | 2003 | 77.7 | 22.3 | 100 |
| Mexico | Female | 1994 | 35.3 | 64.7 | 100 |
| | | 2004 | 17.6 | 82.4 | 100 |
| | Male | 1994 | 58.0 | 42.0 | 100 |
| | | 2004 | 42.7 | 57.3 | 100 |
| Nicaragua | Female | 1993 | 20.4 | 79.6 | 100 |
| | | 2001 | 28.5 | 71.5 | 100 |
| | Male | 1993 | 74.4 | 25.6 | 100 |
| | | 2001 | 76.4 | 23.6 | 100 |
| Panama | Female | 1994 | 9.5 | 90.5 | 100 |
| | | 2004 | 18.7 | 81.3 | 100 |
| | Male | 1994 | 59.0 | 41.0 | 100 |
| | | 2004 | 61.1 | 38.9 | 100 |
| Paraguay | Female | 1999 | 42.8 | 57.2 | 100 |
| | | 2000 | 49.5 | 50.5 | 100 |
| | Male | 1999 | 71.0 | 29.0 | 100 |
| | | 2000 | 70.1 | 29.9 | 100 |
| Peru | Female | 2001 | 72.3 | 27.7 | 100 |
| | | 2003 | 75.7 | 24.3 | 100 |
| | Male | 2001 | 82.2 | 17.8 | 100 |
| | | 2003 | 84.7 | 15.3 | 100 |
| Venezuela | Female | 1994 | 12.8 | 87.2 | 100 |
| | Male | 1994 | 64.7 | 35.3 | 100 |

*Note*: [a]Based on occupied population.
*Source*: Compiled from data made available to the author by ECLAC, Women and Development Unit; based on household surveys.

In the 1990s in only Bolivia, Brazil and Peru were the majority of active rural women employed in agriculture; in 12 out of 15 countries the majority of rural women were employed in non-agricultural activities (see table 4.4). The gender differences are striking, for in all but two countries in this period (Costa Rica and the Dominican Republic), the majority of active rural men were employed in agriculture.

Between the 1990s and the 2000s the share of rural women employed in agriculture fell significantly in Guatemala, El Salvador and Mexico; in the latter two countries, the share of rural men in agriculture fell as well. Most interesting, however, is that in four countries—Chile, Honduras, Nicaragua and Panama—there was a reversal of this trend, with the share of rural women employed in agriculture increasing. In Chile this reversal was due to significant new employment opportunities for women in agriculture, principally as wage workers in non-traditional agro-exports. Such might also account for part of the increase in the Central American countries, although it is likely that the growth in the share of women in agricultural activities may reflect their greater visibility as own-account farmers.

One of the most important findings of recent econometric work is the tendency in Ecuador, El Salvador and Northeast Brazil for economically active rural women to be more likely than men to engage in low productivity, poorly remunerated non-agricultural activities, with the latter measured with respect to either the average agricultural wage or the rural poverty line (Ferreira and Lanjouw 2001; Elbers and Lanjouw 2001; Lanjouw 2001). Controlling for similar individual, household and regional characteristics, in Ecuador it was found that women earn 29 per cent less than men with respect to non-agricultural labour earnings (Lanjouw 2001). With respect to non-agricultural wage earnings, controlling for other factors, women earn about 70 per cent less than men (Elbers and Lanjouw 2001). The work by Lanjouw and colleagues suggest that non-agricultural employment can be thought of as representing two paths, one consisting of "safety net" or "last resort" jobs to keep households from destitution, and the other a means of household upward mobility. That female participation in non-agricultural employment is linked with low productivity, low remunerated activities in many (but not all) countries is particularly worrisome, since economically active rural women are reported to be so concentrated in the non-agricultural sector.

## METHODOLOGICAL PROBLEMS IN ANALYSING CHANGES IN RURAL WOMEN'S WORK

Much of the recent literature on Latin America emphasizes that one of the main tendencies of the last several decades has been the feminization of agriculture. Yet the main conclusion reached earlier was that economically active rural women in Latin America are concentrated in non-agricultural employment. Are these two trends compatible?

The feminization of agriculture can have multiple meanings. It can refer to an increase in rural women's, or rural and urban women's participation rates in the agricultural sector. It can also be measured as an increase in the share of the agricultural labour force that is female. A higher female share can in turn be the result of a higher female activity rate in agriculture and/or a decrease in men's. Moreover, the feminization of the agricultural sector might be the result of the underenumeration of women as unpaid family labour in the past, combined with their greater current visibility as agricultural wage workers or own-account farmers.

The underenumeration of women in agriculture in census data has been a constant theme of the Women/Gender and Development field since the 1970s (Deere and León 1982; Buvinic 1982). Underenumeration in the past could result in an absolute increase in the number of women reporting agriculture as their primary activity while at the same time, if non-agricultural employment is growing at a faster rate, the majority of active women would be concentrated in non-agricultural activities. This would provide one explanation of why a trend towards the feminization of agriculture might be compatible with the reported concentration of rural women in non-agricultural activities. However, the underenumeration of women in agriculture continues to be a problem since census estimates tend to capture the socially appropriate gender division of labour—women's role as housewives and mothers—rather than the economic activities in which they normally engage. Censuses also better capture participation in income-generating activities (what is considered "work"), than participation in subsistence production, which may be viewed as an extension of women's domestic responsibilities. Moreover, agricultural participation tends to be measured quite narrowly, privileging participation in fieldwork, to the detriment of many of the activities commonly carried out by women, such as tending a garden and small animals. Another problem is that participation tends to be measured in terms of engaging in an economic activity for a minimum amount of time the week prior to the census or survey that overlooks the seasonality of crop production. In some cases a minimum time requirement for classification as economically active is utilized for only certain categories of workers, such as unpaid family workers. Since if a man is present, he tends to be considered the own-account worker, the underenumeration of unpaid family workers tends to principally affect women.[3]

Another difficulty in accurately measuring rural women's economic participation has to do with the multiple economic activities in which they engage. Over the course of a year, for example, they may participate as unpaid family labour in agriculture while also engaging in wage labour, petty trade and artisan production; moreover, sometimes they engage in multiple activities at the same time (Campaña 1982; Deere 1991). Household surveys (such as the Living Standard Measurement Survey—LSMS) have improved upon census data by usually asking a respondent's primary and secondary activity. However, at the moment of analysis, these tend to focus on an individual's primary occupation. This probably leads to a continued underestimation of women's agricultural activities because cash-generating activities tend to be privileged over subsistence-oriented activities. Moreover, the LSMS surveys (the primary source for the data in tables 4.2, 4.3 and 4.4) have still to address the problem of seasonality, that is, that an individual's most important income-generating activity might not take place the week or month prior to the survey.[4]

Finally, another problem that complicates the analysis of changes in rural women's economic activity rates and its distribution by sectors is that the most visible growth in female employment over the last two decades has been in non-traditional agro-export production and, particularly, in the packing houses for fruit and vegetable export activities. It is not at all clear whether the various estimates of economically active women treat such employment as agricultural or industrial, although it should properly be classified as agricultural, consisting of agricultural services.[5]

In sum, the multiple sources of underenumeration of women's agricultural participation make conclusions regarding trends in rural women's employment quite problematic, particularly with respect to their concentration in non-agricultural activities. My main hypothesis, to be developed in the next two sections, is that the main change over the past few decades is that rural women's work has become more visible than ever, and that rural women have gone from being unpaid family workers in agriculture to remunerated workers in both the agricultural and non-agricultural sectors. But given the problematic nature of the data, the case that the main trend points to a feminization of agriculture rests primarily on case study evidence. These suggest an increase both in women's participation as agricultural wage workers and as own-account workers in agriculture.

## AGRICULTURAL LABOUR MARKETS AS GENDERED INSTITUTIONS

The boom in non-traditional agro-export production associated with the crisis-ridden 1980s in Latin America has led to a plethora of studies on women's agricultural wage work. Almost uniformly, the incorporation of women workers in the new fruit, vegetable and flower export industries has been deemed a process of feminization of agriculture. Here we try to establish what exactly is new. This is a difficult task for, although the literature on the current period is much more abundant than on women in traditional agro-export production, it suffers from the same deficiency. There are few reliable estimates of the magnitude of women's employment in these industries, partly because of its precarious and temporary nature. Also, what is considered non-traditional agro-export production varies by country, depending on the specific crops developed for export over the past three decades (Barham et al. 1992). Since in most Latin American countries these include fresh fruit and vegetables, and sometimes flowers, we concentrate on these commodities in the discussion following.

Non-traditional agricultural exports began making an appearance in the 1960s in Mexico and Chile. In Mexico this development was associated with the expansion of irrigation in the arid northwestern region of the country, bordering the United States, and with the expansion in US demand related to rising incomes and changes in consumer tastes favouring fresh over canned fruits and vegetables. Among the first non-traditional Mexican agricultural exports were tomatoes, strawberries, cucumbers, cauliflower and broccoli, geared to the US winter market when Mexican production was complementary to that of the United States and tariff levels were lower (Lara 1992).

The development of non-traditional agro-export production in Chile largely responded to the imperatives of the neoliberal economic model instituted after the military coup of 1973. Chile was the first country in Latin America to restructure its economy along the lines of comparative advantage by drastically reducing tariffs and other support to import substitution industries, including domestic-oriented agriculture. Liberalization of external markets had profound effects, reorienting the agricultural sector toward the production of temperate crops that could compete in Northern markets during their winter season. Between 1972 and 1988 Chile's fruit exports witnessed a 26-fold increase, becoming the world leader in the export of fresh fruit by the end of that decade (Thrupp et al. 1995; Lara 1995; Barrientos et al. 1999).

In the 1970s other Latin American countries, such as Colombia and Brazil, also began to promote export diversification, motivated by growing competition among countries in the South in traditional agricultural exports such as coffee, bananas, sugar and cotton. The promotion of non-traditional agricultural exports became a generalized policy throughout the region with the debt crisis of the 1980s and the adoption of structural adjustment policies. Export promotion became a necessary complement to external liberalization if a trade surplus was to be generated for external debt repayment. In the Caribbean and Central America the promotion of non-traditional agricultural exports was facilitated by the Reagan administration's Caribbean Basin Initiative (CBI), which provided duty-free treatment of certain rubrics to the US market. Among the more successful country responses to these initiatives were by the Dominican Republic, Costa Rica and Guatemala.

In sum, the combination of economic crises, neoliberal policies and trade agreements have led to a fundamental restructuring of Latin America's agricultural sector. Mexico, Brazil and Chile are now among the leading world exporters of fresh and processed fruits and vegetables (Raynolds 1998). By 2001 fruit and vegetable exports constituted the largest agricultural export rubric of Latin America and the Caribbean, reaching US$8.9 billion, and made up 15 per cent of the region's total agricultural, forestry and agro-industrial exports (García Pascual 2003:table 1).

There is consensus that women are an important component of the wage labour force engaged in fieldwork for non-traditional agro-export crops, perhaps constituting at least half of these workers. Moreover, they usually constitute a majority of the wage labour force employed in the packing operations required for agricultural exports. However, women were always an important component of the temporary labour force of a number of traditional export crops, such as coffee and cotton. Since their participation in the past was largely undercounted, it is difficult to assess whether the *net* wage employment of women has increased and, in particular, their relative participation with respect to men. Further, the underenumeration of peasant women as unpaid family workers on family farms is notorious. What is perhaps new is that rather than being invisible workers on family farms they are now quite visible participants in agro-export production. Thus rather than a change in their (unofficial) labour force participation rate, what we may be seeing is a change in their labour *market* participation rate, and particularly, as independent wage workers.

The main factor that supports the argument that the development of non-traditional agricultural exports has increased absolute employment opportunities for women in agriculture is the fact that production and packing activities are particularly labour-intensive and much more so than traditional agricultural exports. For example, flower production in Colombia and Ecuador is estimated to involve an average of 200 person-days per hectare, compared to 44 for coffee, 33 for bananas and 150 for potato production. In Guatemala traditional corn and beans production require only around 60 person-days per hectare, whereas the production of broccoli requires 197, cauliflower 276 and snow peas 663 days per hectare (Thrupp et al. 1995: table 9).

Good macro data on the size and gender of the wage-intensive force employed in non-traditional agro-export production is not even available for Mexico, the country where it has been studied in most depth (Lara 1992). The 1991 National Employment Survey enumerated a total of 5.4 million agricultural wage workers, 26 per cent of whom were women (1.4 million) (Robles 2000:41). The degree of potential underenumeration in these estimates is apparent from some of the state-level studies on agro-export employment. In the state of Sinaloa alone, in the early 1990s it was estimated that 950,000 wage workers were employed in vegetable production for export, with women constituting 40 per cent of the field-workers and around 90 per cent of those employed in the packing houses (Lara 1995). In a study of fruit and vegetable production in six northern Mexican states it was estimated that women represented at least half, if not more, of the field-workers (Collins 1995). The most feminized of all non-traditional exports is cut-flower production, where women are estimated to make up 70 to 80 per cent of the workers (Lara 1998; Becerril 1995).

In the mid-1990s in Chile it was estimated that 150,000 women were employed in the fruit industry, with women constituting over half of the temporary workers (Barrientos 1997). In the Dominican Republic in 1990 the 120 non-traditional agricultural export firms employed 25,589 workers, 42 per cent of whom were women; they represented over two-thirds of those employed in the production of plants and flowers and processed vegetables and horticulture (Raynolds 2001). Other large concentrations of female workers include those for grape production in Brazil's São Francisco Valley, where they constitute approximately two-thirds of the field labour (Collins 1993), and the flower industry in Colombia where in the 1990s they made up between 60 to 80 per cent of the 75,000 to 85,000 workers (Lara 1995; Meier 1999).

The main conclusions that can be drawn from the review of the case study literature are as follows.[6] First, women are employed for the labour-intensive tasks of non-traditional agro-export production for the same reason that in the past they were employed in the most labour-intensive traditional export crops: Women constitute a source of cheap labour that can be drawn upon seasonally, at the peak periods of labour demand. Thus there is a great deal of continuity in the role that rural women play as a "labour reserve" for agro-export production. Second, as in the past, there is a tendency for the permanent jobs in non-traditional agro-export production to be reserved for men, with women concentrated in temporary jobs. A similar gendered ideology continues to define the employment of women as secondary workers, whose primary responsibility is in the domestic realm. Thus they can be drawn upon seasonally as befits the needs of export production, since they are not viewed as needing or desiring full-time employment.

Third, low wages continue to be maintained by the employment of women for the agricultural tasks that are remunerated as piecework, a general characteristic of harvest labour. This form of remuneration encourages the participation of the whole peasant family, overcoming whatever cultural resistance may be at play regarding rural women's economic participation outside the home. It also increases the intensity of labour.

In some countries, such as Chile, women's large-scale participation in fieldwork around the fruit harvest constitutes a significant break with gender norms (Aranda 1982). In others, where women have always participated in local agro-export harvests, what is new is the spatial dimension. In the past they have rarely been among the contingents of highly mobile seasonal workers that follow the harvest from region to region. This was primarily because of women's responsibility for domestic labour and a gender division of labour sufficiently flexible for women to assume management of peasant agricultural and livestock production during periods of male absence. With the growth in landlessness and falling real wages, combined with the demand for female and child labour, whole families are now among the temporary agricultural migrants, particularly in Mexico, where seasonal rural–rural migration has a strong ethnic dimension (Bonfíl Sánchez 1996; Buechler 2005).

In Chile, Brazil, Colombia and increasingly in Mexico, another new trend is that a significant number of the female agricultural wage workers reside in urban as opposed to rural areas. This is related to growing land shortages in rural areas, the decay of peasant agriculture, and the growth of migration to towns and smaller cities rather than to large metropolitan areas as in the past (Aranda 1982; Lara 1992). Another major change is that one industry, the cut-flower industry in Colombia, Ecuador and Mexico—which developed primarily on the basis of female labour—has generated nearly year-round employment for women.

The large-scale incorporation of women into the packing stage of non-traditional agro-export production probably marks the most important change in women's agricultural participation over the last couple of decades. What appears to be driving this feminization of a stage of production in this period is that fresh fruits and vegetables are produced for a highly competitive market where profits depend on the appearance and quality of the produce. Hence, women's employment is now associated with the most technologically advanced aspect of the production process.

Since the early 1980s the literature on gender and globalization has highlighted the increasing preference among employers for women workers in all sectors of the economy, but particularly in the most labour-intensive industries. This tendency has been linked to the possibility for occupational segregation—the employment of women in specific branches of industry and occupations—where lower wages prevail. In addition, the preference of employers for women has been linked to specific feminine characteristics, such as their greater submission and docility and hence willingness to follow orders while being less likely to organize; greater dexterity or suitability in those production processes that require care and patience; and flexibility with respect to the conditions of work (Elson and Pearson 1981; Benería 2003).

The literature on the employment of women in Latin American non-traditional agro-exports has tended to emphasize this latter process—flexibilization in the context of the increasing precariousness of work—while demonstrating how gender subordination conditions women's integration into the labour force. Flexibilization is usually defined in terms of a firm's ability to move workers from one stage of the productive process to another, and from one product to another, while progressively increasing labour productivity. A flexible labour force is also associated with flexible hours of work, wages and contracts (Martínez Medina 1996). In the case of non-traditional exports such as fresh fruits, vegetables and flowers, the need for flexibility is accentuated, given that these are perishable products and international competition is driven by quality, specifically appearance.

Sara Lara Flores (1991, 1992, 1995, 1998) in her penetrating analyses of non-traditional export production argues that the key to productive reconversion is the adaptability of the labour force to market expansions and contractions. This adaptability can be provided through an upgrading of labour skills combined with decentralization, or by greater reliance on precarious labour, with the specific outcome dependent on the social conditions of each country, particularly the capacity for labour organization. In the context of Latin America, where the consolidation of neoliberalism is associated with the weakening of unions, growing poverty and unemployment, the outcome has been the tendency toward what Lara and others term "primitive or savage flexibilization" or precarious employment.

Thus the modernization of Latin American agriculture, based on increasing mechanization, the use of chemicals and computerized production and processing, has been accompanied by a greater reliance on a mass of temporary workers, often paid by the task or on a piecework basis, and few permanent workers. Women are the ideal social subject for the implementation of all forms of flexible labour because, given their domestic role, they have been socialized to have the flexibility to combine productive and reproductive activities. This is also evident in women's labour market trajectories, with women moving flexibly from one sector to another.

Laura Raynold's (2001) research in the Dominican Republic provides a useful reminder, however, that the flexibilization of the labour force and the devaluation of women do not necessarily always result in the feminization of agricultural employment. Her study of the main corporate pineapple plantation in the Dominican Republic shows how the informalization of the labour force can result in a gender reversal, from a largely female to male workforce, in this case with a switch from a permanent, plantation labour force paid by the day to the use of labour contractors. These paid their workers a piece-rate and preferred to hire men in order to spur competition among them to increase productivity.

It is useful to consider how occupational segregation by gender contributes to lower wages for women. In the gender division of labour in the tomato-packing plants of northwest Mexico in the late 1970s and early 1980s, women predominated in three occupations, those of sorters, classifiers and packers (Roldán 1982). Although women made up 90 per cent of the workers, the few men did all the other tasks in the packing firms such as sealing, carrying and loading the boxes and driving the trucks to market. They also made up all of the supervisors and administrative workers. Equal pay for equal work prevailed in these tomato-exporting firms when payment was by piece-rate. But due to occupational segregation by gender, men's jobs tended to pay above the minimum wage. Thus a loader, paid by contract, could earn up to 5,000 pesos weekly, whereas a sorter, paid by the hour, could never earn more than 1,200 pesos, working for the same number of hours. While most of the positions in the packing house were temporary jobs, lasting only the six months of the harvest season, the few permanent positions were all held by men.

The main change that has occurred over the past 20 years as many of the tomato exporting firms expanded to other regions of Mexico to prolong the growing season is that many of the young women in the packing houses now find employment almost year round. Employers prefer to move this skilled, yet devalued labour force from site to site rather than train new workers in each locale, given the potential loss in productivity. While this has resulted in a growing gap in wage levels between the women field-workers in the tomato harvest (the large majority of whom are indigenous migrants) and the relatively privileged women employed in the "moving maquila" (the majority of whom are mestizo and better educated), the gender wage differentials have not changed much since occupational segregation has continued (Barndt 2002).

The best example of high-tech, productive restructuring favouring female as well as year-round employment is the flower industry in Colombia, Ecuador and Mexico. Production in the cut-flower industry generally takes place in nurseries where workers are assigned a specific physical area that they care for from beginning to end—from the planting of seedlings to the harvest—requiring workers who are particularly adept at multitasking. Employment in this industry is overwhelmingly female, with men employed only for the application of fertilizer and herbicides, in equipment maintenance and as supervisors. In Colombia in the early 1980s the wage gap between female and male workers in this predominantly female industry was 84 per cent (Silva 1982:table 2), but by the 1990s the disparity in male and female wages had pretty much disappeared, with both earning the minimum wage (Friedemann-Sánchez 2006). Moreover, conditions of work on the flower farms have improved considerably since the 1980s—largely due to the pressure of non-governmental organizations (NGOs)—and women are now fairly well represented among the supervisors on these farms. Jobs in this sector were considered the very best jobs to which women could aspire.

Most studies support the proposition that women's packing house jobs are among the best available to women and certainly preferable to work in the fields. In the tomato-packing houses in Mexico in 2000 women could earn from US$13–30 in the highest paid female job of packers; in contrast, field-workers earned only US$5 a day (Barndt 2002). Similarly, in Chile, women in the packing houses earn much more than working in the fields; in either occupation women earn at least twice what they would if employed in non-agricultural activities (Aranda 1982). In the Cayambe region of Ecuador the gender wage gap in the flower industry has almost disappeared, whereas in other sectors in the northern highlands women earn only 64 per cent of what men do (Newman 2002).

Overall, then, there seems to be considerable support for the proposition that occupational segregation by gender in the packing houses serves to maintain lower wages for women, although not always nor everywhere.

Moreover, most studies find that although women workers in the packing houses for agro-export production might be earning only the minimum wage, they earn more in the packing houses than in any other form of employment and thus the gender wage gap in these industries tends to be less than in other pursuits.

## PEASANT AGRICULTURE: ITS VIABILITY AND FEMINIZATION

Several often overlapping processes over the past 30 years have contributed to changes in the gender division of labour and the tendency towards the feminization of peasant agriculture. First and foremost, male participation in temporary wage labour, particularly when it requires seasonal migration, has everywhere been associated with higher female participation in agriculture, giving rise to the often noted inverse relation between farm size and women's participation in fieldwork.[7] It has as its basis the general flexibility of the gender division of labour in peasant agriculture. Few tasks are strictly "male only" tasks—with perhaps ploughing with a team of oxen being the most common exception. And no matter how rigid the cultural construction of agriculture as a male occupation, women participate in a broad range of field activities when it is required of them, albeit as self-defined "helpers" or secondary workers, given their responsibility for domestic labour.

What seems to distinguish women's participation in peasant agriculture in the neoliberal period is that women's participation is no longer only as a "secondary" worker. Rather, in many cases they are emerging as the farm managers and/or the main source of family labour. This change reflects the fact that male absence from the farm is no longer as conditioned by the labour demands of peasant agriculture (with men migrating to seek wage work only in the off-season of basic grain production), as by the imperative to seek off-farm income and the demands of the labour market. The current process of feminization of agriculture is thus associated with an increase in the number of agricultural tasks in which women participate (including traditional male-only activities); an increase in the total labour time that they dedicate to fieldwork; and their greater participation in agricultural decision-making. Hence, when I use the term "feminization of agriculture", I am distinguishing it from the normal inverse relation between women's participation in fieldwork and farm size noted earlier. I argue that it is a phenomenon associated with the lack of viability of peasant agricultural production in the current period.

Besides their general association with falling real wages and rising poverty levels, neoliberal policies have spurred the feminization of agriculture through the withdrawal of the state from direct support to domestic food production, combined with external liberalization. The feminization of agriculture has also been spurred by the decline of traditional agricultural exports as a result of increased international competition. A third process relates to the exceptional case where peasant producers have been able to take advantage of the new conditions for non-traditional agro-export production. This development has increased women's participation in field-work, but not necessarily led to an increase in their participation in farm management. Each case will be examined in turn.

The degree of distress of the peasant economy as a result of neoliberal policies largely depends on the extent to which peasant producers were previously integrated to markets as suppliers of basic foodstuffs and on the degree of state support that they received in earlier periods. Subsistence producers in countries such as Mexico, Peru or Bolivia, for example, have been less directly affected by neoliberal agricultural policies than by changes in urban and rural labour markets (Tejo 2001; Crabtree 2002). Those most negatively affected have been the small and medium producers who were the beneficiaries of previous state rural development policies that supported domestic food production. Not surprisingly, then, the degree of distress of peasant agriculture is related to the breadth of previous state policies along with the pace and intensity of external liberalization measures. It is these factors that distinguish countries such as Mexico and Brazil. By far the most voluminous literature on the feminization of agriculture of any country has been generated on Mexico.[8] In contrast, the term has yet to be utilized with respect to family agriculture in Brazil, largely reflecting the factors noted earlier.[9]

From 1970 through 1982, two successive Mexican governments pursued a policy of food sovereignty, investing in rural social and physical infrastructure and providing increased access to credit and Green Revolution technology to peasant producers. A good share of them thus became net commercial producers of basic grains (Preibisch et al. 2002). Not surprisingly, the adjustment policies associated with the 1982 debt crisis, combined with the general opening of the economy and dismantling of the network of state institutions that had supported the agricultural sector, had severe implications for the profitability of peasant agriculture. Such was compounded after the implementation of the North American Free Trade Agreement (NAFTA) by the abrupt increase in imports of US corn, which drove prices down and made the government's compensatory measures wholly inadequate to maintain peasant incomes.

The feminization of peasant agriculture in Mexico, while already noted in the literature of the late 1970s and early 1980s (Arizpe et al. 1989), is directly associated with the increase in long-distance migration in the decades of the 1980s and 1990s, and particularly, with migration from rural areas to the United States (Aranda 2000; Buechler 2005; D'Aubeterre 1995; González and Salles 1995; Lazos 1995; Marroni 1995; Robles 2000; Suárez 1997). Women, particularly married women, emerge as the farm managers when both sons and husbands are absent from the household for substantial periods of time, thus it is not surprising that this phenomenon is associated with the growth of de facto female household headship.

A case study of an indigenous community in the Mexican Central highlands illustrates how male long-distance migration and the feminization of agriculture are related to neoliberal policies (Preibisch et al. 2002). The decline in the profitability of peasant farming—due to rising input prices and falling crop prices—led men in this community in the late 1990s to migrate to the United States for the first time. These changes did not immediately lead to a reduction in the acreage planted to maize, but rather to a reduction in the proportion that was marketed. Whereas maize production had previously been an activity in which both men and women participated, as it became less a source of cash income it became a female activity, an extension of women's domestic work.[10] With the men absent, women began making most of the decisions regarding its production, provided the bulk of the labour and controlled the output. While maize production might be unprofitable, it guarantees women the ability to feed their households in a context in which male remittances cannot be depended upon, providing an important safety net.

Recent data on Mexican migration to the United States suggests that it is accelerating. Audley and others (2003) report that the Mexican agricultural sector lost 1.3 million jobs between 1994 and 2002, a loss not compensated for by the increase in manufacturing jobs in that country. More research is obviously needed to establish with precision the impact of all these changes on the gender division of labour in rural areas, but it is likely that the reported job loss in agriculture has been more severe for male rather than female workers, and that it has accentuated the feminization of agriculture.

Turning to the decline of traditional agro-exports, between 1979 and 2001 the value of coffee exports from the region fell 50 per cent, principally due to a 63 per cent fall in the price of coffee over this period (García Pascual 2003:table 1). The long-term decline of coffee exports is associated with overproduction and increased global competition as well as the late 1980s breakdown of the quota system managed by the International Coffee Organization. In countries such as Mexico the crisis for coffee producers, both large and small, has been aggravated by the privatization of many of the state institutions formerly charged with financing, storing and marketing national coffee production.

The impact of the decline of coffee exports has again been studied in most detail in Mexico. Josefina Aranda (2000) provides an excellent case study of the impact on peasant producers in the state of Oaxaca, the third largest producer in Mexico. Women in this region have always been involved in planting the coffee seedlings and in weeding and harvesting the coffee trees, with men carrying out the other tasks of land preparation, hilling and fertilization. Women also provided the bulk of the labour for coffee processing, fermenting, washing and depulping the coffee berries prior to their drying and selecting the coffee beans. In recent decades, however, with the mechanization of coffee processing women's post-harvest labour was becoming limited to bean selection.

Aranda (2000) describes how the coffee crisis forced growing numbers of men to migrate in search of wage work, bringing about changes in the gender division of labour. The absence of husbands and sons required women to increase their participation in all of the tasks associated with coffee production, including those in which they did not previously engage, including farm management. Moreover, the decline in the price of coffee impacted the local labour market, since family farmers could no longer afford to contract day-labourers. Female family members also began to replace the wage workers who had previously been contracted for certain tasks. In addition, wages fell so low as a result of the low coffee prices that men refused to take the available jobs, and they were largely replaced by women from smallholder households who had no alternative but to seek local wage work. Thus, in Oaxaca the coffee crisis resulted in both the feminization of peasant agricultural production and of the local wage labour market, often intensely prolonging the working day of rural women.

The only positive aspect of this process, as described by Aranda, is that peasant women, as the de facto household heads, began representing their households in the main organization of coffee producers and in local movements demanding community services, thus increasing their visibility in the public domain.

The most successful cases reported of peasant incorporation into non-traditional agro-export production include those of vegetable production in Guatemala and the Dominican Republic. In such cases, agro-export production has generally intensified women's participation in fieldwork, but led to widely varying outcomes with respect to women's role in agricultural decision-making.

Vegetable production for export among smallholders began in the early 1980s in the central Guatemalan highlands. Dary (1991) and Blumberg (1994) report that it brought about an increase in women's participation in fieldwork, while their previous marketing activities have declined. In addition, in some regions women lost access to land, principally the small garden-plots where they had grown vegetables and herbs for family consumption as well as for sale in local markets. The income generated from such sales had generally been a woman's own to dispose of, as was the income from the sale of her husband's surplus crops. Men now control the commercialization of the export crops and women have thus lost access to an important source of income over which they had control. Thus both Dary (1991) and Blumberg (1994) conclude that women were affected negatively by the introduction of non-traditional agro-export production since the reduction in their own independent activities reduced their bargaining power within the household, and they became more dependent on men's transferring sufficient funds to them to cover household expenses.

Elizabeth Katz (1995) undertook a household survey of adaptors and non-adaptors of non-traditional export crops in this same general region of the central highlands in the early 1990s and also concluded that non-traditional agro-export production was deepening gender inequalities. She found that peasant women were dedicating a significant amount of time to broccoli and snow peas production. With the exception of female household heads, women rarely participated in farm decision-making and received relatively few of the benefits of agro-export production. In her detailed analysis of household spending decisions, Katz found that increasing male agricultural income from non-traditional exports is largely spent on male goods, negatively affecting women's ability to purchase food as well as items that might alleviate the burden of housework.

This same region was subsequently restudied in the 1998–2001 period by Hamilton and others (2001), and Hamilton and Fischer (2003). They conclude that non-traditional agricultural export production has contributed to women's greater role in productive decision-making and, in contrast to earlier studies, women have shared in its benefits. In their 1998 and 2001 surveys over two-thirds of the households reported that women shared or controlled earnings from non-traditional agro-export production. Three-quarters reported that women participated in land use decisions. These studies are not exactly comparable with previous ones, but the high share of women participating in decision-making in roughly the same region suggests that perhaps over time there has been some important changes in gender roles.

The main agro-export activity in which peasant households participate in the Dominican Republic is the production of tomatoes under contract to agro-industry. Raynolds (2002) reports that these contracts are entered into by male household heads, but that this labour-intensive activity has increased the work of wives, both in the fields and in terms of cooking for field-hands. A new phenomenon that she observed was that wives were increasingly demanding that they be paid for their work during the harvest. Such was facilitated by the fact that husbands generally received an advance from the buyers for the payment of harvest wages, and by the fact that generally women provided the majority of harvest labour. This independent income was a source of great pride for wives, for they themselves could decide how to spend this income, not withstanding the fact that most spent their meagre earnings on household necessities. Raynolds (2002:792) suggests that the payment of wives for their harvest labour constitutes a "subtle re-negotiating of inter-twining domestic and production relations".

In sum, what all these processes illustrate is that rural women are working more in agriculture than ever before. The main process of feminization of agriculture is related to the decline of agriculture as the primary economic activity of peasant households and male absence from the farm and is thus correlated with the growth in rural female household headship, either de facto or de jure. As the viability of peasant agriculture is undermined by neoliberal policies, peasant production becomes increasingly oriented towards household food security, becoming an extension of women's domestic responsibilities. A second process related to neoliberal restructuring and less widespread than the first—the integration of smallholders into agro-export production—has undoubtedly also increased women's participation in agricultural fieldwork. The main difference is that in the former process women become the primary farmers, with potentially greater changes in traditional gender roles and household relations.

## CONCLUSION

The main trends associated with the economic crisis, neoliberal restructuring and the growth of rural poverty rates in Latin America include a continued diversification of household income strategies, an increase in the number of household members seeking off-farm employment and the increased participation of rural women as own-account workers as well as wage workers in both the agricultural and non-agricultural sectors.

Household survey data suggest that rural women are more concentrated in non-agricultural activities than are rural men, with roughly half of economically active rural women and only one-third of men in this sector. I have argued that rural women's participation as unpaid family labour, own-account workers and/or temporary wage workers in agriculture continues to be undercounted, casting doubt on this finding.

The feminization of the agricultural sector is taking place through two paths, women's increased responsibility for peasant production and their growing participation as wage workers in non-traditional agro-export production. Neither path is well captured by census or survey measures. Moreover, the particular path to feminization of agriculture is location specific and depends on a myriad of factors, including household-level variables and the gendered nature of local, regional, national and international labour markets as well as other income-generating opportunities.

Women's increased visibility as own-account farmers is associated with relative land shortage, a decline in the profitability of peasant agriculture, an increase in the share of rural female-headed households and male absence from the farm, due either to a growth in long-distance migration or better remunerated off-farm employment possibilities. This trend is best documented by case studies for Mexico and Central America.

The feminization of agricultural wage employment is largely due to the fact that the growth in agricultural employment has been limited to non-traditional agro-exports, the most dynamic activity in the era of neoliberalism. The new crops and products are much more labour-intensive than traditional agro-exports and require a flexible labour force that (with the exception of the cut-flower industry) can be employed only a few months out of the year. In this context, in which few permanent employment opportunities are created, but where the demand for seasonal labour is high, women have become the preferred workers, particularly in the packing houses for vegetable and fruit exports. The case study evidence suggests that women constitute the overwhelming majority of those employed in the packing houses and in cut-flower production and from 40 to 60 per cent of the field labour in these new crops.

Women are the preferred workers partly because their socialization has made them into flexible workers, so they are willing to accept short-term, casual employment, and the fact that they are adept in flexibility combining productive and reproductive activities. Gender socialization has also produced the skills (patience, dexterity, submissiveness) in women necessary for high-quality production in extremely competitive markets. As a skilled, but devalued, workforce women are cheaper to employ than men and less likely to organize.

The available data on the gender wage gap, nonetheless, is mixed. A wage gap in the range of 80 to 90 per cent in agro-export production is frequently cited although some cases of near gender wage parity have also been noted. While there is little outright discrimination with respect to wage levels when men and women perform the same tasks (generally both working at piece-rates), differential earnings by men and women are usually the result of occupational segregation by gender. Men's occupations are more varied than women's and often result in higher average daily or monthly earnings. Men also occupy the vast majority of the permanent as well as supervisory positions, with women workers having limited opportunities for advancement, with perhaps the exception of the flower industry.

Among the new trends related to the employment of women in non-traditional agro-exports has been that in many cases it has provided opportunities for women to become independent wage workers, receiving their own wage for the first time. In most cases it has provided an alternative for young women other than rural–urban migration and employment in domestic service. It has added a new spatial dimension to women's employment, as women, particularly from landless or near-landless households, join men in rural–rural migration, following the harvests. It has also brought an increasing number of urban women into agricultural production, even in regions where rural women have traditionally not formed part of the agricultural wage labour force. Finally, in many regions it offers women employment at a much higher wage than in other rural occupations.

The incorporation of peasants into global markets as producers of non-traditional export products has also had mixed results. Such production has inevitably increased peasant women's workloads. In some cases the expansion of export crops has come at the cost of women's other income-generating activities, or participation in household and crop decision-making. In other cases it has led to more equitable gender household relations, with women participating even more in farm and marketing decisions.

As Raynolds (1998:166) concludes, "the process of labour force restructuring which has driven female employment in expanding non-traditional sectors throughout Latin America and the Caribbean does not represent an unqualified economic or political gain for women." She rightly points to how wage work is often redefined as something women must do to support their children without substantial changes in the gender division of labour within households. At the same time, wage employment has often bolstered their ability to negotiate more equitable household relations.

## NOTES

1. This chapter is an updated and condensed version of Deere (2005). The chapter benefited from the very useful comments of Martine Dirven, Lovell Jarvis, Elizabeth Katz, Wendy Pond and Shahra Razavi.
2. Increases in female economic activity rates are usually associated with increases in education, lower fertility and urbanization. The sharp increase in rural women's economic activity rates in Latin America suggests that other factors are also at play and should be further examined.
3. The censuses for Central America, for example, consistently reported very low female activity rates in agriculture, ranging from 5 per cent in Panama to 12.4 per cent in El Salvador in the 1980s. The Inter-American Development Bank–Inter-American Institute for Cooperation on Agriculture (IDB-IICA) surveys in five countries, by taking into account the full range of agricultural activities in which women engage, revealed that 68 to 90 per cent of the rural women interviewed participated in agricultural and livestock production (Chiriboga et al. 1996). This project recalculated female economic activity rates in agriculture and concluded that in the 19 countries the degree of underenumeration ranged from 69 per cent (Uruguay) to 500 per cent (Guatemala) (Kleysen and Campillo 1996:tl.4).
4. See the excellent analysis of this problem in Barrientos (1997) with respect to women workers in the Chilean fruit industry.
5. Email communication to the author from the International Labour Organization (19 January 2004) and ECLAC Agricultural Unit (19 January 2004). In the United Nations classification of economic activities, International Standard Industrial Classification (ISIC), rev.3.1, packing activities are classified in groups 011 and 014 of the agricultural sector and all workers in these units are considered as part of the agricultural sector irrespective of whether these workers do agricultural-related jobs.
6. See Deere (2005) for the full list of case studies and references.
7. See Arizpe et al. (1989); Chiriboga et al. (1996); Deere (1976, 1991); Deere and León (1982), and the essays in Deere and León (1987).
8. In Central America the process of feminization of agriculture has also been related to the withdrawal of state support to basic grain production by peasant producers (Chiriboga et al. 1996).
9. Mexico also has a much richer tradition of agrarian studies than Brazil, which accounts for the much greater attention to rural women and the peasant economy in feminist scholarship in this country. For an overview of Brazilian policies and how the exclusion of peasant agriculture from state largesse in the 1970s buffeted the peasant economy from what was also in the 1980s and 1990s a more gradual withdrawal of state support to agriculture and opening to foreign competition, see Brumer and Tavares (1998).

124    *Carmen Diana Deere*

10. See also Bonfil (1996) and Katz (2003) on this point.


## REFERENCES

Aranda, J. 2000. "Respuestas campesinas a la crisis del café. Las mujeres cafetaleras se organizan." In J. Aranda, C. Botey and R. Robles (eds.), *Tiempo de crisis, tiempo de mujeres.* Universidad Autónoma Benito Juárez de Oaxaca, Oaxaca.
Aranda, X.B. 1982. "El díptico campesina-asalariada agrícola." In M. León (ed.), *Las trabajadoras del agro.* ACEP, Bogotá.
Arizpe, L., F. Salinas and M. Velásquez. 1989. "The effects of the economic crisis on the living conditions of peasant women in Mexico." In UNICEF (ed.), *Poor Women and the Economic Crisis. The Invisible Adjustment.* The Americas and the Caribbean Regional Office, UNICEF and Alfabeta Impresores, Santiago.
Audley, J.J., D.G. Papademetriou, S. Polaski and S. Vaughan. 2003. *Nafta's Promise and Reality. Lessons from Mexico for the Hemisphere.* Carnegie Endowment for International Peace, Washington, DC. www.ceip.org/pubs, accessed on 15 March 2004.
Barham, B., M. Clark, E. Katz and R. Schurman. 1992. "Non-traditional agricultural exports in Latin America." *Latin American Research Review,* Vol. 27, No. 2, pp. 43–82.
Barndt, D. 2002. *Tangled Routes: Women, Work and Globalization on the Tomato Trail.* Rowman & Littlefield, Landham, MD.
Barrientos, S. 1997. "The hidden ingredient: Female labour in Chilean fruit exports." *Bulletin of Latin American Research,* Vol. 16, No. 1, pp.71–81.
Barrientos, S., A. Bee, A. Matear and I. Vogel. 1999. *Women and Agribusiness. Working Miracles in the Chilean Fruit Export Sector.* Macmillan, London.
Becerril, O. 1995. "¿Cómo las trabajadoras agrícolas de la flor en México, hacen femenino el proceso de trabajo en el que participan?" In S.M. Lara Flores (ed.), *El rostro femenino del mercado de trabajo rural en América Latina.* UNRISD, Geneva and Nueva Sociedad, Caracas.
Benería, L. 2003. *Gender, Development and Globalization: Economics as If All People Mattered.* Routledge, New York.
Blumberg, R.L. 1994. "Women's work, wealth and family survival strategy: The impact of Guatemala's ALCOSA Agribusiness Project." In E. Ngan-ling Chow and C. White Berheide (eds.), *Women, the Family and Policy: A Global Perspective.* State University of New York Press, Albany.
Bonfíl Sánchez, P. 1996. "Las familias rurales ante las transformaciones socioeconómicas recientes." *Estudios agrarios* (Mexico City), No. 5, pp. 64–78.
Brumer, A. and J. Tavares Dos Santos. 1998. "Tensões agrícolas e agrárias na transição democrática brasileira." In N. Giarracca and S. Cloquell (eds.), *Las agriculturas del Mercosur. El papel de los actores sociales.* Ed. La Colmena, Buenos Aires.
Buechler, S. 2005. "Women at the helm of irrigated agriculture in Mexico: The other side of male migration." In V. Bennett, S. Dávila-Poblete and M. Nieves Rico (eds.), *Opposing Currents: The Politics of Water and Gender in Latin America.* University of Pittsburgh Press, Pittsburgh, PA.
Buvinic, M. 1982. "La productora invisible en el agro centroamericano: Un estudio de caso en Honduras." In M. León (ed.), *Las trabajadoras del agro.* ACEP, Bogotá.
Campaña, P. 1982. "Mujer, trabajo y subordinación en la Sierra Central del Perú." In M. León (ed.), *Las trabajadoras del agro.* ACEP, Bogotá.

Carter, M. and B. Barham. 1996. "Level playing fields and laissez faire: Postliberal development strategy in inegalitarian agrarian economies." *World Development*, Vol. 24, No. 7, pp. 1133–1149.

CELADE/CEPAL (Centro Latinoamericano y Caribeño de Demografía/Comisión Económica para América Latina y el Caribe). 2002. "América Latina y el Caribe: Indicadores seleccionados con una perspective de género." *Boletín Demográfico*, No. 70, July.

Chiriboga, M., R. Grynspan and L. Pérez. 1996. *Mujeres de Maíz*. Inter-American Development Bank–Inter-American Institute for Cooperation on Agriculture (IDB-IICA), San José.

Collins, J. 1995. "Gender and cheap labour in agriculture." In R. McMichael (ed.), *Food and Agrarian Orders in the World Economy*. Greenwood Press, Westport, CT.

———. 1993. "Gender, contracts and wage work: Agricultural restructuring in Brazil's São Francisco Valley." *Development and Change*, Vol. 24, pp. 53–82.

Crabtree, J. 2002. "The impact of neo-liberal economics on Peruvian peasant agriculture in the 1980s." In T. Brass (ed.), *Latin American Peasants*. Frank Cass, London.

Dary, F.C. 1991. *Mujeres tradicionales y nuevos cultivos*. FLACSO, Guatemala City.

D'Aubeterre Buznego, M.E. 1995. "Tiempos de espera: Emigración masculina, ciclo doméstico y situación de las mujeres en San Miguel Acuexcomac, Puebla." In S. González Montes and V. Salles (eds.), *Relaciones de género y transformaciones agrarias*. El Colegio de México, Mexico City.

David, M. Beatriz de A., C. Morales and M. Rodríguez. 2001. "Modernidad y heterogeneidad: Estilo de desarrollo agrícola y rural en América Latina y el Caribe." In M. Beatriz de A. David, C. Morales and M. Rodríguez (eds.), *Desarrollo rural en América Latina y el Caribe. La construcción de un nuevo modelo?* CEPAL and Alfaomega, Santiago de Chile.

Deere, C.D. 2005. *The Feminization of Agriculture? Economic Restructuring in Rural Latin America*. Occasional Paper No. 1, UNRISD, Geneva.

———. 1991. *Household and Class Relations: Peasants and Landlords in Northern Peru*. University of California Press, Berkeley.

———. 1976. "Rural women's subsistence production in the capitalist periphery." *Review of Radical Political Economy*, Vol. 8, No. 1, pp. 9–17.

Deere, C.D. and M. León (eds.). 1987. *Rural Women and State Policy: Feminist Perspectives on Latin American Agricultural Development*. Westview Press, Boulder, CO.

———. 1982. *Women in Andean Agriculture: Peasant Production and Rural Wage Employment in Colombia and Peru*. International Labour Office, Geneva.

Deere, C.D., P. Antrobus, L. Bolles, E. Melendez, P. Phillips, M. Rivera and H. Safa. 1990. *In the Shadows of the Sun: Caribbean Development Alternatives and US Policy*. Westview Press, Boulder, CO.

de Janvry, A., E. Sadoulet and L. Wilcox. 1989. "Land and labour in Latin American agriculture from the 1950s to the 1980s." *Journal of Peasant Studies*, Vol. 16, No. 3, pp. 396–424.

ECLAC Women's Unit. 2007. *Estadísticas de Género*. www.eclac.org/mujer, accessed on 12 May 2008.

Economic Commission for Latin America and the Caribbean (ECLAC). 2007. *Social Panorama of Latin America 2006*. ECLAC, Santiago.

Elbers, C. and P. Lanjouw. 2001. "Intersectoral transfer, growth, and inequality in rural Ecuador." *World Development*, Vol. 29, No. 3, pp. 481–496.

Elson, D. 1991. "Male bias in macro-economics: The case of structural adjustment." In D. Elson (ed.), *Male Bias in the Development Process*. Manchester University Press, Manchester.

126    *Carmen Diana Deere*

Elson, D. and R. Pearson. 1981. "Nimble fingers make cheap workers: An analysis of women's employment in Third World export manufacturing." *Feminist Review*, No. 7, pp. 87–107.

Ferreira, F.H.G. and P. Lanjouw. 2001. "Rural non-farm activities and poverty in the Brazilian northeast." *World Development*, Vol. 29, No. 3, pp. 509–528.

Friedemann-Sánchez, G. 2006. "Assets in intrahousehold bargaining among women workers in Colombia's cut-flower industry." *Feminist Economics*, Vol. 12, Nos. 1–2, pp. 247–269.

García Pascual, F. 2003. "El ajuste structural neoliberal en el sector agrario latinoamericano en la era de la globalización." *European Review of Latin American and Caribbean Studies*, No. 75, pp. 3–29.

González Montes, S. and V. Salles. 1995. "Mujeres que se quedan, mujeres que se van...Continuidad y cambios de las relaciones sociales en contextos de aceleradas mudanzas rurales." In S. González Montes and V. Salles (eds.), *Relaciones de género y transformaciones agrarias*. El Colegio de México, Mexico City.

Hamilton, S., L. Asturias de Barrios and B. Tevalán. 2001. "Gender and commercial agriculture in Ecuador and Guatemala." *Culture and Agriculture*, Vol. 23, No. 3, pp. 1–12.

Hamilton, S. and E.F. Fischer. 2003. "Non-traditional agricultural exports in highland Guatemala: Understandings of risk and perceptions of change." *Latin American Research Review*, Vol. 38, No. 3, pp. 82–110.

Katz, E. 2003. "The changing role of women in the rural economies of Latin America." In Benjamin Davis (ed.), *Food, Agriculture and Rural Development: Current and Emerging Issues for Economic Analysis and Policy Research (CUREMIS II). Vol. I: Latin America and the Caribbean.* FAO, Rome.

———. 1995. "Gender and trade within the household: Observations from rural Guatemala." *World Development*, Vol. 23, No. 2, pp. 327–342.

Kleysen, B. and F. Campillo. 1996. "Productoras de alimentos en 18 países de América Latina y el Caribe. Síntesis hemisférica." In B. Kleysen (ed.), *Productoras agropecuarias en América del Sur.* Inter-American Development Bank–Inter-American Institute for Cooperation on Agriculture (IDB-IICA), San José.

Lanjouw, P. 2001. "Non-farm employment and poverty in rural El Salvador." *World Development*, Vol. 29, No. 3, pp. 529–547.

Lara Flores, S.M. 1998. *Nuevas experiencias productivas y nuevas formas de organización flexible del trabajo en la agricultura mexicana.* Juan Pablo Editores and Procuraduría Agraria, Mexico City.

———. 1995. "La feminización del trabajo asalariado en los cultivos de exportación no tradicionales en América Latina: Efectos de una flexibilidad 'salvaje'." In S.M. Lara Flores (ed.), *El rostro femenino del mercado de trabajo rural en América Latina.* UNRISD, Geneva and Nueva Sociedad, Caracas.

———. 1992. "La flexibilidad del mercado de trabajo rural: Una propuesta que involucra a las mujeres." *Revista Mexicana de Sociología*, Vol. 54, No. 1, pp. 29–48.

———. 1991. "Las obreras agrícolas: Un sujeto social en movimiento." *Nueva Antropología* (Mexico City), Vol. 11, No. 39, pp. 99–114.

Lazos Chavero, E. 1995. "De la candela al mercado: El papel de la mujer en la agricultura comercial del sur de Yucatán." In S. González Montes and V. Salles (eds.), *Relaciones de género y transformaciones agrarias*. El Colegio de México, Mexico City.

Marroni de Velázquez, María da Gloria. 1995. "Trabajo rural femenino y relaciones de género." In S. González Montes and V. Salles (eds.), *Relaciones de género y transformaciones agrarias*. El Colegio de México, Mexico City.

Martínez Medina, M.C. 1996. "Elementos que permiten tipificar a las jornaleras agrícolas de México." *Momento Económico* (Mexico City), No. 84, pp. 9–12.

Meier, V. 1999. "Cut-flower production in Colombia: A major development success for Women?" *Environment and Planning*, Vol. 31, pp. 273–289.

Newman, C. 2002. "Gender, time use and change: The impact of the cut flower industry in Ecuador." *The World Bank Economic Review*, Vol. 16, No. 3, pp. 375–396.

Preibisch, K.L., G. Rivera Herrejón and S.L. Wiggins. 2002. "Defending food security in a free-market economy: The gendered dimensions of restructuring in rural Mexico." *Human Organization*, Vol. 61, No. 1, pp. 68–79.

Raynolds, L.T. 2002. "Wages for wives: Renegotiating gender and production relations in contract farming in the Dominican Republic." *World Development*, Vol. 30, No. 5, pp. 783–798.

———. 2001. "New plantations, new workers: Gender and production politics in the Dominican Republic." *Gender and Society*, Vol. 15, No. 1, pp. 7–28.

———. 1998. "Harnessing women's work: Restructuring agricultural and industrial labor forces in the Dominican Republic." *Economic Geography*, Vol. 74, No. 2, pp. 149–169.

Razavi, S. 2002. "Introduction." In S. Razavi (ed.), *Shifting Burdens: Gender and Agrarian Change under Neoliberalism*. Kumarian Press, Bloomfield, CT.

Reardon, T., J. Berdegué and G. Escobar. 2001. "Rural non-farm employment and incomes in Latin America: Overview and policy implications." *World Development*, Vol. 29, No. 3, pp. 395–409.

Robles, R. 2000. "El ajuste invisible." In J. Aranda, C. Botey and R. Robles (eds.), *Tiempo de crisis, tiempo de mujeres*. Universidad Autónoma Benito Juárez de Oaxaca, Oaxaca.

Roldán, M. 1982. "Subordinación genérica y proletarización rural: Un estudio de caso en el Noroeste Mexicano." In M. León (ed.), *Las trabajadoras del agro*, Vol. I. ACEP, Bogotá.

Silva, A.E. 1982. "De mujer campesina a obrera florista." In M. León (ed.), *La realidad colombiana*. ACEP, Bogotá.

Spoor, M. 2002. "Policy regimes and performance of the agricultural sector in Latin America and the Caribbean during the last three decades." *Journal of Agrarian Change*, Vol. 2, No. 3, pp. 381–400.

Suárez, B. 1997. "Flores, hortalizas y mujeres en Morelos." In K. Appendini, B. Suárez and M.L. Macías (eds.), *¿Responsables o gobernables? Las trabajadoras en la agroindustria de exportación*. El Colegio de México, Mexico City.

Tejo, P. 2001. "El modelo agrícola de América Latina en las últimas décadas (síntesis)." In B. David, C. Morales and M. Rodríguez (eds.), *Desarrollo rural en América Latina y el Caribe. La construcción de un nuevo modelo?* CEPAL and Alfaomega, Santiago de Chile.

Thrupp, L.A., with G. Bergeron and W.F. Waters. 1995. *Bittersweet Harvests for Global Supermarkets: Challenges in Latin America's Agricultural Export Boom*. World Resources Institute, Washington, DC.

Weeks, J. 1995. "Macroeconomic adjustment and Latin American agriculture since 1980." In J. Weeks (ed.), *Structural Adjustment and the Agricultural Sector in Latin America and the Caribbean*. St. Martins, New York.

# Part II

# Informalization and Feminization of Labour

# 5 Informalization, the Informal Economy and Urban Women's Livelihoods in Sub-Saharan Africa since the 1990s

*Dzodzi Tsikata*

## INTRODUCTION

This chapter examines urban women's livelihoods in sub-Saharan Africa within the context of economic liberalization, the growing informalization of labour relations and an exponential growth of the informal economy. While historically much of the urban labour force has operated within the informal economy and its interface with the formal, the particular processes of informalization since the economic liberalization of the 1980s are worthy of attention because their impacts on the character, structure and quality of Africa's urban economies and livelihoods have been significant. Livelihoods in most of Africa are rural, agrarian and household-based and employ traditional technologies. However, the rapid pace of urbanization and the exponential growth of aspects of the urban informal economy underscore its increasing importance. Urban women's livelihoods are of particular interest because they best illustrate the segmentation and workings of the informal economy. The differences in women's and men's location also have a bearing on gender inequalities in the wider economy and society.

In spite of its steady growth and extension, the informal economy before the economic liberalization policies of the 1980s was often seen in terms of the failure of the formal sector to absorb surplus labour. Its labour relations were considered exploitative and therefore retarding improvements in incomes, purchasing power and economic growth in general. This analysis implied that labour relations had to move towards formalization for economic growth and development to occur (Mhone 1996). Lourenço-Lindell (2004) recalls that in the 1970s, literature on state–society relations in Africa, which characterized informal activities as disengagement or exit from the state by independent producers, was very influential in political science. This highlighted the resilience and autonomy of traders and the significance of their collective impact beyond the control of the state and provided conceptual support for the state's withdrawal from economic processes under economic liberalization (see Lourenço-Lindell 2004, for a critique of the disengagement thesis).

Economic liberalization discourses of the 1980s promoted the view that labour regulation distorted production costs and thereby threatened sustained economic growth. The informal economy within this new approach was considered critical for coping with growing urban unemployment and poverty. While the International Labour Organization (ILO) supported the employment creation potential thesis of the informal economy, it has argued that those working informally need protection from excesses which depress working conditions (Hansen and Vaa; 2004 ILO 1991:58).

In spite of the existence of several studies pointing to the deterioration of livelihoods within the informal economy, recent policy interest has focused more on the expansion of the revenue base of governments and improving market access for enterprises than on their labour relations. This chapter's focus on gendered labour relations is intended to demonstrate their importance in discussions of the future of the informal economy.

The chapter is organized as follows: The introduction is followed by a discussion of conceptual approaches to the informal economy, informalization and gender. The third section of the chapter is a historical account of the urban informal economy from the colonial period to the era of economic liberalization. The fourth part of the chapter explores three developments which are important to livelihoods in the informal economy. These are the growth in demographic urbanization,[1] the proliferation of various processes of informalization of work and state policy responses to the growth in the informal economy. The penultimate section focuses on women's livelihoods in the informal economy. This is then followed by a summary and conclusions.

## APPROACHES TO THE INFORMAL ECONOMY IN AFRICA

### Defining the Informal

The term "informal sector", which has since the 1970s been used to refer to enterprises operating on a small scale with a low capital base outside the purview of state regulation, has increasingly given way in the literature to the term, "informal economy". This shift was preceded by an extensive critique of the enterprise focus of the concept of the "informal sector". Hansen and Vaa (2004), for example, have argued that it is the extra-legality of the informal which is its defining characteristic and not the type and size of the operations, their capital base or income. Thus, Kamete has noted in his study of home industries[2] in Harare that, while informal economic activities paid taxes as expected, none of them complied with "labour laws such as minimum wage, pensions and other benefits. . . . or business laws such as opening and closing hours, sales taxes, standards and trading licences" (Kamete 2004:128).[3] Heintz and Pollin (2003) have argued that because informal work does not belong to any particular sector of the economy, industry or activity, it is misleading to think of the informal as a sector.

The term informal economy is the outcome of a process in which the ILO together with researchers and activists expanded the term informal sector to incorporate certain types of informal employment which had hitherto not been part of the definition.[4] As Chen notes, this broader concept "includes the whole of informality as it is manifested in industrialized, transition and developing economies and the real world dynamics in labour markets today, particularly the employment arrangements of the working poor" (2006:3). The significance of this expanded concept is that it focuses not only on unregulated enterprises, but also on employment relationships which are not legally regulated or protected even if they occur within enterprises which are legally regulated in other ways (Chen 2006; ILO 2002). Thus, the informal economy in this approach comprises "informal employment (without secure contracts, worker benefits, or social protection) both inside and outside informal enterprises" (ILO 2002:12). The informal economy definition identifies three categories of workers: the self-employed in informal enterprises, wage workers in informal jobs and industrial outworkers.[5]

While the concept of the informal economy is more complete, it does not change the fact that what is informal is complicated and imprecise, and that there are different degrees of informality in economic and legal terms; and that the informal economy is highly segmented. However this broader definition allows us to map women's contributions to the economy more fully.

Settling definitional problems also does not fully address the problem of estimating the size and contributions of the informal economy. Indeed it complicates measurement. In keeping with the informal sector–informal economy divide, some institutions adopt an enterprise-based approach (production units),[6] while others use a labour-based approach (status of employment)[7] and this has implications for what is being measured (Heintz and Pollin 2003). Even more problematic, the changes in definitions and conceptualizations have not been carried through into data collection. Only a handful of countries have data on the informal economy which actually reflects the new definition of informality centred on *labour relations* (rather than *scale of the enterprise*), and these were the countries that were included in the 2002 ILO publication on women and men in the informal economy. The lack of data based on labour relations creates some difficulties for discussing the informal economy in this chapter. Whenever possible, statistics based on the labour-centred definition are used. The limitations of enterprise-based statistics and analysis notwithstanding, they still provide useful insights which have been used in cases where labour-based statistics and analyses were not available.

Presently, the ILO estimates informal employment at between half and three-quarters of the non-agricultural employment in developing countries, with a disproportionate number of such workers being women (ILO 2002). As table 5.1 shows, there are also variations between sub-Saharan Africa and other parts of the world in the size and composition of the non-agricultural informal economy.

*Table 5.1* Informal Employment in Non-Agricultural Employment, by Sex, 1994–2000

| Region | Informal employment as a percentage of non-agricultural employment | Women's informal employment as a percentage of women's non-agricultural employment | Men's informal employment as percentage of men's non-agricultural employment |
|---|---|---|---|
| North Africa | 48 | 43 | 49 |
| Sub-Saharan Africa | 72 | 84 | 63 |
| Latin America | 51 | 58 | 48 |
| Asia | 65 | 65 | 65 |

*Source*: ILO (2002).

Beyond differences about definition is an extensive critique of the concept of the informal as vague and unable to stand alone since it is primarily defined in relation to the formal (Mhone 1996; Ndoro 1996; Teszler 1993). Hart, who is credited with being the first to draw attention to the informal enterprises based on his research in Nima, a low-income neighbourhood of Accra, has recently drawn attention to the fact that the term informal was coined in a period of state-led development to describe activities outside state processes. Therefore in a period of economic liberalization where the market is privileged, the continued appropriateness of the term for discussing a particular set of economic activities and players is in doubt (Hart 2007). While these observations are well founded, in the absence of alternative widely accepted terms, the term "informal economy" is used in this chapter. In cases where there are references to enterprises, the term "informal enterprises" or "informal sector" will be used. More commonly, the term "sector" is used in this chapter to refer to different segments of economic activity such as agriculture, manufacturing and services.

It has also been observed that certain kinds of informal employment are increasing in incidence in various countries, and not all of this can be attributed to improvements in data collection. This situation is of concern because there is overwhelming evidence that formal work often provides more security than informal work and, in general, average incomes in the informal economy are below those in the formal economy in the same industry (Heintz and Pollin 2003; ILO 2002; Mhone 1996). There is also general agreement that the informal sector does not constitute a homogeneous group of low-capital, small-scale and low-remunerative activities which play a common role in the economy, but is instead deeply segmented (Beneria 2001; Lourenço-Lindell 2004). Essentially, these differences have been attributed to the existence of production and distribution chains which link informal and formal segments of the national economy with international economic processes (Lourenço-Lindell 2004:52).

The variability of the informal economy has a gender dimension. While not all women have lower earnings than men, gender differentials in remuneration in the informal economy are wider than in the formal economy. Also, a larger proportion of women than men have low incomes, and gender disparities exist in the range of activities and employment status. These differences have been attributed to women's lower educational attainments and skills, the smaller size of their businesses, their lower levels of capital investment, the structural and legal constraints facing such businesses and their generally lower access to certain networks and social resources (Sethuraman 1998). Often, such arguments downplay the contribution of gender discrimination to these disparities in income, opportunities and employment status.

Recent literature has raised the importance of linking informal production and reproduction with the space in which it occurs (Hansen and Vaa 2004:7). This literature has drawn attention to the growth of informal settlements[8] which are also increasingly the site of informal economic activities (Hansen and Vaa 2004).[9]

These insights underscore the multidimensional character of the informal economy. The relationships between the formal and informal, which have been characterized variously as competitive, complementary, exploitative and stifling of the informal by the formal (Baud 1993), have regulatory, economic and social elements.[10] It has also been suggested that the term interface, which "highlights encounters between entities or processes that are governed by different rules" is a useful way of looking at formal and informal connections (Hansen and Vaa 2004:9). Mhone (1996) has argued that it is the lack of backward and forward linkages within the economy as a whole rather than the character of formal–informal linkages which is responsible for the weaknesses of the informal economy.

## Gender Structures in the Informal Economy

The informal economy has long been a space in which gender inequalities are visible.[11] The majority of women in urban areas make a living there, mostly in self-employment, with the result that their participation in the informal economy is higher than their share in the total labour force (Sethuraman 1998). Long-term gender segregation of work, discrimination in labour markets, access to credit, training, land and infrastructure, women's lower levels of education due to inequalities in social relations and the heavy burden of reproductive work account for women's greater reliance on informal economy activities. For women in formal employment, the informal economy is a source of supplementary livelihood activities, a phenomenon which has been growing since the economic liberalization programmes of the 1980s (Niger-Thomas Agbaw 2000; Pearson 2003). Women's productive activities are often an extension of their unpaid reproductive activities (Gaidzanwa 1996; Pape 2000).

Several authors take a voluntarist view of women's work, arguing that certain productive activities and labour relations in the informal economy (for example, home-based work), are popular with women because they are low-risk, flexible and can be done alongside domestic chores (Carr 1993; Gaidzanwa 1996; Kazimbaya-Senkwe 2004). Pape (2000) takes issue with this kind of voluntarist thinking that explains women's shorter working hours in terms of their "preferences" for accommodating family responsi-bilities, arguing that it is an ideological construct which promotes the posi-tion of women as wives rather than as workers. He distinguishes the context of most African countries from the North where part-time and other flex-ible work arrangements can be combined with social benefits and "quality time" with young children in a context of exorbitant childcare costs. In African countries where wages and social benefits are much lower, where the potential domestic labour pool is wider, where paid domestic work is often very cheap and many women are the sole income earners within their household, flexible working arrangements are not attractive, except that in some situations, they are the only work on offer (Pape 2000).

These two different approaches to women's work should be seen as a corrective of each other. It is the case that there are strong ideological underpinnings which channel women into certain kinds of work. At the same time, their heavy domestic responsibilities are a factor in their choice of work in certain cases. While the potential domestic labour pool may be high, it is increasingly difficult to access because of growing demand, demographic changes, patterns of rural–urban migration and the economic situation of potential users of such services.

An important aspect of the gendered nature of the informal is spatial. Economic liberalization policies have affected the value of land and with it commercial spaces and housing. The increase in prices and competition over urban land is expected to increase gender inequalities in access to land (Whitehead and Tsikata 2003). Hansen and Vaa (2004) have argued that in countries where there has been a widespread privatization of state and municipal housing, not only is this benefiting mainly formal economy workers and likely to deepen the gap between rich and poor in the quality of housing, but it is also gender biased.[12]

Although studies of home-based industries have shown that both men and women work from their dwellings in both affluent and poor neigh-bourhoods (Kazimbaya-Senkwe 2004), more women than men tend to do so. Tati's study of the fishing industry in Pointe-Noire in Congo-Brazzaville also demonstrates that the gendered division of labour in informal enter-prises structures the use of space. In Pointe-Noire, the sea and the beach were considered the domain of men, while the courtyards of informal set-tlements were women's space where they smoked fish and cooked food for sale (Tati 2004). This division was a function of women's activities in the informal economy and their greater responsibility for reproductive activities. Thus women in the informal economy often experienced more actively the environmental and occupational challenges of their living space. These included overcrowding, poor sanitation, infrastructure, power, water, transport and other amenities. This problem, which is especially acute in peripheral urban areas where the poor congregate, is exacerbated by the notions of planning which have not fully factored in the fact that economic activities occur in areas designated as residential.[13] On the other hand, homeless market traders and street vendors, the majority of whom are women, also face challenges of personal security and are vulnerable to physical and sexual violence and robberies in the markets and streets at night. The next section of the chapter is an account of the character and composition of the informal economy within African economies before and after the liberalization policies of the 1980s and 1990s.

## THE URBAN INFORMAL ECONOMIES IN SUB-SAHARAN AFRICA: HISTORICAL PERSPECTIVES

### The Colonial Period

Women's predominance in the informal economy is linked with the history of urbanization and the creation of a formal economy presided over by the colonial state. While several African cities predated colonization, colonial economic policies resulted in predominantly male labour migrations to mining, industrial and administrative centres and promoted the expansion of urbanization in the colonies. Ndoro (1996:22) argues that before colonialism, secondary and tertiary activities in African communities, such as mineral smelting and foundry work, beer-brewing and other crafts, were "legitimate, technologically advanced and accepted activities, central to the autonomous development and evolution of these economies and societies". With colonialism, those activities which survived or were started by Africans in response to socioeconomic developments were either declared illegal, suppressed over long periods or displaced, thus forcing them underground and stifling their development. Alcohol brewing and distillation is the most cited example of this marginalization of African economic activities.

Mhone (1996) and others have distinguished the processes which established the informal economies of Eastern and Southern Africa from what pertained in West Africa. As they argue, the informal economy in Southern Africa is a post-colonial development. The relatively low levels of development of the craft industries and market economies at the start of colonialism coupled with the way in which settler colonialism used African labour and controlled its movement delayed the development of an informal economy across Southern Africa (Mhone 1996; Ndoro 1996).

While West Africa's informal economies have a longer history, with the appearance of a wider range of goods and artisanal services, and larger more populous and more structured marketplaces, Eastern and Southern African countries such as Zimbabwe, South Africa and Kenya have some of the more industrialized economies. However, after two decades of almost identical policies of economic liberalization across Africa, it is not clear what differences remain in the character of informal economies. Some of the statistical data provide clues, but these are not conclusive.

Table 5.2 depicts self-employment and wage employment as percentages of non-agricultural employment in several African countries. There are clear differences between Benin, Chad and Guinea, on the one hand, and Kenya and South Africa on the other. In the former, self-employment is much higher than wage employment, while in the latter it is the other way round. For our purposes, self-employment can be taken as a proxy measure for informal employment. With regard to gender differences, more women are in wage employment than men in Kenya, but not in South Africa, while more men than women are in wage employment in the West African countries. On the other hand, more women than men are self-employed in West Africa and in South Africa. These differences might also be a function of industrialization and the size of the informal economy in the various countries. However, even here, the differences between Kenya and South Africa, both with a history of settler

*Table 5.2* Wage and Self-Employment in Non-Agricultural Formal Employment, by Sex, 1994–2000

| Region | Self-employment as percentage of non-agricultural informal employment. | | | Wage employment as percentage of non agricultural informal employment. | | |
|---|---|---|---|---|---|---|
| | *Total* | *Women* | *Men* | *Total* | *Women* | *Men* |
| North Africa | 62 | 72 | 60 | 38 | 28 | 40 |
| Sub-Saharan Africa | 70 | 71 | 70 | 30 | 29 | 30 |
| Benin | 95 | 98 | 91 | 5 | 2 | 9 |
| Chad | 93 | 99 | 86 | 7 | 1 | 14 |
| Guinea | 95 | 98 | 94 | 5 | 2 | 6 |
| Kenya | 42 | 33 | 56 | 58 | 67 | 44 |
| South Africa | 25 | 27 | 23 | 75 | 73 | 77 |
| Latin America | 60 | 58 | 61 | 40 | 42 | 39 |
| Asia | 59 | 63 | 55 | 41 | 37 | 45 |

*Source*: ILO 2002.

colonialism, are interesting. This issue requires closer examination, but is beyond the scope of this chapter.

The existing literature shows that in countries such as Zimbabwe, Namibia, South Africa and, to a lesser extent, Zambia, laws and regulations controlled labour migrations and urban settlement. This, together with educational, agricultural, taxation and land policies, stifled the development of independent economic activities among Africans and confined them to formal economy activities which were useful to the settlers. Malawi, Botswana, Lesotho, Swaziland and Mozambique became labour reserves of the settler and mining economies, especially that of South Africa, thus delaying urbanization, and with it the growth of their urban informal economies (Banda and Nyirongo 1996; Mhone 1996; Ndoro 1996).

In West Africa, both the urban areas created by economic activities, such as mining, commercial farming and railways, and the older towns which serviced the colonial economy, saw increased in-migration because of the economic opportunities offered by the colonial economic system. Akyeampong and Agyei-Mensah (2006) argue that in colonial Ghana, the abolition of slavery and pawning at the end of the nineteenth century enlarged the wage labour pool which gravitated towards commercial and wage labour opportunities in the urban areas. Both men and women migrated to towns but under different circumstances. Women's interest in migration was strengthened by their weakening control over productive resources such as land and labour as a result of the introduction of cash-crops which as perennials had a profound impact on the availability of land. However, the labour recruited to work in colonial bureaucracy, public and private enterprises, the mines and to build infrastructure was predominantly male. According to Gugler (1989), in many, if not all, African colonies, almost as a rule domestic servants, secretaries and nurses were male. This, and the discriminatory character of colonial education, meant that women participated in the colonial economy on its margins, while performing the critical functions which reproduced the colonial labour force. This also made trading in goods and services an attractive option and resulted in female dominance in this area of the informal economy in many countries (Akyeampong and Agyei-Mensah 2006). Clark (1994) argues that while women were expected to earn their independent incomes in most societies in Ghana, they also had heavy domestic responsibilities. This situation determined their livelihood prospects and also defined trading as women's work.

Gugler describes women as the second sex in urban colonial Africa because of men's predominance in numbers and their wider range of economic options. In spite of their disadvantages, women found avenues for accumulation in the towns, such as supplying goods and domestic service to male migrants—cooked food, a place to sleep and sex. Several historians of colonial gender relations have written about strenuous efforts to control female sexuality, to which was attributed several ills including sexually transmitted diseases (Allman 1996; Roberts 1987). It has been noted that, while the colonial state and men sought to control women's sexuality, freedom of movement and association in the rural areas, sexuality came to be used by some women to make a living in the relative freedom of urban life (Akyeampong and Agyei-Mensah 2006).

Women's activities, however, were often criminalized and in much of sub-Saharan Africa, keeping them out of urban areas was explicit colonial policy at one point or other. As a result, until the late colonial period, women's lives in urban areas were often poorly established. This, together with the education policy of providing women with skills related to their reproductive functions and a pervading ideology of domesticity, kept women out of jobs in the formal economy. In many colonial civil services, women had to resign their jobs either on marriage or on the birth of their first child (Tsikata 1997).

Once colonial regulations against women's migration were relaxed in West Africa, they became key actors in the trade in goods and services. According to Clark (1994), women's participation in commerce in urban colonial Ghana increased dramatically in the 1920s and 1930s when European traders established control over the import–export trade. With these developments, men left commerce and entered into more profitable areas of work in cocoa farming and the civil service. In Eastern and Southern Africa though, the patterns of largely male rural–urban migration remained, particularly in relation to cross-border migration (Mhone 1996; Ngwira 1996).

In time, the independent economic activities taking place in the margins of the formal economies around Africa expanded and provided work for increasing numbers of urban and rural dwellers without formal schooling. This came to be christened as the informal sector. In the old conception of the informal as a temporary place for those who could not be absorbed by the formal economy, more and more of the labour force was expected to move into the formal economy. This did not happen. Instead, the informal workforce grew and became increasingly central to the economies of sub-Saharan Africa.

## The Post-Colonial Period Up to the Era of Structural Adjustment Policies

The 1960s to the early 1980s was the period of import substitution industrialization. While the urban informal economies of African countries grew in this period, they did so at a relatively slower pace than in the late 1980s and beyond. Persuaded that the main route to development lay in industrialization and modernization, newly independent African governments embraced polices such as the expansion of social and physical infrastructure, the protection of infant industries, tax incentives to attract foreign capital and direct state involvement in the establishment of industries.

This strategy necessitated a strongly interventionist state which also assumed responsibility for development in all its dimensions. Along with the state-led push for industrialization, labour codes were passed or strengthened and the new labour unions across Africa organized the small, largely male class of formal sector employees in the mines, manufacturing industries and the service sector. The strategy initially made gains for African countries in terms of economic growth and social development. However, the failure to ensure that capital-intensive industries earned sufficient foreign exchange and the reliance on a narrow range of primary export commodities for foreign exchange proved destabilizing in the longer run. Several countries experienced economic crises from the late 1970s, triggered by the high oil prices and the collapse of agricultural commodity prices (Mkandawire and Soludo 1999). To resolve these crises, structural adjustment programmes (SAPs) were instituted across Africa from the early 1980s. These programmes, which marked an end to import substitution industrialization, explicitly sought to limit the role of the state in the economy, promote private sector operations, remove "distortions" and ensure market determined prices across the board, except for labour.

## The Economic Liberalization Agenda of the 1980s

### *The Aims and Objectives of SAPs*

The package of policies that became known as "structural adjustment" (SAP) combined an International Monetary Fund (IMF) stabilization loan with conditionalities, along with a longer term SAP overseen by both the World Bank and the IMF. The stabilization package, which addressed monetary and fiscal issues, typically sought to reduce inflation, reduce the government's budget deficit and balance of payments problems and deflate government and private domestic demand. The longer term SAPs were to promote production and resource mobilization, through the rehabilitation of commodity exports, public sector reform, market liberalization and institutional reform (Olukoshi 1998; Tsikata and Kerr 2000).

There have been numerous discussions about the rights and wrongs of SAPs. These have focused on issues as diverse as whether SAPs have lived up to their promise of sustained growth and development, their impacts on disadvantaged social groups, questions of ownership and state sovereignty, and alternatives to SAPs (Bakker 1994; Sparr 1994; Tsikata and Kerr 2000). What is most relevant to this chapter is that the combined impacts of certain adjustment policies, namely, trade and investment liberalization, labour market liberalization, industrial sector reforms, privatization and the reform of the public sector have affected informal economies in sub-Saharan Africa.

### *Key Policies: Privatization, Trade and Investment Liberalization, and Industrialization*

Under privatization programmes, state-owned mines, commercial enterprises and manufacturing industries have been put under the hammer across sub-Saharan Africa. This has gone hand in hand with the retrenchment of labour and the closure of certain factories. There have also been massive retrenchments in the civil services and public sector enterprises to create a leaner and more effective administration. The expected impacts of privatization have not been realized, two decades on, and many enterprises slated for privatization have either not been sold or have not resumed full service under the new owners (Mkandawire and Soludo 1999).

In addition, under trade liberalization, industries have been exposed to the harsh climate of global competition and the results have been mixed. Export trade in primary commodities improved in volume, though not in the diversification of the export base. Given Africa's history of economic crisis linked to commodity price fluctuations, there is cause for concern. Between 1985 and 1990, exports of nine major commodities in Africa increased by 75 per cent over 1977–1979 averages. However, earnings from these exports fell by 40 per cent (Mkandawire and Soludo 1999) because of adverse terms of trade. Even more importantly, manufacturing industries and manufactured exports did not fare well under adjustment. Several commentators have argued that there has been some level of deindustrialization in some countries with new primary commodity exports not doing well enough to make up for the loss of those industries (Mkandawire and Soludo 1999; Pape 2000).

Industrial performance under SAPs has been hampered in part by the lack of industrialization programmes in the majority of countries. In both Ghana and Tanzania for example, the growth in manufactures up to the early 1990s has not been sustained.[14] Even more telling has been the fall in employment in manufacturing in Ghana from 78,700 in 1987 to 28,000 in 1993. Part of the problem is the poor response of foreign capital to the industrial sector under adjustment (Mkandawire and Soludo 1999, citing the African Development Bank 1993). There has been a shift from productive to speculative investment in banking and financial services and much of the foreign direct investment (FDI) flows to the real economy have been in the area of extractive industries. These sectors of investment are not known for their job creation properties and have delivered important strategic assets into the hands of transnational corporations.

Along with trade and investment, labour markets were a target for reform. Measures were put in place to remove institutional arrangements protecting labour. Employment was no longer considered a central issue of macroeconomic policy, but a microeconomic concern (Bangura 1997; Tsikata and Kerr 2000). The upshot of over two decades of reform has been that urban workers have been identified as the most adversely affected social group under SAPs, experiencing a dramatic decline in real wages, increased unemployment, deteriorating employment conditions, greater informalization and instability of employment (Mkandawire and Soludo 1999).

The adjustment logic, that the adoption of labour-intensive technologies would provide work for the poor, did not happen in practice. According to

Mkandawire and Soludo, declining wages have not led to a reduction in unemployment. Instead, in 14 countries, the annual growth rate of formal sector employment had fallen from 2.8 per cent between 1975 and 1980 to 1 per cent in the 1980s. The failure of labour market flexibility to increase employment in the formal sector has been attributed to an exaggeration of the problem of labour market "distortions", given low minimum wages and poor enforcement (Mkandawire and Soludo 1999).

Studies of the impacts of SAPs on the informal economy are not common. A rare study commissioned by the ILO on the informal economy in Ghana (Barwa 1995) identified a number of such impacts. For example, the study found that SAP policies of reduction of public expenditure and the downsizing of the civil service and state-owned enterprises encouraged more people to enter the informal economy. Currency devaluation, the imposition of user fees for education and health and retrenchments in the civil service resulted in a net drop in household incomes and an increase in the number of poor households. This reduced the demand for urban informal products. Deregulation of prices of inputs and foreign exchange and trade liberalization as well as incentives for production of exports put larger scale units in an advantageous position in relation to smaller enterprises, and this reduced revenue at the enterprise level. At the same time, deregulation and currency devaluation were creating higher input costs for smaller and medium-sized enterprises in the informal economy. These high input costs resulted in firms looking for cheaper substitutes which affected the quality of their production, the product mix and their markets. This, in turn, affected output, income and employment. Restrictive credit ceilings and liberalization of bank lending rates created credit constraints and increased its costs. This scaled down investments and technology upgrading. Intensified competition from imports led to the reduction in revenues of businesses and their closure in certain cases (Barwa 1995).

After two decades of adjustment, the economic liberalization agenda continues into a post-adjustment phase. In response to the crippling debt burden of many adjusting countries as well as the failure of adjustment to tackle the deepening poverty of large sections of their populations, the World Bank and IMF have injected a poverty focus into the economic liberalization agenda. While the essential macroeconomic policies remain in place, countries seeking support from the World Bank or seeking debt relief through the Highly Indebted Poor Countries (HIPC) Initiative are required to draw up Poverty Reduction Strategy Papers (PRSPs) as the new framework for their economic policies. The main innovation in the programmes is policy continuity combined with an insistence that civil society organizations participate in policy-making, though the fundamental issue of the strategy of economic liberalization is not up for discussion.

This new phase of economic liberalization is taking place in an international context characterized by continuing efforts by industrialized nations and transnational corporations to push for far-reaching liberalization agendas. These include trade negotiations within the World Trade Organization (WTO), United States efforts to enter African markets through the African Growth and Opportunities Act (AGOA), and the European Union's efforts to establish Economic Partnership Agreements (EPAs), which are essentially free trade area agreements with the different regional groups of African, Caribbean and Pacific (ACP) countries. This combination of international processes of economic liberalization and national-level economic reforms is raising concerns that the informalization of work and the deterioration of labour conditions will be deepened rather than reduced in the long term.

## STATE RESPONSES TO THE INFORMAL ECONOMY

This section of the chapter discusses three developments which constituted the context for women's livelihoods in Africa's urban informal economies in the 1990s. These are the growth of demographic urbanization which has been distinguished from urbanization arising from industrialization, the proliferation of varied processes of informalization of labour in the formal economy, which are enlarging the informal economy, and state policy responses to the growth of the informal economy. As we shall see, these three interconnected developments have been important in shaping livelihoods in the urban informal economies of the continent. At the same time, they are also indications of what needs to change with regard to economies and livelihoods.

### Urbanization, Slums, Poverty and the Informal Economy

Potts argues that the assumption that urban areas were privileged in relation to rural ones—an assumption that drove some liberalization policies—was erroneous even at the time of adjustment because many of the advantages of urban dwellers had been largely eroded by the economic crisis of the 1970s. This is what accounts for the devastating impact of the reforms, especially on those who were already poor and vulnerable, caught as they were in a situation of deepening poverty rather than a reduction of privileges. As a result, urban poverty may now have become worse in some senses than rural poverty, given that the ability of poor households to access food is more vulnerable to income fluctuations (Jamal and Weeks 1993; Potts 1997).

Liberalization policies are also implicated in the expansion of urbanization and in the growth of slums. Several writers have argued that the disconnect between urbanization and industrialization, which they directly trace to the debt crisis and the SAPs, is responsible for the enlargement of the informal economy, the rise of slums and urban poverty (Davis 2004; Omari 1995; Rakodi 1997; UN-Habitat 2003). Davis, for example, argues that the economies of cities in Cote d'Ivoire, Tanzania, Gabon and the Democratic

Republic of Congo, to name only a few, were contracting by 2–5 per cent a year, but were having to cope with population growth rates of 5–8 per cent per annum. In Abidjan, which had a manufacturing sector and service sector, SAPs resulted in deindustrialization, and the decline of construction and public transport. The persistent growth of the urban population, in spite of falling real wages, rising prices and rising urban unemployment had to do with policies of agricultural deregulation which continued to make the rural areas unattractive. This resulted in slums characterized by very poor housing, overcrowding, insecurity of tenure of both land and housing, inadequate or missing basic services, such as water and sanitation, and an unhealthy environment. Fifty-seven per cent of urban dwellers in Africa do not have access to basic sanitation such as toilet facilities.[15] While the poor infrastructure has in certain cases created income-generating opportunities for informal operators, it has also deepened the exploitation of consumers who very often cannot afford some of the services on offer (Davis 2004; UN-Habitat 2003). Chant (2007) has drawn attention to the gendered impacts of the infrastructural and environmental problems of slums.

The issue of slums is important because they are both the dwelling places and the workplaces of many urban informal economy workers. Also, their population figures, which are often gross underestimates, are an indication of the levels of urban poverty. While many slum-dwellers are poor and many of the poor are not slum-dwellers, two out of every five slum-dwellers are said to experience life-threatening poverty (UN-Habitat 2003). In Ethiopia and Chad, 99.4 per cent of the urban population are slum-dwellers, while Maputo and Kinshasa are identified as having the poorest urban populations with two-thirds of residents earning less than what is required for their minimum required daily nutrition. The West African coast (from Abidjan to Ibadan and including Lagos) is estimated to have 70 million slum-dwellers, described as "probably the biggest continuous footprint of urban poverty on earth" (Davis 2004:15). The retreat of the state from social provisioning under adjustment apart from worsening poverty and inequality has also exacerbated unplanned urbanization and the rise of slums. Unemployment, which was affecting not only the unskilled workers but also university graduates, was expected to exceed 30 per cent in most cities in sub-Saharan Africa by 2000 and to continue growing. Those most affected by unemployment are the urban youth, aged between 20 and 29 who are said to constitute between 60 to 75 per cent of the unemployed although they are only one-third of the labour force (Rogerson 1997). The urban informal economy is likely to be the next stop of these persons.

## Informalization and the Informal Economy

It is well established that over two decades of economic liberalization has resulted in the stagnation of formal economies along with a significant growth in informal employment in sub-Saharan Africa. By the mid-1980s, as a result of economic growth, the creation of new areas of work and gender equity policies, many more women entered the labour force around the world (Sethuraman 1998). While some entered professions and management jobs in the formal sector, mainly in public service, they were in a minority. The majority of women were self-employed or in waged work in the informal economy. The export processing zones (EPZs) also absorbed some female labour in various African countries. The increase in women's labour force participation however has not seen commensurate increases in women's earnings. This trend of increased labour force participation has been reversed in more recent years because of poor gross domestic product (GDP) growth and structural adjustment policies in Africa (Pape 2000; Sethuraman 1998).

It has been argued that economic liberalization is promoting the feminization of work in the overall economy (Beneria 2001; Deedat 2003; Elson 1999; Pape 2000; Pearson 2003; Sethuraman 1998).[16] While flexible labour relations are most advanced in the areas of the economy where women predominate, such as retail and services, they are spreading to other areas. As Pearson notes of feminization, "the most general conditions of work have come to reflect not the 'labour aristocracy' of organized (unionized) regulated and protected workers (who historically have been men) but the insecure, irregular and unregulated situation in which the majority of working women have, in most countries outside the former centrally planned economies always endured" (1998:5). Feminization can be seen in the growing incidence of practices, such as outsourcing, home-based work, homework,[17] short-term contracts, contract work, piece-rate work and part-time work (Deedat 2003; Elson 1999).

Informalization has been discussed in the literature as (i) the growth in size of the informal economy which has accompanied the reduction in the size of the formal economy; and (ii) the systemic changes in labour relations from formalized to more informal arrangements (Beneria 2001; Charmes 1998; Pape 2000; Pearson 2003; Sethuraman 1998; WCL 1999). Informalization has been attributed to various factors and processes. Heintz and Pollin (2003) identify two broad conceptions of informalization in the literature. One attributes informalization to a reaction by firms to government interventions in the marketplace and the normal activity of firms seeking to increase their profits in a context of poor economic growth, while the second sees it as an outcome of policies of liberalization. Heintz and Pollin argue convincingly that the evidence on informalization does not support the "responses to excessive government" approach[18] or the "informalization and growth arguments.[19] Under economic liberalization, informalization or increased labour market flexibility was not an accident, but a conscious policy outcome (Heintz and Pollin 2003; Tripp 1997; see also Hansen and Vaa 2004; Meagher and Yunusa 1996; Pearson 2003; Sethuraman 1998; WCL 1999).

Certain changes in the organization of work in the formal economy illustrate some of the features of informalization. Two examples—the leather footwear industry in South Africa and the informal activities of formal economy workers in Cameroon—highlight the implications of informalization for women's livelihoods. The Leather Footwear Industry in South Africa was created in the context of import substitution industrialization during a period when South Africa was under sanctions and boycotts because of apartheid. It was protected, subsidized and sheltered until the end of apartheid, when South Africa embarked on economic liberalization and imports began to flood the economy. By the late 1990s, both employment and production in the footwear industry began to decline. Shoe factories which had been in existence for years closed down and others retrenched hundreds of workers, shrunk their operations and in some cases were taken over by foreign investors. Footwear production declined by 13.8 per cent in 1999 and employment in the industry reduced from 24,878 in 1995 to 15,745 in 2000. The hardest hit provinces were the Western Cape, Eastern Cape and KwaZulu-Natal where employment reduced by 38.83 per cent, 52.94 per cent and 62.08 per cent, respectively, between 1989 and 2000.

Along with the reduction of employment was the restructuring of production processes. Drawing on experiences in Southeast Asia, employers began to institute a more flexible wage and job regime. Over the course of the 1990s, employers moved away from having a permanent full-time and organized workforce by increasingly using casual, temporary and seasonal labour. There was also a gradual reduction in the distinction between the work conditions of permanent and temporary workers (Pape 2000). New work forms such as team-work, multitasking, job rotation, outsourcing and subcontracting were introduced. Also, many factories began to retrench workers. Retrenched workers were in certain cases encouraged to buy their equipment and set up in home-based production. Such workers became employers to less fortunate retrenched colleagues.

For those who remained in formal employment, while the amount of work per person has increased, real wages have not increased over the years. The hours of work increased with the working day between eight to nine hours on average, and overtime was not always properly planned, computed and paid. Among the changes enumerated by the workers was the loss of rights to join a union, to earn a fixed salary and to contribute to a pension fund. Conventions such as "first-in, last-out" no longer applied and anyone could be retrenched. Maternity leave was taken at the risk of losing one's work schedule or particular position, or the job altogether. The footwear industry is considered a female industry because the labour force was predominantly made up of women who were concentrated in the preparation and closing rooms where work was less well-paid. Men were in the cutting rooms and were better paid. While more women were taking up jobs in male-dominated sectors, they were not offered the same rates of pay as men because for employers, the point about employing women in such tasks was to reduce the wage bill. The labour laws of South Africa have been revised to create the conditions for a flexible and casual labour force (Deedat 2003).

In Cameroon, under structural adjustment in the mid-1980s, one target for reform was the public sector of the formal economy. In addition to a policy of downsizing through massive retrenchments and retirements (in 1995–1996 alone, seven Ministries fired 3,105 workers), the terms and conditions of service of public sector employees were trimmed. In three years, civil servants had experienced salary cuts of up to 60 per cent (Niger-Thomas Agbaw 2000). This was compounded by arrears in salary payments. Civil servants and other public officials responded to shortfalls in earnings and falling living standards by finding other sources of income.

Forays into the informal economy, although forbidden by law, became common. This strategy of survival or accumulation is known as straddling. A study found that women in Limbe and Mamfe, two towns in the Southwest Province of Cameroon, began to combine certain types of formal work (teaching, nursing and clerical work) with informal activities. Informalization here involved the use of position, equipment and time from a formal work situation for informal transactions for profit. Out of 109 women interviewed in Mamfe, 69 (63 per cent) were involved in this practice. In Limbe, out of 204 women interviewed, 155 (76 per cent) were involved.

The striking characteristics of these informal activities were their relationship with particular formal economy engagements and their gendered character. Thus, while the majority of male teachers were organizing supplementary private tuition for students and selling reproductions of lecture notes (known as polycops) to them, women teachers were mostly involved in small-scale trading in food and non-food items. Seventy per cent of female and 0 per cent of the male teachers were engaged in trading. Female respondents attributed this to the gendered division of labour in the society and what it would imply for men's sense of their position to engage in activities associated with women. However, the earnings from trading in some cases exceeded monthly salaries.

Nurses, like teachers, were involved in informal activities related to their formal work. From being a secretive sporadic activity, private consultations and medicine sales became more open and more widely practised after general and hospital strikes of the early 1990s. In a few cases, profit levels enabled health workers to open a drug-store. Registration and taxpaying transformed what had started as an informal activity into a formal enterprise (Niger-Thomas Agbaw 2000).[20]

The South African example demonstrates several related elements of informalization: the move into the informal economy by workers after large-scale retrenchments; formal economy firms farming out certain production functions to small-scale operators in the informal economy; unilateral changes in working conditions of workers in the formal economy, resulting in the downward pull of terms and conditions of service; and firms employing casual and seasonal labour in place of permanent employees. In the Cameroon case, formal economy employees entering the informal economy to generate supplementary income to improve their deteriorating terms and conditions of service were increasing the size of the informal economy and the range of persons operating within it.

The two examples demonstrate that, while informalization may take different forms and involve varying degrees of change, a common outcome is the downgrading of the status of certain categories of workers and the worsening of their work conditions, bringing them more in line with the much criticized working conditions within the informal economy. Beyond specific terms and conditions of service, the atmosphere of uncertainty created by informalization disables workers from insisting on their rights and protesting labour code violations, thus leaving them open to abuse. Competition between workers for the favours of supervisors, which has been observed in these situations, also weakens organizational potential of the workforce. Women workers are particularly vulnerable under these conditions as they often occupy the most dispensable positions within industrial structures and suffer from pre-existing discrimination from their male counterparts and the management. It is therefore not surprising that the South Africa case recorded an increased incidence of transactional sex and sexual abuse of women workers (Deedat 2003).

## Changing State Policies and the Informal Economy

State policy towards the informal economy during the period before adjustment was variously tolerant, ambivalent or hostile. In Zimbabwe, for example, while the informal economy was expected to provide short-term solutions to the problem of unemployment, in the long term, it was considered that the solution to the employment problems lay in formalizing the sector and bringing it into the mainstream (Ndoro 1996). In countries such as Ghana, informal economy activities such as small-scale mining continued to be criminalized for decades. Market traders, most of whom were women, or from particular ethnic and religious groups, had a long history of fractious relations with the state in Ghana, Nigeria, Guinea Bissau, Zambia and Zimbabwe, among others. Often becoming scapegoats for shortages and high prices of consumer goods, they suffered periodically from state harassment and prosecution, and seizures and destruction of goods in times of economic crisis. Infractions of planning regulations through the construction and use of unauthorized structures were often punished by demolitions (Dennis 1987; Hansen 2004; Lourenço-Lindell 2004; Robertson 1983; Tsikata 1997).

By the late 1980s, however, long-term economic stagnation, growing rates of urban unemployment and liberalization policies affected confidence in the ability of the formal sector to absorb more labour. In 14 African countries, the average annual growth rate of formal sector employment fell from 2.8 per cent between 1975 and 1980 to 1 per cent in the 1980s. The informal economy, on the other hand, grew. As table 5.3 shows, informal employment in sub-Saharan Africa grew from 68.1 per cent of non-agricultural employment in the 1980s to 74.8 per cent in the 1990s. Table 5.4 shows that the percentage of female self-employment in the non-agricultural labour force grew from 38.1 per cent in the 1970s, to 59.8 per cent in the 1980s, and to 62.8 per cent in the 1990s.

The relaxation of planning bye-laws in some of the better planned African cities and the entry of formal economy operators into the informal economy has resulted in the proliferation of small trading concerns in residential areas. In countries such as Ghana and Nigeria, roadside selling of snacks, bread, fruit, small electrical goods such as water-heaters and decorative lights, handkerchiefs, artefacts and sweets by young men and women is a visible indication of the livelihood trajectories of school leavers and drop-outs.

*Table 5.3* Trends in Informal Employment, 1980–1999

| Regions | Informal employment as % of non-agricultural employment | | % of women in informal employment (1990–1999) | % of self-employment in the informal economy (1990–1999) |
|---|---|---|---|---|
| | 1980–1989 | 1990–1999 | | |
| North Africa | 38.8 | 43.4 | – | 51.5 |
| Sub-Saharan Africa | 68.1 | 74.8 | 52.3 | 90.0 |
| Latin America | 52.3 | 56.9 | 45.9 | 50.4 |
| Asia | 53.0 | 63.0 | 39.9 | 63.0 |

*Source*: Charmes 2000, cited in Beneria 2001.

*Table 5.4* Self-Employment in the Female Non-Agricultural Labour Force

| | % of self-employed in female non-agricultural labour force | | |
|---|---|---|---|
| | 1970 | 1980 | 1990 |
| Developed | 10.4 | 9.7 | 11.1 |
| Africa | 38.1 | 59.3 | 62.8 |
| Latin America | 28.6 | 29.2 | 32.1 |
| Asia | 27.9 | 26.7 | 28.7 |
| World | 24.0 | 28.4 | 27.6 |

*Source*: Charmes 2000, cited in Beneria 2001.

While there is disagreement about whether its growth was an involuntary response to economic liberalization (Banda and Nyirongo 1996; Mhone 1996), or the result of conscious policy (Lourenço-Lindell 2004; Ndoro 1996; Tripp 1997), at the very least, developments dictated a more positive attitude to the informal economy. This was manifested by governments commissioning studies of the informal economy in several countries and the establishment of institutions and programmes to support the informal economy in Zambia, Zimbabwe and Ghana (Adu-Amankwah 1999; Hansen 2004; Mhone 1996; Ndoro 1996).

State support for the informal economy, however, has not been unequivocal. As Hansen's study of Zambia shows, a few years on, there have been street clearing programmes and demolitions of stalls, in some cases to make space for large transnational distribution chains or more up-market stalls. These events have threatened the livelihoods of poorer informal economy operators, not least because, even when relocated, many have been either unable to afford the price of new stalls and market tolls or to recover from the dissipation of their capital and loss of clientele which accompanies the disruption of their activities (Hansen 2004).

Recent demolitions in Zimbabwe and continuing discrimination against workers in the informal economy also demonstrate the complicated and changing character of state–informal economy relations. Kamete notes that Harare City Council's policies towards the informal economy tend to be welfarist and informed more by sociopolitical calculations than economic considerations. While the council has an economic unit staffed by economists dealing with industrial and commercial enterprises, home industries are under the department of housing and community services, which is predominantly staffed by social workers. Incentives offered to industries such as tax holidays, reduced rates and service charges are not extended to home industries. The two sectors also make demands differently, the industrialists preferring the "use of facts, figures and discussions," while the home industry operators use demonstrations and frame their demands in terms of "livelihood, votes, politics, colonial rule, discrimination, black empowerment and threats" (Kamete 2004:134). This observation deserves comment. The strategies of the two sectors have more to do with differences in class, gender, positioning within the political economy and access to power than with a lack of appreciation of methods of advocacy.

What is most striking about state policies in this period is a lack of recognition of how liberalization policies are fuelling the expansion of the informal economy and the nature of the expansion. The overall framework of economic policy continues unchanged, while much of the concern these days is to formalize the operations of enterprises and provide them with certain incentives in order to improve tax revenue collection. Labour relations in the informal economy continue to be a neglected area in spite of efforts by trade unions across Africa to promote decent work, as defined by the ILO (FIAS-ISSER 2007; ILO 2002).

## LIVELIHOODS IN THE URBAN INFORMAL ECONOMIES OF THE 1990S

### The Structure and Composition of the Urban Informal Economy

The urban informal economy has since the 1990s become the leading employer in several African countries (see tables 5.1–5.4 in this chapter). Much of this growth, though, has been in trading activities and this has gone hand in hand with the decline of manufacturing (Potts 1997). The urban informal economies in various countries in sub-Saharan Africa might be specific in overall size, composition and sizes of their various parts. However, their main components—services, construction, manufacturing and urban agriculture—are consistent across the continent. In Ghana for example, the informal economy's large service sector consists of food traders and processors (who include foodstuffs and fruit-sellers in the market, itinerant wholesalers and retailers, bakers, caterers and cooked food sellers) who are mostly women; non-food and imported food traders who deal in a range of goods (including clothing, cloth, shoes, cooking pots, other non-food items and canned and factory-processed food and drinks) who are also mostly women; health and sanitation workers who are mixed in terms of their gender, employment status and capital base and include a wide range of actors (such as chemical sellers, drug-store operators, funeral undertakers, refuse collectors, traditional/herbal healers, attendants in private maternity homes and traditional birth attendants). There are also domestic workers who are mostly women; repairers of watches, refrigeration equipment, radios and other electrical and electronic and mechanical equipment; service providers (such as auto mechanics, sprayers, welders, vulcanizers and auto electricians); graphic designers and audio-visual workers (such as photographers, cinema/video operators, performers, musicians, filmmakers) who are mostly male; seamstresses, tailors, hairdressers and barbers made up of both men and women; and private security employees, mostly young men. A smaller construction sector (made up of masons, carpenters, steel benders, small-scale plumbers, electricians) involves mostly men, while an also small manufacturing sector (made up of food processing, textile and garments, wood processing and metalworks) employ both men and women but in different sectors, with women dominating the food processing, textiles and garments and men dominating wood processing and metalworks (Adu-Amankwah 1999).[21]

Many of those involved in hawking and trading in foodstuffs and cooked food in front of dwellings, sidewalks and the markets depend on credit arrangements with suppliers, their insecurity exacerbated by the perishable character of their goods and lack of proper storage facilities. The vast majority of them use little or no hired labour and some are involved in income-generating groups on a part-time basis (Carr 1993). Those who work for the owners of micro and small enterprises, whether as family members, apprentices or hired casual labour, have very poor or no pay and uncertain terms and conditions of service. Apprentices even have to pay for the privilege of being taken on to learn new skills (Teszler 1993).

Urban agriculture, either on home gardens or in the urban peripheries, has been described as an increasingly important activity within the urban informal economy. Its growth in prevalence and economic significance since the early 1980s has been attributed to the impacts of economic liberalization on the urban poor (Mbiba 1994; Niger-Thomas Agbaw 2000; Rogerson 1997). Studies have documented the growth of full-time and part-time urban farming in the Democratic Republic of Congo, Uganda, Tanzania, Kenya, Nigeria, Lesotho, Zambia, Zimbabwe and South Africa. In Kenya, Zambia and Zimbabwe, women have been major participants in urban agriculture, an activity critical to the survival of low-income women (Rogerson 1997). With poor urban households in Kenya, Mali and Tanzania, spending between 60 to 89 per cent of their incomes on food, and city dwellers paying between 10 to 30 per cent more for their food than rural dwellers, the expansion of urban agriculture in the period of adjustment is easy to understand. Urban agriculture, though, has not been the preserve of the poor (Rogerson 1997).

Many women in the urban informal economy are working for others or have done so at some point in their lives. As Davis has pointed out, these employer–employee relations, which he describes as "ubiquitous and vicious networks of micro-exploitation of the poor exploiting the very poor", are not properly discussed in the literature on the informal economy (Davis 2004:22). An example of this class of exploited and very poor workers are the head porters known as *kayaye* in urban markets in Southern Ghana. Composed predominantly of young female rural–urban migrants, but increasingly of locals, they eke out a living carrying goods meant for sale as well as the purchases of shoppers usually for loose change. The only equipment they require are large aluminium wide-brimmed basins usually purchased or acquired second-hand and a large piece of cloth to serve as a buffer between the head and the basin. For many of these women, the marketplaces are all at once a workplace, shelter for the night and the place to bring up children.

The *kayaye* in Ghana operate in marketplaces which are highly segmented and organized, as is the case in much of West Africa. For example, sellers of different food items are organized with their own leaders in a hierarchical order in which the overall leader of the market is the market queen (Clark 1994; King and Oppong 2000). This traditional hierarchy which also has a governance function is implicated in questions of power and influence over the allocation of stalls and over the wholesaling of goods. These hierarchies together with the capital base of traders account for the many layers of economic and political power in the markets. Those who retail small quantities of fruits and vegetables are better off than the head porters.

However, their capital base and earnings are often lower than those trading in proteins, canned and imported foods and non-food consumer goods. Clearly the scale of operations and the capital base are critical determinants of whether the activity is itinerant, that is, whether the items are being hawked around neighbourhoods, in the markets or along the streets, or if it is done from a stationary point, for example, in the sun, in an open shed shared by others, in shop-fronts and on pavements, in kiosks or small shops of various sizes. Whether the enterprise is wholesale or retail and whether it involves travelling within the region or further afield are also a function of the capital base of the traders. All these different factors affect livelihood outcomes (Darkwah 2002).

Processes such as industrial subcontracting, which have helped to create informal economy employment, have been significant in only a few sub-Saharan African countries such as South Africa and Cote d'Ivoire mainly because of their history of industrialization. Instead, subcontracting has been mostly between commercial firms in the formal economy and traders in the informal economy, the latter retailing the products procured by the former (Brand et al. 1995; Meagher and Yunusa 1996; Rogerson 1997).

Several elements of the growth of the urban informal economy have raised grounds for concern. While manufacturing and construction have shrunk, the growth of trade in goods and services has been identified as a sign of the crisis of the informal economy. Also, it has been pointed out that those areas which are expanding are those at the level of sub-subsistence, or what has been also described as survivalist. These have been distinguished from the microaccumulation or growth enterprises (Chhachhi and Pittin 1996; Rogerson 1997). In other words, microenterprises employing one to five workers and apprentices, technicians and artisans are not growing at the same pace as hawking, petty trading and domestic work. Thus the growth of the informal economy is a process of replicating existing enterprises and activities instead of these growing through the upgrading of capital, skills and technologies and employing a greater number of people. A 1993 study of seven Eastern and Southern African countries, cited in Rogerson, found that over 90 per cent of informal enterprises had fewer than five workers, at least 50 per cent of them having only one person (Rogerson 1997). The studies of the urban informal economy in Lesotho, Angola, Zambia, South Africa and Namibia show that women are overrepresented in the sub-subsistence enterprises and underrepresented in the growth enterprises. It is these sub-subsistence enterprises which were hardest hit by the saturation which has occurred under SAPs. Also, they continue to be involved in a narrower range of activities than men.

Within informal enterprises, increases in prices of inputs and the credit squeeze resulting from fiscal and monetary policies and trade liberalization have led to tremendous jumps in their capital requirements. Many of the much touted characteristics of the informal sector—smaller capital requirements and ease of entry—are being undermined in relation to micro and small-scale enterprises. Problems with capital have been exacerbated by the cumbersome processes involved in accessing formal credit, unfavourable conditionalities and the social stigma associated with borrowing. Those enterprises which rely on imported inputs and equipment have turned to local, poorer quality substitutes, lowering the quality of their own products, and in many cases, unable to increase or sustain existing levels of production (Adedokun et al. 2000). Many of the activities that constitute informal livelihoods depend on demand from wage workers and other formal economy operators. Therefore the expansion of the informal economy to the point of saturation, when the formal economy is contracting, raises questions about its sustainability. With the formal urban wage so low, the competition for its patronage in the informal economy has become very fierce.

## SUMMARY AND CONCLUSIONS

This chapter has highlighted urban women's livelihoods in sub-Saharan Africa within the context of growing informalization of labour relations attributed to economic liberalization programmes and an accompanying shift in policy attitudes towards the informal economy. The chapter discussed the difficulties of mapping and accounting for the informal economy, which have been only partially reduced by improvements in data collection arising from the ILO's adoption of the term the informal economy which consists of both informal enterprises and informal labour relations.

A key concern in the chapter is the exponential growth of the informal economy, particularly its survivalist segments, which are largely concerned with trade in goods and services and which are dominated by women. The gendered nature of the informal economy in sub-Saharan Africa—in enterprise structure, labour relations and spatial construction—have been a running theme of the chapter. How this came to be was outlined in a brief discussion of historical patterns which showed that long-term segregation of work, discrimination in labour markets, access to resources and the burden of reproductive work all accounted for women's dominance in these segments of the informal economy. The chapter identified differences in the analysis of women's location in the informal economy, highlighting the structuralist and voluntarist approaches and arguing that both positions were partial and each should be seen as a corrective of the other. As the history of women's involvement in the informal economy showed, colonial discriminatory policies, which saw a consensus between the colonial state and traditional authorities to control women's mobility and sexuality, kept them out of the commercial, administrative and industrial labour. Women responded to these challenges by migrating to urban areas where they rendered domestic service to men and engaged in informal commerce, and thus became the backbone of the distribution trade in many important African cities. In the chapter, certain differences in the informal economies and in women's location in these economies between West Africa and Eastern and Southern Africa were identified. This issue could not be fully explored for lack of research data and space.

The impacts of the economic crises of the 1970s and economic liberalization and adjustment since the 1980s on the informal economy and its livelihoods were examined. Policies such as the rationalization of public sector employment, privatization of state-owned enterprises, trade and investment liberalization, labour market reforms and the neglect of industrialization and employment were discussed for their indirect and direct impacts on the informal economy. It was argued that while the direct impacts of these policies on the informal economy have not been extensively studied, existing studies suggest that the informal economy is suffering from reduced demand for its products, reduced revenues and an impaired ability to employ wage labour. The upshot of all these processes were the growth in demographic urbanization without industrialization, processes of informalization which were affecting both formal and informal enterprises and industries, and the amendment of state policies in recognition of the increasing importance of the informal economy. All of these buttressed the exponential growth of the informal, particularly its survivalist segments. While women's labour force participation had increased over the years, informalization had resulted in the feminization of labour in both the formal and informal economies, often blurring the distinctions between them. Two situations of informalization in the formal economy—the labour regimes of a formal economy industry ravaged by retrenchments and new labour policies, and the straddling strategies of women working in the formal economy—were discussed to highlight the nature of informalization, the similarities and differentials in impacts on men and women in terms of entry, participation, conditions of work and security as well as livelihood outcomes. The discussion concluded that straddling the formal and informal economies offered locational, supplementary and indirect advantages to the few who were able to adopt this strategy. The hardest hit by informalization processes are the smallest or survivalist self-employed operators of the urban informal economy, most of whom are women. They were competing with workers straddling the formal–informal divide and new entrants into the informal economy.

The last substantive section of the chapter provided an account of women's livelihoods in the urban economy. The chapter argued that in spite of their specificities, several urban informal economies in sub-Saharan Africa shared similarities in their composition and their gender segregation and segmentation. Except for those countries where women are secluded, urban informal economies were composed of food and non-food trading sectors dominated by women, artisanal services which were gender segregated, manufacturing and construction services which were dominated by men, and urban agriculture in which both men and women were increasingly involved. Complicating these gender differences were hierarchies related to capital base and scale of operations and labour relations. It was noted that there were three elements of the growth of the informal economy which were matters of concern: the growth of the informal in the face of the shrinking formal economies; the growth of trade in goods and services at the expense of manufacturing and construction; and the growth in its survivalist segments as opposed to its growth segments.

The implications of these changes have been experienced in particular ways by women, whose quality of life and livelihoods were at risk from the growth of urban poverty. This situation requires a major rethinking of economic and social policies beyond PRSPs, debates about formalizing informal enterprises and creating decent work. Such strategies need to tackle the enduring gender, class and regional discrimination and arrest trends such as demographic urbanization and the informalization of work.

## NOTES

1. The term demographic urbanization distinguishes urbanization which involves only population growth from urbanization which is also accompanied by socioeconomic changes and infrastructural developments.
2. Home industries in Zimbabwe are distinguished from home-based enterprises which take place within the housing unit. These are "located in officially designated industrial estates set aside for the informal sector units" (Kamete 2004:120).
3. The issue of legality, however, is complicated. At a recent regional conference on formalizing informal enterprises in Africa, organized by the Foreign Investment Advisory Service (FIAS) of the World Bank, participants noted that the legality of enterprises was along a continuum with enterprises having different shades of informality (FIAS-ISSER 2007).
4. The international definition of the informal sector that was adopted by the 1993 International Conference of Labour Statisticians (ICLS) included only those who work in informal enterprises. The new expanded definition of informal employment has been endorsed by the 2002 International Conference of Labour Statisticians (ILO 2002:11).
5. See ILO (2002) for a detailed list of the different kinds of employment in these three categories.
6. For example, the ICLS.
7. For example, the International Classification of Status in Employment (ICSE).
8. Three forms of illegality or extra-legality of informal settlements are identified by Hansen and Vaa (2004). These relate to the illegal occupation of customary and statutory land, the subdivision of land or conversion of land to uses against planning regulations and construction of buildings without permission or against planning regulations.
9. The Central Statistical Office in Zambia is said to have reported in 1997 that 50 per cent of those in the informal economy work from home, and this was not only in poor neighbourhoods. While this statistic is probably based on an enterprise definition of the informal, it points to an important issue which city planners often ignore. This trend has been attributed to either planning failures, lack of formal employment or its reduced appeal or the growth of poverty across all social groups (Kazimbaya-Senkwe 2004:100).

10. The regulatory element pertains to state control of the use of space, work conditions and safety, rent control, labour relations, access to energy, other utilities, and infrastructure, and taxation. Economic relations include participation in production and distribution chains, the sharing of an overlapping labour pool and skills, credit, infrastructure and other resources produced in one or other economy, while the social refers to their sharing of the production and use of social goods such as health, education and social security.

11. Other forms of segmentation in the informal economy are based on caste, ethnicity, region, training and occupation (Baud 1993).

12. A study in the Zambia Copperbelt they cite found that very few women tenants were able to purchase the houses which were privatized because of their lack of credit (Chellah 2001, cited in Hansen and Vaa 2004:12).

13. Kazimbaya-Senkwe (2004) argues that home-based work reduces production costs, allows the use of non-market resources such as neighbourhood networks in times of need and enables children to benefit from free skills training and income-generation opportunities not available in formal settings.

14. The early improvements in manufacturing have been put down to the short-term restoration of supply of inputs to existing industries which had not been able to source them because of the economic crisis. As liberalization deepened and the climate became more competitive, firms used up their excess capacities and began to stagnate, and this was reflected in the general deceleration of industrial growth.

15. Global Urban Observatory, 2003:25, cited in Davis (2004:16).

16. Feminization of the labour force is manifested in various ways: the increase in female labour force participation rates relative to men; the substitution of men by women who take over traditional "male" jobs; an increase of women's involvement in invisible work such as family labour and home-working; and changing the character of industrial work on the basis of new technologies and managerial strategies whereby work is decentralized, low paid, irregular, with part-time or temporary labour contracts making them increasingly like women's work but not necessarily done by women (Chhachhi and Pittin 1996:8).

17. Home-based workers are those who carry out market work at home or in adjacent premises whether as self-employed or as paid workers. Home-workers are those home-based workers who do paid work for others usually on a piece-rate basis (ILO 2002:44; Pearson 2003).

18. It has been pointed out that government intervention in the economy, particularly in labour markets, has been decreasing over the same period that informalization has been rising (Heintz and Pollin 2003).

19. The relationship between economic growth and informalization, however, is not straightforward. Baud (1993) argues that growth on its own does not address the problem of informalization in the absence of explicit conditions directed at the labour markets.

20. Activities involved minor consultations and drug sales to patients within the health workers' area of residence, the sale of drugs within hospital premises during working hours, rural home-care nursing during the week and after working hours, and a combination of informal health care and trading in other consumer goods.

21. The situation is largely similar to Zimbabwe where 75 per cent of women's enterprises were in clothing, textiles, crochet and basket-making, while in Lesotho, 50 per cent of 500 women surveyed were engaged in food and textiles (Carr 1993).

# REFERENCES

Adedokun, O., O. Akande, A. Carim, and N. Nelson-Twakor. 2000. "Economic liberalisation and women in the informal sector in rural Nigeria." In D. Tsikata and J. Kerr (eds.), *Demanding Dignity: Women Confronting Economic Reform in Africa.* The North South Institute and Third World Network-Africa, Ottawa and Accra.

Adu-Amankwah, K. 1999. "Ghana, in trade unions in the informal sector: Finding their bearings." *Labour Education*, No. 116. ILO, Geneva.

Akyeampong, E. and S. Agyei-Mensah. 2006. "Itinerant gold mines? Mobility, sexuality and the spread of gonorrhea and syphilis in twentieth century Ghana." In C. Oppong, M.Y.P.A. Oppong and I.K. Odotei (eds.), *Sex and Gender in an Era of AIDS: Ghana at the Turn of the Millennium.* Sub-Saharan Publishers, Legon, Accra.

Allman, J. 1996. "Rounding up spinsters: Gender chaos and unmarried women in colonial Asante." *The Journal of African History*, Vol. 37, No. 2, pp. 195–214.

Bakker, I. 1994. "Introduction: Engendering macro-economic policy reform in the era of global restructuring and adjustment." In I. Bakker (ed.), *The Strategic Silence: Gender and Economic Policy.* Zed Books in association with North South Institute, London and Ottawa.

Banda, M. and G. Nyirongo. 1996. "Zambia: The informal sector in a beleaguered economy." In G.C.Z. Mhone (ed.), *The Informal Sector in Southern Africa: An Analysis of Conceptual Research, and Policy Issues.* Southern Africa Regional Institute for Policy Studies, SAPES Books, Mount Pleasant, Harare.

Bangura, Y. 1997. *Policy Dialogue and Gendered Development: Institutional and Ideological Constraints.* Discussion Paper No. 87, UNRISD, Geneva.

Barwa, S.D. 1995. *Structural Adjustment Programmes and the Urban Informal Sector in Ghana.* Issues in Development Discussion Paper No. 3, ILO, Geneva.

Baud, I. 1993. "Introduction." In I.S.A. Baud and G.A. De Bruijne (eds.), *Gender, Small-Scale Industry and Development Policy.* Intermediate Technology Publications, London.

Beneria, L. 2001. *Shifting the Risk: New Employment Patterns, Informalization, and Women's Work.* Mimeo, Cornell University, New York.

Brand, V., R. Mupedziswa and P. Gumbo. 1995. "Structural adjustment, women and informal trade in Harare." In P. Gibbon (ed.), *Structural Adjustment and the Working Poor in Zimbabwe.* Scandinavian Institute of African Studies, Uppsala.

Carr, M. 1993. "Women in S-scale industries—Some lessons from Africa." In I.S.A. Baud and G.A. De Bruijne (eds.), *Gender, Small-Scale Industry and Development Policy.* Intermediate Technology Publications, London.

Chant, S. 2007. *Gender, Cities, and the Millennium Development Goals in the Global South.* New Series Working Paper, Issue 21, LSE Gender Institute, London.

Charmes, J. 1998. *Women Working in the Informal Sector in Africa: New Methods and Data.* Paper prepared for the United Nations Statistics Division, The Gender and Development Programme of UNDP and Women in Informal Employment: Globalizing and Organising (WIEGO). ORSTOM, Paris, October 1998.

Chen, M. 2006. "Rethinking the informal economy: Linkages with the formal economy and the formal regulatory environment." In B. Guha-Khasnobis, R. Kanbur and E. Ostrom (eds.), *Linking the Formal and Informal Economy, Concepts and Measures.* Oxford University Press, Oxford.

Chhachhi, A. and R. Pittin. 1996. "Introduction." In A. Chhachhi and R. Pittin (eds.), *Confronting State, Capital and Patriarchy: Women Organizing in the Process of Industrialization.* Macmillan, London.

Clark, G. 1994. *Onions Are My Husband: Survival and Accumulation by West African Market Women.* University of Chicago Press, Chicago, IL.

Darkwah, A.K. 2002. "Trading goes global: Ghanaian market women in an era of globalization." *Asian Women*, Vol. 15, pp. 31–47.

Davis, M. 2004. "Planet of slums: Urban involution and the informal proletariat." *New Left Review*, Vol. 26, March/April, pp. 5–34.

Deedat, H. 2003. *Women Workers in the Leather and Footwear Industry in South Africa*. Research Report, GERA Programme, Third World Network-Africa, Accra North.

Dennis, C. 1987. "Women and the state in Nigeria: The case of the federal military government 1984–85." In H. Afshar (ed.), *Women, State and Ideology—Studies from Africa and Asia*. Macmillan, London.

Elson, D. 1999. "Labor markets as gendered institutions: Equality, efficiency and empowerment issues." *World Development*, Vol. 27, No. 3, pp. 611–627.

Foreign Investment Advisory Service–Institute of Statistical, Social and Economic Research (FIAS-ISSER). 2007. *Preliminary Report of a FIAS-ISSER Regional Conference on the Formalisation of Informal Enterprises, 8–10th January 2007, Accra*. Mimeo: FIAS, www.fias.net/ifcext/fias.nsf/content/InformalityHome.

Gaidzanwa, R.B. 1996. "The ideology of domesticity and the struggles adjustment programme." In A. Chhachhi and R. Pittin (eds.), *Confronting State, Capital and Patriarchy, Women Organizing in the Process of Industrialization*. Macmillan, London.

Global Urban Observatory, 2003. *Slums of the World: The Face of Urban Poverty in the New Millennium*, UN-Habitat, New York.

Gugler, J. 1989. "Women stay on the farm no more: Changing patterns of rural-urban migration in sub-Saharan Africa." *The Journal of Modern African Studies*, Vol. 27, No. 2, pp. 347–352.

Hansen, K.T. 2004. "Who rules the streets? The politics of vending space in Lusaka." In K.T. Hansen and M. Vaa (eds.), *Reconsidering Informality: Perspectives from Urban Africa*. Nordiska Africainstitutet, Uppsala.

Hansen, K.T. and M. Vaa. 2004. "Introduction." In K.T. Hansen and M. Vaa (eds.), *Reconsidering Informality: Perspectives from Urban Africa*. Nordiska Africainstitutet, Uppsala.

Hart, K. 2007. *The African Revolution: Urban Commerce and the Informal Economy*. Opening Lecture of the ISSER-Merchant Bank Lecture Series 2007, University of Ghana, Accra, 8 January.

Heintz, J. and R. Pollin. 2003. *Information, Economic Growth and the Challenge of Creating Viable Labor Standards in Developing Countries*. Working Paper Series, No. 60, Political Economy Research Institute (PERI), University of Massachusetts, Amherst, MA, June.

International Labour Organization (ILO). 2002. *Women and Men in the Informal Economy: A Statistical Picture*. ILO, Geneva. www.ilo.Org/Public/English/Employment/Gems, accessed in 2003.

———. 1991. *The Dilemma of the Informal Sector*. Report of the Director General, International Labour Conference, 78th Session, ILO, Geneva.

Jamal, V. and J. Weeks. 1993. *Africa Misunderstood*. Macmillan, London.

Kamete, A.Y. 2004. "Home industries and the formal city in Harare, Zimbabwe." In K.T. Hansen and M. Vaa (eds.), *Reconsidering Informality: Perspectives from Urban Africa*. Nordiska Africainstitutet, Uppsala.

Kazimbaya-Senkwe, B.M. 2004. "Home based enterprises in a period of economic restructuring in Zambia." In K.T. Hansen and M. Vaa (eds.), *Reconsidering Informality: Perspectives from Urban Africa*. Nordiska Africainstitutet, Uppsala.

King, R. and A. Oppong. 2000. "Influencing policy: Urban market women and the Kumasi central market." In D. Tsikata and J. Kerr (eds.), *Demanding Dignity:*

*Women Confronting Economic Reform in Africa*. The North South Institute and Third World Network-Africa, Ottawa and Accra.

Lourenço-Lindell, I. 2004. "Trade and the politics of informalisation in Bissau, Guinea-Bissau." In K.T. Hansen and M. Vaa (eds.), *Reconsidering Informality: Perspectives from Urban Africa*. Nordiska Africainstitutet, Uppsala.

Mbiba, B. 1994. "Institutional responses to uncontrolled urban cultivation in Harare: Prohibitive or accommodative?" *Environment and Urbanisation*, Vol. 6, pp. 188–202.

Meagher, K. and M. Yunusa. 1996. *Passing the Buck: Structural Adjustment and the Nigerian Urban Informal Sector*. Discussion Paper No. 75, UNRISD, Geneva.

Mhone, G.C.Z. 1996. "Conceptual and analytical issues." In G.C.Z. Mhone (ed.), *The Informal Sector in Southern Africa: An Analysis of Conceptual Research and Policy Issues*. Southern Africa Regional Institute for Policy Studies, SAPES Books, Harare.

Mkandawire, T. and C.C. Soludo. 1999. *Our Continent, Our Future: African Perspectives on Structural Adjustment*. CODESRIA and Africa World Press, Inc., Dakar and New Jersey.

Ndoro, H. 1996. "Zimbabwe: The informal sector in decontrolling formerly 'Socialist' economy." In G.C.Z. Mhone (ed.), *The Informal Sector in Southern Africa: An Analysis of Conceptual, Research and Policy Issues*. Southern Africa Regional Institute for Policy Studies, SAPES Books, Harare.

Ngwira, A.B. 1996. "Malawi: The informal sector in an inequitable and statist market economy." In G.C.Z. Mhone (ed.), *The Informal Sector in Southern Africa: An Analysis of Conceptual, Research and Policy Issues*. Southern Africa Regional Institute for Policy Studies, SAPES Books, Harare.

Niger-Thomas Agbaw, M. 2000. *"Buying Futures": The Upsurge of Female Entrepreneurship Crossing the Formal/Informal Divide in South West Cameroon*. PhD thesis, CNWS Research School, University of Leiden.

Olukoshi, A.O. 1998. *The Elusive Prince of Denmark: Structural Adjustment and the Crisis of Governance in Africa*. Nordiska Afrikainstitutet, Uppsala.

Omari, C.K. 1995. *Women in the Informal Sector*. Professorial Inaugural Lecture, Dar es Salaam University Press, Dar es Salaam.

Pape, J. 2000. *Gender and Globalisation in South Africa: Some Preliminary Reflections on Working Women and Poverty*. International Labour Resource and Information Group, Cape Town.

Pearson, R. 2003. *The Global Context: Home-Based Work and Policy Options*. Leeds: Mimeo, Home Workers Worldwide Mapping Project, August.

———. 1998. "Nimble fingers revisited: Reflections on women and Third World industrialisation in the late twentieth century." In C. Jackson and R. Pearson (eds.), *Feminist Visions of Development: Research, Analysis and Policy*. Routledge, London.

Potts, D. 1997. "Urban lives: Adopting new strategies and adapting rural links." In C. Rakodi (ed.), *The Urban Challenge in Africa: Growth and Management of Its Large Cities*. United Nations University Press, Paris and Tokyo.

Rakodi, C. 1997. "Global forces, urban change and urban management in Africa." In C. Rakodi (ed.), *The Urban Challenge in Africa: Growth and Management of Its Large Cities*. United Nations University Press, Paris and Tokyo.

Roberts, P. 1987. "The state and the regulation of marriage: Sefwi Wiawso (Ghana), 1900–1940." In H. Afshah (ed.), *Women, State and Ideology: Studies from Africa and Asia*. Macmillan, London.

Robertson, C. 1983. "The death of Makola and other tragedies." *Canadian Journal of African Studies*, Vol. 17, No. 3, pp. 469–495.

Rogerson, C.M. 1997. "Globalization or informalization? African urban economies in the 1990s." In C. Rakodi (ed.), *The Urban Challenge in Africa: Growth and Management of Its Large Cities*. United Nations University Press, Paris and Tokyo.

Sethuraman, S.V. 1998. *Gender, Informality and Poverty: A Global Review— Gender Bias in Female Informal Employment and Incomes in Developing Countries*. Poverty Reduction and Economic Management, World Bank, Washington, DC, and WIEGO, Geneva.

Sparr, P. (ed.). 1994. *Mortgaging Women's Lives: Feminist Critiques of Structural Adjustment*. Zed Books, London.

Tati, G. 2004. "Sharing public space in Pointe-Noire, Congo-Brazzaville: Immigrant fishermen and a multi-national oil company." In K.T. Hansen and M. Vaa (eds.), *Reconsidering Informality: Perspectives from Urban Africa*. Nordiska Africainstitutet, Uppsala.

Teszler, R. 1993. "Small-scale industry's contribution to economic development." In I.S.A. Baud and G.A. De Bruijne (eds.), *Gender, Small-Scale Industry and Development Policy*. Intermediate Technology Publications, London.

Tripp, A.M. 1997. *Changing the Rules: The Politics of Liberalisation and the Urban Informal Economy in Tanzania*. University of California Press, Berkeley and London.

Tsikata, D. 1997. "Gender equality and the state in Ghana: Some issues of policy and practice." In A. Imam, A. Mama and F. Sow (eds.), *Engendering African Social Sciences*. CODESRIA Book Series, Dakar.

Tsikata, D. and J. Kerr. 2000. "Introduction." In D. Tsikata and J. Kerr, with Cathy Blacklock and Joycelyn Laforce (eds.), *Demanding Dignity: Women Confronting Economic Reforms in Africa*. North South Institute, Third World Network-Africa, Ottawa and Accra.

UN-Habitat. 2003. *The Challenge of the Slums: Global Report on Human Settlements*. UN-Habitat, London.

Whitehead, A. and D. Tsikata. 2003. "Policy discourses on women's land rights in sub-Saharan Africa." *Journal of Agrarian Change*, Vol. 3, Nos. 1 and 2, pp. 67–112.

World Confederation of Labour (WCL). 1999. *Gender and Informal Sector*. WCL Women and Work Department, Brussels.

# 6 Informalization and Women's Workforce Participation
## A Consideration of Recent Trends in Asia

*Jayati Ghosh*

## INTRODUCTION

The countries of the Asian region differ in size, resource endowment, the nature of the ruling regimes, particular social and political configurations, conditions of poverty and human development, patterns of constraints and features such as the extent of internal political conflict. Despite these differences, there is some commonality of economic experience across these very disparate countries, and there are also similarities in the types of economic strategy that have been pursued over time. Indeed, the apparent synchronicity of economic policies and processes across the region, despite very different histories and widely varying external and internal social and political pressures, is quite remarkable.

All the economies of the region had import-substituting industrialization strategies, with the attendant development of some industry and associated dualism in the economy, as well as regulation of much economic activity, for some decades after the mid-twentieth century. In some countries, notably in East Asia, these policies were associated with "developmental states" that were very successful in the project of industrialization. In other countries, especially in South Asia, the strategy did lead to some degree of economic diversification, but structural weaknesses persisted and meant that the development project fwas largely incomplete. These differences, in turn, can be traced, at least partly, to the fact that the more successful economies were those in which some asset redistribution (typically through land reform) had broken the power of previously existing monopolies to retard development, whereas in the less successful countries traditional structures continued to inhibit growth. In addition, developmental states in Asia paid much greater attention to improving the quality of the workforce through substantial public investment in health and education services, unlike countries in South Asia where health and education provision was generally underfunded and continues to be inadequate.

While some of the developmental states of East Asia were export oriented from the 1960s onwards, the emphasis on export-led growth permeated to the rest of Asia in stages. And this, in turn, was associated with much more extensive liberalization of other aspects of the economy. From the 1980s onwards, almost all of the countries of Asia moved, to varying degrees, to a strategy of development based on export orientation, internal deregulation, trade liberalization and privatization. Subsequently, and more strongly from the early 1990s, almost all the governments in the region went through fairly comprehensive policies of internal and external liberalization, reduction of direct state responsibility for the funding and provision of a range of goods and services, and privatization of state assets and public utilities.

The explicit aims of a process of economic reform such as has characterized most Asian countries have been: (i) to do away with, or substantially reduce, controls on capacity creation, production and prices, and let market forces influence the investment and operational decisions of domestic and foreign economic agents within the domestic tariff area; (ii) to allow international competition and therefore international relative prices to influence economic decisions; (iii) to reduce the presence of state agencies in production and trade; and (iv) to liberalize the financial sector by reducing controls on the banking system, allowing for the proliferation of financial institutions and instruments and permitting foreign entry into the financial sector. These were all based on the notion that greater freedom given to private agents and market functioning would ensure more efficient and more dynamic outcomes. The government's aim was also to restructure production toward areas of international "comparative advantage" (defined in static rather than dynamic terms). These areas were seen as inherently more labour-intensive, which led to the further prediction that, after an initial brief period of net job loss, such a strategy of trade liberalization would actually create more employment over time in more sustainable ways.

These aims translated into successive changes in the pattern of regulation in different sectors as well as in aggregate macroeconomic policies, and typically involved the following policy changes, to differing degrees in different countries:

- reduction in direct state control in terms of administered prices and regulation of economic activity;
- privatization of state assets, often in controversial circumstances;
- rationalization and reduction of direct and indirect tax-rates, which became associated with declining tax–gross domestic product (GDP) ratios;
- attempts to reduce fiscal deficits which usually involved cutting back on public productive investment as well as certain types of social expenditure, reducing subsidies to farmers and increasing user charges for public services and utilities;
- trade liberalization, involving shifts from quantitative restrictions to tariffs and typically sharp reductions in the average rate of tariff protection, as well as withdrawal of export subsidies;

- financial liberalization, involving reductions in directed credit, freeing of interest rate ceilings and other measures which raised the real cost of borrowing, including for the government;
- shift to market-determined exchange rates and liberalization of current account transactions;
- capital account liberalization, including easing of rules for foreign direct investment (FDI), permissions for non-residents to hold domestic financial assets, easier access to foreign commercial borrowing by domestic firms and in some cases even freedom for domestic residents to hold limited foreign assets.

This commonality of policy experience meant, in turn, that outcomes were also quite similar in most of the economies, despite the very different initial conditions in the different economies, and also notwithstanding the varying institutional and political conditions that have operated in the different countries. First, in terms of clearly positive results, there has been some increase in private investment in all of these countries due to the immediate effects of liberalization and increased export orientation. Growth rates on average have typically increased and the Asian region has been the most economically dynamic region of the world for the past decade and more. However, this has been associated with increasing inequalities of income in all the economies of the region. These growing inequalities are evident in terms of differences between rural and urban residents; between subregions within countries, between different economic classes and, of course, across the gender divide. The widening of income gaps has also in some cases been associated with increased social and political tensions, which have often been expressed not so much as direct demands for redressal of income imbalances, but in terms of ethnic, social, cultural or regional demands.

Despite the aggregate growth, across most of the countries in the region there has been deceleration of employment generation. In general, employment generation has not kept pace with the increase in population, and in several countries this has expressed itself not only in higher rates of unemployment and underemployment, but also in declining labour force participation, which is not fully explained by increased involvement in education. Further, the quality of employment appears to have deteriorated, with declines in regular work and increases in either casual contracts or self-employment in adverse conditions. Wage shares of income have typically declined and in some countries real wage rates have stagnated or declined despite the economic growth.

These changes have had direct and indirect effects on the conditions affecting women, in ways that are by now well documented. In terms of conditions of work, the most obvious changes have been: a phase of increase in female employment in some export-oriented industries, followed by a relative decline in such work; the growing insecurity and casualization of work contracts, and much greater dependence upon informal work; the increase in women's unpaid labour because of policies and processes that reduce public provision of important goods and services. This chapter will examine one of these outcomes—the issue of informal work—in more detail. In the next section, some conceptual issues involved in understanding the nature, and measuring the extent, of women's work are briefly discussed. In the third section, the macroeconomic processes which form the context for changing work patterns of women are described. The fourth section takes up the issue of export-oriented employment, and the fifth section discusses services employment. The concluding section considers some implications for public policy.

## CONCEPTUAL ISSUES IN ASSESSING WOMEN'S WORK

Work defines the conditions of human existence in many ways. This may be even more true for women than for men, because the responsibility for social reproduction—which largely devolves upon women in most societies—ensures that the vast majority of women are inevitably involved in some kind of productive and/or reproductive activity. Despite this, in mainstream discussion, the importance of women's work generally receives marginal treatment simply because so much of the work regularly performed is "invisible" in terms of market criteria or even in terms of socially dominant perceptions of what constitutes "work". This obviously matters, because it leads to the social underestimation of women's productive contribution. Even more importantly, as a result, inadequate attention is typically devoted to the *conditions* of women's work and their implications for the general material conditions and well-being of women.

This is particularly true in developing countries, where patterns of market integration and the relatively high proportion of goods and services that are not marketed have implied that female contributions to productive activity extend well beyond those which are socially recognized, and that the conditions under which many of these contributions are made entail significant pressure on women in a variety of ways. In almost all societies, and particularly in developing countries, there remain essential but usually unpaid activities (such as housework and childcare and community-based activities) which are seen as the responsibility of the women of the household. This social allocation tends to operate regardless of other work that women may perform. For working women in lower income groups, it is particularly difficult to find outside labour to substitute for household-based tasks, which therefore tend to devolve upon young girls and aged women within the household or to put further pressure on the workload of the women workers themselves. In fact, as Elson (1987) has pointed out, it is wrong to assume that unpaid tasks by women would continue to be performed regardless of the way resources and incomes are allocated. "Gender neutral" economic policies may thus imply possible breaking-points within the household or the collapse of women's capacity. Social provision for at least a significant part of such services and tasks, or changes in the gender-wise division of labour with respect to household tasks, therefore become important considerations when women are otherwise employed.

This makes the consideration of work participation by women a more complex matter than is often recognized. Since most women are actually engaged in some kind of productive/reproductive work, whether or not this is recognized and quantified by statistics, the issues relating to female employment are qualitatively different from those of male employment. Thus, the unemployment-poverty link which has been noted for men in developing countries is not so direct and evident for women: Many women are fully employed and still remain poor in absolute terms, and adding to their workload will not necessarily improve their material conditions. Nor is the pressing policy concern that of simply increasing the volume of explicit female employment, since simply adding on recognized "jobs" may in fact lead to a double burden upon women whose household obligations still have to be fulfilled. Instead, concern has to be focused upon the *quality*, the *recognition* and the *remuneration* of women's work in developing countries, as well as the *conditions* facilitating it, such as alternative arrangements for household work and child-care. All of these are critically affected by broader economic policies as well as by government interventions at micro and meso levels, in ways that will be elaborated in the following. And it is these together which determine whether or not increased labour market activity by women is associated with genuine improvements in their economic circumstances.

The relative invisibility of much of women's work has been the focus of a substantial amount of discussion. Since many of the activities associated with household maintenance, provisioning and reproduction—which are typically performed by women or female children—are not subject to explicit market relations, there is an inherent tendency to ignore the actual productive contribution of these activities. Similarly, social norms, values and perceptions also operate to render most household-based activity "invisible". This invisibility gets directly transferred to data inadequacies, making officially generated data in most countries (and particularly in developing countries) very rough and imprecise indicators of the actual productive contribution of women.

All this means that the data on the labour force participation of women are notoriously inaccurate. Not only are the problems of undercounting and invisibility rife, but there are often substantial variations in data across countries which may not reflect actual differences but simply distinct methods of estimation. Further, even statistics over time for the same country may alter dramatically, as a result of changed definitions of what constitutes "economically active" or because of more probing questions put to women, or simply due to greater sensitivity on the part of the investigators.[1]

The impact of social structures is reflected not merely in the data, but in the actual determination of explicit labour market participation by women.

Thus, in many Asian developing countries social norms determine the choice between participation in production and involvement in reproduction, and consequently inhibit the freedom of women to participate in the job market or engage in other forms of overt self-employment. The limitations on such freedom can take many forms. While the explicit social rules of some societies limit women's access to many areas of public life, the implicit pressures of other supposedly more emancipated societies may operate no less forcefully to direct women into certain prescribed occupational channels. It is also evident that, since the activities of reproduction and care (of children, elderly, sick and so on) put so many and varied demands upon women's labour and time, combining these activities with other forms of productive work is only possible when other members of society (whether within the household or outside it) share the burden, at least partially. The issue of social responsibility for such activities is therefore critical. Certainly, involving women in other forms of work without ensuring for the sharing of tasks and responsibilities associated with child-rearing and household work puts tremendous pressure on both mothers and children.

Notwithstanding these difficulties with the available data, there are some shifts in employment patterns that are so striking and substantial that they cannot be ignored. The most significant change that has occurred for women throughout the developing Asian region since the early 1980s has been the increase in labour force participation rates, which has only recently been followed by a decline in the early years of this century. The earlier pattern was similar to a worldwide pattern of increasing work participation of women, but the Asian experience was somewhat different, in that (unlike, say, Latin America) the increasing work participation of women was part of—and even led—the general employment boom created by export-led economic expansion. It has been suggested (Horton 1995) that over a longer period the pattern of labour force participation among women in various Asian countries shows a U-shaped curve, first decreasing with urbanization (as women stop working on family farms and on other household production activities) and then rising again once the demographic transition is completed. Clearly, however, what happened in many countries of Asia was a sharper and more decisive process than this more gradual long-term tendency, which is discussed in more detail in the second section of this chapter.

Assessing women's work in the informal sector is even more complicated. The informal sector has typically been categorized as a residual, catch-all sector, of all economic activities outside the "formal", "organized" or "registered" sectors. One of the major problems with studying informal sector employment of both men and women is the sheer difficulty of defining, identifying and quantifying it. Because the sector is effectively defined as a residual, it becomes very difficult to piece together any estimates of aggregate employment, and much of the information is necessarily based on micro-level studies which can yield valuable qualitative data even if not much in terms of aggregate analysis. In the case of women workers, as noted earlier, the problem is further complicated by the fact that so much of their informal work is unrecognized and unpaid, and therefore does not enter many standard labour force and employment indicators.

The early perception of these activities was that they reflected the failure of the organized or formal sector to generate sufficient employment, and that those who could not find paid work in the formal sector were therefore forced into informal activities. However, from the 1970s, more positive definitions of the informal sector have emerged. Among the first such was from the International Labour Organization (ILO), which in 1972 defined the main characteristics of the informal sector as ease of entry; reliance on local resources; family ownership of enterprises; small-scale operations; labour-intensive work, using adaptive technologies; use of skills acquired outside school; an irregular and competitive market. The ILO discussion incorporated the idea—new for its time—that this informal sector had untapped development potential because of its flexibility and potential for creative responses to economic change. Subsequent discussions have tended to take this more positive angle, and have stressed the idea of the informal sector as opportunity rather than failure.

Despite this recent more positive spin, there is no question that typically work in the informal sector is less remunerative and under conditions which are inferior to organized sector work, even when it is home-based or in very small family-owned units. There is much greater vulnerability of workers who are outside the reach of labour legislation or trade union organization, and within this, women workers are particularly vulnerable. It has been noted that the only real specificity of the informal sector is the absence of workers' rights and social protection. In every other sense, formal and informal work form an integral whole, and much of what is the "formal" sector today relies on informal activities, through subcontracting and related arrangements, simply so that employers can take advantage of the absence of workers' rights to ensure much lower wage shares than would otherwise be the case.

More recent work by the ILO, especially in the context of its formulation of "decent work", shares this perspective. In 2002, the ILO argued for defining the informal economy as "comprising the marginalized economic units and workers who are characterized by serious deficits in decent work—labour standard deficits, productivity and job quality deficits, and organization and voice deficits. Reducing these deficits in the informal economy will promote the transition to recognized, protected, legal—and, therefore, 'formal'—activities and ensure decent work" (ILO 2002a:4–5).

The influential work of de Soto (2000) has paved the way for another slightly newer attitude to informal sector activities, which is that their expansion and development into formal activities are constrained by the lack of an adequate legal institutional framework for property rights. The non-recognition of some forms of property which are effectively controlled, if not formally owned, reduces access to institutional credit because it cannot be used as collateral. This perception is also evident in the *Report of the World Commission on the Social Dimensions of Globalization* which argues that "the legalization of *de facto* property rights is therefore a vital step in the transformation of the informal economy" (ILO 2004:61).

This position assumes that the informal economy is inherently vibrant, flexible and dynamic, and that it can effectively compete with larger units in the "formal sector" once constraints such as credit access are removed. Such an understanding assumes away a number of features and problems typically associated with informal sector activities. First, market access is not fundamentally dependent upon legal status—it does tend to be affected by size simply because of the organizational economies of scale involved. Increased access to markets by tiny and cottage units therefore has almost always required some degree of cooperation across units or involvement with a larger unit or public intervention through marketing bodies. Second, credit access is typically more difficult for all small units, even in the formal sector, not only because of the lack of collateral but because they are perceived to be inherently more risk-prone for a number of other reasons. Third, recognition of de facto property rights (such as land which is squatted upon) is not only fraught with a number of problems, but typically has little or no meaning for a large number of informal sector workers who do not even have this kind of "property" and are engaged in informal activities only because they cannot find work in the formal sector. Most women workers would be in this category.

Fourth, and perhaps most crucially, it is a mistake to assume that all informal activity is effectively self-employment and that employer–workers relationships do not exist in this residual sector. In fact, one of the main attractions of the informal economy for employers is precisely the absence of labour regulation, which allows for more intensive exploitation of workers. This is true in a whole range of service activities, and also in manufacturing which relies on outsourcing to tiny and home-based units. Increasingly, there is tremendous dependence upon so-called "informal sector" production, by units in the so-called "formal sector" through subcontracting and other relationships, so much so that the line has become much harder to draw. This means that the most basic difference between formal and informal "sectors" is not the access to credit or markets, but the absence of labour protection in the informal economy.

It is frequently argued that women are found to be overrepresented in the informal economy because the flexibilities of work involved in such activities, especially in home-based work, are advantageous to women workers, given their other needs and the other demands upon their time in the form of unpaid labour. This is certainly the case to a significant extent, because much employment in the formal economy is based on the "male breadwinner" model that does not give adequate space or freedom to women who are also faced with substantial domestic responsibilities, given the gender construction of societies and the division of labour within households. However, these constraints upon women's time and freedom to choose—which are imposed by society rather than self-created—are exploited by employers to ensure much more work for less pay being performed by women. Thus, home-based work or work in very small enterprises can be for long hours and very demanding in other ways, and with conditions of remuneration (such as piece-rate wages) that effectively ensure the maximum tendency for self-exploitation. In addition, other basic responsibilities of employers, such as minimum safety conditions at work, basic health care and pension provision, are all entirely missing, which constitutes a massive reduction of the effective wage for employers and a substantial loss for workers. The recent tendencies toward greater informalization of women's work must be viewed in this context. In general, these represent retrograde moves from the perspective of women's empowerment in both economic and social terms, and reflect the worsened bargaining power of labour in general in recent years across Asia.

## THE MACROECONOMIC CONTEXT OF WOMEN'S WORK IN ASIA

Several recent processes in the international economy have a direct bearing upon labour markets and work conditions in countries across the world. Despite some revival in growth recently, the world economy is still operating substantially below capacity. Income disparities have greatly increased, both within countries and between countries. In addition, the bulk of the people across the world find themselves in more fragile and vulnerable economic circumstances, in which many of the earlier welfare state provisions have been reduced or removed, public services have been privatized or made more expensive and therefore less accessible. Since 2002, there has been a net transfer of resources from the less developed countries to the developed North, and particularly to the United States, in a reversal of the traditional expectations regarding international capital flows. This follows a period in which the "emerging markets" of developing countries experienced much greater economic and financial volatility because of their exposure to boom-and-bust cycles created by rapid and unsustained capital flows of relatively large magnitudes. Instability has been associated with the growing concentration of ownership and control in the international production and distribution of goods and services, and also among the agents of international finance. Crises in emerging markets are typically associated with further concentration, as the attempt to resolve such crises within the basic neoliberal paradigm have involved further liberalization and privatization, thus allowing the sale of domestic business units to large multinationals. Very recently, there has been an apparent breakdown of multilateralism, with growing reliance on bilateral and regional trade and investment agreements to direct world trade and investment.

These changes in the international economy have affected national and international labour markets. The most significant change is the increase in open unemployment rates across the world. By the turn of the century, unemployment rates in most industrial countries were higher than they had been at any time since the Great Depression of the 1930s. But even more significantly, open unemployment was very high in developing countries, and has continued to grow thereafter. This marks a change, because developing countries have typically had lower open unemployment rates simply because of the lack of social security and unemployment benefits in most such societies, which usually ensures that people undertake some activity, however low paying, and usually in the form of self-employment. Therefore disguised unemployment or underemployment has generally been the more prevalent phenomenon in developing societies. The recent emergence of high open unemployment rates therefore suggests that the problem of finding jobs has become so acute that it is now captured even in such data, and may also herald substantial social changes in the developing world.

The Asian region typically has the lowest rates of open unemployment in the world, but even here, these rates have been historically high and rising, especially in Southeast Asia where it has been as high as 9 per cent in recent years (ILO 2005). Furthermore, in most Asian countries, youth unemployment is particularly high. In many Asian economies, moreover, underemployment continues to be the most significant concern. This is especially true in Southeast and South Asia. In Nepal, underemployment is officially estimated to be as high as half of the workforce, while in Indonesia and the Philippines, disguised unemployment is high and rising, especially in the informal economy.

Another very significant change in the recent past is the decline in formal employment. In developing countries, this substantial reduction in the share of organized sector employment has been associated not only with increased open unemployment, but also the proliferation of workers crowded into the informal types of work, and typically more in the low-wage and low-productivity occupations that are characteristic of "refuge sectors" in labour markets. While there are also some high value-added jobs increasingly being performed by non-formal workers (including, for example, computer professionals, and some high-end information technology/IT-enabled services) these are relatively small in number and certainly too few to make much of a dent in the overall trend, especially in countries where the vast bulk of the labour force is unskilled or relatively less skilled. In turn, this has meant that the cycle of poverty—low-employment generation—povertyhas been accentuated because of the diminished willingness or ability of developing country governments to intervene positively to increase employment generation.

The decline in aggregate employment elasticities of production[2] is a tendency which is especially marked in developing countries (ILO 2003a). To some extent this reflects the impact of international concentration of production and export orientation, as the necessity of making products that will be acceptable in world markets requires the use of new technologies developed in the North and inherently labour saving in nature. But what is interesting is the extent to which declining employment elasticities in developing Asia have marked all the major productive sectors, including agriculture. This is evident from table 6.1, which describes the employment elasticity of GDP growth in the key productive sectors over 1990–2000 in the major economies of Southeast and South Asia. Agriculture is clearly no longer a refuge sector for those unable to find employment elsewhere—the data indicate low or even negative employment elasticity in this sector, reflecting a combination of labour-saving technological changes such as greater use of threshers and harvesters, and changes in landholding patterns resulting in lower extents of the traditional small peasant farming, because of the reduced economic viability of smallholder cultivation across the region. The service sector, by contrast, seems to have emerged as the refuge sector in this region, except possibly in countries like Sri Lanka and India.

The emergence of global production chains is another very important feature of the recent past. These are not entirely new, and even the current chains can be dated from at least the 1980s. However, two major changes have dramatically increased the relocation possibilities in international production. Technological changes have allowed for different parts of the production process to be split and locationally separated, as well as created different types of requirement for labour, involving a few highly skilled professional workers and a vast bulk of semi-skilled workers for whom burnout is more widely prevalent than learning-by-doing. Organizational

*Table 6.1* Employment Elasticities of GDP Growth, 1990–2000

|  | *Agriculture* | *Industry* | *Services* |
|---|---|---|---|
| Indonesia | -0.43 | 0.76 | 1.23 |
| Malaysia | -2.51 | 0.54 | 0.54 |
| Philippines | 0.04 | 0.57 | 0.9 |
| Singapore | - | 0 | 0.5 |
| Thailand | -1.25 | 0.65 | 1.35 |
| Viet Nam | 0.33 | 0.3 | 1.12 |
| Bangladesh | 0.21 | -0.5 | 1.94 |
| India | 0.02 | 0.29 | 0.76 |
| Pakistan | 0.36 | 0.22 | 1.08 |
| Sri Lanka | -0.94 | 0.16 | 0.22 |

*Source*: ILO, 2003a.

changes have been associated with concentration of ownership and control as well as greater dispersion and more layers of outsourcing and subcontracting of particular activities and parts of the production process.

Therefore, we now have the emergence of international suppliers of goods who rely less and less on direct production within a specific location and more on subcontracting a greater part of their production activities. This has been strongly associated with the increase in export-oriented production in manufacturing in a range of developing countries, especially in textiles and garments, computer hardware, consumer electronics and related sectors. It is true that the increasing use of outsourcing is not confined to export firms; however, because of the flexibility offered by subcontracting, it is clearly of even greater advantage in the intensely competitive exporting sectors and therefore tends to be even more widely used there.

Much of this outsourcing activity is based in Asia, although Latin America is also emerging as an important location once again. Such subcontracted producers, in turn, vary in size and manufacturing capacity, from medium-sized factories to pure middlemen collecting the output of home-based workers. The crucial role of women workers in such international production activity is now increasingly recognized, whether as wage labour in small factories and workshops run by subcontracting firms, or as home-workers paid on a piece-rate basis who deal with middlemen in a complex production chain. This is considered in more detail in section 3.

Finally, there is the very significant effect of international migration, in determining changes in both national labour markets and macroeconomic processes within home and host countries. In Latin America, migration is a response to the lack of productive employment opportunities within the country—at least 15 per cent of the labour force of most Central American countries (in particular El Salvador, Guatemala and Honduras) is estimated to be working in the United States, mostly in underpaid, oppressive and precarious jobs (UNDESA 2002). Migration flows are especially marked for Asia over the past two decades, and within the broad Asian region. South Asian migrant workers in the Gulf and West Asia have contributed huge flows of remittance income which have stabilized the current account in India and Bangladesh, for example. What is noteworthy about Asian migration is the significant role played by women migrants.

The Asian region as a whole is seen as the part of the world that has benefited most from the process of globalization. In terms of growth rates of aggregate GDP, this region—and especially East Asia—far outperformed the rest of the world. It is now commonplace to note that this economic expansion was fuelled by export growth. What is noteworthy is that until 1996, for most high-exporting economies except China, the rate of expansion of imports was even higher, and the period of high growth was therefore one of rapidly increasing trade-to-GDP ratios. For the whole of East and Southeast Asia and the Pacific, trade amounted to more than 60 per cent of GDP in the 1990s and 70 per cent in the first half of the current decade, which is historically unprecedented.[3]

This very substantial degree of trade integration has several important macroeconomic implications. First, since these economies are heavily dependent upon exports as the engine of growth, they must rely either on rapid rates of growth in world trade or increase their shares of world markets. In the last decade the second feature has been more pronounced, but of course such a process has inevitable limits (Ghosh and Chandrasekhar 2003). These limits can be set either by rising protectionist tendencies in the importing countries, or by the competitive pressures from other exporting countries which give rise to the "fallacy of composition" argument (that is, the fall in prices of export items on the global market if many countries simultaneously increase their export volumes). It has been noted that such tendencies remain strong and have adversely affected the terms of trade of high-exporting developing countries over the past decade, indicating that rapid increases in the volume of exports have not been matched by commensurate increases in the value of exports. This, in turn, means that the search for newer or increased forms of cost-cutting or labour productivity increases is still very potent. This is one reason why employment elasticities of export production have been falling throughout the region, and have also affected women's employment in these sectors.

Second, the high rates of growth are matched or exceeded by very high import growth in almost all the economies of the region, barring China and Taiwan Province of China, which are still generating substantial trade surpluses. The net effect on manufacturing employment is typically negative. This is obvious if the economy has a manufacturing trade deficit, but it is also the case even with trade balance or with small manufacturing trade surpluses, if the export production is less employment-intensive than the local production that has been displaced by imports. This is why, barring China and Malaysia, all the economies in the region have experienced deceleration or even absolute declines in manufacturing employment despite the much hyped perception of the North "exporting" jobs to the South (Ghosh 2003a, 2003b). It should be noted that China, which accounted for more than 90 per cent of the total increase in manufacturing employment in the region, could show such a trend because imports were still relatively controlled until 2001, and because state-owned enterprises continued to play a significant role in total manufacturing employment.

The East and Southeast Asian regions have experienced very sharp and large swings in capital flows over the past decade, which have also been associated with relatively large swings in the real economies. Between the mid-1980s and the crisis period of 1997–1998, this region experienced the largest volumes of capital flows in the developing world. Thereafter, the Southeast Asian financial crises put a sharp brake on such inflows (except in the form of FDI). Net flows into the region as a whole have been negative or close to negative since 2003. Instead, there has been a large build-up of foreign exchange reserves by the Central Banks of the countries in the Asian region over the past two years, much of which is being held as securities or in safe deposits in the developed world, especially the United States. The current capital export is really the result of reserve build-up because of Central Bank policies in the region attempting to prevent currencies from appreciating, as some of the lessons from the 1997 crisis are still retained by policymakers.

The accumulation of foreign exchange reserves means that domestic savings are higher than domestic investment, so that economies in the region are generally operating below the full macroeconomic potential. This, in turn, affects employment conditions, especially for women workers. In many countries of the region, as is evident from table 6.2, there has been a decline in female labour force participation rates since 1995. In some countries, such as Cambodia and Thailand, the decline has been drastic. Very few economies reported an increase (Philippines, Singapore, Hong Kong SAR being exceptions), and these were relatively much less in magnitude. It is likely that reduced opportunities for productive employment have been responsible for the tendency for fewer women to report themselves as being part of the labour force, what is known in the developed countries as the "discouraged worker" effect.

*Table 6.2* Labour Force Participation Rates[a]

| | Men | | | Women | | |
|---|---|---|---|---|---|---|
| | *1990* | *1995* | *Latest year[b]* | *1990* | *1995* | *Latest year[b]* |
| Bangladesh | 88 | 87 | 88.8 | 65.4 | 65.9 | 55.9 |
| China | 85 | 85.6 | | 73 | 73.7 | |
| Hong Kong SAR | 78.9 | 76.6 | 75.5 | 46.6 | 47.6 | 48.5 |
| Cambodia | 84.3 | 87.1 | 81.2 | 82 | 82.6 | 73.5 |
| India | 51.5 | | 51.9 | 22.3 | | 25.7 |
| Indonesia | 82.7 | 82.3 | 84.6 | 44.6 | 52.8 | 51.5 |
| Malaysia | 81.9 | 83.2 | 82.8 | 45.2 | 48.9 | 44.7 |
| Pakistan | 84.9 | 82.3 | 82.4 | 11.3 | 12.7 | 15.2 |
| Philippines | 81.8 | 82.1 | 81.8 | 47.5 | 49 | 50 |
| Singapore | 79.2 | 78.4 | 77.5 | 50.3 | 50 | 51.3 |
| South Korea | 74 | 76.5 | 74.4 | 47 | 48.3 | 47.4 |
| Sri Lanka | 77.9 | 74.8 | 77.5 | 45.3 | 35.8 | 37.6 |
| Thailand | 87.7 | 86.4 | 80.3 | 76.3 | 73.5 | 64.2 |
| Viet Nam | 85.2 | 83.5 | | 75.9 | 74.6 | |

*Notes*: a The data relate to population aged 15 years and above. b The latest year varies according to country, from 1998 to 2001.

*Source*: ILO 2003b (except for India, for which Census of India year).

Table 6.2 points to some interesting variations across major Asian economies. Cambodia, Thailand and Sri Lanka show continuous and very sharp declines in female labour force participation rates since 1990, while male rates also declined, albeit less dramatically. In the Republic of Korea (hereafter South Korea), Indonesia and Malaysia, female labour force participation rates increased until 1995, but have declined thereafter. In East Asia, only China and the Philippines—the two economies whose manufacturing exports remained buoyant over the 1990s and subsequently—show rising rates of female labour force participation.

In South Asia, the picture is more mixed. While women's labour force participation appears to have been rising in India, this is mainly due to the increase in "marginal work" (defined in the Census as less than 183 days of work per year), while in Pakistan such rates have been increasing over a very low base. Overall, the picture across most of the Asian region is of reduced employment opportunities for women translating into reductions in labour force participation as well as higher rates of open unemployment. Only in China did paid employment for women workers, including in the manufacturing sector, continue to grow—but even in China, services employment dominated in total employment for women, at more than 35 per cent of total female employment.

In addition to these changes in labour force participation, evidence suggests that in general the paid work performed by women has become less permanent and more casual or part-time in nature. In South Korea, one of the few countries for which such data is available, the proportion of employed women with casual contracts nearly doubled between 1990 and 1999; over the 1990s, around 60 per cent of all casual jobs were held by women workers (Lee 2001). Gender wage gaps have narrowed slightly in most countries of the region, but they remain very high compared to other regions of the world. Thus, in South Korea, the average female wage in manufacturing as a ratio of the male wage increased from 0.51 in 1985 to 0.58 in 1993, and to 0.63 in 2002. But the 2002 ratio is still below the ratio even in most other developing Asian countries. In other countries of the region, this ratio currently varies from 0.7 to 0.85.[4]

## TRADE LIBERALIZATION, EXPORT EMPLOYMENT AND WOMEN'S WORK

From the early 1980s onwards, the increasing importance of export-oriented manufacturing activities in many developing countries had been associated with a much greater reliance on women's paid labour. This process was most marked over the period from 1980 to 1995 in the high-exporting economies of East and Southeast Asia, where the share of female employment in total employment in the export processing zones (EPZs) and export-oriented manufacturing industries typically exceeded 70 per cent. It was also observed in a number of other developing countries, for example in Latin America in certain types of export manufacturing (Brachet-Marquez and de Oliveira 2004).

Thus, the dramatic economic boom in East and Southeast Asia over the 1980s and first half of the 1990s, based on rapid export expansion, was itself based on the growing use of women as wage workers. Indeed, it is now widely appreciated that the Asian export boom was driven by the productive contributions of Asian women in the form of paid labour in export-related activities and in services, through the remittances made by migrant women workers, and through the vast amounts of unpaid labour as liberalization and government fiscal contraction transferred many areas of public provision of goods and services to households (and thereby to women within households). It has even been argued (Seguino 1997, 2000) that those Asian economies that disadvantaged women the most actually grew fastest from 1975 to 1990, because high gender gaps, low female wages and the more "flexible" contracts for women's work substantially lowered unit labour costs, thereby spurring exports and investment.

This trend toward feminization of employment in Asian countries resulted from employers' needs for cheaper and more "flexible" sources of labour, and was also strongly associated with the moves toward casualization of labour, shift to part-time work or piece-rate contracts and insistence on greater freedom for hiring and firing over the economic cycle. All these aspects of what is now described as "labour market flexibility" became necessary once external competitiveness became the significant goal of domestic policymakers and defined the contours within which domestic and foreign employers in these economies operated.

Feminization was also encouraged by the widespread conviction among employers in East and Southeast Asia that female employees are more tractable and subservient to managerial authority, less prone to organize into unions, more willing to accept lower wages because of their own lower "reservation"[5] and "aspiration" wages and easier to dismiss using life-cycle criteria such as marriage and childbirth. This was made more relevant because of technological changes which encouraged the use of labour which could be replaced at periodic intervals.

This was the received wisdom, at least until the crash of mid-1997 which dramatically altered both the potential for continued economic activity at the same rate, as well the conditions of employment in the region. When the export industries started to slow down from the middle of 1995, it became evident that continued growth of employment in these export-oriented industries could not be the same engine of expansion that they had served as over the previous decade. It also became clear, therefore, that there could be some setback to the feminization of employment that had been occurring, since the export industries had become the most important new employers of women. Indeed, the very features which had made women workers more attractive to employers—the flexibility of hiring and firing and the more casual, non-unionized nature of labour contracts—are precisely those which are likely to render them to be the first to lose their jobs in any recessionary phase.

The feminization of such activities had both positive and negative effects for the women concerned. On the one hand, it definitely meant greater recognition and remuneration of women's work, and typically improved the relative status and bargaining power of women within households, as well as their own self-worth, thereby leading to empowerment. On the other hand, it is also true that most women are rarely if ever "unemployed" in their lives, in that they are almost continuously involved in various forms of productive or reproductive activities, even if they are not recognized as "working" or paid for such activities. This means that the increase in paid employment may lead to an onerous double burden of work *unless* other social policies and institutions emerge to deal with the work traditionally assigned to women on an unpaid basis.

Given these features, it has been fairly clear for some time now that the feminization of work need not be a cause for unqualified celebration on the part of those interested in improving women's material status (Seguino 1997). However, it has recently become evident that the process of feminization of labour in export-oriented industries may have been even more dependent upon the relative inferiority of remuneration and working conditions than was generally supposed. This becomes very clear from a consideration of the pattern of female involvement in paid labour markets in East and Southeast Asia, and more specifically in the export industries, over the entire decade of the 1990s. What the evidence suggests is that the process of feminization of export employment really peaked somewhere in the early 1990s (if not earlier in some countries) and that thereafter the process was not only less marked, but may even have begun to peter out. This is significant because it refers very clearly to the period *before* the effects of the financial crisis began to make themselves felt on real economic activity, and even before the slowdown in the growth rate of export production. So, while the crisis may have hastened the process whereby women workers are disproportionately prone to job loss because of the very nature of their employment contracts, in fact the marginal reliance on women workers in export manufacturing activity (or rather in the manufacturing sector in general) had already begun to reduce *before* the crisis (Ghosh 2003a).

The relative increase in the share of women in total export employment, which was so marked for a period, especially in the more dynamic economies of Asia, has turned out to be a rather short-lived phenomenon. Already by the mid-1990s, women's share of manufacturing employment had peaked in most economies of the region, and in some countries it even declined in absolute numbers (see Table 6.3). Some of this reflected the fact that such export-oriented employment through relocative foreign investment simply moved to cheaper locations: from Malaysia to Indonesia and Viet Nam; from Thailand to Cambodia and Myanmar, and so on. But even in the newer locations, there have been problems with certain export-oriented industries—garments in some countries, electronic goods in others.

*Table 6.3* Trends in Manufacturing Employment and Share of Women Workers Before the East Asian Crisis

| Country and year | Total manufacturing employment, 000s | Women employed in manufacturing, 000s | Share of women workers (per cent) |
|---|---|---|---|
| South Korea, 1992 | 4,828 | 1,931 | 40 |
| South Korea, 1997 | 4,474 | 1,594 | 35 |
| Malaysia, 1992 | 1,637 | 767 | 47 |
| Malaysia, 1997 | 2,003 | 807 | 40 |
| Indonesia, 1990 | 7,693 | 3,483 | 45 |
| Indonesia, 1996 | 10,773 | 4,895 | 45 |
| Thailand, 1990 | 3,133 | 1,564 | 50 |
| Thailand, 1996 | 4,334 | 2,065 | 48 |
| Singapore, 1991 | 423 | 189 | 44 |
| Singapore, 1997 | 414 | 166 | 40 |
| Hong Kong SAR, 1990 | 751 | 314 | 42 |
| Hong Kong SAR, 1997 | 444 | 160 | 36 |

*Source*: Ghosh (2003b), based on ILO Yearbook of Labour Statistics, various issues.

The reversal of the process of feminization of work has already been observed in other parts of the developing world, notably in Latin America. Quite often, such declines in women's share of employment were associated with either one of two conditions: an overall decline in employment opportunities because of recession or structural adjustment measures, or a shift in the nature of the new employment generation toward more skilled or lucrative activities. A third potential factor is that as women became an established part of the paid workforce, and even the dominant part in certain sectors (as indeed they did become in the textiles, ready-made garments and consumer electronics sectors of East Asia) it became more difficult for employers to exercise the traditional type of gender discrimination at work. Not only was there an upward pressure on their wages, but there were also social pressures for legislation which would improve their overall conditions of work. Social action and legislation designed to improve the conditions of women workers, tended to reduce the relative attractiveness of women workers for those employers who had earlier been relying on the inferior conditions of women's work to enhance their export profitability. The rise in wages reinforced this effect. Thus, as the relative effective remuneration of women improved (in terms of the total package of wage and work and contract conditions), their attractiveness to employers decreased.

The earlier common assessment of the feminization of work in East Asia had been based on what was perhaps an overoptimistic expectation of expansion in female employment.[6] Thus, while female employment in manufacturing was important, the trend over the 1990s, even *before* the 1997–1998 crisis, was not necessarily upward. In most of the countries mentioned, there is a definite tendency toward a decline in the share of women workers in total manufacturing employment over the latter part of the 1990s. In Hong Kong SAR and South Korea, the decline in female employment in manufacturing was even sharper than that in aggregate employment. Similarly, even in the countries in which aggregate manufacturing employment increased over the period 1990–1997, the female share had a tendency to stabilize or even fall. Thus, in Indonesia the share of women workers in all manufacturing sector workers increased from an admittedly high 45 per cent to as much as 47 per cent by 1993, and then fell to 44 per cent by 1997. In Malaysia the decline in female share was even sharper than in South Korea: from 47 per cent in 1992 to only 40 per cent in 1997. A slight decline was evident even in Thailand (Ghosh 1999, 2003a).

This fall in women's share of employment is evident not just for total manufacturing but even for export-oriented manufacturing, and is corroborated by evidence from other sources. Thus Joekes (1999) shows that the share of women employed in EPZs declined even between 1980 and 1990 in Malaysia, South Korea and the Philippines, with the decline being as sharp as more than 20 percentage points (from 75 per cent to only 54 per cent) in the case of Malaysia.

In the post-crisis period, manufacturing has tended to occupy a much less significant position in the total employment of women. In Malaysia the share of women workers in manufacturing to all employed women fell from its peak of 31 per cent in 1992 to 26 per cent in 1999; in the Philippines from 13.3 per cent in 1991 to less than 12 per cent in 1999; in South Korea from its peak of 28 per cent in 1990 to 17 per cent in 2000; and in Hong Kong SAR from 32 per cent in 1990 to 10 per cent in 1999.[7] Recent evidence from India (Varma and Neetha 2003) suggests that export-oriented production does not always result in the feminization of the workforce, which is essentially dependent upon the relative inferiority of wages and work conditions of women. Where both male and female workers are forced by the state of the labour market to accept adverse low-paid and insecure work contracts, there appears to be less preference for young women workers than was previously observed.

In any case, the nature of such work has also changed in recent years. Most such work was already based on short-term contracts rather than permanent employment for women; now there is much greater reliance on women workers in very small units or even in home-based production, at the bottom of a complex subcontracting chain (Harrison and Kelley 1999). Already this was a prevalent tendency in the region. For example, labour flexibility surveys in the Philippines have shown that the greater the degree of labour casualization, the higher the proportion of total employment consisting of women and the more vulnerable these women are to exploitative conditions (ILO 2002b). This became even more marked in the post-crisis adjustment phase. A study by Ofreneo and others (2002) suggests that the declining competitiveness of the garments industry of the Philippines has led to the development of complex and demanding subcontracting arrangements involving more than six million home-based workers.

In Southeast Asia, women have made up a significant proportion of the informal manufacturing industry workforce, in garment workshops, shoe factories and craft industries. Many women also carry out informal activities as temporary workers in farming or in the building industry. In Malaysia, over a third of all electronics, textile and garments firms were found to use subcontracting. In Thailand, it has been estimated that as many as 38 per cent of clothing workers are home-workers and the figure is said to be 25–40 per cent in the Philippines (Sethuraman 2000). Home-based workers, working on their own account or on a subcontracting basis, have been found to make products ranging from clothing and footwear to artificial flowers, carpets, electronics and teleservices (Carr and Chen 1999; Lund and Srinivas 2000).

This is, of course, part of a wider international tendency of somewhat longer duration: The emergence of international suppliers of goods who rely less and less on direct production within a specific location and more on subcontracting a greater part of their production activities. Thus, the recent period has seen the emergence and market domination of "manufacturers without factories", as multinational firms such as Nike and Adidas effectively rely on a complex system of outsourced and subcontracted production based on centrally determined design and quality control. It is true that the increasing use of outsourcing is not confined to export firms; however, because of the flexibility offered by subcontracting, it is clearly of even greater advantage in the intensely competitive exporting sectors and therefore tends to be even more widely used there. Much of this outsourcing activity is based in Asia, although Latin America is also emerging as an important location once again (Bonacich and Waller 1994). Such subcontracted producers, in turn, vary in size and manufacturing capacity, from medium-sized factories to pure middlemen collecting the output of home-based workers. The crucial role of women workers in such international production activity is now increasingly recognized, whether as wage labour in small factories and workshops run by subcontracting firms, or as home-workers working on a piece-rate basis who deal with middlemen in a complex production chain (Beneria and Roldan 1987; Mejia 1997).

A substantial proportion of such subcontracting in fact extends down to home-based work. Thus, in the garments industry alone, the percentage of home-workers to total workers was estimated at 38 per cent in Thailand, between 25 to 29 per cent in the Philippines, 30 per cent in one region of Mexico, between 30 to 60 per cent in Chile and 45 per cent in Venezuela

(Chen et al. 1998). Home-based work provides substantial opportunity for self-exploitation by workers, especially when payment is on a piece-rate basis; also these are areas typically left unprotected by labour laws and social welfare.

A study of women working in the garments industry in Sri Lanka brings this out very clearly (TIE-Asia 2003). This sector is typically presented as the most dynamic export activity in Sri Lanka today, accounting for nearly 70 per cent of non-agricultural exports, and becoming the second largest source of foreign exchange earnings after remittances from Sri Lankan workers abroad (again mainly women). The garments industry in Sri Lanka, like those in many other Asian countries, is involved in producing for international subcontracting chains organized and marketed by major multinational brand names. Of the women surveyed for this study, 24 per cent of those who worked in factories defined themselves as "self-employed", since they had been instructed to do so by their employers, in order to avoid legal obligations of paying into the employees' provident fund and fulfilling other employers' responsibilities. The research team however found it very hard to find actual home-based workers for a number of reasons. These included the absence of such workers from official data; the atmosphere of anxiety and fear of management which made workers anxious to avoid identification and possible retribution; and the disinclination of subcontracting agencies such as factories and smaller agents to disclose the extent of dependence upon such work. Nevertheless, it appeared that more than half of the women workers involved in this sector were engaged either through home-based work or in very small factories.

Recent research by Mazumdar (2004a) in India indicates that even such home-based work may be experiencing some sort of crisis, as the textile and garments exports from developing countries face increasing difficulties in world markets and the pressure of competition forces exporters to seek further avenues for cost-cutting. The extreme volatility of employment that characterizes factory-based, export-oriented production has also become a feature of home-based work for export production

## SERVICE SECTOR EMPLOYMENT OF WOMEN

Women have always been major sources of service sector work, but they have not always been classified as engaged in such employment, because much of the work they typically perform comes into the category of unpaid labour, performed within the household or local community. The care economy dominates in such work: thus, all activities such as cooking and cleaning for household members, care of the young, the old and the sick and provisioning of necessary goods (such as fetching water and fuel wood in rural areas) are typically seen as the responsibility of women members of the household in most Asian economies. It is only recently that women's involvement in paid services has increased across Asia. While there has been some increase in women's share of paid employment in the formal sector (especially in public employment) in general, women workers tend to be concentrated into the lower paid and more informal types of service activity.

The paid employment of women in services has been most marked not only in these, but also in petty trading activities. Such work comes dominantly in the form of self-employment, and because most of it is conducted informally, it is extremely difficult to get reliable estimates of the extent of such employment or its remuneration. Table 6.4 provides such data as exist on the share of self-employment in all recognized work by women; note, however, that this refers to all sectors and not services alone.

Recent data from India point to an increase in female self-employment in unorganized industry and services (NSSO 2006). For women in both rural and urban areas, the share of regular work has increased but that of casual employment has fallen so sharply that the aggregate share of wage employment has fallen. Self-employment now accounts for nearly two-thirds of all jobs among rural women and nearly half among urban women. But this work is evidently taking place under more precarious conditions, as the survey data show not only that real wages of regular women workers have been falling, but also that around half of self-employed women workers find their remuneration inadequate for survival.

Across Asia, two types of work appear to dominate in the service sector employment of women: petty trade, as mentioned earlier, typically as self-employment on the part of the individual woman or the household; and personal services, especially in what can be broadly described as the "care" industry, ranging from domestic service to skilled and unskilled activities in health care and related areas, as well as in the "entertainment" industries

*Table 6.4* Self-employed Women as Per Cent of All Employed Women

|  | *1990* | *1995* | *Latest year** |
|---|---|---|---|
| Bangladesh | 94.8 | - | - |
| Indonesia | 76 | - | - |
| Malaysia | 35.3 | - | - |
| Pakistan | 77.4 | 66.9 | 66.9 |
| Philippines | 58.8 | - | - |
| Singapore | 7.6 | 8.5 | 8.5 |
| South Korea | 36.9 | 39.2 | 39.2 |
| Sri Lanka | 57.3 | - | - |
| Thailand | 99.4 | 98.8 | 98.8 |

*Source*: ILO 2002.

*Note*: "Latest year" refers to 1999–2001, depending on the country.

which can be seen as a catch-all for a very wide range of legal and illegal activities. Except for East Asia (China, Taiwan Province of China, South Korea) formal sector service employment of women remains quite limited.

One new area of service activity that is currently widely discussed relates to the new IT-enabled services, which have become important especially for workers with educational achievements in a number of Asian countries, especially India, China and the Philippines. Aside from software industries (in which the share of women remains quite small), the emergence of business process outsourcing has been seen as one of the most important future tendencies, which will affect not only domestic labour markets and the status of women workers, but also the possibilities of increased foreign exchange inflows through export of this type of resident labour.

It is possible that some of the optimism surrounding this new source of employment generation may be exaggerated, especially as far as women workers are concerned (Chandrasekhar 2003). Consider recent trends in India, where the buoyancy of IT-enabled services has already received much international attention. The microevidence suggests that women workers are reasonably involved in this sector, and in particular activities their share of employment is much higher than that for the formal sector as a whole. However, this sector shows clear signs of labour market segmentation by gender, caste and class. Since almost all of those involved are from the urban upper-class (and mostly upper-caste) English-speaking elite of Indian society, it has been argued that the pattern of development of the software and IT-enabled services sector brings into sharp relief the tendency of the market to reinforce or aggravate existing socioeconomic inequities (Vijaybhaskar 2000). While it will certainly draw more educated women into paid jobs and reduce the problem of unemployment among those with education to some extent, it would not bring about any major transformation in aggregate employment patterns in the near future.

Further, the nature of the work involved in Business Process Outsourcing (BPO) activities can be compared to export-oriented employment, with the difference that a greater degree of education and skill is required of the workers. Recent studies of call centres in Delhi and New Okhla Industrial Development Authority (NOIDA) (Mazumdar 2004b, Babu and Neetha 2004) point to the lack of opportunities for development and promotion in such activities, as well as the high degree of burnout, suggesting the absence of what could be called a "career track" in such work. It has been found that since the "productivity" of call centre workers is determined by the number of calls handled while maintaining appropriate "quality levels", the work is subject to constant monitoring and supervision. High premium is also placed in increasing productivity through intensification of the labour process. Even in a few years, there is evidence of a downward trend in wages in such activities, even though the wages in these call centres remain higher than the average wages of private sector clerks, teachers and nurses.

On average, female call centre workers are young and do not last in this activity beyond a few years because of the sheer pressure of the work.

So even in this emerging sector, women's work tends to be concentrated in low-end, repetitive activities with little chance of upward mobility, recreating the pattern already observed in export-oriented manufacturing production. And there are also possibilities of the future reversal of the process of feminization of such work, in this case because changes in technology may require less of such work to be outsourced to developing countries in the first place. Such technological changes are likely to be accentuated by the protectionist pressures that are already being felt in the developed countries.

## ISSUES FOR PUBLIC POLICY

The picture of women's employment in Asia today is much more complex than it has appeared for some time. There have been some clear gains from the relatively short-lived process of feminization of export-oriented production of the region. One important gain is the social recognition of women's work, and the acceptance of the need for greater social protection of women workers. The fact of greater entry into the public sphere of paid work may also have provided greater recognition of women's unpaid household work. At the same time, however, unpaid work has tended to increase because of the reduction in government expenditure and support for many basic public services, especially in sanitation, health and caregiving sectors. This is evident from several time use surveys tracking women's work at the micro level, and also emerges in countries like India from the data from the National Sample Surveys. These show an increase in the proportion of those women who say that they have to perform unpaid domestic work out of necessity rather than choice (NSSO 2006).

Recent reversals in the feminization of paid employment also point to the possibility of regression in terms of social effects as well. Already, we have seen the rise of revivalist and fundamentalist movements across the Asian region, which seek to put constraints upon the freedom of women to participate actively in public life. The speed and extent of such processes in Asia have the capacity for creating major social changes which can have destabilizing effects on gender relations and on the possibilities for the empowerment of women in general. At the same time, advances in communication technology and the creation of the "global village" provide both threats and opportunities. They encourage adverse tendencies such as the commodification of women along the lines of the hegemonic culture portrayed in international mass media controlled by giant US-based corporations, and the reaction to that in the form of restrictive traditionalist tendencies.

In this context, there are important measures which governments in the region can, and must, take in order to ensure that work processes and the growing informalization of work do not add to the complex patterns of oppression of women that continue in Asian societies today. More stable and less exploitative conditions for work by women cannot be ensured without a revival of the role played by governments in terms of macroeconomic management for employment generation and provision of adequate labour protection for all workers. Changes in labour market regulation alone do little to change the broad context of employment generation and conditions of work if the aggregate market conditions themselves are not conducive to such change. More direct employment generation through increased public investment and provision of public services is useful; in addition, indirect employment generation through encouraging the expansion of activities which use female labour in stable and remunerative ways should be encouraged through fiscal incentives and other means. Given that across the region, external competitive pressures are creating tendencies for more exploitative and volatile use of all labour, including women's labour, this has to be counteracted with proactive countercyclical government spending policies. Further, for women in particular who on average tend to be less trained and with fewer marketable skills, there is need for systematic vocational training to allow for greater worker mobility and ability to find other jobs.

In addition, the regulatory framework remains important essentially as a basic premise that can affect the bargaining position of workers. It is a necessary condition (but not a sufficient one) for improving wages and conditions of work. That is why it is both important and necessary to ensure that laws and provisions guaranteeing workers' protection and safety are in place, even if they are not well enforced. These should be seen not as welfare measures granted by a benevolent state, but rather as government's recognition of the basic socioeconomic rights of workers. While the existence of such laws does not ensure compliance, and indeed compliance or implementation is impossible to ensure for the whole population in the current circumstances in most Asian countries, it does provide a basis for workers themselves to bargain and organize collectively to try and ensure their enforcement. The regulation should also be such as to prevent employers from being vindictive or punitive toward workers who do organize and mobilize for better conditions of work and wages.

At the same time, of course, it is clear that such laws cannot be so rigid as to make it difficult for employers to respond effectively to what are much more fluid and volatile conditions of production and competition. In essence this means that the laws should be such as to allow for closures and job loss where these cannot be avoided. But these should always be with adequate compensation and with encouragement and assistance for mobility of workers across activities and even, if possible, across regions. There should also be a greater attempt to make such laws applicable across all sectors of productive employment, including in agriculture, and to encourage the mobilization and association of rural, as well as urban, workers.

In sum, therefore, appropriate legislation needs to be in place to ensure workers their basic rights and especially to allow them the power to associate and bargain collectively for claiming what are recognized to be their socio-economic rights. But even more important than this is the recognition from governments that a focus on macroeconomic policies for employment generation should dominate the overall economic strategy and determine specific policies as well.

## NOTES

1. In India, for example, the sharp increase in female labour force participation rates, evident in the 1991 Census (as in the 1961 Census before it), was related to the changed nature of the questions posed and the slightly different training given to enumerators, and the same holds true for the surveys conducted by the National Sample Survey Organization in India over the 1990s. Such a shift is even more marked for Bangladesh, where a change in definition was associated with an increase in female activity rates between 1983 and 1989 by 35 percentage points—an eightfold increase.
2. In other words, the additional employment created at a given level of economic growth appears to have fallen over time.
3. World Bank World Development Indicators online: http://web.worldbank.org, accessed in February 2007.
4. ILO Labour Statistics database: http://laborsta.ilo.org, accessed in February 2007.
5. This is a concept used in labour economics which suggests that each worker has a specific wage rate whereby they are induced to perform paid market work. Wages offered below a worker's reservation wage would keep said worker from participating in the labour force.
6. Such optimism was implicit or explicit in discussions such as those of Joekes and Weston (1994), Horton (1995), Heyzer (1998), and even to some extent Wee (1998).
7. Data from ILO (2002b).

## REFERENCES

Babu, R.P. and N. Neetha. 2004. *Women Workers in the New Economy: Call Centre Work in NOIDA*. Paper presented at National Seminar on Globalization and Women's Work, VV Giri National Labour Institute, NOIDA, Gautam Budh Nagar, UP, 25–26 March.

Beneria, L. and M. Roldan. 1987. *The Crossroads of Class and Gender: Homework Subcontracting and Household Dynamics in Mexico City*. University of Chicago Press, Chicago, IL.

Bonacich, E. and D.V. Waller. 1994. *Mapping a Global Industry: Apparel Production in the Pacific Rim Triangle*. Temple University Press, Philadephia, PA.

Brachet-Marquez, V. and O. de Oliveira. 2004. "Gendering the debate on the welfare state in Mexico: Women's employment and welfare entitlements in the globalized economy." In S. Razavi, R. Pearson and C. Danloy (eds.), *Globalization, Export-Oriented Employment and Social Policy: Gendered Connections*. Palgrave, Basingstoke.

Carr, M. and M. Chen. 1999. *Globalization and Home-Based Workers*. WIEGO Working Paper No. 12, WIEGO, Cambridge, MA.

Chandrasekhar, C.P. 2003. "The diffusion of information technology: The Indian experience." *Social Scientist*, Vol. 31, Nos. 7 and 8, pp. 42–85.

Chen, M.A., J. Sebstad and L. O'Connell. 1998. "Counting the invisible workforce: The case of homebased workers." *World Development*, Vol. 27, No. 3, pp. 603–610.

de Soto, H. 2000. *The Mystery of Capital: Why Capitalism Triumphs in the West and Fails Everywhere Else.* Basic Books, New York.

Elson, D. 1987. *The Impact of Structural Adjustment on Women: Concepts and Issues.* Zed Books, London.

Ghosh, J. 2003a. "Globalization, export-oriented employment for women and social policy: A case study of India." In S. Razavi, R. Pearson and C. Danloy (eds.), *Globalization, Export-Oriented Employment and Social Policy: Gendered Connections.* Palgrave, Basingstoke.

———. 2003b. "Where have the manufacturing jobs gone? Production, accumulation and relocation in the world economy." In J. Ghosh and C.P. Chandrasekhar (eds.), *Work and Well-Being in the Age of Finance.* Tulika Books, New Delhi.

———. 1999. *Trends in Economic Participation and Poverty of Women in the Asia-Pacific Rregion.* United Nations Economic and Social Commission for Asia and the Pacific (UN-ESCAP), Bangkok.

Ghosh, J. and C.P. Chandrasekhar (eds.). 2003. *Work and Well-Being in the Age of Finance.* Tulika Books, New Delhi.

Harrison, B. and M. Kelley. 1999. "Outsourcing and the search for flexibility: The morphology of contracting out in US manufacture." In Stroper, Michael and Allen J. Scott (eds.), *Pathways to Industrialization and Regional Development in the 1990s.* Unwin and Hyman, Boston, MA.

Heyzer, N. (ed.). 1988. *Daughters in Industry: Work Skills and Consciousness of Women Workers in Asia.* Asia and Pacific Development Centre, Kuala Lumpur.

Horton, Susan (ed.). 1995. *Women and Industrialization in Asia.* Routledge, London.

International Labour Organization (ILO). 2005. *Global Employment Trends 2004–05.* ILO, Geneva.

———. 2004. *Report of the World Commission on the Social Dimensions of Globalization.* ILO, Geneva.

———. 2003a. *Global Employment Trends.* ILO, Geneva.

———. 2003b. *Key Indicators of the Labour Market.* ILO, Geneva.

———. 2002a. *Decent Work and the Informal Economy. Report VI, International Labour Conference 90th Session.* ILO, Geneva.

———. 2002b. *Key Indicators of the Labour Market. Fourth Edition.* ILO, Geneva.

Joekes, S. 1999. "A gender-analytical perspective on trade and sustainable development." In *Trade, Gender and Sustainable Development.* UNCTAD, Geneva. http://r0.unctad.org/trade_env/test1/topics/UNCTAD19999poedm_m78.en.pdf#page=57, accessed on 12 March 2008.

Joekes, S. and A. Weston. 1994. *Women and the New Trade Agenda.* UNIFEM, New York.

Lee, H. 2001. *Evaluation and Promotion of Social Safety Nets for Women Affected by the Asian Economic Crisis.* Paper presented at the Expert Group Meeting on Social Safety Nets for Women, UNESCAP, Bangkok, 2–4 May.

Lund, F. and S. Srinivas. 2000. *Learning from Experience: A Gendered Approach to Social Protection for Workers in the Informal Economy.* ILO, Geneva.

Mazumdar, I. 2004a. *Impact of Globalization on Women Workers in Garment Exports: The Indian Experience.* Mimeo, Centre for Women's Development Studies, New Delhi.

———. 2004b. *Neither Mental Nor Manual Labour: The Service Factories of the "New Economy."* Mimeo, Centre for Women's Development Studies, New Delhi.

Mejia, R. 1997 "The impact of globalisation on women workers." In *The Impact of Globalisation on Women Workers : Case Studies from Mexico, Asia, South Africa and the United States.* Oxfam, London.

National Sample Survey Organization (NSSO). 2006. *Employment and Unemployment Situation in India.* Government of India, Ministry of Statistics and Programme Implementation, Kolkata, October.

Ofreneo, R.P., J.Y. Lim and L.A. Gula. 2002. "The view from below: Impact of the financial crisis on subcontracted workers in the Philippines." In R. Balakrishnan (ed.), *The Hidden Assembly Line: Gender Dynamics of Subcontracted Work in a Global Economy.* Kumarian Press, Bloomfield, CT.

Seguino, S. 2000. "Accounting for gender in Asian economic growth." *Feminist Economics*, Vol. 6, No. 3, pp. 22–58.

———. 1997. "Gender wage inequality and export-led growth in South Korea." *Journal of Development Studies*, Vol. 34, No. 2, pp. 102–132.

Sethuraman, S.V. 2000. *Gender, Poverty and the Informal Sector.* WIEGO. www.wiego.org, accessed on 24 July 2006.

TIE-Asia. 2003. *Women Working in the Informal Sector in Sri Lanka.* Transnational Information Exchange, Colombo.

United Nations Department of Economic and Social Affairs (UNDESA). 2002. *International Migration Report 2002.* United Nations, New York.

Varma, U.K. and N. Neetha. 2003. *Labour, Employment and Gender Issues in EPZs: The Case of NOIDA Export Processing Zone.* Research Report VV, Giri National Labour Institute, NOIDA, Gautam Budh Nagar, UP.

Vijaybhaskar, K. 2000. *What Happens to Formal Employment in the Indian Software Industry?* Paper presented at 42nd Annual Conference of Indian Society of Labour Economics, Jabalpur University, Jabalpur, 9–11 December.

Wee, V. (ed.). 1998. *Trade Liberalization : Challenges and Opportunities for Women in Southeast Asia and Beyond.* United Nations Development Fund for Women (UNIFEM), New York/ENGENDER, Singapore.

# 7 Informalization of Labour Markets

## Is Formalization the Answer?

*Martha Alter Chen*

## INTRODUCTION

The overarching theme of this volume is gendered differences in the impact of economic liberalization on livelihoods, employment opportunities and labour markets. As the chapters in this volume have illustrated, this requires an understanding of, first, overall impact and, then, gendered differences in impact. It is now widely understood that the impact of trade and market liberalization on livelihoods and employment is diverse. Indeed, the way that women and men workers experience market and trade liberalization is determined not only by their sex but also by the sector and type of unit in which they work; by their employment status; by their race, ethnicity, age and class; by where they live and work; and by the complex interplay of all these factors.

In general, policies that increase access to export markets, facilitate imports of scarce inputs and encourage investment in domestic production are thought to have positive effects on livelihood and employment opportunities (Heintz 2006). And policies that facilitate imports of consumer goods, over imports of scarce inputs, and/or do not encourage investment in domestic production are likely to have negative effects on livelihood and employment opportunities. In brief, the relative size of exports compared to imports—not the total volume of trade—appears to determine the impact of trade openness on employment (Heintz 2006). However, market and trade liberalization are often associated with the informalization of labour markets. So it is important to assess the impact of liberalization on the *quality* as well as the *quantity* of livelihood and employment opportunities.

Further, the employment impacts of trade openness tend to be gender specific and may change over time. In the first phase of trade openness, women tend to disproportionately gain from the jobs created from export growth and men are disproportionately impacted by the job losses associated with import penetration (Heintz 2006). However, in the second phase of trade openness, when export-oriented activities often become more profitable and mechanized, men may take over from women: as happened in the export assembly and processing sector in Mexico (Polaski 2004; UNIFEM 2000; White et al. 2003).

In addition to exports and imports, the third main pathway by which trade liberalization affects livelihoods and employment is through labour migration and related migration policies. But there are barriers to labour mobility, especially across borders, and to the flow of remittances, which undermine the ability of migrant workers to earn decent incomes and develop skills in host countries and reduce the potential benefit of their remittances on employment creation back home (Heintz 2006).

As other chapters in this volume have illustrated, it is also now widely understood that trade and market liberalization create risks as well as opportunities. But the contradictory impacts on employment and livelihoods are not well understood. First, it is still widely assumed that trade liberalization leads to employment creation. But this is not always the case. Countries—or sectors within countries—can experience so-called "jobless growth", when economic output expands but formal employment stagnates or declines. At the sector level, jobless growth is often due to choice of technology or, more specifically, to mechanization. But at an aggregate country level, jobless growth is also often due to the privatization of public enterprises, downsizing of the public bureaucracy and competition from cheap imports. Second, it is still widely assumed that the jobs that are created are "good jobs". But this too is often not the case. In fact, trade liberalization is associated with a global production system that favours subcontracting production of low value-added labour-intensive activities to producers, suppliers and workers in developing countries. Near the bottom of the global supply chains are the unprotected workers in export processing zone factories or small export-oriented production units. At the very bottom are the industrial outworkers—or home-workers—who produce for a piece-rate for suppliers (or their intermediaries) and have to bear most of the costs of production other than wages and raw materials.

Finally, it is still widely assumed that informal employment results from underdevelopment or poor economic performance. But trade liberalization and economic growth are, in some contexts, associated with the informalization of labour markets. When not enough jobs are created to meet the demand, people turn to self-employment in the informal economy. When the self-employed cannot compete with cheap imports, they often shift into low-skilled and low-paid wage jobs. When people can no longer afford public services once they are privatized, they may be forced to supplement their existing earnings with self-employment in the informal economy. When the new employment opportunities are linked to the global production system or labour migration, they are often "bad jobs".

This chapter considers what can and should be done about labour market informalization. The chapter opens with a brief overview of informal labour markets in developing countries and labour market informalization in (mainly) developed countries, including gendered patterns and trends. It then considers whether "formalization" is the answer to informalization, by considering what formalization should consist of for both the self-employed in informal enterprises and wage workers in informal jobs. Finally it outlines a broad approach to informal labour markets that goes beyond formalization per se, including reorienting economic policies, reforming the formal regulatory environment and empowering informal workers.

## INFORMALIZATION OF LABOUR MARKETS

Broadly defined, the informalization of the labour market represents a situation in which the ratio of the informal labour force to the formal labour force—or the share of the informal labour force in the total labour force—increases over time. However, the term is often used, more narrowly and specifically, to refer to the informalization of once-formal jobs in (mainly) developed countries. In this chapter, the term is used in the broad sense to refer to informalization of work over time in both developing and developed countries. But a distinction is drawn between informal employment in developing countries and nonstandard work in developed countries.

In developing countries, labour statisticians have used the term "informal sector" to refer to employment in informal enterprises (that is, unregulated and small enterprises). Recently, they have adopted the term "informal employment" to refer, more broadly, to all forms of informal employment (that is, unregulated and unprotected employment) both inside and outside informal enterprises. Increasingly, labour economists and other observers are also drawing the distinction between the "informal sector" and the broader concept of "informal employment".

Broadly defined, the informal labour force includes the *self-employed in informal enterprises* (that is, small and unregulated) as well as the *wage labourers employed in informal jobs* (that is, unregulated and unprotected) in both urban and rural areas (Chen et al. 2005; ILO 2002). So defined, informal labour markets encompass *rural self-employment*, both agricultural and non-agricultural; *urban self-employment* in manufacturing, trade and services; and various forms of *informal wage employment* (including casual day-labourers in construction and agriculture, industrial outworkers, and more).

In developed countries, relatively few labour statisticians, economists or other observers use the concepts of informal sector or informal employment. Rather, the more common concept and term for forms of work that have been flexibilized or informalized is "nonstandard work". Nonstandard work refers to forms of work that do not—or no longer—conform to regular, year-round, full-time employment with a single employer. The most commonly cited categories of nonstandard work in developed countries, for which official data are readily available, are self-employment, part-time work and temporary work. It is important to note that, in addition to self-employment, two categories of nonstandard work—day labour and domestic work—that are often informal (that is, unprotected) are fairly common in developed countries. Also, some part-time and temporary workers in some developed countries are not covered by legal or social protections and could, therefore, be considered as informally employed.

## Developing Countries

To date, relatively few developing countries have measured informal employment broadly defined and fewer still have measured trends in informal employment over time. This is because the expanded concept of "informal employment" was ratified only in 2003. However, an indirect measure of informal employment can be—and has been—used to estimate the size of informal labour markets and the informalization of labour markets over time: namely, estimating informal employment as the difference between *total* employment (estimated by labour force surveys or population censuses) and *formal* employment (estimated by enterprise surveys or economic censuses).

What follows is a summary of findings regarding the size of the informal economy in 25 developing countries (ILO 2002) and changes in informal employment over time in 20 of these countries (Heintz and Pollin 2003). Official national data were used to estimate informal employment in each of the countries using the indirect measure noted earlier.[1] Findings on labour force segmentation and average earnings are based on two recent reviews of available data (Chen et al. 2004, 2005).

### Informal Labour Markets

Informal employment broadly defined comprises one-half to three-quarters of *non-agricultural* employment in developing countries: specifically, 47 per cent in the Middle East and North Africa; 51 per cent in Latin America; 71 per cent in Asia; and 72 per cent in sub-Saharan Africa. If South Africa is excluded, the share of informal employment in non-agricultural employment rises to 78 per cent in sub-Saharan Africa; and if comparable data were available for countries other than India in South Asia, the regional average for Asia would likely be much higher.

Some countries include informal employment in *agriculture* in their estimates. This significantly increases the proportion of informal employment: from 83 per cent of *non-agricultural* employment to 93 per cent of *total* employment in India; from 55 to 62 per cent in Mexico; and from 28 to 34 per cent in South Africa.

The main segments of informal employment, classified by employment status, are as follows:

### Self-Employed:

- *employers*: owner operators of informal enterprises who hire others;

- *own-account workers*: owner operators in single-person units or family businesses/farms who do not hire others;
- *unpaid contributing family workers*: family workers who work in family businesses or farms without pay.

*Wage Workers:*

- *informal employees*: unprotected employees with a known employer: either an informal enterprise, a formal enterprise, a contracting agency or a household;
- *casual wage workers*: wage workers with no fixed employer who sell their labour on a daily or seasonal basis;
- *industrial outworkers*: subcontracted workers who produce for a piece-rate from their homes or small workshops.

While average earnings are higher in formal jobs than in informal employment, there is also a hierarchy of earnings within informal employment. In Tunisia, for example, informal employers earn four times the minimum wage and over two times (2.2) the formal wage. Their employees earn roughly the minimum wage, while industrial outworkers—mostly women home-workers—earn less than one-third (30 per cent) of the minimum wage. In Columbia and India, informal employers earn four to five times the minimum wage, while own-account operators earn only 1.5 times the minimum wage (analysis of national data by Jacques Charmes, cited in Chen et al. 2004).

In brief, within informal labour markets, there is a marked segmentation in terms of average earnings across the different employment statuses outlined earlier. Research findings suggest that it is difficult to move up these segments due to structural barriers (state, market and social) and/or cumulative disadvantage. Many workers, especially women, remain trapped in the lower earning and more risky segments. To statistically test whether there are structural barriers to mobility across the different segments will require better data on key variables—such as education or assets—across these different segments.

## Informalization of Labour Markets

As noted earlier, there is a widespread assumption that the informal economy is countercyclical: that is, it expands during economic downturns and contracts during periods of economic growth. However, recent analyses of data over time from different developing countries suggest a more complex and dynamic picture, with substantial variation in patterns of informalization across countries. As might be expected, sharp economic downturns are associated with a rise in informal employment. But in some countries, steady rates of economic growth are associated with an increase in informal employment. This is because certain forms of informal employment expand during downturns in the economy, such as survival activities and subcontracted and outsourced activities linked to formal firms trying to cope with recession. While certain other forms of informal employment expand during upturns in the economy, such as the more entrepreneurial small firms as well as sub-contracted and out-sourced activities linked to the global production system.

Consider the findings from 20 countries in Asia, Africa and Latin America at two points in time—generally in the 1980s and the 1990s. For each of the countries, the rate of change in informalization is compared to the rate of growth in average per capita gross domestic product over the same time period (Heintz and Pollin 2003, cited in Heintz 2006). Most of the countries (14 out of 20) experienced growth in informalization; four experienced a decline; and two experienced little, if any, change. What is interesting to note, and which goes against the common assumption, informalization increased in three countries with respectable per capita growth rates (>2 per cent) and declined in two countries with poor per capita growth rates (<1 per cent). "These patterns suggest that informal employment has been increasing faster than formal employment, even in countries with strong rates of growth" (Heintz 2006:17). But the authors conclude that "[h]igher rates of growth are generally associated with smaller increases in the rate of informalization. At very high levels of growth, informalization may decline" (Heintz 2006:18; Heintz and Pollin 2003). But they also note that such cross-country comparisons do not include all types of informal employment: this is because the available data often exclude own-account production and informal wage employment, especially industrial outwork. High levels of growth driven by export production may be associated with increases in certain types of informal employment: notably, industrial outwork for global supply chains (see evidence from Tunisia in the following section).

In sum, cyclical patterns cannot fully explain the rate of informalization: Structural factors also play a role. When it comes to informal self-employment, there is a widespread notion that excessive bureaucracy and costly regulations are what drives informality. But economic liberalization is associated with fewer regulations, not more. So what contributes to *structural* informal self-employment? First, the markets in which the smallest informal enterprises compete are often not deregulated in at least the first generation of economic reforms: they often remain either outside the reach or control of government (for example, traditional street-trading in many countries around the world) or under the control of government (for example, minor forest products in India). Second, as noted earlier, people turn to self-employment in the informal economy when they lose a job (which happens under conditions of economic growth as well as economic decline or stagnation) or when they need to supplement their earnings. When it comes to informal wage employment, certain forms of subcontracted and outsourced jobs are associated with the global production system and trade liberalization.

## Developed Countries

Few labour statisticians, economists and other observers in developed countries use the concepts of informal sector or informal employment: the more common concept is that of "nonstandard" work. And the most common categories of nonstandard work for which official data are available are self-employment, part-time work and temporary work. Although not all part-time workers and temporary workers are informally employed, in the sense of being unprotected, many receive few (if any) employment-based benefits or protection.[2] Comparable data on other categories of employment that are even more likely to be informal in nature—namely, contract work, industrial outwork and casual day labour—are not readily available in developed countries.

In North American, European Union (EU), and other Organisation for Economic Co-operation and Development (OECD) countries, available evidence suggests that the workforce has become flexibilized or informalized. In these regions, statisticians and researchers use the concept "nonstandard" work for the forms of work that are flexible or informalized. The term "nonstandard work" as commonly used includes: (i) jobs that entail an employment arrangement that diverges from regular, year-round, full-time employment with a single employer without secure contract; and (ii) self-employment with or without employees (Carré and Herranz 2002). The common categories of nonstandard wage work are temporary work, fixed-term work and part-time work. Increasingly, interfirm subcontracted work in the service sector (such as janitorial services and home care) and in the manufacturing sector (such as garment-making and electronic assembly) are also included. However, data on the following categories of "nonstandard work", which are very likely to be informal (that is, unprotected), are not readily available in developed countries: informal wage work for informal enterprises (employees of the self-employed), for households (domestic workers) or for no fixed employer (casual day-labourers).

What follows is a brief summary of trends in three categories of non-standard work—part-time work, temporary work and self-employment—in Europe (Carré 2006; Carré and Herranz 2002).

### Part-Time Work

Since the early 1970s, there has been a marked growth in the proportion of part-time workers in total employment. By 1998, part-time workers accounted for 16 per cent of total employment in EU countries and 14 per cent of total employment in OECD countries.

### Temporary Employment

For the EU as a whole, and in a majority of EU nations, the share of workers in temporary employment, including both direct hire and agency hire, increased from the mid-1980s to the late 1990s. By 1998, temporary employment accounted for around 10 per cent of total employment in EU countries.

## Self-Employment

Self-employment, including both employers and own-account workers, has increased in many OECD countries over the past 25 years.[3] Indeed, outside of agriculture, self-employment has grown at a faster rate than total employment in 14 (out of 24) OECD countries where data were available. Also, as self-employment has been growing, so has the share of own-account self-employment within total self-employment. As a result, in OECD countries today, more self-employed persons are own-account workers than employers.

## Gendered Patterns

### Informalization of Labour Markets by Sex

The last two decades have seen a marked increase in women's labour force participation: most significantly in the Americas and Western Europe, and more modestly in sub-Saharan Africa, Southeast Asia and East Asia (Heintz 2005; UNRISD 2005). Only in two regions—Eastern Europe and South Asia—has women's labour force participation rate actually fallen. The marked increase in women's labour force participation worldwide has given rise to the notion of the "feminization of the labour force". But this notion has been defined and used in two distinct ways. First, to refer to the situation in which the ratio of women's labour force participation rate to men's labour force participation rate increases over time. Second, to refer to a situation in which the structure of the labour force itself is "feminized": that is, when jobs take on features associated with women's work such as low pay, drudgery, uncertainty and precariousness (Heintz 2005; Standing 1989, 1999).

Whether or not there is a causal link between the increase in women's labour force participation and the growing precariousness or informality of work is not clear—and has been hotly debated. Are the expansion of women's labour force participation and the informalization of labour markets over the past two decades linked in some way, or do they represent parallel but distinct processes? The pervasive segmentation of labour markets by gender, which we will discuss later, suggests that women's labour did not simply substitute for men's labour. Rather, that there has been some parallel process at work creating low-paid and poor quality informal employment opportunities for (primarily) women (Heintz 2005; Standing 1989, 1999).

Estimates of changes over time in the degree of informalization within the female and male labour force are not available. However, a recent analysis of trends in the Tunisian labour market, with a special focus on informal employment, suggests the kind of analysis required and the trends that might be found elsewhere.

Between 1975 and 1997, informal employment in Tunisia grew at a very fast rate. During the economic slump of the 1980s, the share of informal employment increased, accounting for almost 40 per cent of non-agricultural employment by 1989. This trend confirmed the conventional notion that the informal economy is countercyclical, expanding during economic downturns and shrinking during economic growth. However, during the rapid economic growth and trade liberalization of the 1990s, the share of informal employment grew even faster, accounting for over 47 per cent of non-agricultural employment by 1997. In brief, while informal employment grew at an annual rate of over 5 per cent in the late 1970s and 1980s, it grew at an annual rate of 7.5 per cent between 1989 and 1997 (Charmes and Lakehal 2006).

How can this apparent contradiction be explained? The authors make the case, with supporting data, that the distinction between informal employment *inside* the informal sector (that is, small non-registered enterprises) and informal employment *outside* the informal sector is behind this seeming contradiction. During the late 1970s and 1980s, it was largely informal employment *inside* the informal sector that grew. During the economic growth of the 1990s it was largely informal employment *outside* the informal sector that grew: notably, informalized and subcontracted labour for larger enterprises, most of it undeclared. By 1997, less than half of the informal workforce (46 per cent) was employed in small informal enterprises (that is, the informal sector), while over half (54 per cent) was employed as *undeclared informal workers* for both formal and informal enterprises, most of whom are women outworkers for export-oriented firms. In brief, the evidence from Tunisia suggests that, while employment inside the informal sector may be countercyclical, informal employment outside the informal sector may be procyclical (Charmes and Lakehal 2006).

The Tunisian example confirms what the cross-country analysis, summarized earlier, suggests: namely, that certain forms of informal employment—notably, subcontracted work linked to the global production system—expand during periods of economic growth, especially when growth is driven by trade and financial liberalization. What is important to note is that women workers tend to be overrepresented in global production systems, at least in the early stages of industrialization and trade liberalization, when a premium is placed on export-oriented light manufacturing and low-skilled (and low-paid) workers (Chen et al. 2005).

### Informal Employment in Developing Countries by Sex

Informal employment is generally a larger source of employment for women than for men in the developing world. Other than in the Middle East and North Africa, where 42 per cent of women workers (and 48 per cent of male workers) are in informal employment, 60 per cent or more of women non-agricultural workers in the developing world are informally employed. Among non-agricultural workers in sub-Saharan Africa, 84 per cent of women workers are informally employed, compared to 63 per cent of men workers; in Latin America, 58 per cent of women workers, compared to 48 per cent of men; and in Asia, 73 per cent of women workers, compared to 70 per cent of men workers (ILO 2002).

### Segmentation of Informal Employment in Developing Countries by Sex

Available evidence from several developing countries suggests that, as a general rule, relatively high shares of informal employers are men and relatively high shares of industrial outworkers are women. In India, for example, 6 per cent of informal employers, 19 per cent of own-account operators, 16 per cent of informal wage workers and 59 per cent of industrial outworkers are women.[4]

In brief, men tend to be overrepresented in the top segments of the informal economy; women tend to be overrepresented in the bottom segment; and the relative shares of men and women in the intermediate segments vary across sectors and countries. Available evidence also suggests that there are significant gaps in earnings within the informal economy: informal employers have the highest earnings on average; followed by their employees and informal employees of formal firms; then own-account operators, casual wage workers and industrial outworkers. These two stylized facts are depicted graphically in figure 7.1.

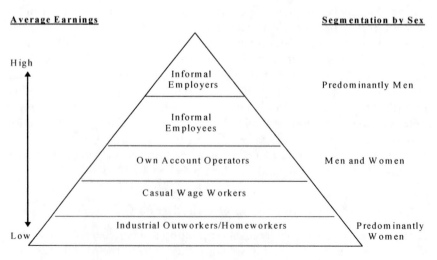

*Figure 7.1* Segmentation of informal employment, by average earnings and sex.

The available data on poverty risk—that is, the likelihood that a worker from a given segment of the labour force is from a poor household—indicate a similar hierarchy. Workers in the formal economy, particularly in public sector formal jobs, are less likely than workers in the informal economy to be from a poor household. Within the informal economy, informal employees are more likely than their employers to be from poor households, own-account operators are more likely than informal employees to be from poor households and so forth down the segmentation pyramid illustrated earlier (Chen et al. 2005). However, analysing the poverty risk of workers, as opposed to their average earnings, is complicated by whether or not a worker is the sole earner, the primary breadwinner or a supplemental earner in her household. For example, because their earnings are so low, women industrial outworkers are likely to be supplemental earners in households with male earners. Whether or not an industrial outworker is from a poor households depends on whether the earnings of the whole household, including her earnings, fall below or above the poverty threshold. If she is the sole or primary breadwinner, the household of a women industrial outworker is very likely to be poor (Chen et al. 2005).

An additional fact, not captured in figure 7.1, is that there is gender segmentation and earning gaps *within* these broad employment status categories. Women tend to work in different types of activities, associated with different levels of earning, than men—with the result that they typically earn less even within specific segments of the informal economy. Some of this difference can be explained by the fact that men tend to embody *more human capital* due to educational discrimination against girls, especially in certain societies (for example, in North India and Pakistan). This difference can also be explained by the fact that men tend to have *better tools* of the trade, operate from *better worksites/spaces* and have *greater access to productive assets and financial capital*. In addition, or as a result, men often *produce or sell a higher volume or a different range* of goods and services. For instance, among street vendors in many countries, men are more likely to sell non-perishables while women are more likely to sell perishable goods (such as fruits and vegetables). In addition, men are more likely to sell from pushcarts or bicycles, while women are more likely to sell from baskets, or simply from a cloth spread on the ground.

In sum, there is a significant range of average earnings and poverty risk within the informal economy by employment status with a small entrepreneurial class (comprised of most informal employers and a few own account operators) and a large working class (comprised of most informal employees, most own-account operators, all casual workers and all industrial outworkers). There is also gender segmentation within informal labour markets, resulting in a gender gap in average earnings with women overrepresented in the lowest paid segments and earning less on average than men within most segments.[5]

### Nonstandard Work in Developed Countries by Sex

#### Part-Time Work

In virtually all EU and OECD countries, the incidence of part-time work is much higher among women than men: in some countries it is twice as high. By 1998, women represented 82 per cent of all part-time workers in EU countries. Further, rates of part-time work are high for women, but not men, in their prime working years.

#### Temporary Employment

Temporary employment, like part-time work, is primarily a female phenomenon, although there is wide variation among EU countries. In all countries except Austria, the incidence of temporary employment among female workers is higher than among all workers. And, like part-time work, temporary employment is concentrated in the service-producing industries. Interestingly, in regard to temporary agency employment, women account for the majority of agency temps in countries where such employment concentrates in services, while men account for the majority of agency temps in countries where such employment concentrates in manufacturing and construction: that is, "the gender composition of employment mirrors that of the sectors in which temporary agency assignments take place" (Carré 2006:13).

#### Self-Employment

In 1997, women comprised one in three self-employed persons in OECD countries and this proportion is growing. For EU countries as a whole, the incidence of own-account work is greater for men (11 per cent) than for women (7 per cent). But, in some countries, a higher proportion of women than men are own-account work. Age is a factor in own-account work, with workers aged 45 and above more likely than younger workers to be own-account workers (Carré 2006).

## IS FORMALIZATION THE ANSWER?

### The Formalization Debate

Over the years, the debate on the informal economy has crystallized into four dominant schools of thought regarding the causes, composition and nature of the informal economy, and what should be done about it. The *dualist* school, popularized by the International Labour Organization (ILO) in the 1970s, sees the informal sector as comprised of marginal and survivalist activities—distinct from and not related to the formal sector—that provide income for the poor and a safety net in times of crisis (ILO 1972; Sethuraman 1976; Tokman 1978). According to this school, the persistence of informal activities—and, thus, a dualistic labour market—is due largely to the fact that not enough modern employment opportunities have been created to absorb surplus labour in developing countries, due to slow rates of economic growth and/or faster rates of population growth.

The *structuralist* school, popularized by Caroline Moser, Alexandro Portes and others in the late 1970s and 1980s, sees informal enterprises and informal wage workers as subordinated to the interests of large capitalist firms, supplying cheap goods and services. In the structuralist model, in marked contrast to the dualist one, formal and informal modes of production are seen to be inextricably connected and interdependent (Moser 1978; Portes et al. 1989). According to this school, the nature of capitalist development (rather than a lack of growth) accounts for the persistence and growth of the informal economy.

The *legalist* school, popularized by Hernando de Soto in the 1980s and 1990s, sees the informal sector as comprised of "plucky" microentrepreneurs who choose to operate informally in order to avoid the costs, time and effort involved in formal registration (de Soto 1989).[6] According to de Soto, cumbersome government rules and procedures create barriers to formalization and thus stifle the productive potential of informal entrepreneurs (de Soto 1989).

The *voluntarism* school, popularized by neoclassical and neoliberal economists across the decades, sees informal entrepreneurs as deliberately seeking to avoid regulations and taxation. According to this school of thought, informal entrepreneurs choose to operate illegally—or even criminally—in order to enjoy the benefits of avoiding taxation, commercial regulations, electricity and rental fees and other costs of operating formally (Maloney 2004). Some voluntarists see the informal economy as dealing with illegal, even criminal, goods and services and, therefore, refer to it as the underground or black economy.

Since these schools of thought focus on different segments of the informal economy—from survivalists to subcontracted producers and workers to independent entrepreneurs—they see different linkages between economic liberalization and informalization. The dualists argue that the informal sector is countercyclical, the structuralists highlight how informal workers and units are subordinated to the global production system, and the legalists and volunteerists focus on regulation and taxation. Each of the schools of thought has distinct notions of what formalization of the informal economy should entail, as follows.

- The *dualists* argue that governments should provide credit and business development services to informal operators as well as basic infrastructure and social services to their families.

- The *structuralists* argue that governments should address the unequal relationship between "big business" and subordinated producers and workers by regulating both commercial and employment relationships.
- The *legalists* argue that governments should introduce simplified bureaucratic procedures to encourage informal enterprises to register and extend legal property rights for the assets held by informal operators in order to unleash their productive potential and convert their assets into real capital (de Soto 1989, 2000).
- The *voluntarists* focus on bringing informal enterprises under the formal regulatory environment in order to increase the tax base and reduce unfair competition by informal enterprises.

Given the heterogeneity of the informal economy, there is merit to each of these perspectives as each school reflects one or another "slice of the (informal) pie". But the informal economy, as a whole, is more heterogeneous and complex than the sum of these perspectives would suggest. Therefore, the common policy prescription of "formalizing the informal economy" needs to be reexamined to reflect all forms of informality.

## Rethinking Formalization

To begin with, it is important to recognize that formalization has different meanings for different segments of the informal economy. To date, the formalization debate has focused primarily on the self-employed in informal enterprises; and often, more specifically, on microentrepreneurs who hire others. At a minimum, the formalization debate needs to distinguish between wage workers in informal jobs and self-employed in informal enterprises. Ideally, it should further distinguish between different segments of the self-employed and wage employed in the informal economy as each segment has its particular needs and constraints.

Second, it is important to ensure that formalization offers the benefits and protections that come with *being* formal and does not simply impose the costs of *becoming* formal. For the self-employed, formalization should not mean just obtaining a license, registering their accounts and paying taxes: these represent, to them, the costs of entry into the formal economy. What they would like is to receive the benefits of operating formally in return for paying these costs, including: enforceable commercial contracts; legal ownership of their place of business and means of production; tax breaks and incentive packages to increase their competitiveness; access to government procurement bids; membership in trade associations; protection against creditors and clear bankruptcy rules; and government contribution to the social protection of themselves and their employees. What about informal wage workers? For them, formalization would involve paying taxes and making some kind of regular social security contribution. In return, formalization would mean obtaining a formal wage job—or converting their current job into a formal job—with a secure contract, worker benefits, membership in a formal trade union and government and employer contributions to their social protection (Chen 2006).

What is required is an approach to formalization of the informal economy that seeks to promote good or appropriate regulations—not deregulation or reregulation—and is comprehensive in design but context-specific in practice. A comprehensive design for formalizing the informal economy should include the elements listed in box 7.1.

---

*Box 7.1* Formalization of the informal economy: A comprehensive approach

*1. Formalization of informal enterprises*

- Registration and taxation:
    - simplified registration procedures
    - progressive registration fees
- Legally-recognized property rights
- Benefits of operating formally:
    - access to finance and market information
    - access to public infrastructure and services
    - enforceable commercial contracts
    - limited liability
    - clear bankruptcy and default rules
    - access to government subsidies and incentives, including procurement bids and export promotion packages
    - membership in formal business associations
    - access to formal system of social security

*2. Formalization of informal jobs*
- Legal recognition and protection as workers
- Rights and benefits of being formally employed:
    - freedom from discrimination
    - minimum wage
    - occupational health and safety measures
    - employer contributions to health and pensions
    - right to organize and bargain collectively
    - membership in formal trade unions
    - access to formal system of social security

In formalizing specific groups of informal workers, policymakers and practitioners should choose appropriate elements from this framework and tailor interventions to meet local circumstances. Consider, for example, the specific conditions of several informal occupations in which large numbers of working poor women tend to be concentrated.

## Street Vendors

The common problems faced by street vendors around the world include:

- insecure place of work, due to competition for urban space;
- capital on unfair terms, due to dependence on wholesale traders;
- uncertain quantity, quality and price of goods, due to dependence on wholesale traders;
- lack of infrastructure: shelter, water, sanitation;
- ambiguous legal status, leading to harassment, evictions and bribes;
- negative public image.

What do street vendors want in exchange for registering their businesses and paying taxes? They want:

- secure vending sites;
- access to capital on fair terms: a loan product tailored to their daily need for working capital;
- bargaining power with wholesale traders;
- infrastructure services at vending sites: shelter, water, sanitation;
- license to sell and identity cards;
- freedom from harassment, evictions and bribes;
- positive public image.

Except in societies where gender norms restrict women's mobility, women account for a major share of street vendors. However, with a few notable exceptions in mainly African countries, women traders are more likely than men traders to have the more risky work situations, by: operating from the street rather than a cart or staff; operating from an insecure or illegal space; trading in perishable goods; generating a lower volume of trade; working as commission agents or employees of other vendors; and not employing others to work for them (Cohen et al. 2000). Consequently, women vendors also tend to earn less than men vendors (Cohen et al. 2000).

## Waste-Collectors

It is estimated that 2 per cent of the world's urban population lives off collecting and recycling waste (Medina 2007). Waste-collectors commonly suffer:

- very low average earnings;
- fluctuations in quantity, quality and price of waste;
- harsh working conditions and related occupational hazards;
- negative public image.

In many waste-collection communities, women and children often collect and sort the waste—thus adding to their exposure to the waste and associated health risks—while the men sell the waste. Since they have to move around different neighbourhoods to collect waste, women and girls face teasing, touching and other forms of sexual harassment (Paula Kantor, personal communication, 2005).

Given these conditions, many waste-collectors would like to find alternative employment opportunities. This can be done within the waste-recycling sector by training them in waste-recycling skills or by organizing them into cooperatives and negotiating contracts for these cooperatives to provide cleaning services to, or collect waste from, government and private offices or institutions.

What would formalization mean for those who continue to work as waste-collectors? It would mean:

- legal recognition and positive public image as waste-collectors (who contribute to the upkeep and cleanliness of the cities they work in);
- identity cards to protect them;
- bargaining mechanisms to negotiate with: (i) those to whom they sell the waste they collect, and (ii) municipal officials and police;
- organization and bargaining power;
- appropriate implements and protective gear (gloves and aprons) to help them avoid dangerous and toxic waste.

## Industrial Outworkers

Around the world, women represent the vast majority (80 per cent in some countries) of industrial outworkers who work from their home (ILO 2002). Industrial outworkers, whether in the garment, shoe or electronic sectors, face a number of common problems:

- low piece-rates and earnings;
- irregularity of work;
- irregular and (often) delayed payments;
- costs of providing/maintaining workspace, utilities and equipment.

In addition, some endure harsh or dangerous working conditions: for example, shoemakers are exposed to toxic glues. Many also suffer sore backs and deteriorating eyesight from working in badly equipped and poorly lit workplaces (often their own homes).

What would formalization mean for industrial outworkers? It would mean:

- regular, secure and enforceable work orders;
- regular and timely payments;
- piece-rates that are equivalent to minimum wages;
- occupational health and safety measures;
- capital to improve their workspace (often their home) and upgrade their equipment.

In today's global economy, there is probably no greater difference in terms of market power and wealth than between the chief executive officer of a multinational corporation that sells garments, footballs or electronic goods, and the woman industrial outworker who stitches or assembles these goods for that firm in her home.

## Construction Workers

In many developing countries, where the industry has not been mechanized, the construction workforce is comprised largely of casual day-labourers, often migrants. Many such construction workers are unskilled and engaged in lifting and carrying loads of cement, bricks and concrete. Except in societies where gender norms restrict women's mobility, women represent a significant share of the unskilled construction workforce.

What are the common problems of unskilled construction workers? They include:

- irregular days of work;
- low and erratic earnings;
- arduous and hazardous work: frequent accidents and occasional deaths;
- lack of occupational health and safety measures;
- lack of accident or disability insurance.

What would formalization mean to construction workers? It would mean:

- more regular work;
- higher wages;
- skills training: masonry, carpentry and other construction skills;
- safety regulations;
- accident insurance and workers' compensation;
- identity cards;
- registers or other proof of days of work.

## Horticulture Export Workers

In Latin America and (less so) Africa, there has been a notable increase in women agricultural workers in the non-traditional agro-export sectors: specifically, in the production and packaging of fresh flowers, fruit and vegetables (see chapters by Deere and Whitehead in this volume; see also Barrientos and Barrientos 2002; Barrientos et al. 2004).

What are the common problems of women workers in these agro-export sectors? They include:

- temporary contracts;
- uncertain days and hours of work, associated with "flexible" contracts;
- piece-rate payments and low wages;
- occupational segregation by gender (especially in packing houses).

What kind of formalization would these agricultural workers want? They would want:

- permanent contracts;
- regular days and hours of work;
- wage payments and higher wages;
- opportunities to shift to better paid work within occupation.

## Challenges to Formalization

Admittedly, implementing a comprehensive yet context-specific approach to formalization will not be easy or straightforward. Among the key policy challenges facing such an approach are what to do about informal employers. Many informal wage workers work for informal firms. The policy challenge is whether and how to make informal employers comply with labour regulations and offer their employees formal benefits and protections. This is what the ILO has referred to as "the dilemma of the informal sector" (ILO 1991). It is genuinely difficult for many informal employers to offer legal benefits and protection to their employees at their present level of operations and profits. This suggests that formalization may need to be sequenced as follows: by first providing incentives and benefits to informal enterprises that register and then progressively enforcing compliance with taxation and labour regulations (ILO 1991).[7] But available evidence suggests that many informal employers are not poor (Chen et al. 2004, 2005). For this more entrepreneurial class of informal operators, the issue is less whether they are *able* to comply with commercial and employment regulations than whether they are *willing* to comply.

Another related challenge is what to do about *formal* employers who hire workers under informal employment relations or subcontract production to a chain of suppliers. Faced with global competition, formal firms or employers often prefer to hire workers under flexible contracts or to outsource or subcontract production. In today's global production system, suppliers are often small informal enterprises who, in turn, hire workers under informal contracts or subcontracts. Hence, for producers of labour-intensive products, such as garments, who operate in global markets where demand is sensitive to price, there needs to be simultaneous change in all countries, otherwise they will be squeezed out of the market if they are the only ones to have to increase their prices as a result of meeting higher labour costs.

In sum, both formal firms and larger informal firms need a special package of incentives and sanctions to encourage them to provide benefits and protection to their workers. Admittedly, there is the risk of offering unnecessary incentives for them to extend benefits/protection to their workers or creating perverse incentives for them to continue to deny benefits/protection to their workers. But, this risk notwithstanding, appropriate labour standards and social protection can, and should, be developed for informal wage workers through tripartite negotiations, including employers (formal or informal), the government and informal workers. The Self-Employed Women's Association (SEWA), the well-known trade union of women informal workers in India, has effectively negotiated with the government and employers/contractors to obtain wage increases, annual bonuses, health benefits and/or pension contributions for a wide range of informal workers, including: day-labourers in construction and agriculture and industrial outworkers who produce garments, embroidered goods, incense sticks and *bidis* (cigarettes) at home.

Those who run single-person or family businesses present a different kind of challenge. To begin with, they do not hire workers. Second, they often earn so little that they fall into the lowest tax brackets. What *are* burdensome to these operators are the bureaucratic regulations and fees related to registering their businesses. For them, formalization requirements need to be made simpler and less costly through, for instance, a single-window registry system and differentiated registration fees (that is, depending on the size, output or location of their enterprises). For them, formalization should be seen as an incremental process that begins by introducing appropriate incentives and benefits of formality and then progressively enforces compliance with the costs and regulations associated with operating formally. This would create the conditions under which the working poor in the informal economy would be entitled to the benefits of formality while, at the same time, being enabled to comply with the duties of formality.

## Limits to Formalization

As outlined in this chapter, formalization of the informal economy can, and should, take different forms, including: creating incentives for the informal self-employed to register their enterprises and benefits for them once they do; and creating a mix of incentives and sanctions for employers, both formal and informal, to extend benefits to their informal workers.

However, the limits to formalization need to be understood. First, it should be recognized that formalization is *not* a one-time process involving a specified set of steps. Rather, formalization should be seen as a gradual ongoing process involving incremental steps and different dimensions leading towards varying degrees and types of formality. Second, it should be recognized that formalization will *not* proceed quickly or automatically for all those who choose to formalize. The bureaucratic procedures and incentives for registered informal businesses need to be retooled and streamlined. Labour standards and benefits for informal workers need to be carefully negotiated by employers, workers and government. Third, it should be recognized that formalization will *not* be feasible or desirable for all informal enterprises or all informal wage workers. Rather, it should be assumed that many informal enterprises and informal wage workers will remain informal or semi-formal for the foreseeable future. In other words, informality—in varying degrees and forms—is here to stay.

Other fundamental challenges, then, are to create more formal employment opportunities and to decrease the costs and increase the benefits of those who continue to operate informally or semi-formally.

## BEYOND FORMALIZATION

### Reorienting Economic Policies

Clearly, there are limits to thinking of formalization in narrow "one size fits all" or "magic bullet" ways. While streamlining registration procedures for informal enterprises and extending property rights to informal operators are critically important, they are hardly sufficient. The informal economy is simply too big, too heterogeneous and too segmented for simple solutions. The global development community needs to recognize that to reduce poverty and inequality, including gender inequality, it has to deal with the informal economy in a comprehensive way that goes beyond formalization per se. Too many people—especially the working poor and women in particular—earn their living in the informal economy for it to be treated as a legal problem requiring formalization or a social problem that can be redressed by social policies alone. The challenge is to reorient development strategies—and development economics—to deal front and centre with the informal economy.

To deal effectively with the informal economy—and those who earn their livelihoods in it—will require a comprehensive economic strategy with three interrelated components: (i) creating more employment opportunities through employment-intensive growth; (ii) formalizing informal enterprises and informal jobs through a context-specific mix of incentives and regulations; (iii) improving conditions and increasing returns of those who continue to work informally.

Component (i) requires putting employment creation back at the centre of macroeconomic policies, ensuring that employment is labour-intensive and targeting investments at low-income communities and under-developed areas. Component (ii) requires implementing context-specific elements of the comprehensive approach to formalization outlined earlier. Component (iii) requires a complimentary set of policies to help those who continue to operate informally improve their working conditions and get higher returns to their labour by increasing assets and competitiveness, assuring better terms and conditions of work, securing appropriate legal frameworks and addressing risk and uncertainty.[8]

## Reforming the Regulatory Environment

An essential dimension of this reorientation of economic policies is the reform of existing laws, regulations and institutions. This does not mean deregulation but *appropriate regulations*. As the evidence presented in this volume has highlighted, work is increasingly informal in today's global economy, rendering obsolete many of the features of existing legislation, regulations and institutions modelled on the modern industrial era job. To legitimize and protect all types of workers today will require, in the end, reforming the laws, regulations and institutions that govern both commercial and employment relations. Laws, regulations and institutions governing commercial relations need to reflect the reality that most economic units are very small with few hired workers and that many working poor operate on their own account. Similarly, laws, regulations and institutions governing employment relations need to reflect the reality that most wage workers are not formal employees. Also, biases in existing laws, regulations and institutions that favour large enterprises over small enterprises, formal workers over informal workers and men over women in both categories need to be addressed. In the absence of new more appropriate laws, regulations and institutions, most of the working poor in the informal economy will remain unprotected, insecure and vulnerable.

Changing the existing regulatory regime should not be seen simply in "either-or" terms—regulation versus deregulation. The goal is, rather, appropriate regulations. Changing the existing regulatory regime in appropriate ways should not be seen as a pipe dream. Proposals have been made and measures have been taken to deal with the growing numbers of nonstandard wage workers in developed countries. To address the new employment relationship in the United States, which renders obsolete many features of the existing labour law regime, several types of legal reforms have been proposed and/or tested: benefit portability and broader safety nets; new anti-discrimination strategies; the legal right to organize across employer units; broader notions of bargaining units; and labour organizations that operate across industries and across firms in local or regional geographic areas (Stone 2004).

The EU has issued directives on part-time work (1997) and fixed-term employment (1999) to uphold the principle of "non-discrimination" between such workers and workers in formal contracts. The extent to which workers in part-time and fixed-term jobs are protected by these directives depends on the degree to which these directives are implemented in member states as well as pre-existing national regulations or collective bargaining agreements in those states. In particular, eligibility criteria such as mandated thresholds of employment continuity, work hours and years of experience need to be adjusted to ensure part-time and fixed-term workers are eligible for social protection measures such as unemployment insurance and pensions (Carré 2006).

Some EU countries have extended the right to representation in collective bargaining arrangements to nonstandard workers. In some EU countries, depending often on their length of experience, fixed-term workers have the right to attend meetings of workplace representative bodies as well as to vote and present their candidacy in elections. Temporary agency workers tend to participate in representation structures, if any, within the temporary agency itself, rather than in that of the user firm. In several countries, union membership is not a precondition for coverage under collective bargaining agreements. For the self-employed, the main option is belonging to, or building, an association of similar workers. But there are a few examples of trade unions reaching out to and incorporating the self-employed (Carré 2006).

In developing countries, there have also been efforts to extend existing labour and social protection regimes to cover informal workers. In Ghana, the Ghana Trades Union Congress (GTUC) carried out a review of national labour laws and found that the laws were outdated, fragmented and did not match either the work realities or the Ghanaian constitution. The GTUC resolved to push for reforms of existing laws to extend protection enjoyed by formal workers to informal workers. The resulting New Labour Act (2003) was negotiated through a tripartite process involving the government, trade unions and employers. The act allows temporary and casual workers to benefit from provisions of collective agreements on equal pay for work of equal value, access to the same medical provisions available to permanent workers and a full minimum wage for all days in attendance and public holidays. In addition, the act mandates that a temporary worker employed by the same employer for a continuous period of six months or more must be treated as a permanent worker (Kofi Asamoah, personal communication, 2004, cited in Chen et al. 2005; Owusu 2003).

In India, a national policy on street vendors was officially adopted in early 2004. Jointly drafted by the Government of India and the National Association of Street Vendors of India (NASVI), this policy includes provisions mandating legal status, special hawking and vending spaces, fee-based licenses, organization and representation and social security and financial services for street vendors. Other bills which would provide social protection to, and guarantee minimum working conditions for, all informal workers were being debated in the Indian parliament in late 2007.

## Empowering Informal Workers

To promote and sustain this major reorientation of economic policies and regulations, two preconditions are essential. First, increased *visibility* of informal workers—especially working poor women and men—in labour force statistics and other official data used in formulating policies. Second, the *representative voice* of informal workers—especially working poor women and men—in the processes and institutions that determine economic policies and the formal regulatory environment. Arguably, official visibility and representative voice are the two most *essential* and *enabling* dimensions of formalization for the working poor in the informal economy. Being visible in official statistics and to policymakers, and having representative voice in policy-making institutions and processes is what will ensure that the working poor can demand and ensure that both formalization per se and the broader economic strategy outlined earlier meet their needs and suit their circumstances.

Again, increasing the voice and visibility of informal workers should not be seen as a pipe dream. Over the past two decades, organizations of informal workers have been coming together to form a growing international movement of informal workers. There is now a global alliance of street vendor organizations (called StreetNet) as well as national and regional networks of organizations of home-based workers (called HomeNets) (see chapter 6 in Chen et al. 2005). And, over the past decade, concerted efforts have been made by the ILO, the International Expert Group on Informal Sector Statistics and the Women in Informal Employment: Globalizing and Organizing (WIEGO) network to improve statistics on informal employment, and to make these accessible to informal workers and their organizations (see chapter 4 in ILO 2002).

## Engendering the Process

Further, it is important to recognize that both informal and formal markets are gendered institutions: that there is gender segmentation and a gender gap in earnings/pay within both informal and formal labour markets. In the informal economy, women are concentrated in the segments of the informal economy associated with the lowest earnings and highest risks. But even when women and men do similar kinds of informal work, there is often a gender gap in earnings.

In part, this gender gap in earnings reflects differences in the amount of time that women and men are able to spend in paid work. Most societies around the world share a common gender division of labour whereby women are associated with reproduction (unpaid care work) and men with production (paid market work). As a result, many women are forced, or conditioned, to engage in paid employment that is home-based. Formalization should include the provision of childcare services to allow women the choice of whether to engage in paid work outside their homes. In addition to the greater demands on their time, women's access to property is typically less than that of men and often mediated through their relationship to men; women's access to education, finances and other resources are typically less than that of men; and women often face greater social constraints on their physical mobility than men. Formalization could address these constraints as well.

## BEYOND FORMALITY AND INFORMALITY

In closing, it is important to consider that informality may not be the problem, and that formalization may not be the answer. After all, in developing countries, the majority of all workers and the vast majority of the working poor, especially women and other disadvantaged groups, work in the informal economy. And in developed countries, nonstandard work is expanding. After all, many of the existing formal economic institutions are now obsolete, modelled in the mid-twentieth century on mass production, large factories, firms and so-called "modern" jobs in industrialized countries. Given the persistence and growth of informal employment in developing countries—and the informalization of once modern jobs in developed countries—much of economic reality in the new millennium does not fit the twentieth-century industrial model. Imposing the existing narrow set of formal economic institutions on the large diverse set of informal economic activities may be neither desirable nor feasible. What is needed are twenty-first century institutional arrangements—a creative mix of formal and informal—for twenty-first century economic realities.

## NOTES

1. This summary is based on recent analyses of available national data, as indicated, as well as earlier summaries of these analyses in Chen and others (2004, 2005). The authors of ILO (2002), as well as Heintz and Pollin (2003), analysed a common set of official national data collected and compiled by Jacques Charmes.
2. It should be noted that part-time work is often not informal (that is, unprotected). In the Nordic countries, part-time work is often long-term with social protection. In the United States, however, part-time workers are offered very few benefits: in the mid-1990s, less that 20 per cent of regular part-time workers had employer-sponsored health insurance or pensions (Hudson 1999).
3. Statisticians distinguish three main subcategories of self-employment: (i) "employers", the self-employed who hire others; (ii) "own-account workers", who do not hire others; and (iii) "unpaid contributing family workers".

However, many statistical analyses, such as those by the OECD reported by Carré (2006), exclude unpaid family members because they are considered "assistants", not "entrepreneurs". Since the majority of unpaid family workers in most contexts are women, this exclusion understates the real level of women's labour force participation and entrepreneurship (Carré 2006).

4. These figures were computed by Jeemol Unni, using the individual records of the Employment and Unemployment Survey, 1999–2000, 55th Round of the National Sample Survey Organization, New Delhi.

5. For a detailed analysis of available statistics on the gender segmentation of the informal economy and the linkages between working in the informal economy, being a woman or man and being poor, see Chen and others (2004, 2005).

6. In a similar vein, neoclassical and neoliberal economists argue that labour market regulations (for example, dealing with minimum wage or hiring/firing) encourage employers to shed workers or to hire workers under informal contracts, thus justifying the deregulation of labour markets.

7. For a similar argument, including the need for government industrial policies, see Tendler (2004).

8. For a detailed elaboration with good practice examples of the comprehensive yet context-specific response to informal employment, see Chen and others (2005).

## REFERENCES

Barrientos, A. and S.W. Barrientos. 2002. *Extending Social Protection to Informal Workers in the Horticulture Global Value Chain.* Social Protection Discussion Paper No. 0216, World Bank, Washington, DC.

Barrientos, S., A. Kritzinger and H. Rossouw. 2004. "National labour regulations in an international context: Women workers in export horticulture in South Africa." In M. Carr (ed.), *Chains of Fortune: Linking Local Women Producers and Workers with Global Markets.* Commonwealth Secretariat, London.

Carré, F. 2006. *Flexibility, Informalization, and New Forms of Work: Non-Standard Work Arrangements in Western Europe.* Working Paper prepared for joint ILO-WIEGO project on Labour and Informality: Rethinking Work.

Carré, F. and J. Herranz, Jr. 2002. "Informal Jobs in Industrialized 'North' Countries." Background paper for *Women and Men in the Informal Economy: A Statistical Picture,* ILO, Geneva.

Charmes, J. and M. Lakehal. 2006. "Industrialization and New Forms of Employment in Tunisia." Working Paper prepared for joint ILO-WIEGO project on Labour and Informality: Rethinking Work.

Chen, M. 2006. "Rethinking the informal economy: Linkages with the formal economy and informal regulatory environment." In B. Guha-Khasnobis, R. Kanbur and E. Ostrom (eds.), *Linking the Formal and Informal Economy: Concepts and Measures.* Oxford University Press, Oxford.

———. 2005. *Self-Employed Women: The Membership of SEWA.* Self-Employed Women's Association, Ahmedabad, India.

Chen, M.A., J. Vanek and M. Carr. 2004. *Mainstreaming Informal Employment and Gender in Poverty Reduction: A Handbook for Policy-Makers and Other Stakeholders.* Commonwealth Secretariat, London.

Chen, M.A., J. Vanek, F. Lund, J. Heintz, with R. Jhabvala and C. Bonner. 2005. *Progress of the World's Women 2005: Women, Work, and Poverty.* UNIFEM, New York.

Cohen, M., M. Bhatt and P. Horn. 2000. *Women Street Vendors: The Road to Recognition.* SEEDS Pamphlet Series, Population Council, New York.

De Soto, H. 2000. *The Mystery of Capital: Why Capitalism Triumphs in the West and Fails Everywhere Else.* Basic Books, New York.
———. 1989. *The Other Path: The Economic Answer to Terrorism.* Harper Collins, New York.
Heintz, J. 2006. "Growth, Employment, and Poverty Reduction." Discussion paper prepared for the Growth, Employment and Poverty Reduction Workshop, Department for International Development, London, 17 March.
———. 2005. "Globalization, Economic Policy and Employment: Poverty and Gender Implications." Employment Strategy Paper No. 6, Employment Policy Unit, Employment Strategy Department, ILO, Geneva.
Heintz, J. and R. Pollin. 2003. "Informalization, Economic Growth and the Challenge of Creating Viable Labor Standards in Developing Countries." Political Economy Research Institute Working Paper No. 60, Political Economy Research Institute, University of Massachusetts Amherst, Amherst, MA.
Hudson, K. 1999. "No Shortage of 'Nonstandard' Jobs: Nearly 30% of Workers Employed in Part-Time, Temping, and Other Alternative Arrangements." Economic Policy Institute Briefing Paper 89, Economic Policy Institute, Washington, DC.
International Labour Organization. 2002. *Women and Men in the Informal Economy: A Statistical Picture.* ILO, Geneva.
———. 1991. *The Dilemma of the Informal Sector, Report of the Director-General, International Labour Conference, 78th Session.* ILO, Geneva.
———. 1972. *Employment, Incomes and Equality: A Strategy for Increasing Productive Employment in Kenya.* ILO, Geneva.
Maloney, W.F. 2004. "Informality revisited." *World Development,* Vol. 32, No. 7, pp. 1159–1178.
Medina, M. 2007. *The World's Scavengers: Salvaging for Sustainable Consumption and Production.* AltaMira Press, Blue Ridge Summit, PA.
Moser, C.N. 1978. "Informal sector or petty commodity production: Dualism or independence in urban development." *World Development,* Vol. 6, pp. 1041–1064.
Owusu, F.X. 2003. "Ghana: Where the strong help the weaker." In Federatie Nederlandse Vakbeweging (FNV) (ed.), *From Marginal Work to Core Business: European Trade Unions Organising in the Informal Economy.* FNV, Amsterdam.
Polaski, S. 2004. "Jobs, wages and household income." In John Audley (ed.), *NAFTA's Promise and Reality: Lessons from Mexico for the Hemisphere.* Carnegie Endowment for International Peace, Washington, DC.
Portes, A., M. Castells, and L.A. Benton (eds.). 1989. *The Informal Economy: Studies in Advanced and Less Developed Countries.* Johns Hopkins University Press, Baltimore.
Sethuraman, S.V. 1976. "The urban informal sector: Concept, measurement and policy." *International Labour Review,* Vol. 114, No. 1, pp. 69–81.
Standing, G. 1999. "Global feminization through flexible labour: A theme revisited." *World Development,* Vol. 27, No. 3, pp. 583–602.
———. 1989. "Global feminization through flexible labour." *World Development,* Vol. 17, No. 7, pp. 1077–1095.
Stone, K.V.W. 2004. *From Widgets to Digits: Employment Regulation for the Changing Workplace.* Cambridge University Press, New York.
Tendler, J. 2004. "Why social policy is condemned to a residual category of safety nets and what to do about it." In T. Mkandawire (ed.), *Social Policy in a Development Context.* Palgrave Macmillan, Basingstoke.
Tokman, V. 1978. "An exploration into the nature of the informal-formal sector relationship." *World Development,* Vol. 6, Nos. 9 and 10, pp. 1065–1075.

United Nations Development Fund for Women (UNIFEM). 2000. *NAFTA's Impact on the Female Work Force in Mexico.* UNIFEM, Mexico City.

United Nations Research Institute for Social Development (UNRISD). 2005. *Gender Equality: Striving for Justice in an Unequal World.* UNRISD, Geneva.

White, M., C. Salas and S. Gammage. 2003. *NAFTA and the FTAA: A Gender Analysis of Employment and Poverty Impacts in Agriculture.* Women's Edge Coalition, Washington, DC.

# 8 Women's Migration, Social Reproduction and Care

*Nicola Yeates*

## INTRODUCTION

If liberalization and the global economic restructuring that accompanied it set free both financial and industrial capital to roam the world in search of the highest return, so also did streams of people begin to flow in partial response to the local, national, regional and global social changes that these transformations brought. Responses to these movements of people showed the limits of the supposed hypermobility that is a much praised characteristic of globalization: While elites have been free to flow across state borders with ease and in comfort, increased regulation and restrictions have been placed on the movement of those not blessed with elite membership. Thus, the European Union (EU) began to construct not just a Social Europe but also a Fortress Europe restricting entry into Member States by non-EU citizens from poorer countries. Similarly, the United States, a country built on successive waves of migration, began to construct a fence/wall between itself and its southern neighbours. Other regional concentrations of economic wealth also maintain highly controlled access regimes for non-nationals.

The energetic attempts to regulate, indeed restrict, international migration sit uneasily alongside the proclaimed removal of regulatory barriers to international exchanges and transfers. More than this, these responses to international migration confound the basic tenets of liberal theory that presents globalization as the welcome loosening of political constraints upon economic production and exchange, as creating greater choice and prosperity for all those participating in the new global economy and as a force leading to greater political and economic integration worldwide. The contradictory nature of responses to recent waves of international migration are further thrown into relief when we consider that current migration levels are not the highest recorded historically: "migration has now reached the level of the 1920s but far below that recorded before the First World War" (Samers 1999:170). In addition, international migration is dwarfed by the scale of internal rural–urban migration prompted by agricultural restructuring, depeasantization and urbanization resulting from ongoing transformations of national and global economies (Araghi 1995:338). One of the greatest population movements currently underway is happening within the borders of one country, China, where recent calculations estimate the floating population, driven from the land by the market system and drawn to the cities by the prospect of work in world factories, at 140 million in 2003 (Ping and Shaohua 2005:2).

Migration, whether within or between countries, raises important questions about the nature of social transformations accompanying economic liberalization. It invites closer examination of the ways in which social reproduction systems are embroiled in the global restructuring of production. It opens up for analysis individual, household, family and community strategies in response to uneven development and socioeconomic insecurity. It begs further investigation into contemporary social morphologies and topographies, including the ways in which global processes intersect with and effect changes to social institutions such as familial, employment and welfare systems. This chapter explores these questions through a discussion of the entanglement between international migration and social reproduction. Through a focus on the ways in which this migration is inextricably caught up in the social reorganization of care, we explore the ways in which social divisions of labour—of class, gender, "race", ethnicity and caste—are (re)constituted on a global scale.

Following an overview of the literature on women's international migration, the chapter examines how the relationship between globalization and social reproduction has been addressed in the research literature. Developing recent theorizations of this relationship that focus on the international mobility of social reproductive labour, the subsequent sections review how different migrant groups illustrate the socio-spatial restructuring of care. This discussion includes a reflection on the ways in which this migration is caught up with the restructuring of welfare states in the Global North and the "care drain" in the Global South.

## FEMALE MIGRATION IN CONTEXT

While many analysts profess to have discovered an increasing feminization of international migration, available evidence shows only a slight overall increase in female migration in recent decades. As the International Organization on Migration (IOM) reports,

> the participation of women in international migration has been high for a long time . . . while it is true that the participation of women in certain types of flows, and from certain countries, has risen, the main finding is that, already by 1970 overall female migration had nearly reached parity with male migration. (IOM 2005:394)

This is confirmed by a useful data analysis for the Organisation for Economic Co-operation and Development (OECD) and the European Commission which concludes that "[o]ver the last decade, according to the available data, there has been a slight upward trend in the feminization of migration flows to OECD member countries" (Casas and Garson 2005:13). These feminization processes have developed somewhat unevenly. As table 8.1 shows, since 1960 the proportion of female migrants in the more developed regions increased from 47.9 per cent in 1960 to 50.9 per cent in 2000, while in the less developed regions it was the same in 2000 as in 1960 (45.7 per cent). The most marked increases (four percentage points or more in 2000, compared with 1960) were in sub-Saharan Africa, Oceania, Latin America and Eastern and Southeastern Asia. Only in South Asia has there been a "de-feminization" of migration (46.3 per cent in 1960, compared with 44.4 per cent in 2000).

The general flow from the Global South to the Global North is interlaced with regional divisions of labour. Regarding health-worker migration, for example, one significant destination area is the Middle East, specifically the states of the Arabian Gulf, where the recent development of health services has mainly drawn on non-national labour forces, with the Gulf States' need for health workers being supplied by migrants from the Philippines, Egypt, Bangladesh and India. Another example of a regionally important

*Table 8.1* Female Migrants as a Percentage of Migrants Living Outside Their Country of Birth, by Area, 1960–2000

| Major area | 1960 | 1970 | 1980 | 1990 | 2000 |
|---|---|---|---|---|---|
| World | 46.6 | 47.2 | 47.4 | 47.9 | 48.8 |
| More developed regions | 47.9 | 48.2 | 49.4 | 50.8 | 50.9 |
| Less developed regions | 45.7 | 46.3 | 45.5 | 44.7 | 45.7 |
| Europe | 48.5 | 48.0 | 48.5 | 51.7 | 52.4 |
| Northern America | 49.8 | 51.1 | 52.6 | 51.0 | 51.0 |
| Oceania | 44.4 | 46.5 | 47.9 | 49.1 | 50.5 |
| Northern Africa | 49.5 | 47.7 | 45.8 | 44.9 | 42.8 |
| Sub-Saharan Africa | 40.6 | 42.1 | 43.8 | 46.0 | 47.2 |
| Southern Asia | 46.3 | 46.9 | 45.9 | 44.4 | 44.4 |
| Eastern and Southeastern Asia | 46.1 | 47.6 | 47.0 | 48.5 | 50.1 |
| Western Asia | 45.2 | 46.6 | 47.2 | 47.9 | 48.3 |
| Caribbean | 45.3 | 46.1 | 46.5 | 47.7 | 48.9 |
| Latin America | 44.7 | 46.9 | 48.4 | 50.2 | 50.5 |

*Source*: Zlotnik 2003.

destination area is South Africa, which is a significant destination for nurses migrating from, for example, Swaziland (Buchan et al. 2005:11) and Zambia, demonstrating that a nearby regional developed country can be as important a destination as the Northern developed countries of Europe and North America (Munjanja et al. 2005:21). Within the Global North, it has long been observed that the "brain drain" occurs at different levels from Canada to the United States, and the United Kingdom and Ireland to the United States (Wickramasekara 2003). While much of the literature tries to identify "importing" and "exporting" countries, it is important to recognize that many countries simultaneously import and export labour. Thus, Ireland and England, which draw on peripheral countries for their nursing staff, export nurses to other core economies such as the United States and Australia.

Immigration regimes and policies impact differently on women and men due to their different labour market positions and social roles. Women are less likely than men to enter on economic grounds as fewer of them fall into the designated occupational categories. For example, even though in Western Europe and North America information technology (IT) workers and paid domestic workers are both in short supply, the former enjoy a considerable array of rights and freedoms compared with the latter (Piper 2005). Moreover, although many emigrant women are well qualified with marketable skills, they are disproportionately concentrated at the lower rungs of the services and manufacturing sectors (Piper 2005:8). This is well documented in the care services sectors. Regarding health care, qualified nurses' migration often results in their downward occupational mobility and they tend to be used as a temporary stop-gap to fill labour shortages. Many of them end up working as care assistants in residential nursing homes if their nursing qualification is not recognized in the destination country; others are channelled into lower grade, lower status and "non-career" nursing and nursing auxiliary posts that are not concomitant with their skills (Bach 2003:17; Hardill and Mac-Donald 2000).

The intersection between gender and ethnicity in the formation of global services labour markets is relevant here. In the nursing sector, there are reports of discriminatory wage and occupational structures between European and Asian nurses in the Middle East: "health services are mainly staffed by Egyptians, Indians, Pakistanis and Filipinos in base level nursing positions, and North Americans and the British in senior or administrative positions" (Ball 2004:128). The domestic services sector, which is in many ways an archetypal gender-specific industry providing a key occupational niche for migrant women, is also stratified by skin colour and cultural considerations, with employers expressing a preference for those with (assumed or real) behavioural, cultural, linguistic or religious traits thought to bear on the quality of the service provided. Maher (2003) has shown that the market for foreign domestic workers in California and

Chile is underpinned by a discourse that sees imported Mexican maids and Peruvian nannies as, respectively, "submissive" workers and "natural mothers", echoing narratives about the "nimble fingers" of female Asian electronics workers. While these discourses legitimate the segmented labour market, they also indicate the special domestic and nurturing skills that employers often hope to extract from these workers. A similar dual function is performed by the stereotype that considers Filipino nurses to possess exceptional nurturing qualities, or Thai sex workers to possess exceptional sexual skills. Various studies of domestic workers have reported the prevalence of a racialized global hierarchy among representations of European and Asian nannies based on skin colour and ascribed cultural attributes. This hierarchy is reproduced in wages and working conditions, with European nannies being considered more as professionals and Filipina nannies perceived more as servants. While Filipinas are situated lower down in North American hierarchies, in Italy and Jordan they occupy a higher position in the hierarchy compared with Sri Lankan and African women due to being lighter skinned and English-speaking (Tyner 1999).

While the foregoing may seem to present women as subject to various global pressures beyond their control, recent feminist research emphasizes the role of women as agents within the migration process and migrant social networks, together with the importance of social expectations of the women as responsible for the family, be it sited in a single national location or transnationally across countries. Thus, Asis and others (2004) note that in the Southeast Asian context it is often women who initiate the idea of migration rather than having the household decide for them: Migration represents "convergence between family aspirations and individual aspirations" (Asis et al. 2004:205, citing Oishi 2001 and Wille and Passel 2001). At another level, the role of women in enabling and supporting individual migrants and sustaining international migration is also emphasized, with migrants drawing on personal, familial and community networks to provide care labour for relatives "left behind". Thus it is the sustained care labour of female members of families and wider community for children that enables the migration of their mothers (and fathers). Other research has similarly emphasized the role of women as agents in migrant social networks. In a study of Mexico–United States migration, Kanaiaupuni (2000) highlighted how women maintain family cohesion, mobilize origin networks and ensure economic provision of families; they not only initiate but perpetuate international migration.

The presentation of migrant women as victims of international economic and local patriarchal structures is increasingly being countered by the emphasis on how (in this case, specifically Asian) migrant women "develop greater individual autonomy, engage in everyday resistance and take collective action" (Yamanaka and Piper 2005:6). The growth of national and transnational activism among these women is indeed a sign of change. Ally (2005), for example, has traced the international spread of organizing among migrant domestic workers using associational rather than trade union forms. While this activism has yet to achieve substantial gains, it is an indication of interesting times to come. Associated with this is a growth in the national and transnational operations of a wide variety of non-governmental organizations (NGOs) prioritizing the protection of migrant workers' rights (Yamanaka and Piper 2005).

## GLOBAL RESTRUCTURING, MIGRATION AND SOCIAL REPRODUCTION

There has been a sustained line of research inquiry focusing on the relationship between the global restructuring of production, social reproduction and international migration. Much of this literature has highlighted the adverse social impacts of this restructuring, focusing on the impacts of the globalization of production upon the socioeconomic livelihoods and survival strategies of individuals, households/families and communities. It has pointed to the ways in which migration is a key response to the restructuring of the manufacturing and agricultural sectors on a global scale, and to the uneven nature of "development" more generally. A vast literature has developed around the ways in which the growth of export-oriented production has used female labour. In manufacturing employment "the appearance of duty-free zones has caused an increase in female migration flows in developing countries, particularly in Latin America, Asia and the Caribbean" (Casas and Garson 2005:4). There is a large literature on capital's predilection for women workers in these world market factories: "In Asia these are mostly unmarried women aged between 17 and 23, with the highest densities being 88 per cent in Sri Lanka, Taiwan and Malaysia, and around 75 per cent in Republic of Korea and the Philippines" (De Angelis 1997:49). This type of migration tends to be internal rather than international, as in the "classic" example of Mexican women moving to the Mexican–US border to work in the *maquiladoras*. This industrialization by supposed "modern" methods has benefited from state and local patriarchal social structures.

In world-systems theory, international migration is a response to the penetration of capitalist social relations to less industrialized countries that releases individuals from production in the traditional subsistence economy to participate in the market economy. Migration, first to cities and then to wealthier industrial countries, for paid work is pursued by semi-proletarian households to enable their below subsistence and unstable wages to be supplemented to a level necessary for labour reproduction (Wallerstein and Smith 1992). Although this body of literature makes explicit the connections between the global restructuring of production and social reproduction, the gender dimensions of these processes are often obscured. While such accounts may have identified the range of ways in which household production subsidizes global production (Sassen 2002), they stop short of recognizing the importance of women's reproductive labour in sustaining production in global production processes and networks. Yet as Dunaway (2001) correctly argues, before the expropriations underpinning the inequitable division of surplus among the core, semi-periphery and periphery can occur "the commodity chain structures the maximal exploitation of underpaid and unpaid labour" (Dunaway 2001:10), flowing from the subsistence, informal and illegal economies; not only the kinds of work at the margins of the market economy, but that which lies outside that economy—care work, eco-medical knowledge—which is essential to the survival of the household. This unequal exchange is "embedded in the gendered relations of households" (Dunaway 2001:11). These relations underpin the production of surplus between every node in the global network as well as within every node, and are as essential to understanding the transnational basis of capital accumulation as is waged labour undertaken in the firm or factory or the territorial basis of production (Dunaway 2001).

Supplementing and extending this work, recent feminist analyses of globalization have been concerned with the ways in which social reproductive labour is also being reorganized on a global scale. In the mid-1990s, Truong (1996:47) noted that the transfer of reproductive labour across international borders was attracting increased scholarly attention and commented that, "[no] production system operates without a reproduction system and it should not be surprising that the globalization of production is accompanied by its intimate 'Other' that is reproduction." Over the last decade, a substantial literature loosely framed around the globalization of social reproductive labour has emerged which utilizes a global perspective to explain these international transfers of reproductive labour and their impacts.

In this literature the social division of reproductive labour is regarded as being organized on a global scale rather than on a purely national one. The suggestion is that the "new international division of labour" (NIDL) associated with the globalization of production is paralleled by the "new international division of reproductive labour" (NIDRL), whereby reproductive labour previously provided by women in "core" countries is increasingly provided by women from "peripheral" countries who have migrated to the "core" countries to undertake this labour (Parreñas 2000). Like the NIDL, this global division of reproductive labour is also accompanied by varied regional and subregional divisions of labour tethered to global structures. Thus, young women from poorer Asian countries typically travel to richer countries of Southeast Asia and Western Asia/the Middle East, as well as to Western Europe and the United States to work in various branches of the international care service economy (Heyzer et al. 1994; Chang and Ling 2000). Young women from

Mexico and Central and South American countries travel to the United States, while others from Central and Eastern Europe travel to Western Europe and the United States. Whereas the NIDL is generally expressed as the differences between nation states' (immobile) labour forces (for example, China takes up low wage work which is then lost to Mexico), the NIDRL relates to labour forces that are no longer wholly anchored in their nation-states, but migrate to serve the changing international market in social reproductive labour. These substantial global transfers of paid and unpaid care labour connect children, parents and other family members in different parts of the globe, forging global social inequalities based on gender, class, "race" and ethnicity and caste (Hochschild 2000; Parreñas 2001, 2005; Sassen 2002; Yeates 2004, 2005, 2006).

These processes and transfers are generating changes in both the form and function of family caregiving. With the formation of transnational families come adaptive practices of caregiving from afar. Not only are emigrant mothers providing financial support for their own children (and sometimes those of their relatives), but assisted by advances in communications technologies they retain substantial involvement in the emotional care of their children, and provide tangible, regular educational and health-care support. With an overall emphasis on the adaptability of the family and the durability of family ties and practices among generations across long distances, there has been considerable attention to the reconstitution of gendered parenting roles consequent upon this migration. In the case of Filipino families involving the emigration of the mother, Parreñas reports that most husbands in her sample did not take over the nurturing role of the absent mother: "In working class families, other women usually took over the work left behind by migrant mothers. In middle-class families, fathers usually relied on paid domestic help" (Parreñas 2005:332). Thus even with migration the traditional gender roles of caregiving are maintained: "Mothers both provide economically and nurture emotionally from afar while fathers are physically present but emotionally absent from their children's lives" (Parreñas 2005:327). At the same time, women's migration opens up various gender contestations in family life. These contestations are expressed over issues such as to whom remittances are transmitted and women's continued involvement in the micromanagement of household finances; such arrangements challenge male and other adult authority in the family. A similar variety of responses to the central role of women in-migration can be seen in the case of nurses migrating from Kerala to the United States: While some marriages show a rearrangement of roles to recognize the central place of the women's employment, others attempt to maintain the traditional structure (George 2005).

In the following sections, these themes are explored through a focus on the principal migrant groups that have been the subject of scholarly focus. We begin by examining what are in many ways archetypal workers in the new global social reproductive economy—domestic workers (section 4), while section 5 focuses on the migration of more skilled workers, in particular those moving to take up employment in health and welfare services.

## DOMESTIC WORKERS

A large number of studies have grappled with the intersection between globalization and gender processes through an examination of the international migration of female domestic workers (for example, Anderson 2000; Chang and Ling 2000; Chin 1998; Cock 1984; Gamburd 2000; Heyzer et al. 1994; Hochschild 2000; Hondagneu-Sotelo 2001; Lutz 2002; Momsen 1999; Parreñas 2000, 2001). There has been considerable attention in this literature to the individual person providing a service to one household, with high-class childcare workers in individualized settings—nannies—being a particular focus. The international trade in domestic services is also increasing for household cleaning and eldercare in North America and Western Europe, and this is occurring in a context of a growing market sector served by commercial companies. In the United States, home health care and cleaning are among the fastest growing areas within an expanding care services sector. At the end of the 1990s, nearly four million beneficiaries of home health-care services were served by over 10,000 home health agencies (ITC 1998). Folbre underlines the significance of the health- and social-care industry through the following comparison: "nursing homes employ more workers in the US than the auto and steel industries combined" (Folbre 2002:186). The workers of this "new" service economy are increasingly sourced from outside the United States, particularly from poorer countries. Non-US citizens are overrepresented[1] in household services in the United States. In Western Europe, too, foreigners are overrepresented in household services in Belgium, France, Germany, Greece, Italy, Luxembourg, Spain and Switzerland (Folbre 2002). Household services work is an increasingly significant source of employment of non-nationals—in all continental European countries listed in table 8.2, it accounts for a greater share of foreigners' employment in 2004 compared with 1994; in 2004 it accounted for the employment of over 20 per cent of foreigners in France compared to over 40 per cent in Greece. Migrant domestic workers in Spain, Germany and France number over two million and the demand for their labour is rising (Cancedda 2001). In Britain, household spending on paid domestic labour quadrupled over the space of a decade (1986–1996) and the number of people employed as domestic workers increased by 17 per cent during the late 1990s when average growth in employment was just 3 per cent (Anderson 2001; Cox 2000; Gregson and Lowe 1994).

*Table 8.2* Change in Employment of Women by Nationality in Key Care Service Sectors (Per Cent, 1994 and 2004), Selected Eu Member States

|  | 1994 Foreigners | 1994 Nationals | 2004 Foreigners | 2004 Nationals |
|---|---|---|---|---|
| *Household services* | | | | |
| Spain | 27.1 | 6.9 | 36.0 | 4.6 |
| France | 14.7 | 3.5 | 21.1 | 3.8 |
| Greece | 35.0 | 1.5 | 42.4 | 1.3 |
| Italy | 10.3 | 2.3 | 27.9 | 1.6 |
| UK | 3.7 | 1.1 | 3.1 | 0.6 |
| *Education* | | | | |
| Belgium | 6.8 | 15.3 | 7.5 | 14.8 |
| Germany | 3.4 | 7.9 | 5.7 | 8.8 |
| Spain | 9.5 | 9.8 | 3.8 | 120.2 |
| France | 4.8 | 11.3 | 6.8 | 10.5 |
| Italy | 16.1 | 14.8 | 4.2 | 14.0 |
| UK | 12.5 | 11.4 | 11.4 | 14.4 |
| *Health and social services* | | | | |
| Belgium | 14.5 | 19.3 | 15.9 | 22.4 |
| Germany | 11.9 | 11.7 | 15.7 | 19.6 |
| Denmark | 37.6 | 28.9 | 27.4 | 32.6 |
| France | 10.5 | 16.9 | 12.1 | 20.3 |
| UK | 21.0 | 18.8 | 25.0 | 20.6 |

*Source*: Casas and Garson 2005:12.

Underpinned by a massive and increasing demand for migrant care workers throughout wealthier countries of the world and a supply of them by less wealthy ones, this global "labour intimacy regime" (Chang and Ling 2000) entails massive international transfers of "motherly" care labour. For some, these transfers signify the establishment of a "post-industrial household structure with pre-industrial values" (Parreñas 2001:80). For others, it denotes a massive transfer of care resources, from children and households in poorer countries to children and households in richer countries, what Hochschild (2000) calls the "care drain".

Neither the outsourcing of household tasks nor the international domestic service economy is historically unprecedented. Various historical studies clearly showed the importance of waged domestic work and the part played by migrants in the domestic service economy dating back at least to the nineteenth century. In contexts as diverse as Britain (McBride 1976), Latin America (Chaney and Castro 1991; Jelin 1977), the Caribbean (Chaney and Castro 1991), the United States (Katzman 1978; Palmer 1997, 1990), Australia (Hammerton 2004) and South Africa (Cock 1984), various studies have demonstrated the use of both domestic and foreign labour to perform much of the hard labour involved in household tasks. They also highlight the ways in which migrant domestic workers linked rural to urban parts of national economies, as well as linking the economies of sending and destination countries. Katzman (1978), for example, showed that the concentration of Irish women in domestic service in the United States reflected its significance in Ireland, where it was the major area of employment for women at the time. These global migration patterns contributed to industrialization processes in both labour-exporting and labour-importing countries in ways that have been observed in the contemporary industrialization strategies of certain Asian countries (Chin 1998; Huang and Yeoh 1996). Perhaps the most important contribution foreign domestic workers have made to industrialization projects is freeing local female labour to take up paid employment. As Chin (1998:202) notes, "[f]rom the perspective of the labour-receiving state of Malaysia, the utility of the labour in-migration policy is discerned from the fact that Filipina and Indonesian domestic workers allow working-class and middle-class Malaysian women to participate in the labour force, and ultimately the modernity project" (see also Radcliffe 1989; Tacoli 1995, 1996 on the implications for internal and international migrants of working in the confines of middle-class and elite homes). The importance of this does not need to be stressed in industrialization projects in which the mobilization of female labour is of major importance.

While there are historical continuities in the development of this international domestic services economy, there are also important disjunctures. Although cross-border migration to undertake care work is a traditional route for women, what is new is the number of women following this route and its expansion from cross-border to regional and global scales Thus, recent works emphasize the increasing numbers of women who are migrating abroad (often alone) in search of paid employment, together with the very long distances they travel, and the fact that more mothers of young children migrate without their children than previously (Ehrenreich and Hochschild 2002; Parreñas 2000, 2005; Pessar and Mahler 2003; Sassen 2002; Truong 1996). Also new are the corporatization of service provision and the spread of the domestic services market outside elite sections of society. The corporate care industry is a major area of employment generation (especially for women) in many advanced industrialized and newly industrializing countries. In the United States, "house cleaning professionals" are still strongly drawn from immigrants and ethnic minority groups (Ehrenreich 2002).

There is growing attention to the ways in which the demand for paid care workers generally, and migrant workers specifically, is an integral feature of the restructuring of care regimes in Western Europe and North America. The expansion of low-paid, flexible female employment, associated with the growth of household and personal care services markets, is shaped by a combination of an ageing population, changes in family structure, the unavailability of plentiful supplies of flexible female labour consequent upon the feminization of the labour force and the masculinization of women's employment patterns (women taking up "male" patterns of employment such as lifetime involvement in the labour force with career development emphasized rather than family/household responsibilities), a shortage of public care services, the existence of a sizeable affluent population unable to provide for their own care needs and the ability to use public subsidies to purchase care services (Anderson 1997, 2000, 2001). In this context, female migrant workers substitute for, or supplement, that which women have traditionally provided: In doing so, they are compensating for the inadequacy of public care services (Bettio et al. 2006; Ehrenreich 2002; Escrivá 2004; Ungerson 2002).

The study by Bettio and others (2006) of the interconnections between the feminization of migration and changes to South European care regimes (Greece, Italy, Portugal and Spain) is one such example. These countries have traditionally relied upon informal, unpaid care and general economic support by family members for each other, and there has been limited public and private (commercial) social-care provision. In a context of pressures on women arising from rapid socioeconomic changes, together with familialist care regimes, immigrants have filled the resultant care gap. In recent decades in Italy "[l]arge numbers of female immigrants have moved in to fill this gap, replacing unpaid work by native female family members" (Bettio et al. 2006:274). The use of immigrants to provide personal care services is concentrated in the North Centre of Italy and in large urban areas of Rome, Milan and Naples, but employment of migrant labour for personal care is no longer confined to high-income groups. The low cost of South American and Eastern European migrant labour rendered the cost of private personal care affordable for middle-income families, while low-income families could avail themselves of the state social security attendance allowance to help meet the costs of employing a care worker (Bettio et al. 2006).

The provision of benefits that can be used by those in need of care to employ domestic care workers (including family members) is contributing to the reorganization and status of care work and the development of personal care markets in which women migrants play an important role. Ungerson's (2002) study of the use of these benefits in five European countries (Austria, United Kingdom, the Netherlands, Italy, France) shows how this has involved non-EU, and in many cases undocumented, migrant labour. In Italy and Austria where there are few regulations prescribing how the allowances are to be spent, the allowances' use builds on pre-existing cultures of employment of undocumented foreign labour for housework and personal care. In Italy, recruitment draws on Eastern European, Asian and South American labour, while in Austria recruitment is more localized, drawing from the bordering transition countries of Hungary and Slovakia. In Austria and France, commercial and voluntary sector intermediaries are involved in organizing the labour to supply these care markets.

While the focus on migrant domestic workers has been mainly confined to the realm of paid domestic services, there is also attention to unpaid domestic/sexual services through a focus on marriage and international migration. The question of marriage is of considerable importance in female migration and research in this area has centred on two themes: wives accompanying their migrant spouses or joining them through family reunification policies, and the international "mail-order bride" business. Analytically, this focus widens conceptualizations of the globalization of social reproduction to the non-paid but commercialized sphere in which care services are provided. It also blurs the binary distinctions between the two main analytical categories used to study women's migration—wife or worker (Piper and Roces 2003). Practically, marriage migration is now the main mechanism whereby women gain access to European countries (Kofman and Raghuram 2006).

Most attention has focused on the commercialized form of the marriage-migration nexus. The "bride trade" is one part of a growing international traffic in women: This trafficking of women is estimated to be the third most profitable illegal trade after drugs and arms smuggling, with annual profits estimated at between US$7 and US$12 billion (UNFPA 2006). There are reportedly over 800,000 sites on the Internet appealing to a mass market and resembling industrial characteristics. In the United States one "mother" site (goodwife.com) describes itself as "The Mail Order Bride Warehouse" and receives 12 million visits annually, while another (planetlove.com) receives 10 million visits each year (Gaburro 2004). Concerns centre on the practices of matchmaking agencies and the lack of power of the "imported" bride vis-à-vis her spouse. These render women "vulnerable to domestic slavery, violence and abuse" (Gaburro 2004), given that their continued residence in the host country is totally dependant on her continuing in a (possibly abusive) marriage. Against this should be placed mainly anecdotal evidence which points to some women utilizing marriage as a path to residency and abandoning such marriages as soon as the period required to qualify for residency has elapsed. Transnational business and criminal networks are involved in the international trafficking of women in a host of ways and various shades of il/legality: Major attention has centred on the ways in which this trade operates to illegally recruit women into sex slavery. Like paid domestic work, the supply of female "marital" labour is conditioned by uneven development worldwide (Jeffreys 1999). As Pettman (1996:198) argues, "We find the international, too, in the ways that some countries become acquirers of

brides and others supply them, roughly reflecting their reactive positioning in the international political economy."

## HEALTH AND WELFARE PROFESSIONALS

Social- and health-care services are also provided in a range of collective and institutional settings: care homes; hospitals, hospices, clinics and
health centres; childcare centres, nurseries, schools and colleges provided
by the public, commercial, charitable, and voluntary and community sectors. These "sites" embrace a wide range of human service occupations
(for example, nurses, doctors, educators, social workers) involving different types and levels of "skill", position within the occupational hierarchy
(managerial, supervisory and operative), and working under quite different
conditions (Yeates 2004, 2005). The recent focus of research on the role of
migrant workers in the provision of these various kinds of welfare services
is expanding the realm of research to institutional settings and widening
the focus of research to the migration of more skilled women (Kofman and
Raghuram 2006). This focus is placing the globalization of social reproductive labour and the dependence of care systems on migrant workers in a
new and broader perspective.

Health care is one of the major areas in which skilled women migrate.
Migrant doctors constitute a growing proportion of registrants in many
countries. In the UK context, "about 54 per cent of new full registrants
to the General Medical Council in 2002 [were] women" (Kofman and
Raghuram 2006:292). It is, however, the international migration of nurses
and midwives that has attracted most research and policy attention.
Although data on international nurse migration is incomplete, the available evidence indicates the major flow of migrants is from developing to
industrialized countries. More than 90 per cent of nurses who migrate go
to North America, Europe and the high-income countries of the western
Pacific (Sarfati 2003:120). Several countries stand out in the nurse trade literature as predominantly nurse exporters or importers. Regarding source
countries, the Philippines has dominated international nurse emigration to
a variety of recruiting countries, in particular the Gulf States (especially
Saudi Arabia) and the United States (Sarfati 2003; Brush et al. 2004),[2]
and has "become dependent on health human resource out-migration to
address surpluses and other employment related issues" (Buchan et al.
2005:14). The Gulf States are major importing states which are dependent
on foreign nurses for the functioning of their health services. However,
many countries simultaneously import and export nurses: Australia, Canada, Ireland and the United Kingdom, for example, are all both significant
importers and exporters of nurses. A recent review of the literature on
nurse migration listed the primary nurse "donor" countries as Australia,
Canada, the Philippines, South Africa and the United Kingdom, while the

primary receiving countries are Australia, Canada, Ireland, the United Kingdom and the United States (Buchan et al. 2005:13).

In some cases, outmigration of nurses leads to the need for in-migration of nurses to fill resulting staffing shortages and, in many cases, a dependence upon foreign sources of nursing labour for the basic functioning of the health-care system. This global sourcing of nursing labour and its growing dependence on foreign nurses is best exemplified by Ireland (Yeates 2006). Over the decade 1995–2005, the total numbers of nurses registering in Ireland who were trained overseas (EU and non-EU) increased from 35 per cent to 84 per cent of all nurses registering in Ireland; since 2002 non-EU sources of nursing labour supply have overtaken EU sources. In this latter period, the geographical spread of countries from which overseas nurses were recruited had considerably broadened, but Asia has predominated among these in terms of the volume of nurses being supplied, with Indian nurses from 2005 vying with the Philippines as a principal source of nurse labour. The extent of Ireland's dependence on overseas nursing labour is extremely high by international standards: In the early 2000s, 69 per cent of nurses recruited were of foreign origin, compared with 52 per cent for the United Kingdom, 28 per cent for Norway and 3–4 per cent for the United States (Buchan et al. 2003:53). According to the Irish Nurses Organization (INO), some units in Dublin hospitals had "well in excess of 50 per cent of the staff comprising foreign recruits on short term contracts" (INO 2006).

The need for migrant health-care workers has arisen from the reduction in investment in training nurses and doctors in Australia, Canada and the United Kingdom, resulting from "neoliberal attempts to reduce the cost of social reproduction" (Kofman and Raghuram 2006:291). Fewer nurses are being trained due to the combination of a shortage of training personnel and changes to health-care provision. In addition, though, fewer women are now choosing nursing as a career option, and of those who enter the profession, significant numbers leave due to low pay, long and stressful working hours, unfavourable employer policies and reduced time for patient care (Thomas et al. 2005).

Among nurse labour exporting countries, such as the Philippines and India, the growing international demand for nurse labour has been accompanied by an expansion in nurse training and education. The Philippines, which has over 85 per cent of employed Filipino nurses working abroad (about 150,000 nurses in all) (Buchan et al. 2003), has experienced a 1,000 per cent increase in the number of nursing schools since the adoption of its export-oriented labour policy in the mid-1970s (40 such schools in the 1970s, rising to 439 in 1995; Osteria 2003). For India, too, gearing itself to a global market has also involved a similar proliferation of nursing schools. The Indian Nursing Council (INC) plans to convert all 700-odd Indian nursing schools offering diplomas in nursing into nursing colleges offering BScs in nursing, beginning in 2005 and finishing in 2010 (Dutta 2003).

One Indian state, Kerala, had 62 nursing schools in 1991, while currently it has 163 private and 15 government nursing colleges; in 2003 alone, 17 new private nursing schools opened in the state (Jacob 2005; Pazhanilats 2003.). Like the Philippines, this expansion of export-oriented nursing education programmes has been accompanied by an expansion of the number of recruitment companies and the organization of industry interests (the Overseas Health Care Staffing Association [OHSA] was set up in India in October 2003 to represent companies in the industry). Nurse training for the world market has various beneficial economic consequences for the exporting country: As well as remittances (which have become essential inputs into the economies of Indian states such as Kerala) benefits include employment and wealth creation in the nursing colleges themselves as well as various ancillary services such as recruitment and travel companies, while also providing employment in states whose level of economic development leave large number of citizens facing unemployment.

The extent to which other occupational branches of the health- and social-care system or other parts of the welfare system, such as education, are drawing on overseas labour has not been the focus of extensive research. Some labour force studies are, however, now beginning to report on this matter. In Ireland, for example, it is clear that its health-care system's dependence on foreign labour is not confined to nursing. FÀS, the state employment agency, recently reported that of the 604 physiotherapists who registered for the first time between July 2001 and July 2003, 46 per cent were registered outside the EU, 34 per cent were EU-registered and the remaining 20 per cent were Irish-qualified (FÀS 2005:70). Similarly, it reports that "the increase in speech and language therapists working for the health service between 2001 and 2003 came mainly from non-nationally qualified sources" (FÀS 2005:107). Furthermore, between January 2001 and December 2003, 469 foreign-trained occupational therapists had their qualifications accredited with the result that "[n]on-nationally qualified occupational therapists probably account for a high proportion of occupational therapists currently working in Ireland" (FÀS 2005:104). In the personal social services, the IOM reports that "Ireland's social services are becoming increasingly dependent on both professionally qualified migrant workers and those prepared to take up unskilled or minimum wage jobs" (IOM 2006:143). By 2001 some 10 per cent of social work occupations were held by non-nationally qualified social workers (IOM 2006); since then, accreditation of social work professionals has continued and Ireland recruits from 21 countries (NSWQB n.d.).

While not denying the problematic working conditions that migrant nurses face, it is also important to emphasize that the international competition for scare supplies of skilled nursing labour allows migrant women to play the market to their own—and their families'—advantage. Due to the possession of a globally tradable certified skill in the context of a global nursing shortage, nurses have greater options for international mobility and greater choice/freedom of action than other groups of migrant care workers. As a result, nurses are better able to make greater demands of their employers and destination country governments. Part of this is attributable to the fact that nurses are based in public sector organizations in which there is a strong trade union presence. The significance of the latter in particular is underlined by Bach: "there are frequently differences between the experiences of employment in a nursing care/aged care environment compared to a hospital setting . . . It is in private nursing that some of the worst abuses have been documented" (Bach 2003:19). More generally, it is worth noting that in some countries trade union growth is now seen as being dependent on the unions' abilities to organize migrant labour and major efforts have been made to extend trade union organization to hitherto unorganized economic sectors where migrant labour predominates. The organization of migrant nurses is also putting pressure on governments to reform immigration policy and associated social policies. In the realm of family reunification policy, issues such as satisfying the demand for spouses to be able to take paid work in the destination country are assuming greater importance to state recruitment and retention strategies in a global health economy.

## EFFECTS ON SOURCE COUNTRIES

There has been a great deal of concern over the effects of the export of care labour, in particular in those cases where the migrating mother has left her children behind in her country of origin. Much discourse on Filipino female migration concerns the potentially damaging effects of female migration on the Filipino family: "the need to provide for the economic well-being of her family pushes the worker to a foreign land: in the process, she deprives her family of the social and emotional support that a mother alone can provide" (Licuanan 1994, cited in Carling 2005:10). Of particular concern are the effects of this mass migration on the children "left behind". In the Philippines, NGOs estimate that approximately nine million children—some 27 per cent of the overall youth population—are growing up without their mother, father or both parents (Parreñas 2006).

There is some disagreement as to the deleterious effects on children left behind. Piper cites a 1998 report on the Philippines which indicated "that children with parents away suffered in their social development and psychological well-being, especially when the mother was abroad" (Piper 2005:25). More recent research, while reporting that "parental absence creates displacements, disruptions and changes in caregiving arrangements", concluded that, "despite the emotional displacement, the children of migrants are not disadvantaged vis-à-vis the children of non-migrants in many dimensions of well-being" (SMC 2004:56). Parreñas's (2005) research reports that many of the children of migrant mothers do not feel abandoned, given their mothers' practices of nurturing from afar.

There is greater consensus about the deleterious effects of health-care worker migration on care provision in countries of origin, with critics arguing that this global solution to core country problems essentially entails the export of staffing and training crises to poorer countries (Yeates 2006). While many governments support the export of nurses, there are major concerns that the recruitment of these nurses is adversely impacting upon the health system in source countries and the health status of those countries' populations. In this regard, it is worth reiterating that the Philippines health system experiences chronic nursing shortages (Tan et al. 2005) and, according to the president of the Philippine Medical Association, if the exodus of workers is not tackled, the health system will "certainly collapse". Of course, the threat is not confined to the Philippines. The Director-General of the World Health Organization (WHO) recently argued that "[i]f the worldwide public health community does not correct this trend the ability of many health systems to function will be seriously jeopardized" (Conde 2004). A WHO study of medical migration in six countries showed that

> the emigration of skilled health personnel has important negative effects on the accessibility and equitable distribution of health care, for the departure of skilled health personnel has a direct effect on reducing the quality of health care in the institutions concerned. Marginal and disadvantaged areas such as rural areas have been worst effected, as the skilled workers tend to shun such areas. (Awases et al. 2004:58)

These negative effects are of course regionally varied. "It is amongst African countries that the effects of 'brain drain' have exacerbated a deepening health sector human resources crisis. This catastrophe is reflected in the extent to which the proportion of health workers to the population has stagnated or declined in nearly every African country since 1960" (Bach 2006:6). This is impacting upon the health status of African populations. This migration of health professionals has been described as a "fatal flow", due to its severe effects on health services in African countries (Chen and Boufford 2005). The balance of benefits and losses involved in this medical migration are best summarized as follows:

> The potential benefits to the origin countries include financial gains through remittances, skills transfer, and possible investment if workers return. However, all these are trivial compared with the losses, which include loss of public educational investment, loss of intellectual capital, reduced range of available services, chronic understaffing of health facilities, and poor health care services. In extreme cases, a widening of the population health gap may result in reduced productivity, loss

of national economic investment, and potential damage to economic development. (Ahmad 2005)

More generally, this migration represents a "perverse subsidy" and a regressive redistributive impact in the form of a net flow of benefits from poor to rich country health services (Mensah et al. 2005:4). These global transfers in care are contributing to, and exacerbating, rising international inequity in health care and, in many cases, exceed the volume of international medical aid to developing countries. Nor can this be considered a recent phenomenon. In 1969 Adams estimated "the United States would have to build and operate 12 new medical schools to produce the manpower [sic] provided through immigration . . . the annual dollar value of this 'foreign aid' to the United States approximately equals the cost of all its medical aid, private and public, to foreign nations" (quoted in Hugo and Stahl 2004:184).

## CONCLUSIONS

This chapter's examination of the female migration–social reproduction nexus raises fundamental questions about the social (gendered) impacts of liberalization. At least some of the results appear paradoxical. There is no question that social reproduction is being restructured at a global level, yet this restructuring is exacerbating global inequalities. There is indeed growing integration of care markets and a growing demand for care workers of various skills levels associated with the restructuring of welfare systems. Yet this growing global integration is accompanied by increasingly stringent regulation, indeed restriction, of international migration and concomitant illegal migration and trafficking. Furthermore, health- and social-care worker migration is contributing to continued global inequities in health, with benefits accruing to the host countries of the industrialized core and the costs being borne by peripheral countries and their citizens. Here the new global economy depressingly resembles the old global economy, with uneven development structuring international economic exchange and labour forces still operating under racial, ethnic and caste hierarchies.

For the women migrants themselves, the experience of migration is contradictory. Freed from at least some of the patriarchal and other structures that restrain women in their countries of origin, they mainly find themselves constrained by other factors in their countries of destination, in particular racial and ethnic stereotypes which channel them into low-paid occupational niches, such as domestic work, occupational and credentialization barriers which deskill them, and state migration regimes which deny them full family lives and other benefits of citizenship. Against this, for some skilled care workers migration does represent an opportunity for both increased personal prosperity and a family life denied to many other migrants, while the emergence of various forms of organization among unskilled migrants shows the possibility of change in their marginal and precarious positions also.

Despite the clear advances that the feminist literature on international migration and global restructuring has brought, in particular the weight it accords to female agency and autonomy, it is still limited by its restricted focus on the household as its unit of analysis to the neglect of other sites and institutional settings of care provision, as well as on a relatively narrow range of occupations within the care services sector. Widening the focus of research attention to different settings and occupations is therefore badly needed. Part of this expanded research focus involves highlighting shifts in the restructuring of public services and the development of a market sector increasingly being served by commercial companies which are providing services by paid labourers whether in the house or in more institutional, collective settings such as hospitals, nursing homes, nurseries or childcare centres. This expanded framework effectively locates the study of women's migration in the context of internationalizing state and non-state strategies and enhances the comparative dimensions of analyses of global care economies (Yeates forthcoming). Central to this future research agenda must be more detailed analyses of how care regimes in the South are being transformed by female emigration, given the Northern-driven and Northern-focused nature of the scholarly literature which focuses on what happens to women who migrate from poorer countries to richer ones and what happens to welfare settlements in the richer countries as a result of the availability of migrant females.

To conclude, it is not at all apparent that the restructuring of social reproduction and global integration of care markets resulting from liberalization represents a new dawn of greater prosperity and choice promised by liberal apologists for globalization. Instead, a balancing of the distribution of the risks, costs and benefits involved sees once again the benefits accruing to state and non-state actors in core countries, the costs borne by state and citizens in peripheral countries and a varied mixture of costs and benefits to the migrant care workers and their families themselves. Weighing the conflicting interests of state, commercial, professional, labour and household agents is a difficult but essential task. On the current evidence, the old inequities between core and periphery are being reified in this new global system of social reproduction.

## NOTES

1. The share of foreign employment in that sector being higher than the share of foreign employment in total employment.
2. According to a 1993 World Health Organization (WHO) report, nurses made up 93 per cent of Filipinos working overseas, 80 per cent of whom migrated to the Gulf States, especially Saudi Arabia. In 1987, for example, some 23,000 Filipino nurses migrated to the Gulf and 3,000 migrated to the United States (Sarfati 2003:122). The Philippines was the lead supplier of

nurses to the United States from 1969 to 1979, while "until the mid-1980s Filipino nurses represented 75 per cent of all foreign nurses in the US nurse workforce. Their representation dropped to 43 per cent by 2000 as more countries began sending nurses abroad" (Brusch et al. 2004:79).

## REFERENCES

Ahmad, O.B. 2005. "Managing medical migration from poor countries." *British Medical Journal*, Vol. 331, pp. 43–45. www.bmj.com/cgi/content/full/331/7507/43, accessed on 18 November 2006.

Ally, S. 2005. *Caring about Care Workers: Organizing in the Female Shadow of Globalization.* www.globaljusticecenter.org/papers2005/ally_eng.htm, accessed on 3 May 2006.

Anderson, B. 2001. "Why madam has so many bathrobes: Demand for migrant domestic workers in the EU." *Tijdschrift voor Economische en Sociale Geografie*, Vol. 92, No. 1, pp. 18–26.

———. 2000. "Different roots in common ground: Transnationalism and migrant domestic workers in London." *Journal of Ethnic and Migration Studies*, Vol. 27, No. 4, pp. 673–683.

———. 1997. "Servants and slaves: Europe's domestic workers." *Race & Class*, Vol. 39, No. 1, pp. 37–49.

Araghi, F.A. 1995. "Global depeasantization, 1945–1990." *Sociological Quarterly*, Vol. 36, No. 2, pp. 337–368.

Asis, M.M.B., S. Huang and B. Yeoh. 2004. "When the light of the home is abroad: Unskilled female migration and the Filipino family." *Singapore Journal of Tropical Geography*, Vol. 25, No. 2, pp. 198–215.

Awases, M., A. Gbary, J. Nyoni and R. Chatora. 2004. *Migration of Health Professionals in Six Countries: A Synthesis Report.* WHO, Regional Office for Africa, Brazzaville. www.afro.who.int/dsd/migration6countriesfinal.pdf, accessed on 19 November 2006.

Bach, S. 2006. *International Mobility of Health Professionals: Brain Drain or Brain Exchange?* Research Paper No. 2006/82, United Nations University. www.wider.unu.edu/publications/rps/rps2006/rp2006–82.pdf, accessed on 18 November 2006.

———. 2003. *International Migration of Health Workers: Labour and Social Issues.* Working Paper WP.209, ILO, Geneva. www.ilo.org/public/english/dialogue/sector/papers/health/wp209.pdf, accessed on 18 November 2006.

Ball, R.E. 2004. "Divergent development, racialized rights: Globalized labour markets and the trade of nurses—The case of the Philippines." *Women's Studies International Forum*, Vol. 27, pp. 119–133.

Bettio, F., A. Simonazi and P. Villa. 2006. "Change in care regimes and female migration: The 'care drain' in the Mediterranean." *Journal of European Social Policy*, Vol. 16, No. 3, pp. 271–285.

Brush, B.L., J. Sochalski and A.M. Berger. 2004 "Imported care: Recruiting foreign nurses to U.S. health care facilities." *Health Affairs*, Vol. 23, No. 3, pp. 78–87.

Buchan, J., M. Kingma and F.M. Lorenzo. 2005. "International migration of nurses: Trends and policy implications." *The Global Nursing Review Initiative*, Issue Paper 5, International Council of Nurses, Geneva.

Buchan, J., T. Parkin and J. Sochalski. 2003. *International Nurse Mobility: Trends and Policy Implications.* WHO/International Council of Nursing/Royal College of Nursing, Geneva.

Cancedda, A. 2001. *Employment in Household Services*. European Foundation for the Improvement of Living and Working Conditions, Dublin.

Carling, J. 2005. *Gender Dimensions of International Migration*. Global Migration Perspectives, No. 35, Global Commission on International Migration, Geneva.

Casas, L.O. and J.P. Garson. 2005. *The Feminization of International Migration*. OECD/European Commission, Brussels.

Chaney, E.M. and M.G. Castro. 1991. *Muchachas No More: Household Workers in Latin America and the Caribbean*. Temple University Press, Philadelphia, PA.

Chang, K.A and L.H.M. Ling. 2000. "Globalization and its intimate other: Filipina domestic workers in Hong Kong." In M.H. Marchand and A.S. Ryan (eds.), *Gender and Global Restructuring: Sightings, Sites and Resistances*. Routledge, London.

Chen, L.C. and J.I. Boufford. 2005. "Fatal flows—Doctors on the move." *New England Journal of Medicine*, No. 353, pp. 1850–1852.

Chin, C.B.N. 1998. *In Service and Servitude: Foreign Female Domestic Workers and the Malaysian "Modernity" Project*. Columbia University Press, New York.

Cock, J. 1984. *Maids and Madams: A Study in the Politics of Exploitation*. Ravan Press, Johannesburg.

Conde, C.H. 2004. "A sick health care system." *Bulatlat*, Vol. IV, No. 37. www.wulatlat.com/news/4-37/4-37-sick.html, accessed on 18 December 2007.

Cox, R. 2000. "Exploring the growth of paid domestic labour: A case study of London." *Geography*, Vol. 85, No. 3, pp. 241–251.

De Angelis, M. 1997. "The autonomy of the economy and globalization." *Common Sense*, No. 21, pp. 41–59.

Dunaway, W. 2001. "The double register of history: Situating the forgotten woman and her household in capitalist commodity chains." *Journal of World-Systems Research*, Vol. VII, No. 1, pp. 2–29.

Dutta, R. 2003. *Government to Convert All Nursing Schools into Colleges Post 2005*. Indian Express Newspapers, Mumbai. www.expresshealthcaremgmt.com/20031130/coverstory01.shtml, accessed on 18 December 2007.

Ehrenreich, B. 2002. "Maid to order." In B. Ehrenreich and A. Hochschild (eds.), *Global Woman: Nannies, Maids, and Sex Workers in the New Economy*. Metropolitan Books, New York.

Ehrenreich, B. and A. Hochschild (eds.). 2002. *Global Woman: Nannies, Maids, and Sex Workers in the New Economy*. Metropolitan Books, New York.

Escrivá, A. 2004. *Securing Care and Welfare of Dependants Transnationally: Peruvians and Spaniards in Spain*. Working Paper WP.404, Oxford Institute of Ageing, Oxford.

FÀS. 2005. *Health Care Skills Monitoring Report*. FÀS, Dublin, August.

Folbre, N. 2002. "Accounting for care in the United States." In M. Daly (ed.), *Care Work: The Quest for Security*. ILO, Geneva.

Gaburro, G. 2004. *Domestic Slavery: Servitude, Au Pairs and Mail Order Brides*. Council of Europe, Strasbourg. http://assembly.coe.int/Documents/WorkingDocs/doc04/EDOC10144.htm, accessed on 18 December 2007.

Gamburd, M.R. 2000. *The Kitchen Spoon's Handle: Transnationalism and Sri Lanka's Migrant Housemaids*. Cornell University Press, Ithaca, NY.

George, S.M. 2005. *When Women Come First: Gender and Class in Transnational Migration*. University of California Press, Berkeley.

Gregson, N. and M. Lowe. 1994. *Servicing the Middle Classes: Class, Gender and Waged Domestic Labour in Contemporary Britain*. Routledge, London.

Hammerton, A.J. 2004. "Gender and migration." In P. Levine (ed.), *Gender and Empire*. Oxford University Press, Oxford.

Hardill, I. and S. MacDonald. 2000. "Skilled international migration: The experience of nurses in the UK." *Regional Studies*, Vol. 34, No. 7, pp. 681–692.

Heyzer, N., G. Lycklama and N. Weerakoon (eds.). 1994. *Trade in Domestic Helpers: Causes, Mechanisms and Consequences of International Migration.* Asian and Pacific Development Centre, Kuala Lumpur.

Hochschild, A.R. 2000. "Global care chains and emotional surplus value." In W. Hutton and A. Giddens (eds.), *On The Edge: Living with Global Capitalism.* Jonathan Cape, London.

Hondageu-Sotelo, P. 2001. *Doméstica: Immigrant Workers Cleaning and Caring in the Shadow of Affluence.* University of California Press, Berkeley.

Huang, S. and B. Yeoh. 1996. "Ties that bind: State policy and migrant female domestic helpers in Singapore." *Geoforum*, Vol. 27, No. 4, pp. 479–493.

Hugo, G. and C. Stahl. 2004. "Labour export strategies in Asia." In D.S. Massey and J.E. Taylor (eds.), *International Migration: Prospects and Policies in a Global Market.* Oxford University Press, Oxford.

International Organization for Migration (IOM). 2006. *Managing Migration in Ireland: A Social and Economic Analysis.* National Economic and Social Council, Dublin. www.nesc.ie/dynamic/docs/Full%20IOM%20report.pdf, accessed on 18 December 2007.

———. 2005. *World Migration 2005: Costs and Benefits of International Migration.* IOM, Geneva. www.iom.int, accessed on 18 November 2006.

International Trade Centre (ITC). 1998. *Health Services.* UNCTAD/WTO, Geneva.

Irish Nurses Organization (INO). 2006. *Submission to the Labour Court. Eight Claims in Relation to Pay and Conditions of Employment for Nurses and Midwives.* June. http://www.ino.ie/DesktopModules/articles/Documents/Submission%208Claims%2020Jun06.doc, accessed on 18 December 2007.

Jacob, S. 2005. "Nursing a grudge." *The Hindu Business Line Internet Edition*, Vol. 24, June 2005. www.thehindubusinessline.com/life/2005/06/24/stories/2005062400020100.htm, accessed on 18 December 2007.

Jeffreys, S. 1999. "Globalizing sexual exploitation: Sex tourism and the traffic in women." *Leisure Studies*, Vol. 18, pp. 179–196.

Jelin, E. 1977. "Migration and labour force participation of Latin American women: The domestic servants in the cities." *Signs*, No. 3, pp. 129–141.

Kanaiaupuni, S.M. 2000. *Sustaining Families and Communities: Non-Migrant Women and Mexico-US Migration Processes.* Working Paper 2000–13, Centre for Demography and Ecology, University of Wisconsin-Madison, Madison.

Katzman, D.M. 1978. *Seven Days a Week: Women and Domestic Service in Industrializing America.* Oxford University Press, New York.

Kofman, E. and P. Raghuram. 2006. "Gender and global labour migrations: Incorporating skilled workers." *Antipode*, Vol. 38, No. 2, pp. 282–303.

Lutz, H. 2002. "At your service madam! The globalization of domestic service." *Feminist Review*, No. 70, pp. 89–103.

Maher, K. 2003. *Identity Projects at Home and Labour from Abroad: The Market for Foreign Domestic Workers in Southern California and Santiago, Chile.* Working Paper 75, Center for Comparative Immigration Studies, University of California, San Diego.

McBride, T. 1976. *The Domestic Revolution: The Modernization of Household Service in England and France, 1820–1920.* Holmes & Meier, New York.

Mensah, K., M. Mackintosh and L. Henry. 2005. *The "Skills Drain" of Health Professionals from the Developing World: A Framework for Policy Formation.* Medact, London. http://www.medact.org/content/Skills%20drain/Mensah%20et%20al.%202005.pdf, accessed on 14 July 2006.

Momsen, J. 1999. *Gender, Migration and Domestic Service.* Routledge, London.

Munjanja, O.K., S. Kibuka and D. Dovlo. 2005. "The nursing workforce in sub-Saharan Africa." *The Global Nursing Review Initiative*, Issue 7, International Council of Nurses, Geneva.

National Social Work, Qualifications Board (NSWQB). n.d. *Statistics of Accredited Holders of Non-National Qualifications in Ireland*. www.nswqb.ie/qualification/nonnat2.html, accessed on 18 November 2006.

Osteria, T.S. 2006. *Policy Context of Filipino Nurses' Migration to the United States and Canada*. Paper presented at the Workshop on International Migration and Social Development, Asia Research Institute, National University of Singapore, 20–21 November.

Palmer, P. 1997. "Housewife and household worker: Employer-employee relations in the home, 1928–1945." In C. Groneman and M.B. Norton (eds.), *To Toil the Livelong Day: American Women at Work, 1780–1980*. Cornell University Press, Ithaca, NY.

———. 1990. *Domesticity and Dirt: Housewives and Domestic Servants in the United States, 1920–1945*. Temple University Press, Philadelphia, PA.

Parreñas, R.S. 2006. *Understanding the Backlash: Why Transnational Migrant Families Are Considered the "Wrong Kind of Family" in the Philippines*. http://globalchild.rutgers.edu/pdf/Salazar%20Parrenas%20Research%20Note.pdf, accessed on 18 October 2006.

———. 2005. *Children of Global Migration: Transnational Families and Gendered Woes*. Stanford University Press, Stanford, CA.

———. 2001. *Servants of Globalization*. Stanford University Press, Stanford, CA.

———. 2000. "Migrant Filipina domestic workers and the international division of reproductive labour." *Gender and Society*, Vol. 14, No. 4, pp. 560–581.

Pazhanilats, J. 2003. "NURSE-ing NRI dreams, they flock to Cochi." *The Hindu*, 29 September. http://www.thehindu.com/thehindu/mp/2003/09/29/stories/2003092900320100.htm, accessed on 19 April 2006.

Pessar, P. and S. Mahler. 2003. "Transnational migration: Bringing gender in." *International Migration Review*, Vol. 37, pp. 812–846.

Pettman, J.J. 1996. "An international political economy of sex?" In E. Kofman and G. Youngs (eds.), *Globalization: Theory and Practice*. Pinter, London.

Ping, H. and Z. Shaohua. 2005. *Internal Migration in China: Linking It to Development*. Paper presented at the Regional Conference on Migration and Development in Asia, Lanzhou, China, 14–16 March. http://www.sociology.cass.cn/pws/huangping/grwj_huangping_e/P020050701354125464974.pdf, accessed on 23 November 2006.

Piper, N. 2005. *Gender and Migration*. Global Commission on International Migration, Geneva.

Piper, N. and M. Roces. 2003. "Marriage and migration in an age of globalization." In N. Piper and M. Roces (eds.), *Wife or Worker? Asian Women and Migration*. Rowman and Littlefield, Lanham, MD.

Radcliffe, S. 1989. "Ethnicity, patriarchy and incorporation into the nation: Female migrants as domestic servants in Peru." *Environment and Planning D: Society and Space*, Vol. 8, No. 4, pp. 379–393.

Samers, M. 1999. "'Globalization', the geopolitical economy of migration and the 'spatial vent'." *Review of International Political Economy*, Vol. 6, No. 2, pp. 166–199.

Sarfati, H. 2003. "Remuneration of nurses in Islamic countries: Economic factors in a social context." In N.H. Bryant (ed.), *Women in Nursing in Islamic Societies*. Oxford University Press, Oxford.

Sassen, S. 2002. "Women's burden: Counter-geographies of globalization and the feminization of survival." *Nordic Journal of International Law*, Vol. 71, No. 2, pp. 255–274.

Scalabrini Migration Center (SMC). 2004. *Hearts Apart*. SMC, Manila. www. smc.org.ph/heartsapart/pdfs/Hearts%20Apart.pdf, accessed on 5 April 2006.

Tacoli, C. 1996. "Migrating 'for the sake of the family': Gender life course and intra-household relations among Filipino migrants in Rome." *Philippine Sociological Review*, Vol. 44, Nos. 1–4, pp. 12–32.

———. 1995. "Gender and international survival strategies: A research agenda with reference to Filipina labour migrants in Italy." *Third World Planning Review*, Vol. 17, No. 2, pp. 199–212.

Tan, J.Z.G., F.S. Sanchez, and V.L. Balanon. 2005. *The Brain Drain Phenomenon and its Implications for Health*. Paper presented to the University of the Philippines Alumni Council Meeting, 24 June. www.up.edu.ph/forum/2005/Jul-Aug05/brain_drain.htm, accessed on 10 February 2006.

Thomas, C., R. Hosein and J. Yan. 2005. *Assessing the Export of Nursing Services as a Diversification Option for CARICOM Economies*. Caribbean Commission of Health and Development, Washington, DC.

Truong, T.D. 1996. "Gender, international migration and social reproduction: Implications for theory, policy, research and networking." *Asian and Pacific Migration Journal*, Vol. 5, No. 1, pp. 27–52.

Tyner, J.A. 1999. "The web-based recruitment of female foreign domestic workers in Asia." *Singapore Journal of Tropical Geography*, Vol. 20, No. 2, pp. 193–209.

United Nations Family Planning Association (UNFPA). 2006. *A Passage to Hope: Women and International Migration*. http://www.unfpa.org/swp/2006/pdf/press-summary-en.pdf, accessed on 4 May 2007.

Ungerson, C. 2002. "Commodified care work in European labour markets." *European Societies*, Vol. 5, No. 4, pp. 377–396.

Wallerstein, I. and J. Smith. 1992. "Households as an institution of the world-economy." In J. Smith and I. Wallerstein (eds.), *Creating and Transforming Households*. Cambridge University Press, New York.

Wickramasekara, P. 2003. *Policy Responses to Skilled Migration: Retention, Return and Circulation*. ILO, Geneva.

Yamanaka, K. and N. Piper. 2005. *Feminized Migration in East and Southeast Asia: Policies, Actions and Empowerment*. Occasional Paper No. 11, UNRISD, Geneva.

Yeates, N. Forthcoming. *Migrant Workers in Global Care Economies*. Palgrave, Basingstoke.

———. 2006. "Changing places: Ireland in the international division of reproductive labour." *Translocations: The Irish Migration Race and Social Transformation Review*, Vol. 1, No. 1, pp. 5–21.

———. 2005. *Global Care Chains: A Critical Introduction*. Global Migration Perspectives No. 44, Global Commission on International Migration, Geneva.

———. 2004. "Global Care Chains: Critical reflections and lines of enquiry." *International Feminist Journal of Politics*, Vol. 6, No. 3, pp. 369–391.

Zlotnik, H. 2003. *The Global Dimensions of Female Migration*. http://www.migrationinformation.org/Feature/display.cfm?ID=109, accessed on 4 May 2007.

# Part III

# Social Policy and the Search for Security

# 9  Labour Reform and Livelihood Insecurity in China

*Ching Kwan Lee*

## INTRODUCTION

Chinese socialism had constructed an elaborate social structure of inequalities since the establishment of the Communist regime in 1949. In the absence of a market, resources, life chances and welfare benefits were unevenly allocated through bureaucratic redistribution. State power was predicated on people's material dependence on government redistribution, reinforced by a system of political control extending from the military and the police to the Party cells on the shop floor, in urban neighbourhood committees or rural production teams. For the industrial workforce, this web of all-encompassing control entailed organized dependence but also livelihood security (Walder 1986).

Overall, in the Maoist era of state socialism, the working class as a whole made great strides vis-à-vis other social groups, notably the peasants, the bourgeoisie and the intellectuals in terms of political status, wages, welfare and employment security. Thanks to the egalitarian bent of the Maoist road to modernization, which placed dual emphasis on industrialization and public ownership, Chinese workers (including both blue-collar and white-collar employees in urban China) benefited from the "urban bias" in resource allocation commonly found in developing countries. Furthermore, Maoist ideology enhanced the position of workers vis-à-vis the intelligentsia and managerial cadres. The latter groups were required to engage in productive labour periodically, sometimes being sent to the countryside for this purpose, and their salaries were capped, following the Cultural Revolution, at only 10–30 per cent above that of the highest paid skilled workers. In material terms, despite a low wage system, workers' real wage levels in 1970 represented a 35 per cent rise above those of 1952. Despite periodic setbacks, the revolutionary regime made available unmistakable improvements in worker consumption—food, housing, medical care, education and training opportunities (Hoffmann 1974). Politically, state paternalism had led to both dependence and defiance. While, in normal times, the penetration of the state into workers' everyday life pre-empted autonomous political activities among workers, there were also volatile periods when marginal workers who felt deprived of their fair share of socialism's superiority rose in rebellion against the state (Perry 1994, 1996).

## CONSTRUCTING A NEW LABOUR REGIME

This chapter reviews how livelihood security of the ordinary workers has been affected by a quarter century (1980–2005) of market reform and profound changes in social policies. Underlying many of these transformations was first and foremost a fundamental restructuring of the Chinese economy in terms of the ownership pattern of industrial firms. There has been a secular decline in the proportion of state-owned or state-controlled industrial units, whose share in national industrial output has dwindled to a mere 18 per cent over a 25-year period. At the same time, private, foreign owned and joint venture mushroomed, especially in the 1990s when the government made a decisive push to let go of unprofitable small- and medium-sized state firms. Bankruptcy and privatization have significantly undercut the numerical and social prominence of the old socialist working class.

This industrial restructuring has dealt a severe blow to permanent state workers' entitlements, shattering their prized employment and livelihood security, known colloquially as the "iron rice bowl". Workers in collective enterprises, which had always functioned as subsidiaries of state firms, likewise suffer the same fate of massive lay-offs. Women accounted for 44.6 per cent of all laid-off workers in 1999 (*Blue Book of Chinese Employment* 2002:78). On the other hand, the rise of the private and foreign sector has opened up unprecedented employment opportunities for the massive pool of peasant migrants, whose status is marked by their rural household registration. This immense labour reserve was released from agriculture in the wake of decollectivization in the late 1970s, when collective land use rights were redistributed to peasant households. These surplus labourers took advantage of foreign investors' demand for factory-hands and the loosening up of the household registration system by the state at that time. Female migrant workers accounted for about 47.5 per cent of all migrant workers in 2000 (Liang and Ma 2004). Reform therefore has spawned two historical processes: First, the unmaking of an entire generation of workers rooted in Maoist socialist tradition and institutions; and, second, the making of a new and young generation of migrant workers who are inserted into the orbit of capitalism without being fully proletarianized.

A series of labour, social and legal reforms have been initiated by the Chinese state to enable this structural transformation of the Chinese labour force. The cornerstone of reform has been the construction of a labour rule of law, which has come up against rampant resistance by local governments whose interests are more aligned with employers and investors than with workers. Consequently, labour reform has only been unevenly instituted, resulting in widespread erosion of livelihood security for old and young workers alike. In telling this story of labour reform and livelihood insecurity, the following discussion tries to answer two broad questions: What are the imperatives of the state in devising a new labour regime? How have worker rights and entitlements changed over time as a result of reform?

## Labour Contracts

Labour contracts did not exist under the planned economy. Instead, an "iron rice bowl" system, whereby workers were administratively allocated to a de facto job tenure system in urban work units, had been gradually consolidated since the 1950s. Labour power was then not a commodity to be sold and bought by workers and employers in the marketplace. Labour contracts were introduced in the late 1970s for two reasons. The Chinese government was then confronted with the political urgency to alleviate the tremendous unemployment pressure caused by the return of some 15 million sent-down youths. Labour contracts were introduced as a way of expanding employment, by allowing enterprise managers to recruit their own workers and create more new employment channels run by collectives and private enterprises (White 1987). A second reason for introducing labour contracts was the reform leadership's decision to allow foreign investment in special economic zones in south China. In enterprises involving foreign capital, provisions for labour contracts were promulgated alongside a joint venture law in 1979. The government saw the labour contract as an instrument to attract and regulate an experimental economic zone at the margin of the national political economy (Gallagher 2005).

At the beginning, such attempts at overhauling a time-honoured quintessential socialist institution were greeted with ambivalence and debate. Deep disagreement among policy elites and academics, as well as mass anxiety about employment security and worker morale, had stalled the universalization of labour contracts for more than a decade. Although the labour contract system was extended to all new recruits to state factories in July 1986, it was not until 1993 that the government set a timetable for universalizing the policy nationwide, covering enterprises of all ownership types. The Labour Law, which was passed in 1994 and became effective in 1995, formally requires that all employees sign labour contracts with their employers (Gu 2001b). Official statistics show that labour contracts had become universalized in the state sector by the end of the 1990s. However, a more dismal picture for the non-state sector is revealed by surveys suggesting that only about 23–30 per cent of migrant workers in private enterprises have contracts (Dai and Zhu 1999; Li 2002). The political consequences of this contract gap will be discussed later.

## Labour Dispute Resolution

Another early attempt by the Chinese government to regulate employment relations through legalization concerns the resolution of labour disputes. A labour dispute–arbitration system existed briefly in the early years of the People's Republic but was abolished once private industry was socialized by the late 1950s. Under the permanent employment system and the socialist ideology proclaiming workers "masters" of their enterprise, there was no formal mechanism for settling disputes in the workplace. Informal mediation between the workshop director and the aggrieved worker was the preferred method of dispute resolution. But with the introduction of labour contracts in both state and private sectors, the government saw the need to formalize a set of administrative channels for resolving labour conflicts arising from contractual employment relations. In 1987, the State Council promulgated the Provisional Regulations on the Handling of Enterprise Labour Disputes in State Enterprises, which revived the basic three-step procedural structure abolished in the 1950s. It stipulated the mechanisms and the administrative units for mediation, arbitration and litigation. Then, in 1993, the Regulation for the Handling of Labour Disputes replaced the 1987 Provisional Regulations. The new regulation expanded the scope of conflict resolution to include disputes over matters other than contract termination, such as wages, benefits and occupational health and safety. Employees of all kinds of enterprises, not just those in the state sector, were now covered. A national hierarchy of labour dispute–arbitration committees has been set up. By 2003, there were some 222,888 labour dispute–mediation committees in state-owned enterprises, 3,192 labour dispute–arbitration committees at the county, city and provincial levels, and 24,000 labour dispute arbitrators (Ho 2003). These committees theoretically follow a tripartite principle and should consist of representatives from the labour bureau, the trade union and the enterprise. But, in practice, most of the cases are heard by one arbitrator wearing a double hat as representative of the union and of the labour bureau. Appeals against arbitral awards can be made to the courts as civil lawsuits.

The construction of this dispute-arbitration system turns out to be a double-edged sword. On the one hand, a safety valve is created as the state rationalizes the resolution of conflicts, confining and subjecting them to bureaucratic and judicial processing. On the other hand, the dispute-resolution system opens up new opportunities and resources for workers to challenge not only employers who violate the law, but also local state agents who decide what rules must be obeyed and what rights and responsibilities must be recognized.

## National Labour Law and Workers' Rights

If reinvigorating the labour-arbitration system inadvertently encourages labour activism, the legalization of labour rights is an even more direct catalyst. In 1994, China passed its first ever National Labour Law since the establishment of the People's Republic. As a basic law, it stipulates the legal principles for contractual employment relations, elaborates a range of workers' rights, and redefines the role of the state as regulator of labour relations. In terms of workers' rights, the most important, and interestingly also the most commonly violated, are: the right to get paid for one's labour, the right to rest days and holidays, the right to a safe workplace environment and the right to receive social insurance and welfare. Another significant feature of the Labour Law is the minimum wage system, the level of which is set by the provincial legislature. The Labour Law also stipulates special provisions to protect women's interests, such as proscribing gender discrimination in recruitment and remuneration, and setting limits on the types of work that may be performed by pregnant, nursing or menstruating women (Gallagher 2005; Lee 2003).

In several fundamental ways, the Labour Law marks a drastic break between "socialist" and "market socialist" employment systems. First, in recognizing the unequal power and disunity of interest between workers and management, the law jettisons the previous ideological assumption of harmonious relations between employees and employers. The Labour Law is enacted with a view to protecting the legal rights of workers—the weaker party—by placing the state more on their side. Second, the Labour Law abolishes previous distinctions among workers in different types of enterprises—for example, state, collective, private, migrant, temporary or permanent—and provides a uniform legal framework as well as setting labour standards that are applicable to all workers in all types of enterprises. Third, by stipulating a contribution-based social security system for all workers independent of the ownership nature of their factories, the law shifts the financial burden of worker welfare away from the state and toward the employers and workers themselves. Employment is now a private contractual relationship and the state is a regulator of the labour market rather than an administrator of employment.

From the workers' perspective, the most immediate and sensitive concerns in the Labour Law are those relating to pension, unemployment benefits, medical care and housing. In the past decade, the transition from a workplace-based and state-funded welfare regime to an employment- and contribution-based system has wreaked havoc on many working-class lives, as unemployment becomes a national social problem. For female workers, their disadvantaged position in the labour market in the reform period means that they are more likely than men to fall through the cracks in the social safety net (Sainsbury 1996). But it should be pointed out that, even under work-unit socialism, a male household model undergirded the allocation of housing—a practice that has seriously undermined women's prospects of owning their own homes in the reform period. Women's earlier mandatory retirement age also means a lower retirement wage.

## Pensions

Hailed as a manifestation of the superiority of socialism by the government, guaranteed pension was widely considered a sacrosanct entitlement by ordinary workers in state industries. The 1951 Labour Insurance Regulation provided pension, medical, injuries and maternity benefits for workers and their family members in enterprises with more than 100 employees. Such provisions, formulated by party leaders experienced in skilled workers' unions during the Communist Revolution and modelled after artisans' native-place guilds, were later expanded to include government employees and smaller enterprises (Perry 1997; World Bank 1997:15–16). From the 1950s to the mid-1960s, China patterned its social security system after the Soviet model, with insurance schemes administered by the official union and the Ministry of Labour. Work units contributed portions of their total wage bills (about 3 per cent) to a pooled fund to cover the expenses for employees' pension and medical expenses. This system was abandoned during the Cultural Revolution (1966–1976), when the official union and the Ministry of Labour were abolished. Since the late 1960s, pensions, along with other forms of welfare, have become the responsibility of the individual work units, which pay their retirees directly out of current revenue. The retirement age is 60 for male workers and cadres, 55 for female cadres and 50 for female workers. Replacement rate for cash wages stands at a high of 80 per cent (the international average is about 40–60 per cent), with in-kind benefits continuing at the pre-retirement level (World Bank 1997:5). The ratio of pension to pre-retirement compensation therefore reaches 90 per cent, depending on the employee's post, grade and sector (Gu 2001a).

Based neither on taxation nor contribution and accumulation, this "pay-as-you-go" system at first depended totally on central government appropriation after enterprises remitted all profits. With a massive greying working population, the government recognized very early on in the reform process that the old, work-unit-based social security was a fiscal time bomb. Reform of the pension system began well ahead of other types of welfare because of the immense demographic pressure. The number of urban retirees increased 7.3 times in 15 years, from a mere 3.14 million in 1978 on the eve of reform, to 25.98 million in 1992. The corresponding ratios of working to retired employees worsened from 30.3 to 1 in 1978 to 5.7 to 1 in 1992. In 2000, China had 36 million retirees (Zheng 2002). Among the working population, by the mid-1990s, retirees were estimated to represent 37 per cent of the total workforce of large- and medium-sized state-owned enterprises (O'Leary 1998:57). The World Bank estimated that the proportion of the total wage bill that is used for pensions would rise from 7 per cent in 1978 to an alarming 40 per cent by 2030 (Feng 2001:80; World Bank 1997:24). Pension was also a tremendous financial burden on enterprises, depriving them of a level playing field in market competition. The older the enterprise, the heavier the pension burden on enterprise budget, and the less profitable the enterprise became. The rise of new foreign firms, joint ventures and township and village enterprises, which usually employ younger workers, created formidable competitive pressures for state firms saddled with permanent older workers.

After years of local and sporadic experiments, the government gradually imposed a unified system by issuing several circulars and provisional regulations between 1986 and 1997. From 1997 to 2000, the emphasis had been on standardizing local practices into one national system, and centralizing the administration and management of pension insurance schemes in the hands of the provincial governments, not the municipal governments. Employees are required to contribute up to 8 per cent of their monthly wage and employers up to 20 per cent of the total wage bill. The funds are deposited into two kinds of account: a social pooling account and an individual account, the proportions of which are decided by the provincial government. A retiree's pension will therefore have both pay-as-you-go and contributory components. The Labour Law requires that all enterprises, regardless of ownership category, and all employees, including migrant workers, participate in this contributory system. In light of migrant workers' high job mobility, some localities have issued their own policy allowing migrant workers to withdraw their accumulated contribution in their personal account, but not the social pooling account, when they leave their employer. For instance, in Shenzhen, since 2001 migrant workers have been entitled to pension stipends when they reach retirement age if they have made continuous contributions to their pension accounts, and if they have 15 or more years of employment in Shenzhen (Li 2002). In 2001, the average monthly wage of an employee participating in old-age insurance was 695 yuan (US$84) and the average pension received by a retiree was 576 yuan (US$70), or a pension substitution rate of 82.8 per cent (*China Labour and Social Security Yearbook* 2002:256).

The implementation of pension reform has met with serious problems. First, in terms of coverage, the state sector has been most successful in expanding the participation rate, reaching 96 per cent in 1998. The coverage rates for collective and all other non-state enterprises were only 53 per cent and 30 per cent, respectively (Feng 2001:34). Overall, across all types of enterprises, only 40 per cent of firms participate in a pension scheme. A survey on some 1,500 migrant workers in Guangdong (China's export powerhouse and the most popular destination for migrant workers), found that 73.8 per cent of the respondents did not have any form of social security in 2001 (*Southern Metropolis News* 2002:A06). One reason for this limited coverage is the common practice by local governments of allowing employers to enrol only 10–20 per cent of their employees in social insurance, instead of pressing for the impossible goal of full enrolment, as required by law (Liu 2004:44).

A second and more urgent problem is the massive pension default and arrears that occurred in the late 1990s, caused by insolvency of many old state firms with large numbers of retirees on their payroll. Market reform has brought about financial independence for state companies, as enterprise managers enjoy wide-ranging autonomy in setting wages, determining output prices, hiring, firing and allocating investment finances. But such independence also means that welfare expenditures have to be drawn from their profits, too. Unprofitable enterprises have nowhere to turn for funding. Many state firms that have nominally joined the pooling system are in heavy debt and have suspended their contribution. In 2000, for instance, nationwide, of all the work units participating in pension insurance funds, about 25 per cent of them failed to fully pay their contribution. Some 43,617 work units were not able to pay full pensions to some four million retirees. And one-third of these retirees were concentrated in Liaoning province— one of the oldest industrial bases in China (Research Department of the All China Federation of Trade Unions 2001:90). In the provincial city of Shenyang, Liaoning, 26.4 per cent of retirees have reported pension arrears (Giles et al. 2006). Furthermore, pension burdens sometimes spawn wage arrears. Enterprises with pension burdens are often faltering and unprofitable, seriously impairing their solvency and ability to pay wages to their working employees. According to official union statistics, there have been staggering increases in both the number of enterprises and the number of workers involved in wage arrears. A recent five-city survey revealed that 10.6 per cent of working-age adults who worked during the 1996–2001 period experienced wage arrears (Giles et al. 2006). Due to the practice of replacing retiring workers with their own offspring, since the 1970s, it is not uncommon to find entire working-class families suddenly being plunged into financial difficulties when the enterprise for which they all work goes out of business. Under pressure from several years of widespread worker protests in the late 1990s, the central government had infused additional emergency funding to social insurance funds. Nevertheless, in 2001, despite a 349.4 billion yuan transfer, there was still a shortfall of 2 billion yuan for the repayment of owed pensions (*China Labour and Social Security Yearbook* 2002:256). As we shall see in the following, the rampant non-payment crisis has led to numerous petitions and protests in rust belt cities.

## Unemployment Benefits

Unemployment has become an explosive social and political problem since the mid-1990s. In public opinion polls, ordinary citizens and officials alike consistently ranked unemployment the primary threat to social stability in urban China (Ding et al. 2002; Hu 2002). The root of massive unemployment lies in the government policy of allowing enterprise bankruptcy in the late 1990s. By mid-2001, there were 7.69 million officially registered "laid-off" workers and 6.19 million officially registered "unemployed" workers (or *sheye*) (Mo 2002). These two terms denote two groups of workers who are shed from their work units under different conditions and who, in theory, enjoy different entitlements. A "laid-off" worker is one who (i) began working before the contract system was instituted in 1986 and had a formal, permanent job in the state or collectively owned work units (that is, those work units that did not get budgetary allocation from the central or local governments); (ii) was let go because of the firm's problems in business but has not severed relations with the original firm; and (iii) has not found other employment. Many laid-off workers fail to obtain an official laid-off certificate, which they need in order to obtain government assistance, but the provision of which implies financial responsibility for their enterprises (Solinger 2001). "Unemployed" workers are those whose firms have been officially declared bankrupt and whose posts have therefore disappeared. Many former employees who lose their jobs when firms collapse without going through the official bankruptcy procedures cannot be registered as unemployed workers. Therefore, official statistics on both laid-off and unemployed employees are widely considered to be underestimations. Whereas official unemployment rates hovered around 3–4 per cent in the 1990s, academic researchers reported rates that are three to four times higher (Li 2001:3; Tang 2001; Giles et al. 2006).

Initially, women formed a disproportionately large segment of the laid-off population. But, as lay-offs and unemployment increased in tandem with the rise in enterprise bankruptcy, the gender gap began to narrow. For instance, in 1993, the official union found that female workers accounted for 37 per cent of all state workers but 60 per cent of the laid-off and unemployed combined. By 1999, they made up 44.6 per cent of the laid-off and unemployed (Chang 1995; *Blue Book of Chinese Employment* 2002:78). Unemployment now follows more of a sectoral (that is, state-owned industries), class (blue-collar) and regional (old industrial base) than gender-related pattern.

To maintain social stability in the face of the massive and rapid increase in the number of unemployed workers, the central government has devised several policies to guarantee a standard of basic livelihood, independent of paid employment. Collectively known as the "three lines of guarantees", these policies include the unemployment insurance system, the "Re-employment Project" and the policy on basic living allowances. The local governments are the key actors in implementing these national policies, resulting in uneven realization of actual protection for workers, depending on the extent of enterprise compliance, the economic structure and history of the province, and the integrity and competence of local officials.

Let us begin with the unemployment insurance system, which first came about in 1986 with the labour contract reform and the bankruptcy law. Before the mid-1990s, unemployment insurance covered only the state sector where both enterprises and workers contributed to a pooled fund at the "county-ranked" city level. By the mid-1990s, when unemployment increased, all kinds of enterprises were gradually required to participate. Under the 1999 Regulation on Unemployment Insurance, employers contribute 2 per cent of total expenditure on salaries and employees contribute 1 per cent of their salaries, forming a pooled fund at a prefecture-ranked city administration. Insured employees are paid a monthly allowance set by the local government and for a period of 12–24 months, depending on the length of service of the unemployed (*Blue Book of Chinese Society 2002*; Gu 2001b). From the beginning, there have been problems with collections as a result of failing enterprises being unable to pay and profitable companies unwilling to join. While official statistics claim that 78.2 per cent of urban employees are covered by unemployment insurance, surveys reveal a grimmer picture: 11 per cent of the working population in major cities, 2.8 per cent of the unemployed and 4 per cent of those in the private sector at the end of 1999 participated in unemployment-insurance schemes (Solinger 2001:321). An extensive survey revealed that fewer than 30 per cent of unemployed men and 25 per cent of women had access to public unemployment or laid-off subsidies. One-third to one-half of the unemployed aged 40–50—the group most affected by enterprise restructuring—receive no public support at all (Giles et al. 2006).

In short, unemployment creates a huge demand for public assistance that has become the administrative and financial responsibility of the local government. Due to collection problems, misuse of funds and widespread informal bankruptcy, many workers were denied their legal entitlements to unemployment benefits and pensions. This problem became so serious, particularly from the mid-1990s to about 2003, that disgruntled and desperate workers took to the streets and staged numerous protests, undermining social stability. The central government responded with circulars, repeatedly urging local governments to take seriously their task of guaranteeing the livelihood of unemployed and laid-off workers. In 2000, the State Council even stipulated that different levels of local governments should increase their budgeted expenditure for social security. At the same time, the central government began a multi-year appropriation to make up the pension and unemployment fund deficits. This special infusion of funds increased from 12 billion yuan in 1998 to 300 billion yuan in 2000. In addition, in 2000, central appropriation for guaranteeing the livelihood allowance of laid-off and unemployed workers reached 458 billion yuan (Hong 2003).

The nationwide Re-employment Project was the government's response to massive lay-offs. The government could not afford to run the political risk of throwing millions of former permanent workers out into the market. Instead, it gives workers continuing access to their work-unit-based benefits, especially pension contribution by their employers through local re-employment centres. Enterprises with laid-off employees are required to partially fund "re-employment centres", run by individual enterprises, an industry sector or local labour bureaux. These centres assume trusteeship of laid-off workers for three years, providing them with job training, job placement services, disbursement of basic livelihood allowances and payment of their social security insurance. Workers have to sign an agreement to terminate their labour relation with their work units upon entering the re-employment centres. At the end of the three-year period, workers are completely on their own or they can register themselves as unemployed. The Re-employment Project has been funded on a "three-three" principle—that is, a third of the funding comes from each of the three sources: local government, enterprises and unemployment insurance funds (*Blue Book of Chinese Society 2002*; Feng 2001; Gu 2001a; Solinger 2001). In 2001, the central government announced that re-employment centres would gradually disappear as enterprises were allowed to terminate contracts with employees who become unemployed without going through the laid-off transition status.

The last measure of livelihood guarantee for the impoverished is a basic living allowance system established in 1997. It targets all urban residents who fall below certain locally determined household income levels. Laid-off and unemployed workers make up a large part of this group of urban poor, but households with special difficulties, such as those with sick or handicapped household members, are also eligible. The amount of per capita allowance varies according to the living standard of each city, ranging from 100 to 120 yuan (US$12–14.5) in provinces such as Jilin and Helongjiang, and more than 200 yuan (US$24) in Guangdong and Beijing, with a national average of 150 yuan (US$18) in 1996 (Feng 2001). This welfare responsibility falls squarely on city governments, which fund their civil affairs departments to implement this policy. Implementation is far from satisfactory. Many eligible residents are unable to receive benefits due to lack of local funding, or to local officials' unwillingness to recognize the fact that such residents qualify for benefits. For instance, in Shenyang, Liaoning, only 29 per cent of those qualified were paid the basic living allowance in 2000. Again, the central government continued its financial infusion to make up for local deficits. The Ministry of Civil Affairs allocated 8 billion yuan in 2000, 23 billion yuan in 2001 and 46 billion yuan in 2002 to local departments for providing this basic living allowance. Consequently, more people have received the benefits: 3.82 million in 2000, 11.9 million in 2001 and 19.3 million in mid-2002 (Hong 2003:78).

## Medical Care

From the 1950s to just before the reform era, the vast majority of urban employees (some 94 per cent, by 1956) were covered under a free medical-care system (Zheng 2002:123). The enterprise medical-care system provided free services to employees in state-owned and large collective enterprises while the public medical-care system did the same for employees in administrative and non-productive work units. Dependents of employees were either given medical services free of charge or at half price. The financial burden had always been borne by the enterprise, whether budgeted as part of the enterprise's administrative cost or paid from the enterprise's welfare fund, which was apportioned by the state at a rate of 11–14 per cent of the total wage bill. Like the pension systems, after the Cultural Revolution in the late 1960s, work units rather than trans-work unit entities (such as the trade union or local government labour department) became the main provider and administrator of medical welfare. In addition to free medicine and care in outpatient clinics and in hospital, employees on medical leave were paid 60–100 per cent of their basic wage (Feng 2001).

Wastage of resources, hoarding of medicine by patients and the lack of control over medical expenditures contributed to a fiscal crisis. The average annual growth rate of medical-care expenses hovered around 24 per cent during the reform years between 1988 and 1994 (Gu 2001a). The rise and rapid development of the non-state sectors means that a new medical-care system is needed to cover employees outside the state sector. Experimental reforms began in 1988, when the State Council led a multi-ministry committee to study medical reform proposals. Pilot schemes were carried out in the Jiangsu, Jiangxi and Hainan provinces, and they provided the basis for the 1998 State Council decision that required all provinces to implement a basic health insurance scheme. The new system is basically a contributory, social pooling system whereby employers and employees contribute to a local medical insurance fund, and each employee has an account combining personal and socially pooled contributions. All cities have to set up their schemes to be administered by city-level bodies led by the Labour and Social Security Department, and all employers contribute 6 per cent of their payroll and employees 2 per cent of their wages. All employees' contributions and at least 50 per cent of employers' contributions (depending on the length of employment) are deposited into individual accounts, and the remainder to a social pooling account. Below a minimum benefit level, employees have to pay out of pocket for any medical services they need. Above that, payment must first be drawn from employees' personal accounts. Any additional expenses exceeding 5 per cent of employees' income are paid from the social pooling component of their accounts and by employees. The percentage of employees' financial responsibility decreases as the cost of service increases. There are other regulations on proportionate reimbursement of different kinds of drugs and hospital care (Feng 2001). Yet, the overall drift of the reform is to shift the burden of medical care from the state onto employers and employees.

Thus far, as in other arenas of welfare reform, implementation of the new health insurance system has been uneven, both in terms of coverage and actual access to benefits. Much depends on local economic conditions, local leadership's administrative capacity and political will. For instance, a recent multi-city survey revealed that only 55.7 per cent of employed workers had socialized health insurance in 2001, with the highest rate in Shanghai (88.6 per cent), compared to a dismal 9.1 per cent in Shenyang. Even more important than coverage is whether workers can get the benefits to which they are entitled. Overall, the survey revealed that 22.1 per cent of working adults with health insurance experienced expenditure reimbursement arrears. Shanghai has the lowest rate, at 18.9 per cent, while Shenyang registered a high of 27.7 per cent (Giles et al. 2006). Judging from the coverage rates, local governments are not always successful in enforcing the legal responsibility of employers to contribute to their employees' health benefits. The more impoverished the localities, where workers are more likely to be unemployed, the larger the health insurance gap.

## Housing Reform

The trend in housing reform is to turn what was formerly an employee entitlement into a commodity for private ownership. Since 1949, several decades of socialist transformation in cities have basically eradicated private rental housing and substantially reduced owner-occupied housing. Various surveys carried out in the early 1980s concurred that work-unit housing—that is, apartments constructed and allocated by work units to their employees—comprised some 60–75 per cent of the housing stock in urban China, with municipalities housing taking up some 20–25 per cent and private housing about 10 per cent (Wu 1996). The role of the work unit as a provider of housing was far more important in China than in other former state socialist societies, where enterprise housing usually accounted for only 10–30 per cent of housing stock (Wu 1996). State factories drew on their capital construction investment funds, allocated by their supervising government agencies, to construct "welfare housing". Municipalities allocated their housing budgets to municipal housing bureaux to develop public housing for small and street-level collective enterprises that were unable to receive capital construction investment. Enterprises could also rent municipal housing for their employees. The rent charged had remained very low: Between 1949 and 1990, rent in most Chinese cities accounted for only 2–3 per cent of total household income, with monthly rent for a typical flat costing less than a packet of good cigarettes. In the 1980s, the state paid 5–6 billion yuan each year to subsidize housing maintenance (Wang and Murie 1996). Large state enterprises and institutions all had residential quarters adjacent or close to their workshops, and managers and ordinary workers lived in the same compounds, forming very close-knit communities. The basic criteria for housing allocation were urban residence and permanent employment by the work unit. Priorities depended on the status of the employees (for example, cadres were given higher priority than workers) and length of service. In addition, the size of household and the number of dependent children would sometimes be taken into consideration, especially in the more informal negotiation with allocation cadres (Wang and Murie 2000).

Financial burden on the state, chronic shortage and the poor quality of housing stock are key problems that have prompted reform since 1980.

The emphasis has been on commercialization—specifically, the subsidized sale of public housing to current tenants, rent increase and introduction of housing allowances for employees to purchase their own homes on the market. The central government stopped the distribution of housing to urban employees in 1998 and replaced it with a cash subsidy for private purchase of housing. At the same time, local governments were asked to establish a supply system of affordable housing for sale to low-income families. Special central government loans and free land allocation for such housing projects were introduced in 1994. Local governments were to decide when to implement housing reform and most found it hard to come up with the necessary funds to pay subsidies to the many public and enterprise employees (Wang 2000; Wang and Murie 2000).

Overall, housing reform has turned out to be a slow process due to cadres' and workers' vested financial interests in the old system. From the mid-1980s to the early 1990s, when enterprises were given the autonomy to retain after-tax profits for welfare use, a construction craze occurred and many workers were allocated work-unit flats that were subsequently sold to them at subsidized prices (Gu 2001a; Wu 1996). The caveat was that the buyers only bought part of the full property rights, or the right to use and inherit but not the right to sell in the open market without compensating the work unit for a portion of the profit made in the resale. This complicated property rights issue would become even more confusing when work units collapsed in large numbers in the late 1990s, leaving the partial property right of employees ambiguous and the maintenance of housing stock problematic. Some worker protests have emerged due to neighbourhood and housing issues. For younger workers in failing state-owned firms or smaller private enterprises, housing allowances simply do not exist due to enterprise financial difficulties or the unwillingness of employers to contribute. Due to a traditional preference for men in enterprise housing allocation (Ping 1998; Logan et al. 1998), privatization of work-unit housing has tended to confer ownership to men rather than women. But, so far, there are no statistical data to document this gender bias.

For the millions of migrant workers, their rural household registration status excludes them from acquiring either usage rights or ownership rights for municipal and work-unit housing. Housing schemes mentioned earlier are for urban residents only. In some cities, high-income migrants are given special residency permits if they buy housing units locally. But, for the vast majority of migrant workers, dormitories attached to factories or renting private housing are the only options. Seventy-five to 80 per cent of migrant workers in major cities live in institutionally provided dormitory rooms measuring about 26 square metres, shared by an average of 12 people (Wu 1996). This "dormitory labour system" serves employers by having labour available on tap, facilitating flexible extension of the working day, inhibiting workers' job-search time, reducing the cost of social reproduction and strengthening employer control over workers' personal lives (Smith 2002).

## Trade Unions

One would think that unions might play a critical role in defending workers' interests in the midst of all these drastic institutional changes. Yet, if anything, reforms of the union have left it at least as toothless as before. There is only one legal union in China—the All China Federation of Trade Unions (ACFTU). Independent unions are illegal and attempts at forming autonomous unions have been charged by the government as treason or subversion. According to the law, any enterprise with 25 employees or more should establish a grass-roots union under the auspices of the ACFTU. In 2002, there were 165,800 enterprise-level unions, 30 provincial unions and 19 industry unions. Historically, the Chinese official union has been institutionally subordinate to the Communist Party and financially dependent on the enterprise budget. For instance, party organizations at each level are responsible for setting up new unions, the nomination of trade union leaders and the transmission of party policies to workers. Financially, enterprises have to contribute 2 per cent of the total wage bill to their unions and workers pay 0.5 per cent of their wage as membership fees. The Trade Union Law in 1992 transfers the responsibility for paying the salary of full-time union cadres from the unions to the enterprises, making them more dependent than ever on management (Seung 2000).

In the reform era, the Trade Union Law of 1950 has been revised twice (in 1992 and in 2002) with the basic goal of strengthening the legal status of the ACFTU. The unions' right to legally represent workers against intimidation by management and to receive enterprise contributions equivalent to 2 per cent of total wage bills, as well as the unions' legal role of signing collective contracts and engaging in collective bargaining with employers, are stipulated in the 2001 Trade Union Law. Notwithstanding these legislative reinforcements, the official union continues to be plagued by several fundamental weaknesses, which have only been exacerbated by market reform. First, industrial restructuring and the rise of the private and foreign invested sectors have beset the ACFTU with a membership crisis. The shrinkage of the state industrial sector—through bankruptcy, merger or privatization—has substantially depleted the traditional membership base for the official union. Membership in that sector decreased by about 15 million between 1990 and 2000. On the other hand, the private and foreign sectors remain quite impervious to union organizations, with the rates of membership remaining at a low of 9.6 per cent and 31.1 per cent, respectively, in 1998 (Taylor et al. 2003:125). Many workers simply do not know what unions are about (Eckholm 2001).

Second, the contradiction inherent in Communist unions' dual role as representatives of worker interests and promoter of the national, common interest is sharpened under market reform. As market reform has incessantly chipped away at workers' entitlements and tilted the balance of power further toward the employers, the weakness of unions as defenders of labour rights is acutely felt. The conflicts in the union's double institutional identity explain why the ACFTU would spare no effort at pre-empting the emergence of worker protests and collective actions. At best, official unions have represented individual workers and sometimes groups of workers when they make their claims through state-sanctioned channels such as civil litigation or labour dispute arbitration (Chen 2003). This classic dilemma is exacerbated by the particular alignment of interests in the Chinese reform process. Many local governments are establishing partnerships with foreign joint ventures. Their entrepreneurial interests hold enormous sway over city- and county-level unions, which are, themselves, parts of the local state apparatus (Seung 2000:60). In failing and ailing state-owned enterprises, union cadres are often party officials or deputy managers (Lee 1999). The wearing of multiple hats as Communist Party members, managerial staff and union leaders in many state-owned firms severely hampers the role of unions in defending workers when their interests can no longer be camouflaged as unified with that of the enterprise. Likewise, in many of the newly established unions in non-state enterprises, the managerial staffs serve concurrently as union cadres. In Special Economic Zones in Guangdong, where unionization rates are reportedly high among foreign-owned companies, a survey found that almost all enterprise union chairs are also enterprise managers. These enterprise unions are concerned with recreation and welfare rather than with working conditions or labour rights. Management of these firms sees in enterprise unions an additional instrument for better discipline and control over workers—a position that ACFTU shares and promotes (Chan 1998). Guaranteed by the Chinese Constitution until 1982, the right to strike was revoked by the government haunted by the rise and development of the Polish Solidarity movement (Wilson 1990). To date, even after the People's Republic of China ratified the International Covenant on Economic, Social and Cultural Rights, and became a member of the International Labour Organization (ILO), the Chinese Government still refuses to ratify certain core international labour standards. Closer to home, Article 27 of the 2001 Trade Union Law explicitly prescribes a pro-production mediating role for unions. In the case of a slowdown or production stoppage, the law requires unions to assist enterprises in recovering the normal state of production as soon as possible, and to reflect workers "reasonable demands" through negotiation with the enterprise.

## CONCLUSION: LIVELIHOOD INSECURITY AND LABOUR RESISTANCE

The surge of China as the workshop of the world has been founded on, among other things, a fundamental restructuring of the labour force. Massive unemployment in the state industrial sector is taking place simultaneously with momentous migration of peasants into global factories. Both the unmaking and the making of the Chinese working class are heavily shaped by the state— especially its construction of a labour rule of law and a new social security system. Broad discrepancies, however, exist between the stipulation and the implementation of these new labour regulations designed to protect labour rights and entitlements. The institutional source of these gaps lies in two contradictions inherent in the strategy of Chinese reform. First, the imperative to rely on local accumulation to fuel marketization clashes with the imperative to maintain legitimacy by providing a floor of justice and welfare for the most disadvantaged. Local state agents are more interested in the former than the latter, especially when they can count on central government financial intervention to maintain social stability. The second contradiction in Chinese reform conducive to uneven protection of labour rights has to do with the illiberal nature of the Chinese legal system. The state uses the law as a tool of control over society, while allowing itself to remain mostly unrestrained by the law. When it is not in the interest of the local officials to enforce labour regulations, there is hardly enough countervailing authority (from the judiciary, for instance) to preserve the sanctity of the law (Lee 2007).

The result is that many workers, on seeing their legal right and entitlement unjustly denied, and pressured by livelihood needs, become politically restive. Sharp increases in labour conflicts are accompanied by proliferation of labour activism, taking both conventional forms such as petitions, labour arbitration and litigation, and unconventional forms such as protests, marches and roadblocks. The state has responded with measured mixes of concessions and repression. Economic and livelihood demands are recognized by officials and, in many cases, at least partially answered by swift financial compensation doled out by the central or provincial governments. On the other hand, political demands, such as calling for the removal of officials and cross-factory actions, are relentlessly suppressed and harshly punished (Lee 2007).

While this chapter focuses on the condition of the Chinese working class, women among the two segments of the working class examined here do face gender-specific difficulties. The disappearance of enterprise-based welfare means that more demands are put on the family unit to provide service and financial support. These domestic burdens are still borne predominantly by women. Also, women are among the first to be let go when enterprises restructure by shedding the workforce. Facing gendered disadvantages in the labour market, and under a welfare entitlement regime based on employment rather than universal citizenship, women workers are likely to fall through the cracks of the new social safety net. The male bias in terms of socialist allocation of housing has, in the past, inadvertently undermined women's opportunities of becoming home-owners when work units began privatizing welfare housing in the reform period. For young women migrants toiling in global factories, the lack of maternity benefits forces them to truncate their factory careers to give birth and to take care of children and elderly kin in the countryside. Recent legal changes in land use rights have the potential to encroach on women's equal access to land use, with grave long-term implications for women migrant workers' livelihood security. However, gender bias does not begin to capture the plight of millions of Chinese workers during the reform period. Middle-aged workers in the state sector, whether make or female, confront age discrimination, and migrant workers of both genders suffer from their caste-like status of being a rural resident. Unpaid wages and pensions will continue to plague the lives of both men and women in the working class for as long as the legal system and the government fail to enforce the Labour Law.

# REFERENCES

*Blue Book of Chinese Employment 2002.* China Labour and Social Security Publishing House, Beijing [in Chinese].

*Blue Book of Chinese Society 2002.* Social Science Documentation Publishing House, Beijing [in Chinese].

Chan, Anita. 1998. "Labour relations in foreign-funded ventures, Chinese trade unions and the prospects for collective bargaining." In G. O'Leary (ed.), *Adjusting to Capitalism: Chinese Workers and the State.* M.E. Sharpe, Armonk, NY.

Chang, Kai. 1995. "Female employees' working conditions in medium and large state-owned enterprises." *Sociological Research*, No. 3, pp. 83–93.

Chen, Feng. 2003. "Between the state and labour: The conflict of Chinese trade unions' dual institutional identity." *The China Quarterly*, No. 176, pp. 1006–1028.

*China Labour and Social Security Yearbook.* 2002. China Statistics Press, Beijing [in Chinese].

Dai, Jianzhong and Zhu Min. 1999. *A Survey Report on Labour Relations in Private Enterprises and Women Workers' Problems.* Unpublished manuscript [in Chinese].

Ding, Yuanzhu, Hu Angang and Shaoguang Wang. 2002. "Behind China's wealth gap." *South China Morning Post*, 31 October.

Eckholm, E. 2001. "Workers' rights suffering as China goes capitalist." *The New York Times*, 22 August.

Feng, Genxin (ed.). 2001. *21st Century Chinese Urban Social Security System.* Henan Remin Chubanshe, Zhengzhou.

Gallagher, M. 2005. *Contagious Capitalism: Globalization and the Politics of Chinese Labour.* Princeton University Press, Princeton, NJ.

Giles, J., A. Park and Cai Fang. 2006. "How has economic restructuring affected China's urban workers?" *China Quarterly*, No. 185, March, pp. 61–95.

Gu, Edward X. 2001a. "Dismantling the Chinese mini-welfare state? Marketization and the politics of institutional transformation, 1979–1999." *Communist and Post-Communist Studies*, No. 34, pp. 91–111.

———. 2001b. "Introduction" to "Labour Market Reforms: Central government policy." *Chinese Law and Government*, Vol. 34, No. 1, pp. 5–15.

Ho, Virginia E. 2003. *Labour Dispute Resolution in China: Implications for Labour Rights and Legal Reform.* Institute for East Asian Studies Monograph, Berkeley, CA.

Hoffmann, C. 1974. *The Chinese Worker.* State University of New York Press, Albany.

Hong, Dayong. 2003. "The development of Chinese urban poverty alleviation work since economic reform." *Shehuixue Yanjiu (Sociological Research)*, No. 1, p. 78 [in Chinese].

Hu, Angang, 2002. *State of the Country Report*. Tsinghua University Press, Beijing [in Chinese].

Lee, Ching Kwan. 2007. *Against the Law: Labour Protests in China's Rustbelt and Sunbelt*. University of California Press, Berkeley.

———. 2003. "Pathways of labour insurgency." In E.J. Perry and M. Selden (eds.), *Chinese Society: Change, Conflict and Resistance* (Second edition). Routledge, London.

———. 1999. "From organized dependence to disorganized despotism." *The China Quarterly*, No. 157, pp. 44–71.

Li, Clara. 2002. "Thousands of migrants cash in pension plan." *South China Morning Post*, 10 July.

Li, Qiang. 2001. *Shiye Xiagang Wenti Duibi Yanjiu (A Comparative Study of Unemployment and Lay-off)*. Tsinghua University Press, Beijing [in Chinese].

Liang, Zai and Zhongdong Ma. 2004. "China's floating population: New evidence from the 2000 census." *Population and Development Review*, Vol. 30, No. 3, pp. 467–488.

Liu, Kai Ming. 2004. *Listening to Workers' Complaints*. Report by the Institute of Contemporary Observation, Shenzhen.

Logan, J.R., F. Bian and Y. Bian. 1998. "Tradition and change in the urban Chinese family: The case of living arrangements." *Social Forces*, Vol. 76, No. 3, pp. 851–882.

Mo, Rong. 2002. "Employment condition is still difficult." In *The Blue Book of Chinese Society 2002*. Social Science Documentation Publishing House, Beijing [in Chinese].

O'Leary, G. 1998. "The making of the Chinese working class." In G. O'Leary (ed.), *Adjusting to Capitalism: Chinese Workers and the State*. M.E. Sharpe, Armonk, NY.

Perry, E.J. 1997. "From native place to workplace: Labour origins and outcomes of China's Danwei system." In Xiaobo Lu and E.J. Perry (eds.), *Danwei: The Changing Chinese Workplace in Historical and Comparative Perspective*. M.E. Sharpe, Armonk, NY.

———. 1996. "Labour's love lost: Worker militancy in communist China." *International Labour and Working-Class History*, No. 50, pp. 64–76.

———. 1994. "Shanghai's strike wave of 1957." *The China Quarterly*, No. 137, pp. 1–27.

Ping, Ping. 1998. "Gouyou qiye guanlide xingbie celue yu nugong de qiye yilai. (Gender strategy in the management of state enterprises and women workers' dependency on enterprises)." *Shehuixue Yanjiu (Sociology Studies)*, No. 1, pp. 55–62 [in Chinese].

Research Department of the All China Federation of Trade Unions. 2001. *Chinese Trade Union Statistics Yearbook, 1998*. China Statistics Press, Beijing [in Chinese].

Sainsbury, D. 1996. *Gender, Equality and Welfare States*. Cambridge University Press, Cambridge.

Seung, Wook Baek. 2000. "The changing trade unions in China." *Journal of Contemporary Asia*, Vol. 30, No.1, pp. 46–66.

Smith, C. 2002. "Living at work: Management control and the Chinese dormitory labour system in China." *Asia Pacific Journal of Management*, Vol. 20, No. 3, pp. 333–358.

Solinger, D. 2001. "Why we cannot count the 'unemployed'." *The China Quarterly*, No. 167, p. 321.

Tang, Jun. 2001. "Joining WTO and employment policies and strategies." In China College of Labour Movement, Institute of Labour Relations (ed.), *WTO: Laogongchuanyibaoxian* (*WTO: Labour Rights and Protection*). Gongren Chubanshe, Beijing [in Chinese].

Taylor, Bill, Chang Kai and Li Qi. 2003. *Industrial Relations in China*. Edward Elgar Publishing Ltd., Cheltenham.

Walder, A. 1986. *Communist Neo-traditionalism: Work and Authority in Chinese Industry*. University of California, Berkeley.

Wang, Ya Ping. 2000. "Housing reform and its impacts on the urban poor in China." *Housing Studies*, Vol. 15, No. 6, pp. 845–864.

Wang, Ya Ping and Alan Murie. 2000. "Social and spatial implications of housing reform in China." *International Journal of Urban and Regional Research*, Vol. 24, No. 2, pp. 397–417.

———. 1996. "The process of commercialization of urban housing in China." *Urban Studies*, Vol. 33, No. 6, pp. 971–989.

White, G. 1987. "The politics of economic reform in Chinese industry: The introduction of the labour contract system." *The China Quarterly*, No. 111, pp. 365–389.

Wilson, J.L. 1990. "'The Polish lesson': China and Poland 1980–1990." *Studies in Comparative Communism*, Vol. 23, Nos. 3 and 4, pp. 259–279.

World Bank. 1997. *Old Age Security*. World Bank, Washington, DC.

Wu, Fulong. 1996. "Changes in the structure of public housing provision in urban China." *Urban Studies*, Vol. 33, No. 9, pp. 1601–1627.

Zheng, Cheng Gong. 2002. *Zhongguo Shehui Baozhang Zhidu Bianqian Yu Pinggu*. Zhongguo Remin Daxue Chubanshe, Beijing, p. 123 [in Chinese].

# 10 Girls, Mothers and Poverty Reduction in Mexico
## Evaluating Progresa–Oportunidades

*Agustín Escobar Latapí and Mercedes González de la Rocha*

## INTRODUCTION[1]

The survival and social reproduction of the poor in Mexico amidst a general economic climate marked by diminishing local resources increasingly relies on two sources of income: remittances from migration to the United States and other (richer) Mexican regions (for example, where agriculture for export has grown and flourished), and cash transfers from social policy programmes such as *Oportunidades*. The old survival model based on diversified household strategies is increasingly called into question as peasant economies have become marginal (González de la Rocha 2001).

Household change arising from the relationship between poor households and the state, through the operation of a social policy programme, *Oportunidades*, is the central topic of this chapter. Several important questions regarding the impact of the programme on the ability of households to survive and enhance their well-being are assessed. Although well-being is a rather ambiguous term, we use it as shorthand to allude to people's capacities to attain nutrition, education and health care. Well-being is thus an outcome of individuals' and households' efforts, but their capacities to fulfil their needs are socially and contextually shaped. In this sense the rather precarious well-being which characterizes poor households is susceptible to change when a social policy programme such as *Oportunidades* increases households' budgets and augments individuals' possibilities to access education and health care. What dimensions of family well-being have been more clearly modified? Are factors such as the household's structure, its domestic cycle and its incorporation into the labour market influencing the ability of the poor to benefit from services and cash transfers provided through social programmes? In other words, are household changes homogeneous or, rather, are they differentiated? Which factors explain the variance? How are exogenous factors, such as labour market options or restrictions, affecting household well-being? To what extent is a social policy programme such as *Oportunidades* capable of improving the social and economic conditions of poor households when the economic context has deteriorated or is truly depressed? Finally, how has this programme impacted on gender relations?

We argue that there are certain types of households and stages of the domestic cycle in which families are better equipped to benefit from their participation in the *Oportunidades* programme. The domestic cycle shapes well-being and, at the same time, it is one of the factors that crucially influences the impact of social policy programmes. As a corollary of our argument, it could be claimed that there are certain types of households that do not benefit as much as others from social programmes such as *Oportunidades*: female-headed households and those whose members are either very young or very old, among others.

The empirical basis for this analysis is provided by the ethnographic evaluations of the impact of *Oportunidades* at the household level from 2000 to 2005. Over this period we carried out in-depth case studies of 256 poor, beneficiary and non-beneficiary households, drawn from most Mexican states. The localities included rural, semi-urban and urban settlements. A number of the case studies included follow-ups from a baseline prior to incorporation. We have not relied on ethnographic materials alone. The communities and households have been selected from large census and survey databases informed by theoretical and analytical criteria. Some of the findings presented in this chapter are also supported by statistical evidence. These studies (Escobar and González de la Rocha 2000, 2002a, 2002b, 2005a, 2005b; Escobar et al. 2005) focused on the changes observed in the quality of housing, food consumption and access to formal education and health services as well as on the impact of different programme components and ways of operation. Other changes have also been included in our analyses, such as the household division of labour, women's participation in the labour market, women's autonomy and what we see as the *feminization of household survival* (González de la Rocha 2001; Escobar and González de la Rocha 2002b; Chant 2007). We refer to the multiple tasks that women perform for family well-being (income-generating activities as well as reproductive tasks and community work) in a context in which men find it increasingly difficult to comply with their socially expected role as economic providers (without assuming responsibility for household and reproductive tasks).[2] Women almost everywhere in Mexico (rural, semi-urban and urban communities) have become ever more crucial agents for their households' well-being.

*Oportunidades*, a pioneering cash transfer programme, operates on the basis of conditionalities or "co-responsibilities": In return for the entitlements provided by the programme certain obligations are to be assumed by the participating mother. Our analyses and those of other scholars (Molyneux 2006) have pointed out the complexities of cash transfer programmes' operation in contexts where women are already burdened with a significant amount of work (wage work, subsistence tasks, reproductive work and, since they are incorporated to a programme such as *Oportunidades*, co-responsibilities). Several issues emerge from this discussion. Are women primarily instrumental to state policy? Or, without ignoring the complexities and tensions socially created around the multiple roles that women are demanded to perform, are they interacting with the state as conscious agents who intend to enhance their family well-being? In this chapter, we argue that, although conditional cash transfer programmes do place a significant burden on women, and particularly on mothers, participation in the programme has nevertheless generated a number of positive outcomes for women of different age-groups. These include the narrowing of the gender gap in education (which in some regions has not only closed, but reversed), the increasing availability of reproductive health services and women's enhanced self-esteem when they use banking services, attend a talk or participate in community assemblies.

## THE VULNERABILITY APPROACH: HOUSEHOLD RESOURCES AND OPPORTUNITY STRUCTURES

Analysing processes of change as households are exposed to state policies has been one of the main goals of our long-term research. Instead of limiting ourselves to survival mechanisms and household responses or adaptations, our approach to the study of poverty and the ways in which the lives of the poor have been affected by social policy in Mexico has been to analyse these mechanisms without losing sight of the limits of survival and reproduction. In the past we emphasized the ability of poor households to manage their labour and other resources to cope with scarcity (González de la Rocha 1994). With successive Mexican crises and a stagnant formal labour market, however, it became increasingly difficult to rely on that labour to improve the well-being of household members (González de la Rocha and Escobar 1995; González de la Rocha 1999). For this reason, we have shifted to an approach focusing on resources, assets and vulnerability. This approach first analyses household resources, then focuses on the opportunity structures that facilitate (or block) the conversion of resources into assets and finally assesses the processes by which households evolve into situations rendering them more or less vulnerable to internal and external shocks (Moser 1996; Kaztman 1999; González de la Rocha 2000). According to this approach, state intervention may affect households directly or indirectly at any of these three analytical stages (resources, assets, vulnerability levels).

Our studies have analysed household resources and the extent to which the *Oportunidades* programme has broadened them. We concentrate on the ways in which society and the State, through the operation of cash transfer programmes, provide people with the means and opportunities to conduct their lives (Nussbaum and Sen 1993). In our view, this task requires information about people's activities and actions on a daily basis as well as during extraordinary events, as actors face choices and constraints imposed by the social structure and social institutions. The resources, assets and vulnerability approach states that in order to understand changes in the capacity of the poor to face risks (economic, ecological or other types), it is crucial to analyse the changes that occur in the portfolio of household resources and the changes that take place in labour markets and in the provision of goods and services offered by the state (Moser 1996; Kaztman 1999).

The incorporation of households into the *Oportunidades* programme is understood as a change in the economic, social and political context in which these households are embedded, with repercussions for the resources they command, their social organization, their access to public health and education services, and their participation in community life.

Household resources need an appropriate opportunity structure to become meaningful assets: A household which includes adult members does not necessarily have as many income providers. What matters is the household's capacity to convert such resources into assets, or real (not potential) means to reduce vulnerability and enhance well-being. Resources (labour, housing, land, social networks) become assets when people benefit from opportunities provided by markets, society and the state (Kaztman 1999). Opportunities offered by the society define the household's capacity to transform its resources into genuine means for achieving well-being.

Opportunities to obtain goods and services and to perform activities which contribute to people's livelihoods are not randomly distributed. They are structured in such a way that access to employment, services and markets are interrelated. Both the state and the market play an important role in the structuring of opportunities.

In our view cash transfer social programmes may counteract labour market precariousness as they increase household monetary incomes—a substitute for what markets should have provided. However, as it will be shown in the following, the ability to access state-funded social programmes depends on the household's sociodemographic characteristics.

## PROGRESA–*OPORTUNIDADES*: ORIGINS AND DESIGN

What is now *Oportunidades* was initiated as a targeted programme called PROGRESA in 1997. The programme provides cash transfers, food supplements, subsidies on school supplies and health and education services to families below a certain socioeconomic level, after a selection and verification process. In order to remain in the programme, mothers and individual beneficiaries must comply with specified minima of school attendance, health check-up calendars and attendance at health and nutrition talks. Very often, there are also additional community tasks demanded by doctors, nurses or teachers that family members (mainly adult women) have to perform. The minimum transfer is equivalent to US$17 per month, for a family with no school-age children, and the maximum level can reach over US$130 for families with numerous children attending school up to the equivalent of grade nine (in the US system), and US$200 for families with children attending school in grades 10–12. Individual monthly scholarships range from US$13 per month for a third grader, to approximately US$75 for a young *woman* in grade 12.[3] From grade seven onwards, girls receive larger scholarships than boys, in order to reduce the gender gap in schooling. The scholarships provided are more generous than those being provided through similar programmes in other parts of Latin America. The scholarship is also fixed nationally, and therefore independent of the wealth or cost of living in the state or town, the poverty level of the household prior to entry into the programme and the per capita availability of public funds in any given state or municipality.

Scholarships are intended as individual benefits, and mothers are repeatedly told to use that money for the food, clothes, shoes and school costs of the child in whose name the benefit is made. There is a fraction of the transfer, however, that is meant to provide general support for the household (approximately US$17 per month).

At the end of 1997 there were 500,000 households enrolled in the programme; the number reached 2.6 million in 2000, and in early 2005 there were just under five million households (approximately 24 million individuals) enrolled in the programme. The programme was extended to urban areas in 2002. The number of scholarships per household has fallen, signalling that the programme now includes both very old and very young households, with fewer school-age children and youths.

Originally, the main aim of the programme was to *break the cycle of poverty* among the rural poor. This meant that programme impact had to be measured not in the present but in the future, when children who receive support from the programme actively participate in social and economic life. The first presentations of the programme stated its objectives as:

- substantial improvement in the education, health and nutrition of poor families, particularly of girls, boys and their mothers;
- to do this with a comprehensive approach, to avoid the obstacles that poor health and nutrition pose for educational attainment;
- to help households avail themselves of the means and resources necessary to allow their children to complete their basic education;
- to stimulate responsibility and the active participation of parents and all family members in the education, health and nutrition of children and youths;
- to promote community participation in, and support of, PROGRESA's actions, so that educational and health services benefit all families in those communities; and to participate in and promote actions that complement or further the programme's goals (PROGRESA 1997).

These objectives privilege the attainments of girls and boys (through their mothers), and interpret the improvements in household economies as mostly (but not exclusively) instrumental to that end. Short-term impacts on poverty alleviation were also part of the design, but the "light at the end of the tunnel" lay not in permanently supplementing incomes, but instead in enabling the new generation to compete on a more equal footing (with the non-poor) in the labour market, to reduce gender gaps in schooling and (later) in income generation. It was therefore meant as an effort with benefits accruing in the long term. The prevalence of this long-term objective over other possible positive outcomes could be observed in the emphasis that was placed on its various components. Transfers were linked to "co-responsibilities", that is, beneficiaries had to carry out certain individual, family and pro-community activities to receive the transfers. Among co-responsibilities, children's school attendance was privileged, rather than adult literacy, skill acquisition or other training programmes. Similarly, infants received mandatory food supplements during their first six months of life, or later if they were diagnosed as malnourished, while mothers received food supplements only when they were pregnant or breast-feeding, and adult men were never candidates for food supplements. Mothers were trained to use transfers to improve the general quality of food and drinking-water in their households, and to buy clothes, shoes and school supplies for their children. Scholarships were designed so as to encourage girls' schooling more than boys, but there were no components designed to empower housewives, with the exception of their decision-making power in household management, which was expected to yield substantial benefits to their children.

The emphases on co-responsibility and investing in the future generation of citizen/workers entailed several significant limitations in the programme. First, households with low incomes but no children (a low dependency ratio) were, until 2000, likely to be excluded from the programme. Second, households that failed to comply with the conditionalities, for whatever reason, were likely to be dropped, first temporarily and then permanently. These households could either be better off than other households (since transfers were insignificant to them) or they could be much worse off than others (and therefore unable to take time away from basic money-earning activities to comply with the programme's conditionalities), thus weakening the programme's impact as a social protection net.[4] Finally, households in communities lacking access to health or education services were excluded because they had no way to fulfil their co-responsibilities. The argument, from 1997 to 2000, was that less than 5 per cent of the rural poor lived in such isolated, unserviced communities. This gap is today being partially addressed through a new programme: PAL (*Programa de apoyo alimentario*), or Food Support Programme. An effort is also being made, however, to furnish these communities with education and health infrastructure, in order to both provide them with needed services and allow them to enter *Oportunidades*.

The long-term objective the programme seeks is improved labour market performance (and therefore less poverty) for the next generation of workers, through better schooling and health, while the desired impacts in the short- to medium-term include improved nutrition and overall health, longer schooling and increased cognitive performance among children.

It is important to recognize that the programme was not created in a void. Mexico had significant experience in designing social programmes. These past experiences informed the design of this new programme. Although PROGRESA–*Oportunidades* conforms to the new social policy paradigm of the World Bank and the Inter-American Development Bank (IDB), it is to a large extent an endogenous, home-grown programme. This also means that it may be less exportable than is usually assumed. Experiences which were taken into account for the design of PROGRESA include LICONSA, a milk distribution programme in operation since the 1970s. Other programmes were in place to provide incentives to teachers to help them remain in highly marginal communities. The Ministry of Health had programmes to equip clinics in very poor and marginal communities, and to extend coverage by means, among others, of Itinerant Health Teams. The cash transfer mechanism had been tried two years earlier in the state of Campeche. All of these programmes, however, had significant shortcomings. LICONSA and the Campeche programme were badly targeted. *Solidaridad*, operating from 1989 to 1994, was considered very seriously flawed: It was biased in favour of politically sensitive states, tended to metropolitan rather than marginal areas, was mired in widespread corruption and provided less per capita funding to states with the highest marginality and poverty rates (Chávez et al. 1994; Dresser 1991; Molinar and Weldon 1994; Roberts and Escobar 1997). Knowledge of these successes and failures undoubtedly led to the better design of PROGRESA. Also, prior programmes lacked a comprehensive approach. Each targeted a different population, carried out different interventions and abided by different rules. A programme that could, in a coordinated manner, show real improvements in the population at large was deemed necessary.

Policymakers began working on PROGRESA at the outset of Ernesto Zedillo's presidency in 1995. The goal was to design and operationalize a programme that could be shown to be effective, well targeted, free from the electoral and social biases tarnishing previous efforts and transparent in its achievements. The cumulative experience, technology and analysis by an experienced group of policymakers were fundamental. Levy and Rodríguez (2004) provide a detailed review of their experience in the design of PROGRESA. They review in detail the discussions behind the inclusion of key policy components, and other members of that group have also highlighted significant improvements. These include:

- Targeting: PROGRESA for the first time was able to target highly marginal communities, not just the larger territory of municipalities, thanks to CONAPO's (*Consejo Nacional de Población*) [5] information and analysis.[6]

- Within these communities, a census allowed the programme to select only poor households.
- Households were assessed for incorporation not on declared income, but on the basis of a complex function which includes, as its salient elements, household composition, the number, quality and diversity of its assets, and occupations and dependency rates.
- After discussions, the programme opted to rely upon Mexico's public health system, and not to devise an alternative private service in these communities. This entailed subsequent moderate but visible improvements in these services.
- PROGRESA was viewed as the main form of public intervention in these communities and households, and its benefits and services were defined as non-overlapping: Households forfeit other similar federal benefits when they join the programme (but not agricultural subsidies).
- Demographers in the group were concerned that households should not receive an incentive to increase fertility, and so children's transfers are strictly linked to school attendance and they start at third grade.
- A currently controversial provision states that the programme provides temporary support to a household. Households should "graduate", but there is no clear link between the household's passage through the programme and the means by which it should overcome poverty, except for the accumulation of transfers.[7]
- Finally, another sociodemographic emphasis resides in the programme's gender component, which provides a more generous scholarship for girls, to promote more rapid improvements in their school achievement.[8]

To show the extent to which it achieves short-term results in nutrition, health and education, PROGRESA–*Oportunidades* has commissioned a number of evaluations and studies. In the Mexican public policy scene, it is the most carefully studied programme ever,[9] with quasi-experimental evaluations launched at the same time as the programme. It has also implemented internal performance assessment mechanisms, which work through continuous monitoring. In 2004, for the first time, it carried out medium-term achievement evaluations, including an exploratory analysis of labour market performance in accordance with its original design priorities.

Initially, the programme was considered President Zedillo's offspring and seemed to be doomed to disappear at the end of his term. External evaluations, however, were sufficiently robust and showed clear improvements in the programme's intended impact areas. As a result, it has mustered remarkable political support which has led to its survival and expansion over three consecutive presidential terms.

## Targeting

Targeting, in our view, should not be assessed on the basis of the programme's own evaluation databases. Fortunately, the national household income and expenditure survey in Mexico (ENIGH [*Encuesta Nacional de Ingresos y Gastos de los Hogares*], or National Income and Expenditure Household Survey), has included questions on enrolment in social programmes since 2002. This survey shows that *Oportunidades* is the government's best social programme in terms of targeting (in this case, reaching the poor and showing a clear progressive function), but also that if we assume equal average transfers to households regardless of their position in the income distribution structure,[10] then in 2002 the programme provided transfers to 48 per cent of all households in the poorest decile, 43 per cent in the second, 39 per cent in the third, 25 per cent in the fourth and 21 per cent in the fifth (Cortés, special tabulation). This improved in 2004: Slightly over 50 per cent of the households in the poorest decile were enrolled.

There are several potential explanations for the exclusion of just under half of all of Mexico's poorest households. The simplest one is that the programme uses a selection function which shows considerable mismatch with ENIGH's income studies. Until 2008, the official Mexican poverty line was a (unidimensional) total income poverty line, which added monetary and nonmonetary income, while the programme assesses eligibility on the basis of:

- Household composition: The economic dependency ratio is most important.
- The quality of construction and number of rooms in a dwelling, this includes occupants per room.
- Assets: This includes vehicles, electrical appliances and machinery.
- Income plays a very minor role. It is factored in with other variables.

It is not clear though to what extent the difference in how poverty is defined explains the exclusion of less than half of all Mexico's poor households from the programme. Other explanations include persistent exclusions of the poor, particularly in the programme's first years, a "community"-based approach to incorporation which tended to exclude poor households in non-poor communities and a deficiency in the selection process in urban areas (selection procedures were not modified as the programme was extended to urban areas).

## Achievements and Shortcomings

Evaluations arrived at very significant, positive results. The first quantitative evaluation (Skoufias 2005) found that individuals participating in the programme stayed in school longer, by about one year in seven; they also attended school more regularly and were less subject to illnesses; pregnant women, mothers and infants were better nourished, and there were some indications that households not only had higher incomes (as a result of cash transfers) but also that the consumption of fundamental goods and services improved considerably, resulting in higher levels of well-being. This last finding points to a reduction of poverty not in terms of income, but also in the more direct, real sense of an improvement in the satisfaction of needs.[11] More recent analyses of this database, and updates of the database, found a small but significant increase in the percentage of households investing in productive assets (Gertler et al. 2005). A more recent evaluation, contrasting beneficiary households to a sample of slightly better-off non-beneficiary households,[12] found similar results, but some were more modest, probably due to research design. This second, mid-term evaluation (1997–2003) also detected deficiencies in the nutritional supplements provided to mothers and babies, which have since been corrected.

The programme's achievements in terms of schooling should be discussed in some detail. In Mexico in general, the gender gap in schooling has been narrowed at the elementary level, and has disappeared in grades 7–12. This could to some extent be explained by international migration (boys do not need to prepare for skilled jobs in Mexico, since there are unskilled, relatively well-paid jobs available in the United States), a general reduction in fertility (girls are less discriminated against in smaller families) and the increasing incorporation of women into the paid workforce. Nevertheless, in poor rural areas the differential persists, and communities participating in the programme have made more rapid progress towards the elimination of this gender gap.

Our work, however, indicates that the programme seems to have reached a ceiling in terms of schooling dynamics in primary school and grades seven through nine. Enrolment in primary school now reaches roughly 97 per cent of the relevant age-group in beneficiary communities and is stagnant (emigration and demographic change play a role). Secondary (grades seven through nine) schooling is showing small increases, although there is room for improvement. Coverage is limited to 70 per cent of the relevant age-group in grade seven and 50 per cent in grade nine. The tendency is also towards stability in the short term. Finally, however, enrolment in grades 10–12 is booming, and the programme's role in this regard is unmistakable and visible in national enrolment rates for this age-group.[13] In spite of the increased enrolment rates, grades 10–12 still represent a clear bottle-neck (and an unmistakable social divide) in Mexico. Improvements in education, however, are limited by a number of factors. First, teacher absenteeism was very significant at the programme's outset. It is less problematic today, but it persists. Second, less selectivity means schools are receiving children with less talent, time or interest. Third, the quality of public education in poor communities has always been poorer than in urban or non-poor areas. Together, these trends will only lead to the partial success of the programme, in terms of children's future achievements in the labour market. Critics of the programme have therefore called for a major reform of the public education system, a foremost pending issue in Mexico.

In terms of health, the first quantitative evaluation showed that children in the programme reported 17 days less of illness per year than comparable non-beneficiaries. According to our work, the provision of basic free medical supplies (for illnesses diagnosed at the public health clinic) improved from about 50 per cent of the amounts and types of medical supplies that clinics, according to the population they serve, should have in 2000 to approximately 80 per cent in the year 2004. According to the International Food Policy Research Institute (IFPRI) and the National Public Health Institute, babies in the programme were of higher weight, and there was a reduction in levels of malnutrition (Fuentes and Soto 2000; Huerta 2000; Rivera Dommarco et al. 2004). The reduction in maternal mortality was very small, however, and although children's weight increased, anæmia remained a problem. This led to a change in the iron formula in the programme's nutritional supplement.

Our work showed that "micromanagement" in the clinics explained a large part of the differences in local achievements. Also, some clinics opened fewer hours than prescribed, and some of the appointment and revision procedures were very cumbersome and imposed a severe loss of time, particularly for women, who not only have to attend clinics more often than men as they accompany children and others needing care, but also take their children along with them to their own (even more frequent) appointments. On balance, however, and particularly after component improvements and a number of agreements with the Ministry of Health, the health of beneficiaries has improved clearly.

A significant change also lies in the programme's alliances with other significant social policies. Since 2002 "Popular Health Insurance" coverage is increasingly provided free of charge to families enrolled in *Oportunidades*. This should provide free health care for health problems requiring hospitalization, long-term treatment and surgery which are normally provided at a price, even in public institutions. Our *indirect* evidence from *Oportunidades* evaluations, nevertheless, shows that this has led to an expansion in the eligible population without a corresponding expansion in the capacity of local and regional hospitals to deliver the corresponding services. An additional problem in this regard is that poor households not enrolled in *Oportunidades* are also likely to lack access to popular health insurance.

## GENDER AND *OPORTUNIDADES*

### The Programme's Central Gender Component

The programme's designers have, from its inception, defended it as one with a gender perspective. This claim is based largely on the differential scholarship levels for boys and girls. Girls, as was noted earlier, receive more generous scholarships from grade seven onwards, and by grade 12 their scholarship is close to US$75 a month, while boys receive US$15 less. The programme was initially aimed exclusively at the rural poor. As explained earlier, among them girls lagged significantly behind boys in terms of schooling and school attendance. The programme intended to narrow this gap, or to close it altogether. The gap has in fact been narrowed and it has disappeared in grades 7–12. The reasons for the disappearance of this gap may be traced to several factors. First, the *Oportunidades* programme, which has provided differential incentives according to gender, was extended to urban areas where the gap was narrower, and has focused on poor households, where the gap was most evident. Second, the fact that the "opportunity cost" of schooling is higher for boys than girls can also explain why the gender gap has narrowed: Boys can take on low-skilled paid work (and earn a wage) from the age of 12 years on in rural areas, and from about 16 years in urban areas, while girls have fewer options of paid work and tend to earn lower wages (as domestic helpers, part-time shop assistants). Finally, the US labour market is fairly accessible to young men, as undocumented workers, from 16 years onwards. Although this could encourage them to complete as much schooling (grade 9 or 10), as soon as they become teenagers there is a widely held notion that schooling will not help them to get better occupations in the United States, and that it possesses no value. This phenomenon is closely related to the presence of young, idle men in many poor communities. They may perform odd jobs, but they are basically waiting for an opportunity to go to the United States. They have little interest in starting a job in Mexico, an attitude which is reinforced by the sluggish growth of Mexican employment. This is not true for everyone. More than half of all young rural men start their employment path in Mexico, and more than three-quarters of young urban men do likewise. But the notion of the US labour market avidly demanding low-skilled labour, and paying about 10 times what can be earned in Mexico, is very alluring.[14]

The programme can thus be said to have played a significant role in narrowing the gender schooling gap, although other factors may also have played a part. For the time being, this change is restricted to the school-age population. Among the working-age population, the gender gap persists as a result of past inequalities. A difficult question that must be asked is whether the change is permanent, because families have been convinced that it is worthwhile to invest in girls' education, or whether they will need a permanent government incentive to stay close to gender parity. Certainly, mothers, and to a lesser extent fathers, now say more frequently that women need to be educated, because they should not rely on their husbands as economic providers. But there is no clear answer to this question at present, and it would be extremely premature to reduce girls' scholarships to boys' levels.

## Co-Responsibilities: The Programme's Impact on Women's Workloads

The programme targeted women as its agents in the beneficiary households. They are in charge of making sure everyone fulfils their co-responsibilities (in schools and clinics), and in addition they must attend health talks and participate in locally defined *faenas* (collective tasks), which include cleaning the school or clinic, sweeping the streets or participating in sanitary campaigns. To this must be added the inevitable community meetings in which they are informed of news, changes in programme rules and so on. Our evaluations have found that some women find these burdens overbearing. They either drop out of the programme or drop a job in order to comply with their own and their family's obligations to the programme. This is particularly acute among households lacking an additional breadwinner, or where the income from *Oportunidades* is small relative to the household's total income. The latter may be thought of as positive, since the programme can use its savings from better-off households to incorporate poorer households, but the former is not. An assessment of self-excluded households performed by the IDB for *Oportunidades*[15] found, however, that households that had ceased to comply with co-responsibilities and been excluded were on average better off than those staying on in the programme. Some particularly poor households, nevertheless, are in fact excluded from the programme due to non-compliance with their co-responsibilities, and this is worrying. In sum, in terms of responsibilities there is a gender impact of the programme on household mothers, as opposed to fathers, which is clearly negative for some women—particularly those performing paid work—and leads to self-exclusion from the programme.[16]

Initially, PROGRESA–*Oportunidades* did not intend its talks or meetings to be anything other than instruments ensuring compliance with rules or hygienic improvements in the home. To a modest extent, however, women have appropriated these spaces. They complain that they are time-consuming, but at the same time they are also glad to get away from home and to have a space of their own. In a few instances (such as in Tatahuicapan, in Veracruz) women in the programme have mobilized politically (in order to defend their access to water when the new state-sponsored hydraulic system left Tatahuicapan inhabitants without water for household and agricultural use) and they are recognized as a force by the authorities.

## Women's Control of Cash Transfers

If co-responsibilities were a major burden to most women, however, there would be very high rates of attrition: women deciding it is not worthwhile to perform all these duties. But the vast majority stay. We find women may criticize the programme for many reasons, but they evaluate its overall impact on them and their families as positive. The first and foremost reason is that they see improvements in the programme's core areas: household nutrition, schooling and health. The two main kinds of transfer (food and scholarships) are strictly targeted to these two areas, and women are often reminded that they are not to be used otherwise. The transfers are therefore allocated to improving household nutrition, and buying school supplies and clothes. They receive the transfers and they are encouraged to allocate them to these specific needs. Men should not interfere. When the programme started, men often felt that some of the cash transferred from the programme should be allocated to them. They were accustomed to having decision-making power in matters of household budgeting, and to allocating a part of their household's income to their own personal needs. This led to household conflict. But, by and large, men have increasingly accepted the nature of the transfers, and the fact that women decide how to spend them. Women, on the other hand, feel they have gained an area of relative autonomy and power. Naturally, this process is smooth where the household already possessed a fairly consensual and egalitarian organization for decision-making, and much less so where the pattern was authoritarian. But on balance most women see themselves in a better situation to fulfil their roles as care providers and, increasingly, as economic providers. As planned, in furthering the women's key interests in their families, the programme found very significant allies. We believe women in the programme behave more like willing agents furthering their socially bounded responsibilities through the programme, even if sometimes at a cost to their own interests, than as reluctant instruments fulfilling programme objectives.

In addition to improvements in household well-being derived from spending the transfers on basic needs, we have found households in the programme tend to accumulate assets more rapidly. Short-term evaluations found more improvements in housing and an improved ability to pay electricity bills, contributions to the regularization of their land and some asset accumulation in general. In towns with substantial international migration, the main source of housing improvements was remittances. But in those without, *Oportunidades* was a major factor explaining the differences observed. Our medium-term evaluation in 2004 reinforced this finding. According to Gertler, Martínez and Rubio (2005), households that have been exposed to the programme have a 40 per cent greater rate of investment in productive activities (cattle, vehicles, machinery, small shops), although the percentage is still very small (5 per cent among non-beneficiaries, and 7 per cent among beneficiaries). We believe this is the result of sustained higher incomes over the medium term, less vulnerability to shocks produced by a stable income from the programme and, possibly, improved health in the family.[17]

Counting on a stable government transfer has allowed these women to become credit-worthy. Shopkeepers allow them to defer payment until the transfer arrives. This safeguards basic consumption, but also exposes them to debt accumulation.

## Tensions Arising from the Juxtaposition of Co-Responsibilities and Women's Work

Although the demographers in the team that designed the programme were clearly aware of the rising importance of non-nuclear households and the role of women as income earners, the programme does work best, to this day, for households that are nuclear and where the woman does not perform full-time paid work. We have pointed this out repeatedly since 2001. Molyneux (2006) also finds that the design of the programme emphasizes the traditional role of women as mothers. Agudo (2006) develops a similar argument. This may be explained in terms of the co-responsibilities placed on women by the programme, and the fact that most need to be carried out during normal working hours. During the programme's first years, this bias was even stronger: Working women stood very little chance of incorporation into the programme because they were not at home for the interview (interview teams intentionally arrived without warning[18]). When they left their children with a neighbour or relative, those children were often registered as their dependents, thereby increasing the transfers going to the neighbours or relatives that took care of working women's children, and effectively excluding the households of the working women. Working women need to rely on a good network of family and friends to be able to cope with the demands of paid work, unpaid care for their families and co-responsibilities. While many do count on this kind of support, some of those most in need do not.

We also found that with the new self-selection system[19] a few working women could not devote enough time to the selection process and they were therefore not incorporated. This happened when they had full-time jobs and asked for permission to skip work for a day, which did not suffice to complete the selection process because they would be absent for the "verification" interview (when the programme checks the accuracy of the information provided in the interview). The process was even more problematic when the woman worked the entire week in a nearby town or city as a domestic worker. While this is not strictly speaking the result of co-responsibilities, it is a factor leading to the exclusion of some households with working women.

When women work and (or because) there is no male provider, the most common solution is to incorporate another woman into the household. This may be a single relative, a young mother with a child or, if necessary, one of the older daughters of the working woman. These women then perform the role of housewives, and some of the stresses produced by co-responsibilities can be eased (González de la Rocha 1994; Chant 1991). This is not to say that, among these households, there is a clear tendency to extend the household in order to ease compliance with conditionalities. But an extended structure with an additional adult woman does improve compliance.

Of course, households cannot be reduced to the nuclear/non-nuclear dichotomy. They evolve, and many have complex structures. Some of these complex structures can actually interface very positively with the programme. But in general, it is traditional nuclear households that conform best to the programme's design.

## POVERTY AND VULNERABILITY: "OPPORTUNITY WINDOWS" VERSUS "POVERTY TRAPS"

As mentioned in the introduction, a major objective of our work has been to define the household structures and income levels and the contexts in which programme incorporation can/cannot produce marked improvements in well-being and vulnerability. The programme did not intend to lift the vast majority of beneficiary households above the poverty line. Its impact on the overall percentage of poor households nationally is quite small (Escobar et al. 2005). It lifts out of poverty only those households that were already close to the poverty line, or those in which there are many school-age children receiving scholarships. This is so for budgetary reasons, but also because programme designers wanted to avoid the creation of a class of "disincentivated poor" totally dependent on government resources. The programme does not tailor the size of the cash transfer to the household's income and poverty level. In spite of this fact, the programme does significantly reduce the intensity of poverty (the poverty gap) among beneficiaries, and this is visible in national statistics (Escobar et al. 2005).

### Vulnerability and the Domestic Cycle

Our previous work (González de la Rocha 1994) found that the most critical stage in household well-being is that of "expansion", when both parents are in their 30s and their children are still not in school or are just beginning to attend school. It is at this time that it is most difficult for mothers to work full-time, and most households must rely on a single income earner. This leads to a very high dependency ratio, somewhat alleviated today by lower fertility rates, but fertility rates among the rural poor are still higher than average.

Because the programme bases its transfers on a small "food support" or general grant coupled with scholarships, households in the expansion stage often receive only the former kind of transfer (US$17 a month) because the older children have not yet reached grade three. We have repeatedly asserted that this is a critical stage, and that the school attendance of the oldest children is often sacrificed. They are often pressured to take on paid work, or to take on their mothers' housework so they can in turn take on paid employment. Although our evaluations showed that some children were able to work and attend school, when need is too great and children have to perform full-time work they drop out of school. Those children whose schooling is sacrificed will remain trapped in poverty: Quitting school and starting work early often leads to early marriage, no improvement in their job prospects and the intergenerational reproduction of poverty.

If, however, households successfully cross that critical stage, and their children remain in school, their cash transfers rapidly increase. This is the "consolidation stage". Women no longer have to be present in the house at all times: They may work, and the older children may have also started doing some paid work, and their incomes are supplemented by growing scholarships. At this stage, the programme does furnish a clear "opportunity window" for the beneficiary households. We find that they accumulate assets rapidly, and improve their well-being and resilience. The programme both accelerates and strengthens the consolidation stage. It accelerates it because it improves income levels *before* children enter the labour market, and it strengthens it because it increases incomes at a moment when more than one worker is already present. For instance, we have found that women tend to start small businesses at this stage, and that the programme's cash transfers have helped them do so.[20] Also, at this stage households may comprise not just the couple and their children but other adult relatives too, who help supplement income or take charge of housework, which further improves this opportunity window. Households at this stage may in fact benefit from incorporation into the programme in order to accumulate the assets that will lift them out of poverty more permanently.

Finally, households in the "dispersion stage" once again become vulnerable because their older (working) children leave home, and they often have no school-age children, which means their total transfer is once again reduced to the basic grant. At this stage, however, illnesses often impose catastrophic expenses, and the minimum transfer is of little help. Some households in high emigration communities consist of children and elderly persons (their grandparents), because the adult generation is away working. These households may in fact interface positively with the programme, because they have scholarships and the absent parents send remittances, *provided the grandparents are reasonably healthy.*

Since our evaluations laid bare the vulnerability of older households and the irrelevance of the "basic" grant for them, the programme developed a new component for elderly people, which is higher than the grant (each elderly person now receives US$23 per month, and this may still be supplemented by the basic grant).

## Labour Market and Agricultural Production Options

The Mexican labour market stagnated from 1982–1987, grew modestly from 1988–1991, suffered a major setback in 1993–1995, surged in 1996–2000 and stagnated again in 2001–2006. One result is that the networks linking both rural and urban poor to formal urban employment have weakened significantly. This weakens the link between the programme and improved job performance. But employment prospects are context-specific.

Small villages and towns close to prosperous towns and cities often have sufficient employment opportunities at hand. The north is much better supplied with jobs, and those jobs are more formal and higher paying. In the west, northwest and north, also, there are large areas of prosperous agriculture. But there are few opportunities in most of the poorest villages we have studied. Migration, whether individual or of the entire household, is evident. Many are losing population, as is rural Mexico in general. This leads to variations in programme impact. In high emigration towns and villages, the programme may spur emigration of the male head thanks to the provision of a regular income base, which reduces the risk posed by emigration. But the programme also seems to delay the migration decisions of youths, because they are able to stay in school longer. One trend visible in national statistics is the lower labour force participation rates of young men and women, which may to some extent be due to *Oportunidades*. This alleviates pressure on the labour market. But, overall, one aim of the programme in its original design cannot be said to have succeeded (yet). Youths leaving school are not in general finding substantially better employment opportunities than their parents, due to the sluggish growth of employment and, possibly, the low quality of rural schools. This may provide negative incentives for their younger siblings, thus thwarting programme goals. But it is too early to say. Those boys and girls who started receiving scholarships from the age eight to nine years have not yet graduated from grade 12, and others who benefited from the health component and food supplements as babies will take even longer. The current boom in high school enrolment will lead to larger cohorts of better educated persons in two or three years' time, and their subsequent performance will be key for future cohorts.

## Chronic Disease

In the past, the urban and rural poor were not consumers of complex medical care. The public health sector rarely provided it, and private practitioners did not see them as a market. But Mexicans are living longer, which leads to chronic disease, and often even the rural poor may have a relative willing to send remittances to cover some expensive illness or accident. Also, there is much less malnutrition derived from sub-calorie diets. On the contrary, obesity, hypertension and diabetes are increasing public health concerns, and they are closely related to the rise of high carbohydrate, high fat diets among the poor (Gaytán 2006). Alcoholism is not new, but some improvement in health care means severe alcoholics can live longer, through dialysis, organ transplants and medical attention. The provision of health care to the poor is a positive development, but these various trends have led to the long-term presence of ill or not fully able working persons in a large number of households. Finally, emigration tends to "skim" the household of its ablest members, leaving towns and villages to care for the less able and the sick.

There are both direct gender implications, and indirect implications for *Oportunidades*. Often, the care-taker is a woman. If the ill person is a previously working man, this forces household women to make an additional effort to secure an income. If the ill person is a beneficiary, this means she is not able to perform a number of co-responsibilities, which can lead to exclusion from the programme. But a woman caring for a sick person is also overburdened, and she may not perform adequately in the programme. There are formal provisions in the programme for the certification of the illness of a beneficiary, but many are not aware of them, or doctors may not visit the house to provide a certificate. There remains, thus, a certain bias in the programme against the households of the chronically ill. This is negative in itself, but it also has a gender impact, since the women in these households are left with little or no public assistance to deal with the intense care needs that are placed on them.

## CONCLUDING REMARKS

*Oportunidades* has promoted the narrowing of the gender gap in schooling among the young, and provided some modest measure of improvement in the ability of poor mothers to manage their household expenses, and to participate in community or collective efforts as more autonomous actors. We believe it is also significant that women are now perceived (by men) to have the support of powerful actors (the state, teachers and doctors) to carry out certain actions in their communities and households. Women participate in the programme because they see a net benefit mainly for their households, but also for themselves (as they find it easier to have monetary resources and access to health care, and not because they are forced to do so). Labour market impacts, and specifically an impact reducing gender disparity in job attainment, cannot be seen at this time in general, but this could be realized as a result of the improvement in schooling generally and the narrowing in the gender schooling gap specifically.

However, many challenges remain. It is clear that the burden that comes with being registered as a programme beneficiary is almost exclusively borne by mothers. Also, some household structures, particularly women-headed households, are at a disadvantage in both joining and remaining in the programme. The programme does indeed work best among biparental nuclear households where the mother does not perform full-time extra-household work. Important questions have been raised for future research: the labour market performance of the next generation of workers/citizens and the question of the incorporation of particularly disadvantaged ethnic groups,[21] as well as the programme's impacts upon their levels of well-being and their achievements in schooling. Finally, it would be necessary to focus specifically on the programme's impacts on indigenous mothers and girls. These questions are being addressed in current research.

## NOTES

1. This chapter is based on the findings of a long-standing research project: the qualitative evaluations of the Human Development Programme *Oportunidades*, carried out in different urban, semi-urban and rural communities in Mexico since 1999. These studies, directed and coordinated by Escobar and González de la Rocha, can be found in the programme's web page (www. evaloportunidades.insp.mx). A synthesis of our findings together with the analysis of the programme's impact according to household differences are found in González de la Rocha (2006).

2. Men (and women) are increasingly resorting to internal or international migration to fulfil their duties as breadwinners. "Divided households" are increasingly common, and, although this may result in remittances for those remaining at home, it also places particular burdens on the women staying behind, who are left with many responsibilities, often including other income-generating activities.

3. All these figures correspond to "traditional" beneficiaries, who comprise over 90 per cent of the payroll. There is another kind of beneficiary household: Benefits may extend to high school graduates attending college, but that component functions differently and many candidates are not familiar with it.

4. Since 2002 there is a more clearly defined way for these households to rejoin the programme.

5. The National Population Council is an interministerial body coordinating population policy. It possesses a highly developed capacity to diagnose population-related issues.

6. Since 2002, the programme is able to target recruitment interviews to the level of city blocks.

7. We, Escobar, González de la Rocha and Cortés (2005), studied the graduation mechanism in 2005, and concluded that there were significant problems with the mechanisms that target households for graduation, and that the procedure could not be generalized, that is, that participation in the programme does not necessarily lead to a non-poor status after a specified time.

8. In our view these are improvements. They have nevertheless been criticized.

9. This does not mean public policy is not evaluated. Social and public policy paradigms (as entire sets of policy measures and programmes) have been carefully assessed in the past in terms of poverty alleviation, inequality, social mobility and other impact variables.

10. As already noted, a household's cash transfer varies according to the number of school-age children, their sex and the level of schooling they attend.

11. D'Amato worked with the International Food Policy Research Institute (IFPRI) team to carry out qualitative and focus group interviews with participants. Her findings were published together with our work in 2000 (PROGRESA 2000:Vol. 8). Among other things, she concluded that targeting created new divisions in communities.

12. Because the original extremely poor control sample was enrolled.

13. High schools in towns surrounded by *Oportunidades* communities reported an 80 per cent increase in enrolment in two years since the implementation of programme scholarships at this level.

14. In a few villages and towns, where rural–urban migration is also present, families state, however, that schooling is good for migrants too, and that they can access better jobs in the United States if they can read and write and perform arithmetic operations.

15. Carola Alvarez (IDB), personal communication.

16. We are referring to research findings: Self-excluded households concentrate at the top and at the bottom of the eligibility scores. According to the researchers directing that study (see previous reference), among the poorest, self-excluded households were of two main types: indigenous households and women-headed households.
17. The programme has a clear impact on the health of children, as was already noted. Much less is known, however, about the programme's impact on the health of adults. Health problems arising among the middle-aged and the elderly can wipe out a family's assets. Incorporation of programme families into the *Seguro Popular*, which provides free health care, including hospitalization, to members, does not seem to have had a major impact on families' health expenses yet, due to the slow pace of construction of health infrastructure, which leads to substantial backlogs in the public hospitals tending to them.
18. During the first two years, families were not told the purpose of the selection interview, and teams arrived unannounced to avoid creating expectation, the hiding of assets or a mobilization of neighbours demanding collective incorporation.
19. Special non-permanent "modules" are opened in towns and villages in order to receive applications from individuals and households to be incorporated by the programme. A questionnaire is applied and later verification of housing conditions and other socioeconomic features takes place.
20. We could also say, however, that the programme postpones the consolidation stage when all children attend school and school attendance is given priority to labour market participation (González de la Rocha 2006; Paredes 2006).
21. The ethnic differential is being assessed by the 2007–2008 evaluations of the programme. For the first time in 10 years we are analysing the extent to which *Oportunidades* produces a differentiated impact amongst indigenous and non-indigenous populations (González de la Rocha 2007).

## REFERENCES

Agudo, A. 2006. "La confluencia de relaciones intra-domésticas y redes sociales en procesos de acumulación de (des)ventajas." In M. González de la Rocha (ed.), *Procesos domésticos y vulnerabilidad. Perspectivas antropológicas de los hogares con Oportunidades*. Publicaciones de la Casa Chata, Mexico City.

Chant, S. 2007. *Gender, Generation and Poverty: Exploring the "Feminisation of Poverty" in Africa, Asia and Latin America*. Edward Elgar, Cheltenham.

———. 1991. *Women and Survival in Mexican Cities: Perspectives on Gender, Labour Markets and Low-Income Households*. Manchester University Press, Manchester.

Chávez, A.M., D. Moctezuma and F. Rodríguez. 1994. *El combate a la pobreza en Morelos: Aciertos y desaciertos de solidaridad*. Centro Regional de Investigación Multidisciplinaria, Cuernavaca, Morelos.

Dresser, D. 1991. *Neopopulist Solutions to Neoliberal Problems: Mexico's National Solidarity Program*. Center for US Mexican Studies, University of California-San Diego, La Jolla.

Escobar, A. and M. González de la Rocha. 2005a. "Evaluación cualitativa del Programa Oportunidades en zonas urbanas 2003." In B. Hernández and M. Hernández (eds.), *Evaluación externa de impacto del Programa Oportunidades 2003*. Instituto Nacional de Salud Pública, Cuernavaca, Morelos.

———. 2005b. "Evaluación cualitativa de mediano plazo del Programa Oportunidades en zonas rurales." In B. Hernández and M. Hernández (eds.), *Evaluación*

288   *Agustín Escobar Latapí and Mercedes González de la Rocha*

externa de impacto del Programa Oportunidades 2004. Documento de evaluación, Tomo IV, Aspectos económicos y sociales. Instituto Nacional de Salud Pública, Cuernavaca, Morelos.

———. 2002a. *Documento final de diagnóstico cualitativo de hogares semiurbanos, localidades de 2,500 a 50,000 habitantes, 2001.* http://evaloportunidades. insp.mx/441c7c1a3d30adf64e0e724174a9d527/impacto/2001/ciesas_2001_ evaluacion_cualitativa.pdf, accessed on 10 November 2006.

———. 2002b. *Evaluación cualitativa del Programa de Desarrollo Humano Oportunidades, Seguimiento de impacto 2001–2002, comunidades de 2,500 a 50,000 habitantes.* http://evaloportunidades.insp.mx/441c7c1a3d30adf64e0e7 24174a9d527/impacto/2002/ciesas_2002_evaluacion_cualitativa.pdf, accessed on 10 November 2006.

———. 2000. "Logros y retos: Una evaluación cualitativa del Progresa en México." In PROGRESA, *Progresa: Más oportunidades para las familias pobres. Evaluación de resultados del Programa de Educación, Salud y Alimentación, Impacto a nivel comunitario.* PROGRESA, Mexico City.

Escobar, A., M. González de la Rocha and F. Cortés. 2005. "Evaluación cualitativa del Esquema Diferenciado de Apoyos 2005." Documento analítico del Esquema Diferenciado de Apoyos del Programa Oportunidades, Numeral 11. Centro de Investigaciones y Estudios Superiores en Antropología Social (CIESAS)/El Colegio de México (COLMEX).

Fuentes, M. and H. Soto. 2000. "Perfil de la desnutrición de los niños menores de cinco años en comunidades rurales altamente marginadas." In PROGRESA, *Más oportunidades para las familias pobres. Evaluación de resultados del Programa de Educación, Salud y Alimentación.* PROGRESA, Mexico City.

Gaytán, A.I. 2006. *La prevención, reto antiguo de enfermedades contemporáneas: El Instituto Mexicano del Seguro Social-Jalisco frente a la hipertensión y diabetes.* PhD thesis, CIESAS Occidente, Guadalajara.

Gertler, P., S. Martínez and M. Rubio. 2005. "El efecto de Oportunidades sobre el incremento en el consume de los hogares a partir de inversions productivas en micro empresas y producción agrícola." In B. Hernández Prado and M. Hernández Avila (eds.), *Evaluación externa de impacto del Programa Oportunidades 2004, Vol. IV.* Instituto Nacional de Salud Pública (INSP), Mexico City.

González de la Rocha, M. 2007. "Evaluación cualitativa de impacto del Programa Oportunidades, largo plazo, zonas rurales." Unpublished research proposal.

——— (ed.). 2006. *Procesos domésticos y vulnerabilidad: Perspectivas antropológicas de los hogares con Oportunidades.* Publicaciones de la Casa Chata (CIESAS), Mexico City.

———. 2001. "From the resources of poverty to the poverty of resources: The erosion of a survival model?" *Latin American Perspectives*, Vol. 28, No. 4, pp. 72–100.

———. 2000. *Private Adjustments: Household Responses to the Erosion of Work.* United Nations Development Programme (UNDP), New York.

———. 1999. "La reciprocidad amenazada: Un costo más de la pobreza urbana." In R. Enríquez (ed.), *Hogar, pobreza y bienestar en México.* Instituto Tecnológico y de Estudios Superiores de Occidente, Guadalajara.

———. 1994. *The Resources of Poverty. Women and Survival in a Mexican City.* Basil Blackwell, Oxford.

González de la Rocha, M. and A. Escobar. 1995. "Crisis, restructuring and urban poverty in Mexico." *Environment and Urbanization*, Vol. 7, No. 1, pp. 57–76.

Huerta, María del Carmen. 2000. "Evaluación de impacto del PROGRESA en el estado de nutrición de los menores de cinco años en localidades atendidas por el IMSS." In PROGRESA, *Más oportunidades para las familias pobres.*

*Evaluación de resultados del Programa de Educación, Salud y Alimentación.* PROGRESA, Mexico City.

Kaztman, R. (ed.). 1999. *Activos y estructuras de oportunidades. Estudios sobre las raíces de la vulnerabilidad social en Uruguay.* UNDP/ECLAC, Montevideo.

Levy, S. and E. Rodríguez. 2004. "El programa de Educación, Salud y Alimentación, Progresa-Programa de Desarrollo Humano Oportunidades." In S. Levy (ed.), *Ensayos sobre el desarrollo económico y social de México.* Fondo de Cultura Económica, Mexico City.

Molinar, J. and J. Weldon. 1994. "Programa Nacional de Solidaridad: Determinantes partidistas y consecuencias electorales." *Estudios Sociológicos,* Vol. 12, No. 34, pp. 155–181.

Molyneux, M. 2006. "Mothers at the service of the new poverty agenda: Progresa/Oportunidades, Mexico's conditional transfer programme." *Social Policy and Administration,* Vol. 40, No. 4, pp. 425–449.

Moser, C. 1996. *Confronting Crises. A Comparative Study of Household Responses to Poverty and Vulnerability in Four Urban Communities.* Environmentally Sustainable Development Studies, Monograph Series, No. 8, World Bank, Washington, DC.

Nussbaum, M. and A. Sen. 1993. "Introduction." In M. Nussbaum and A. Sen (eds.), *The Quality of Life.* Clarendon Press-Oxford University Press, New York.

Paredes, P. 2006. "Hogares en consolidación. Descripción y análisis de un equilibrio precario." In M. González de la Rocha (ed.), *Procesos domésticos y vulnerabilidad. Perspectivas antropológicas de los hogares con Oportunidades.* Publicaciones de la Casa Chata, Mexico City.

PROGRESA. 2000. *¿Está dando buenos resultados PROGRESA?, Informe de los resultados obtenidos de una evaluación realizada por el IFPRI, Síntesis de la evaluación de impacto.* http://evaluacion.oportunidades.gob.mx:8010/es/docs/docs_eval_2000.php, accessed on 13 January 2008.

———. 1997. *Programa Educación, Salud y Alimentación.* PROGRESA, Mexico.

Rivera Dommarco, J., D. Sotres-Alvarez, J.P. Habitch, T. Shamah and S. Villalpando. 2004. "Impact of the Mexican Program for Education, Health and Nutrition (Progresa) on rates of growth and anemia in infants and young children. A randomized effectiveness study." *Journal of the American Medical Association,* Vol. 291, pp. 2563–2570.

Roberts, B. and A. Escobar. 1997. "Mexican social and economic policy and emigration." In F.D. Bean, R.O. de la Garza, B. Roberts and S. Weintraub (eds.), *At the Crossroads: Mexico and U.S. Immigration Policy.* Rowman and Littlefield, Lanham, MD.

Skoufias, E. 2005. *Progresa and its Impacts on the Welfare of Rural Households in Mexico.* Research Report No. 139, International Food Policy Research Institute (IFPRI), Washington, DC.

# 11 Gender, Citizenship and New Approaches to Poverty Relief
## Conditional Cash Transfer Programmes in Argentina

*Constanza Tabbush*[1]

## INTRODUCTION

Recent years have seen poverty and social exclusion debates attain renewed attention in international policy circles and donor agencies. The "lost decade" and the negative social outcomes of structural adjustment programmes (SAPs), the persistence of poverty and inequality in many Latin American countries and the current international consensus around the Millennium Development Goals invigorated attempts to tackle poverty and to provide, at least rhetorically, market liberalism a more inclusive face. New approaches to address poverty in the form of conditional cash transfer programmes (CCTs) provide an example of the new "inclusive liberalism" (Porter and Craig 2004) developed in Latin America. With the intent of re-embedding the market and mitigating the social consequences of market-led liberalism, a discourse of "investment" has emerged, aimed at including the *par excellence* liberal subject: the vulnerable. Efforts to fight poverty are articulated in targeted and demand-led programmes that provide assistance to poor families conditional on the performance of socially valued activities, such as paid work, or investing in children's health and education. Their objective is to fight immediate poverty by giving cash directly to families, and to diminish vulnerability in the long term by investing in the human capabilities of poor children—the "citizen-workers" of the future (Lister 2003).

These programmes build on notions of targeting and conditionality already present in residual approaches to social policy. Yet observers also identify some innovative features that include the unprecedented coverage of poor households, the multidimensional understanding of poverty and deprivation, the linking of social assistance to minimal social rights, the perception of beneficiaries as co-responsible and active partners, the emphasis on families and, in particular, the identification of women as the primary targets for addressing poverty. Various evaluations signal that the new generation of programmes offers unprecedented and much needed support to vulnerable sections of the population (Barrientos and DeJong 2004;

de la Briere and Rawlings 2006; González de la Rocha 2003, 2005; IPC 2006; Rawlings 2004; Rawlings and Rubio 2003; Serrano 2005a, 2005b; Villatoro 2004).

Either explicitly written into their legislation, or in practice, women constitute the main recipients of the cash stipends offered to beneficiary households, and are positioned as the key social actors expected to perform the required co-responsibilities. Research in Mexico, Costa Rica, Nicaragua and Argentina presents some initial assessments of the gender assumptions underpinning these programmes, the roles prescribed to women in relation to other household members, and, to a lesser extent, their impact on gender relations (Adato et al. 2000; Bradshaw 2008; Bradshaw and Linneker 2003; Bradshaw with Quirós Víquez 2007; Chant 2008, 2006; González de la Rocha 2003, 2005; Molyneux 2007, 2006; Pautassi 2004; Rodriguez Enriquez 2006). Given the special role played by women in poverty management, CCTs are said to encompass a degree of renegotiation of the reproductive bargain[2] between state institutions and poor households. So how these programmes of "inclusive liberalism" articulate citizenship,[3] gender and state mechanisms in order to build social inclusion is the guiding question of this chapter. Drawing on the Argentine case, the chapter explores the gender-differentiated rights and obligations expected of poor citizens, the mechanisms put in place for "including" poor women and men within mainstream society and finally reflects upon the gender implications of new forms of social protection developed in the region, hand in hand with the rise of the new social policy paradigm (Abel and Lewis 2002).

More specifically, the chapter compares two phases of CCT programmes set up in Argentina after the economic crisis of 2001, a first phase defined by "Plan Jefes y Jefas de Hogar Desocupados: Derecho Familiar a la Inclusión Social"[4] (*Plan Jefas*) and a second one embodied in its successors, "Plan Familias por la Inclusión Social"[5] (*Plan Familias*) and "Seguro de Capacitación y Empleo"[6] (*Seguro*). These particular programmes were selected taking into account their national salience, their rights-based rationale and the distinct mechanisms they put in place to achieve the promised "social inclusion" of the poor. The data and ideas presented are based on a review of the existing academic literature, a textual analysis of legislation and implementation manuals, an examination of programme evaluations and official statistics, and interviews with state bureaucrats and key informants in non-governmental organizations (NGOs) and grass-roots organizations, as well as selected beneficiaries.

The chapter is organized as follows. The first section presents the socioeconomic background of the case study. The second section discusses the main features of *Plan Jefas* and its consequences in terms of poverty, employment creation and gendered inequalities in entitlements. The third part builds upon the results of the previous programme and presents the reasons and the shape taken by the new CCT programmes

(*Plan Familias* and *Seguro*). The last section draws together the main conclusions and findings.

## THE SOCIAL-ECONOMIC CONTEXT TO POVERTY ALLEVIATION IN ARGENTINA

Argentina is a middle-income country and a regional pioneer in social policy terms (Mesa-Lago 1991). Until the 1980s, some social policy experts classified Argentina as a "universally-stratified social state", along with other Southern Cone countries like Uruguay and Chile (Filgueira 2005). Inspired by conservative welfare systems (Esping-Andersen 1991, 2003) and developed hand in hand with the rise of Peronism in 1945, the social state provided protection to the vast majority of the population by means of a social security system and basic health services. However, it did so in a stratified manner, along occupational lines which conferred better entitlements to state workers, professionals, urban service workers and urban manufacturing workers (Filgueira 2005; Filgueira and Filgueira 2002; Mesa-Lago 1991). Simultaneously, those working informally, rural workers and the unemployed were side-lined from state-provided social security mechanisms. Their sources of insurance were limited to family and kinship networks, church and community, and paid work. This combination of formal work-based social insurance described by Filgueira (2005), and the informal networks of survival, leads other regional analysts to classify this period of the Argentine welfare system as a "conservative-informal" welfare regime (Barrientos 2004).

After the turbulent decade of the 1970s, the new democratic government in 1983 initially experimented with economic heterodoxy. As the "lost decade" unfolded, Raul Alfonsin's administration faced various general strikes, military uprisings and an economic turmoil that triggered hyper-inflation. These critical political and economic conditions put an early end to his presidency and facilitated support for more orthodox economic recipes supposedly to achieve economic stability. The first of Carlos Saúl Menem's presidencies (1989–1995) embraced these ideals which continued to be applied during his second term in office (1995–1999). Argentina became subject to SAP policies and was regarded by the International Monetary Fund as one of its "best students" in the region. State reforms in this direction entailed, in addition to the privatization of state-owned enterprises, fiscal constraint and the opening up of the economy; a fixed currency exchange plan and the flexibilization of labour markets via diluting employment legislation and payroll taxes (Lo Vuolo et al. 2002; Barrientos 2004; Vinocur and Halperin 2004).

Fiscal retrenchment meant that Argentina neglected its old system of social security and in turn advanced moderately into a "liberal-informal" welfare regime type that invokes residual forms of welfare and poverty alleviation programmes (Barrientos 2004; Filgueira 2005). The new policy scenario brought significant changes and deterioration in labour market conditions. While coverage of social insurance declined, some components of the "welfare state" were dismantled and established social rights partially curtailed (Vinocur and Halperin 2004; Pautassi 2006; Rodriguez Enriquez 2006).

To contain the negative effects of adjustment, policymakers resorted to minimal and targeted social assistance and food programmes. Social Funds[7] proliferated throughout this decade to address particular needs and to provide income and temporary paid work. In overall terms, they were limited in coverage and meagre in resources, as well as poorly articulated. They created a juxtaposition of initiatives with similar design and objectives (Kessler and Roggi 2005; Pautassi 2006). In the year 2000 there were 20 employment programmes in simultaneous operation. Not surprisingly, social policy in this period has been characterized as, at best, chaotic, fragmented and overlapping[8] (Auyero 2000).

These adjustment measures resulted in strong negative impacts on social development indicators (Lo Vuolo et al. 2002; Kessler and Roggi 2005). With escalating extreme poverty and inequality, both unemployment and informal work also rose to unprecedented levels. Impoverishment peaked in 2002 when 57.2 per cent of the population was living in poverty and 27.5 per cent in extreme scarcity. Unemployment also reached its highest level in May 2002 when it stood at 21.5 per cent, and underemployment at 18.6 per cent of the workforce. The dire social scenario at the beginning of the new millennium was one of the main causes of the institutional and economic crisis set off in 2001 (Pautassi 2006).

Economic stagnation deepened after 1998 and was followed by the breakdown of the monetary regime and by a political and economic crisis at the beginning of the new millennium that generated broad social mobilizations and put an abrupt end to the Presidency of Fernando de la Rúa (1999–2001). The fragile political legitimacy and high levels of social unrest saw the succession of four interim presidents until national elections were called. The new government of Néstor Kirchner (2003–2007) in the post-crisis scenario, with its own reinterpretation of the historical legacy and vision of Peronism, pledged its adherence to fighting scarcity and inequality and, in practical terms, secured political stability by adopting broad poverty alleviation measures to deal with the extreme social and economic consequences of the crisis.

The attempts at providing more inclusive forms of liberalism built upon the experience of the Social Funds and the public work programmes of the 1990s (Golbert 2004; Pautassi 2004). In addition to CCTs which attempted to tackle deprivation and surpass previous deficiencies in reaching the poor, the state also envisaged active policies to encourage formal employment and to extend basic health and pension insurance to those previously dependent on informal mechanisms. The most prominent example of such formalization was the campaign for the registration of domestic workers. Table 11.1 summarizes the main features of each historical period.

*Table 11.1* Welfare Regimes and Type of Social Protection in Argentina

| Welfare regime | Conservative-informal (1950s–1970s) | Liberal-informal (1980s–1990s) | Inclusive liberalism (2000s) |
|---|---|---|---|
| Main forms of protection | Work-based social insurance. Informal networks for rural informal or unemployed workers. | Residual social assistance. Dilution of social rights and increasing reliance on informal work and informal survival networks. | Widespread coverage of minimal social assistance. Policy to expand formal work, and provide basic insurance for informal workers. |
| Paradigmatic Examples | Social insurance | Social funds | CCTs |

In order to rapidly expand the coverage of social assistance programmes in 2002, two conditional cash transfer programmes were launched. The biggest in reach and the more visible in the public sphere was the programme for unemployed heads of households or *Plan Jefas*, while a more modest strategy was linked to the protection of vulnerable groups. Three years later with a more stable socioeconomic situation and the need to move from emergency measures to long-term ones, the structure of social protection was reassessed and modified into the programme for families for social inclusion—*Plan Familias*—and the insurance for training and employment.[9] These two phases in the design and development of CCTs assumed and encouraged particular constructions of gendered identities and citizenship practices.

## THE FIRST PHASE: *PLAN JEFAS*

*Plan Jefas* constituted the high point of emergency programmes launched at a time of extreme social tensions. Initiated by interim President Eduardo Duhalde (2002–2003), the programme was later redefined and expanded during the administration of Néstor Kirchner. In the decree of 4 April 2002 it was defined as the main strategy to fight the adverse employment consequences and the loss of income triggered by the economic crisis of 2001.[10] With its extensive regional coverage and magnitude, reaching in 2002 16 per cent of all households, this initiative is without historical precedence in Argentine social protection (MTESS 2004b).

The programme targets unemployed "heads of households" regardless of sex who are responsible for a child below the age of 18 or caring for a disabled child or a pregnant spouse[11] (Decree 565/2002:art. 2). A monthly stipend of

150 Argentine pesos (ARS)[12] is offered to each family conditional on the performance of 20 hours of paid work per week. In its legislation *Plan Jefas* articulates two simultaneous objectives: to supply a minimal monthly income to all unemployed families by means of the cash provided, as well as to secure families' right to social inclusion and future labour reinsertion through involvement in productive, communal or educational activities (Decree 565/2002). These conditionalities are, in turn, assumed to encourage a "real work culture", and reduce the vulnerability of families (Decree 1506/2004; Resolution MTESS 406/2003). Initially the Ministry of Labour, Employment and Social Security was assigned as the overseeing state entity (Decree 565/2002:art. 14), because it had the adequate institutional and human resources to do so (Golbert 2004). Since 2004 the task is shared with the Ministry of Social Development (MSD) (Decree 1506/2004:art. 4 and 5).

The selection of beneficiaries was carried out by a massive call to the population. To avoid delays due to complex targeting methodologies, the programme did not fix regional targets; instead, individual self-selection was taken as the path. As a result, the requirements of household headship and unemployment were defined by beneficiaries themselves through a signed declaration of their alleged status. Given the problematic nature of defining household headship,[13] it is not surprising that it was not clearly defined in the legislation of the programme, and thereby left to the beneficiaries and those implementing the programme to do so. From the legislation, for example, it is not clear if the notion of "household head" refers to the main economic provider, to the main decision-maker or to the person whom others designate as the head. Furthermore since the targeting criteria was not vigorously enforced, those actually not heading a household or informally employed could in practice access the programme. The only factor precluding participation in *Plan Jefas* is social security contributions attached to formal employment.

The selection process had a further particularity. Initially all citizens fulfilling the stated criteria were entitled to receive benefits through the programme but, given the large number of applicants and budgetary considerations, an arbitrary decision was taken to stop receiving new applicants after 17 May 2002 (CELS 2003). Even though the programme has been continued annually since 2002 by presidential decree, this restriction has effectively closed the programme to new applicants.[14]

Despite these shortcomings, 90 per cent of those participating in the programme fall below the poverty line (Ronconi et al. 2006). The accelerated intake of participants registered in 2002 peaked in 2003 when all those that applied before 17 May 2002 were finally enrolled at slightly over two million beneficiaries. But as economic conditions improved, formal and informal work opportunities became more widely available, and other social programmes captured part of *Jefas'* beneficiaries; the number of beneficiaries decreased, so that by 2007 the figure stood at about half of the initial figure.

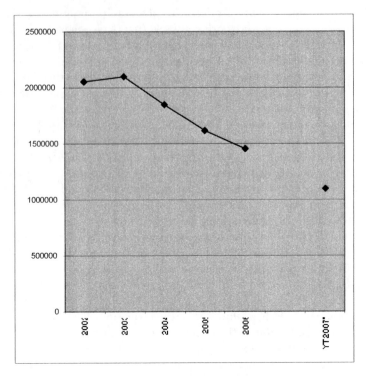

*Figure 11.1* Total number of beneficiaries of *Plan Jefas*, per year.

*Note:* * 2007 only includes the period January–May.

*Source:* Author's own elaboration based on data provided by the Ministry of Labour (MTESS).

Even though the cash provided by the programme was not sufficient to have a major impact on poverty levels, it did have an effect on the incidence of indigence.[15] The impact on levels of indigence, though, has decreased over time, along with a reduction in the number of beneficiaries and the real value of the stipend. Figure 11.2 shows that, while in 2003 the programme reduced the level of indigence by 3 per cent, the impact was reduced to 0.9 per cent in 2006.[16] Furthermore, given that programme beneficiaries were counted as "employed" in official statistics, another outcome of the programme was to reduce the level of unemployment (MTESS 2004a, 2004b). Assessments signal, for instance, that the reduction in the level of unemployment a year after the programme was roughly equivalent to the number of participants in *Plan Jefas* (Galasso and Ravallion 2003). Finally the contribution of the income provided is calculated at 37 per cent of overall household income of beneficiaries (Pautassi 2004).

As these results indicate, *Plan Jefas* "did partially compensate many losers of the crisis and reduce extreme poverty" (Galasso and Ravallion

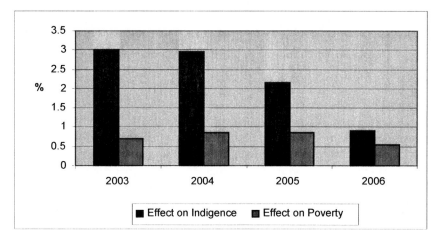

*Figure 11.2* The impact of *Plan Jefas* on levels of poverty and indigence, 2003–2006.

*Note*: The impact of *Plan Jefas* was calculated by computing the difference between levels of poverty and indigence per ye ar with and without the income provided by the programme.

*Source*: Author's own elaboration with data from INDEC, Household Survey.

2003:1). Furthermore it played an important part in diminishing levels of social tension produced by the crisis not only due to the distribution of plans, but also through the alliances carved between key social actors: the unemployment movement, government officials, NGOs and faith-based organizations (Golbert 2004).

Programme evaluations and academic studies describe the main characteristics of beneficiaries. They often use different data sets. The analysis provided in this chapter, for the sake of consistency, uses official statistics to the extent possible. When there are important inconsistencies, and reason to believe that the data may be misleading, other sources are used.

The available data suggests that close to 71 per cent of participants in the programme are women, with low educational levels (primary school) and in their reproductive years (between 30 and 40 years of age) (MTESS 2004b). Household surveys carried out by independent researchers[17] indicate that programme beneficiaries are from the poorest sectors of the population, with the following characteristics: They tend to live in large households with, on average, five household members; they have low levels of economic activity and experience high unemployment rates (Cortés at al. 2004).

In spite of targeting heads of households, around half of female participants defined themselves in later surveys as spouses. So, as shown in table 11.2, male and female beneficiaries of *Plan Jefas* occupy different positions within their respective households.[18] In terms of their links with the labour market, the great bulk of beneficiaries were not only unemployed—the

*Table 11.2* Proportion of Male and Female Participants and Their Household Status

| Position within household | Male beneficiaries (%) | Female beneficiaries (%) |
|---|---|---|
| Head | 81.4 | 25.9 |
| Spouse | 0.9 | 49.4 |
| Other | 17.8 | 24.7 |

*Source*: Pautassi 2004.

original target of the programme—but 37.6 per cent of female and 10.5 per cent of male beneficiaries reported being economically inactive before joining the programme. Compared to the unemployed population more generally, participants of the programme encounter greater difficulties in re-entering the labour market (MTESS 2004b).

Gender analyses of *Plan Jefas* point out that despite women's visibility in the programme, much like previous Social Fund initiatives it lacks a serious concern with gender equity. The main question these studies raise is the significance and impact of the programme on the lives of poor women. Does it help overcome exclusionary labour market mechanisms through its work-related and training conditionalities? Or does it simply provide some additional income in a moment of crisis (Pautassi 2004, 2006)? The effects of the programme on intrahousehold dynamics as well as the gender ideologies underpinning policy formulation have remained, however, largely unexplored. Little consideration has also been given to the resonance with liberal feminist ideas of promoting women's equality with men. The title selected for the programme explicitly recognizes *both* women and men as potential beneficiaries—*Plan Jefes y Jefas*. Does this equal recognition given to both sexes mean that women's interests and constraints are sufficiently reflected in the design of the programme?

The next section considers from a gender perspective the significance of the cash stipend for both women and men, as well as the gender-differentiated responsibilities required by the programme in the form of the labour conditionality. The section will also explore the exit strategies that are available to beneficiaries, in particular, the extent to which they can re-enter the labour market.

## Programme Entitlements: Cash, Gender and Household Structure

Given that programme participants were self-selected, the income provided by the programme seems to have mainly attracted poor women with limited possibilities of accessing other sources of income. While economists foresaw that the gender division of household tasks and the different constraints and possibilities of accessing the labour market would probably mean that more women would be attracted to the programme than men, as a way of complementing their other meagre sources of income, policymakers claim that they did not expect the high levels of female intake.

Because of women's high levels of inactivity and underemployment during the 1990s, and the extent of labour market segmentation and gender wage gaps, it is not surprising that the programme would have been more attractive to women than to men in low-income households. Contrary to men's employment rates that declined during the 1990s (ILO 2005), women's economic activity rates grew. Yet instead of entering employment, women's increased economic activity resulted in rising levels of female unemployment and underemployment. In 2002 these two figures rose to 18.9 per cent and 25 per cent of the female workforce, respectively. The work trajectory of beneficiaries a year and a half before the programme follows this general trend and indicates that labour vulnerability for women was mainly related to either inactivity or unemployment (Cortés et al. 2004).

Almost half of female participants in the programme are spouses, and 43 per cent of them declared to be economically inactive a year before joining the programme, mainly due to labour market constraints, discouragement and/or incompatibility of paid work with their unpaid household responsibilities (Pautassi 2004). It appears that for women, entering or increasing their labour market participation was not as feasible or attractive as joining the programme, the latter providing a more sustained source of income than they would have obtained through the labour market. Thus, the extended feminine presence in the programme can be explained as a household strategy to maximize resources by bringing women out of forced inactivity in a context of crisis (MTESS 2004b; Rodriguez Enriquez 2006; Pautassi 2006).

The households of women beneficiaries, many of them spouses, show better economic conditions and an income 30 per cent higher than those households with male *Plan Jefas* beneficiaries. The former tend to be large families with a higher number of income earners and links to the labour market, while households of male beneficiaries tend to be nuclear families with fewer members who are economically active[19] (Pautassi 2004). Yet information on how earnings and/or power are distributed within each household arrangement to evaluate overall well-being is not presently available.

The use of *Plan Jefas* became increasingly feminized during the consolidation of the programme. Figure 11.3 shows this development with a near 10 per cent increase in the number of female participants over the designated period (2002–2007).

It seems that men resorted to *Plan Jefas* only in the immediate aftermath of the economic crisis as a temporary measure, but as social conditions improved, many found other sources of income. By contrast, poor women in households with multiple income earners accessed the stipend on a more permanent basis. They relied on it as one of several strategies they call upon to secure household survival, along with their tenuous participation in the informal economy and unpaid care responsibilities.[20] The households of male beneficiaries that remain in the programme over time constitute a

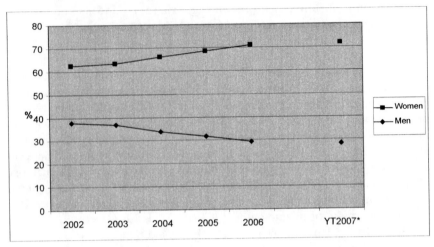

*Figure 11.3* Percentages of female and male beneficiaries of *Plan Jefas*, by year.

Note: * 2007 only includes the period January–May.

Source: Author's own elaboration based on data provided by the Ministry of Labour (MTESS).

particularly vulnerable group, given that many of them have fewer income earners, and the fact that the contribution of the programme to their overall household income is 11 per cent higher than the equivalent figure for female beneficiaries (Pautassi 2004). This group of male participants experience a stronger tendency to engage in sporadic work, persistent unemployment or toddle from inactivity to unemployment at an intensity superior to that of female programme participants (Cortés et al. 2004).

## Programme Obligations: Gender Dynamics, Work Conditionality and Market Inclusion

The Argentine strategy targets unemployed—not poor—heads of households and its long-term strategy of inclusion is based on paid labour and not human capital development. In practical terms, the contribution of the work conditionality to labour market inclusion remains debatable (Pautassi 2004, 2006; Rodriguez Enriquez 2006). The ambiguity of the work component was partly a result of the conditionality appearing as an afterthought to the initial design—a mechanism that was later put in place to reduce the large number of applicants in a context of budgetary constraints (Galasso and Ravallion 2003; Módolo 2004) in order to ensure that the cash transfer would go to those in "real need" (Giovagnoli 2005).

The implementation of the work requirement was decentralized to local governments. General assessments on its significance would therefore have to be tampered by the variance of local experiences. These often differ depending on the characteristics of municipalities, the number of beneficiaries, the role of social movements and faith-based organizations, as well as local labour market dynamics. In many cases, local governments did not have the organizational capacity to develop and monitor activities, which compromised the quality of the work being provided, limiting it to low-skill tasks and occupations (Pautassi 2004, 2006; Rodriguez Enriquez 2006). However, some scholars argue that even where beneficiaries are required to perform cheap labour for regular municipal tasks this should not be seen as entirely negative (Kessler and Roggi 2005). Yet what is also clear is that participation in labour activities declined over the life of the programme. Initially beneficiaries saw them as an obligation in order to access the cash stipend, but when the poor monitoring and low enforcement of municipalities became apparent, work requirements were progressively discouraged.

In spite of these ambiguities and limitations, at least in principle, the work rationale of the programme should be able to supply poor women some opportunities for labour market inclusion that go beyond the little productive prospects opened by other CCT programmes with human development prerogatives—a point to which we will return later.

### The Tasks Involved

Community projects provided the main form of work conditionality and involved 60 per cent of beneficiaries, while administrative tasks drew 20 per cent, followed by microenterprise development (8 per cent), finishing school (6 per cent), training (4 per cent) and work for the private sector (2 per cent). Each of these activities and social spaces attracted women with particular sociodemographic characteristics and offered different opportunities for social interaction and empowerment. Community projects—the main form of work conditionality—attracted women from low-middle income backgrounds with higher educational levels. These spaces stirred social exchanges, autonomy and self-valorization, as well as knowledge exchange on how to maximize benefits from the *Plan*. At the same time, finishing school was taken up by women experiencing poverty for more than a generation and with no primary education. Adult education offered a chance to break their social isolation. It does not seem to enrich social networks and participation, but it enhances self-esteem, cultural capital and a perception of more autonomy in the eyes of their children (Di Marco et al. 2006).

The majority of beneficiaries fulfilled work requirements, but women did so more frequently than men, 93.4 per cent and 81.6 per cent, respectively (MTESS 2004b; Pautassi 2004). For men, over time, the labour requirement lost its significance as their main occupation. In contrast, for women the work performed as part of the programme continued to be significant (Calvi and Zibecchi 2006), concurring with the aforementioned differential usages of the programme by gender.

The tasks generally carried out are mostly low skill and similar to those required by previous employment programmes: construction, repairs, care of children and old people, tourism activities (CELS 2003). A closer look at gender disaggregated data shows that these activities reinforce patterns of gender segmentation already present in low-skill occupations, with women overwhelmingly clustered into reproductive tasks or other typically "feminine" occupations (Daeren 2004). Women's work in community projects, for instance, was geared towards care-related tasks involving cleaning, caring, repairing shoes and clothes, and less prominently clerical responsibilities. Men tended to specialize in general maintenance and construction related activities (Pautassi 2006; Rodriguez Enriquez 2006). In addition to providing poor training opportunities, the lack of skill generation was further reinforced by a general low intake of training as a form of co-responsibility.[21]

Despite the low skills involved and the lack of training available to female beneficiaries, for many of them the conditionalities represent a way of temporarily escaping the confines of family life and being included in public spaces of social interaction (Di Marco et al. 2006).[22] Further, anthropologists suggest that women's employment in social work and clerical activities at the municipality or neighbourhood level has given them a sense of doing socially valued work, compared to men who are often engaged in physically demanding tasks. The conditionality of *Plan Jefas* might therefore offer women a way of building social capital, of learning new skills for personal or family use and of fostering a new sense of social inclusion and social status that is more desirable than that of being "unemployed" or "economically inactive" (Kessler and Roggi 2005). Beneficiaries interviewed underlined the positive effects of being offered socially useful work. Notwithstanding these positive outcomes, it is also clear that the new mechanisms of inclusion are essentially without any form of social protection (and are being used to cut personnel costs in public administration) (Colmegna 2004). Nor did *Plan Jefas* offer women any assistance by providing childcare services (Kessler and Roggi 2005). The legislation of the programme makes no explicit reference to childcare provision (Pautassi 2004).

### Exiting the Programme: Inclusion in Formal Work and Social Mobility

The available evidence suggests that almost 40 per cent of those exiting *Plan Jefas* entered registered employment (MTESS 2007); in total nearly 600,000 beneficiaries found formal work between 2002 and 2007.[23] Labour reinsertion has been partially stimulated by the high growth rates during the last four years of close to 9 per cent (World Bank 2006) that translated into a 30 per cent increase in registered employment (MTESS 2006b). This was facilitated by explicit government efforts to promote employment creation.[24] Yet access to formal work has provided different opportunities for female and male programme participants. Time-series data suggest an initial bias towards men, but over time, the gender gap appears to have narrowed as shown in figure 11.4.

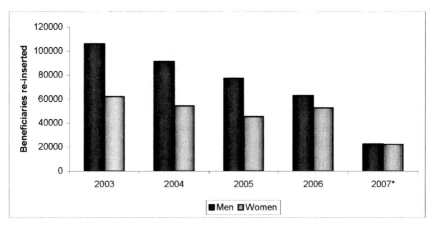

*Figure 11.4* Beneficiaries (re)incorporated into the formal labour market, by sex and by year.

Note: Beneficiaries suspended or cancelled per year due to formal labour insertion.
* 2007 only includes the period January–May.
Source: Author's own elaboration based on data provided by the Ministry of Labour (MTESS).

Women formed the bulk of the beneficiaries, yet until 2006 women had a much lower chance of graduating from the programme into formal work than their male counterparts. While in 1996 and 1998 job creation was driven by the service sector, which provides relatively easier entry for women (MTESS 2004a), since 2003 the growth in employment has risen in the construction sector which typically provides low- and semi-skilled occupations for men (MTESS 2006a, 2006b). Not surprisingly, 65 per cent of the posts created in 2006 were occupied by men (MTESS 2006a). Moreover, there is a high correlation between the prior work experience of beneficiaries and the sectors of the economy in which they find employment. For example, 83 per cent of those beneficiaries hired in the construction sector and 80 per cent of those in industry had already worked in those sectors (MTESS 2007). Male beneficiaries, concurring with employers' expectations, had previously worked in the required sectors, while women had significantly lower formal work experience, most having worked as paid domestic workers (see table 11.3) (MTESS 2004b; Pautassi 2004). In other words, women's employment histories, more than men's, tend to be geared toward informal activities. This is confirmed by qualitative research suggesting that women beneficiaries are actively involved in the informal economy, including domestic work and industrial home-based production for small enterprises.

Hence, the initial employment bias in favour of males was for the most part determined by factors external to the programme: changes in growth patterns, higher levels of overall male employment and employers'

*Table 11.3* Previous Occupation of *Plan Jefas* Beneficiaries Transferring to the *Seguro**

| Women: Previous occupation | % | Men: Previous occupation | % |
|---|---|---|---|
| Domestic service | 22.6 | Construction | 26.9 |
| Administration and planning | 9.9 | Industrial and craft production | 14.2 |
| Industrial and craft production | 9.2 | No data | 6.1 |
| Gastronomical services | 9.2 | Transport | 5.5 |
| Non-domestic cleaning services | 8.8 | Non-domestic cleaning services | 5.1 |

*Notes*: Information until 30 May 2007.
*The Seguro is one of the CCTs that replaces Plan Jefas; it maintains the work-related approach of Plan Jefas.
*Source*: Author's own elaboration based on data provided by the Ministry of Labour (MTESS).

preferences for those with previous formal occupations in their own sectors (be it manufacturing or construction).

As the presence in *Plan Jefas* of male beneficiaries with the required characteristics declined, women's and men's patterns of labour market entry slowly converged. Unfortunately there is no sex-disaggregated data on the types of occupations into which programme beneficiaries enter.

### Quality of Jobs Being Created

After 2004 the entry into the labour market of male *Plan Jefas* participants progressively declines (see figure 11.4). The jobs obtained seem to have become more precarious; temporary employment has increased and constituted 55 per cent of men's total employment in 2007. At the peak of men's labour market entry, the number of programme beneficiaries obtaining work for short-term periods was low and much of it confined to women. As men's entry into employment diminished, the re-entry of beneficiaries back into the programme grew (see figure 11.5). Furthermore, male beneficiaries who find additional barriers in accessing paid work and who remain in *Plan Jefas* tend to enter insecure forms of paid work, highlighting that men's vulnerability is mostly linked to intermittent employment (Cortés et al. 2004).

In the case of women, at the start of *Plan Jefas* not only did they experience difficulties in accessing formal work, but even for those who did access paid work, close to 60 per cent returned to *Plan Jefas* within three months. After 2005 the situation for women appears to have improved: Not only do a larger proportion of programme beneficiaries appear to find employment, but the paid work that they find seems to be more stable. Short-term occupations have declined, despite the slight increase in the percentage of women who returned to the programme after 2006. In spite of women participants being incorporated into the labour market at a much lower rate, it is worth

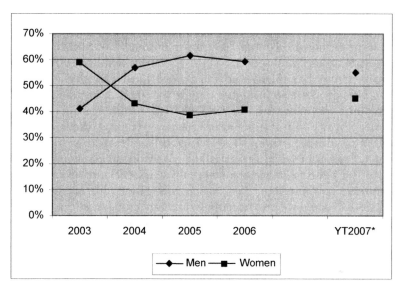

*Figure 11.5* Percentages of beneficiaries that return to *Plan Jefas* after gaining employment, by sex and by year.

*Note:* * 2007 only includes the period January–May.
*Source:* Author's own elaboration based on data provided by the Ministry of Labour (MTESS).

noting that many of those who are entering had no recent experience of formal sector work (MTESS 2004a), and are slowly cultivating links with the formal labour market.

In addition to the instability of jobs found by beneficiaries, their salaries tend to cluster below ARS350 (MTESS 2007). Some studies suggest *Plan Jefas* tends to promote informal or precarious forms of work. These critics suggest that the programme encourages the substitution of formal work with informal part-time jobs and non-registered employment, because those who are formally employed are not able to access the programme (Rodriguez Enriquez 2006).

As noted earlier, domestic work appears to be the most common prior occupation of female beneficiaries. However, since programme evaluations focus on formal employment, domestic work that generally belongs to the informal economy does not appear in official documentation. And despite recent efforts to formalize it, the labour market conditions of domestic workers remain poor with the level of pay at the discretion of individual employers. Moreover, even if the wages offered for domestic work are comparable to wages offered in jobs involving similar levels of skill, hourly wages tend to decrease concomitant with the number of hours worked, discouraging such workers from working full- or overtime (MTESS 2005).[25]

## *Plan Jefas:* Gender, Social Inclusion and Work

*Plan Jefas* sees paid work as the key mechanism of social integration (Resolution MTESS 256/2003), which has some parallels with the "welfare-to-work" policy thrust into the United States and social democratic prescriptions for social inclusion in Europe (Gerhard et al. 2002). Liberal feminist concerns with equality, embedded in the design of such programmes, assume that the strategy of inclusion through the labour market provides equal opportunities for women and men. The earlier analysis, however, suggests that in practice the manner in which women and men enter such programmes and the extent to which they are able to exit such programmes and enter the labour market are gender differentiated.

Three different groups of beneficiaries can be identified. First, women, a high percentage of whom are spouses, discouraged from participation in economic activities and living in large families with several income earners. These women tend to resort to the programme because the stipend it provides compares favourably with their poor labour market prospects. Given the multiple income earners, the households of these female beneficiaries seem to have a higher level of income than those of male participants. Little is known about the incidence of other forms of risk in their lives related to time poverty and their economic insecurity; because of their economic dependence on other household members, especially male partners, they do face particular risks associated with divorce, separation and widowhood. Although some of these women may have been able to benefit from the programme in terms of entering some form of economic activity and social networks, their involvement appears to be disarticulated from the economic citizenship and long-term labour inclusion called upon by programme regulations. Up until 2005 women's labour market prospects were highly unstable; in more recent years there has been some improvement, thanks to the dynamism of the manufacturing and administrative sectors. Some women seem to be entering more stable forms of employment.

Second, men resorted to *Plan Jefas* in the immediate aftermath of the social emergency, but once the economy showed signs of recovery those with stronger links to formal work re-entered employment in construction and industry. Formal labour market participation is an opportunity mostly enjoyed by one-third of male programme beneficiaries. And even in these cases new jobs provide wages that are significantly lower than the average wage in the economy as well as being unstable.

Finally, there is a group of male beneficiaries who could not take advantage of formal work openings, and who still remain in *Plan Jefas*. This remnant male group shows signs of intense vulnerability: Their households have fewer income earners and relatively lower levels of income than those of female participants. Furthermore, as the next section suggests, this group of men will not be included in the new programme that is intended to replace *Plan Jefas*, and is likely to become side-lined from the state's efforts at providing social protection.

### Beneficiaries: Subjects of Rights or Assistance

From a rights-based perspective, *Plan Jefas* signals improvements in terms of coverage,[26] and the core logic of the programme, the right to social inclusion, signals a growing valorization of citizenship, social rights and capability enhancement (CELS 2003; Golbert 2004; Pautassi 2006). Notwithstanding these nominal gains, the amount of cash provided is insufficient to have made a significant dent into poverty.

In principle *Plan Jefas* attempts to surpass "assistential" social programmes. However, equality of access and entitlements, and state accountability to programme beneficiaries, are curtailed in three respects. First, there is little effort to monitor the extent to which the state performs its side of the "co-responsibility", nor are there clear and timely complaints procedures available to beneficiaries. Centralized structures of administration in the programme further jeopardize effective appeal mechanisms (CELS 2003, 2007). Second, informal and/or arbitrary deadlines for beneficiary enrolment (in this case 17 May 2002) act as barriers to entry. Finally, even if discretionary allocations are less prevalent than in previous decades, research still shows that beneficiary participation rates are significantly higher in Peronist than in non-Peronist municipalities (Giovagnoli 2005), pointing to the persistence of politicized forms of enrolment.

The aforementioned ambiguities are also evident in how beneficiaries perceive the programme. *Plan Jefas* is mostly interpreted by the target population as a form of assistance to the poor, aimed at gaining some form of political support for ruling parties. As shown in Table 11.4, only one-tenth of beneficiaries think that the programme can meet their rights as citizens, while the majority see it as a form of "social aid."

*Table 11.4* The Meaning of *Plan Jefas* from the Perspective of Beneficiaries

| The programme is | % |
| --- | --- |
| An act of charity | 7.0 |
| A right | 10.4 |
| A political manoeuvre | 16.1 |
| A social aid | 63 |
| Other | 1.1 |
| No answer | 2.4 |

*Source*: MTESS 2003.

Special consideration should finally be given to the growing emphasis placed on citizens' obligations, to the detriment of their claims/rights. In the context of targeted efforts to alleviate poverty, emphasizing the obligations of the poor in exchange for access to minimal rights can end up being detrimental for the extension of those same entitlements (Levitas 2005; Kessler and Roggi 2005).

## THE SECOND PHASE OF INCLUSIVE LIBERALISM: "THE PLAN FAMILIAS"

After the immediate years of the social emergency had passed, various criticisms voiced by Catholic organizations, the association of national industry and international donors on grounds of "clientelism" and of not encouraging a culture of work (Clarín 2006b; CTA 2006) signalled the need to re-evaluate the strategies of social protection put in place during the emergency period. In response, *Plan Jefas* underwent major modifications, and, though it is still in operation, it has sought to downsize the number of beneficiaries by transferring them to two other CCT programmes—the *Plan Familias* and the *Seguro*—each supposedly targeting a specific profile of *Jefas* beneficiaries.[27]

Government authorities divided the occupational profiles of beneficiaries of *Plan Jefas* into different groups based on their employment prospects. Beneficiaries with higher educational levels and previous work experience, those with low levels of education yet with a motivation to continue their studies, and those facing added difficulties (older beneficiaries with low levels of education and no labour skills) were identified as having different degrees, yet still possessing some employment prospects. Consequently, they continue to receive their benefits under the umbrella of the Ministry of Labour. "Inactive beneficiaries, women or the elderly", in contrast, form a group that is considered to be socially vulnerable yet "not employable". This group is seen as highly vulnerable and therefore in need of income support or human development in the form of *Plan Familias* which is being implemented by the MSD (MTESS 2004b; Decree 1506/2004).

The rationale behind these changes is that different measures are needed to deal with extreme poverty and unemployment. First, to secure training and productive employment, the *Seguro* reproduces the *Jefas'* work rationale and continues to prioritize reinsertion into formal paid work (Resolution 336/2005). It targets the unemployed or informal workers and helps promote a "real work culture" (Decree 1506/2004).[28]

The need to develop institutional capacity and build employment agencies at the municipal level almost from scratch meant that by April 2007 the *Seguro* was operating in only 99 municipalities in the country. Hence, only a small number of beneficiaries of *Plan Jefas* (nearly 44,000) had transferred to this new initiative. However, contrary to expectations, women were strongly represented among those who agreed to move to this initiative (77 per cent), slightly older than *Jefas'* participants[29] and only 61.7 per cent of them had previous work experience.[30]

The second objective, the strengthening of vulnerable families was to be pursued through *Plan Familias* (Resolution MSD 648/2006). In its current format *Plan Familias* was launched in October 2004 with the aim of combating the social exclusion of poor families through the promotion of human development and capacity-building of children's health and education (Resolution MSD 825/2005). Those eligible to participate are previous beneficiaries of *Plan Familias*' predecessor—the programme income for human development (IDH)[31]—and female beneficiaries of *Plan Jefas* who have low education levels, two or more children and who reside in one of the 403 municipalities or surrounding areas identified as geographical priorities[32] (MSD 2006c, 2006d). In terms of design and objectives, *Plan Familias* mirrors the Mexican programme, *Oportunidades*, and other subsequent human development strategies developed in Latin America. It provides cash transfers dependant on family size directly to women, conditional on school attendance and health checks of their children between 5 and 19 years of age.[33] The minimum monetary provision is ARS185[34] for families with two children, and offers a top-up of ARS30 per child, up to a maximum of ARS305[35] per month for a family with six or more children[36] (Resolution MSD 693/2007). A second component only targeting 60 municipalities nationwide also offers optional community and family activities focused on training in health promotion and school progress for children and adolescents (MSD 2005b). Currently, programme beneficiaries can have other sources of income, through either work or pensions, as long as the total amount of household earnings does not exceed the minimum salary.[37] The programme has an estimated annual budget of US$322.5 million (MSD 2005b), with an estimated funding of US$2 billion for the next five years. The Inter-American Development Bank (IDB) currently provides 70 per cent of this funding, and the national government the remaining 30 per cent.

To date 203,402 beneficiaries have migrated from *Plan Jefas* to *Plan Familias*, which, together with the IDH beneficiaries, brings the total number of programme beneficiaries to 427,282 (see figure 11.6). Yet, it was expected that close to 500,000 households would migrate from *Plan Jefas* to *Plan Familias* in 2006 and 700,000 in 2007 (MSD 2006d). Delays in programme expansion have to do with poor administrative capacity, as well as scepticism on the part of *Plan Jefas* participants towards any effort to downsize and modify the programme. *Plan Jefas* enjoyed a level of legitimacy, durability and public visibility that gives beneficiaries a sense of security. As a result, beneficiaries are resisting the changes being proposed; they nevertheless opt for *Plan Familias* mainly due to the larger stipend it offers (MSD 2005b).

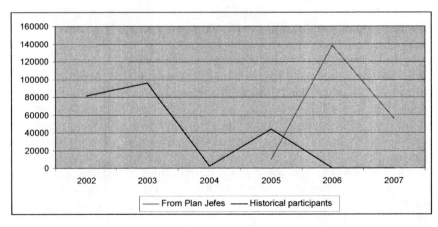

*Figure 11.6* Number of new participants in *Plan Familias* coming from *Plan Jefas* and previous IDH programmes, by year.

*Note*: The figure excludes those entering the programme by decree or judicial ruling; in total: 906 beneficiaries from 2002 until 2007.
*2007 only includes until March
*Source*: Author's own elaboration with data from MSD.

Since the programme has been recently implemented there is little information regarding its outcomes. However the data available shows beneficiaries that opt to transfer to *Plan Familias* are mostly women (95.79 per cent) in reproductive ages and with large households; 64 per cent of these beneficiaries describe themselves as heads of households.[38] The cash received is generally used for satisfying needs such as purchasing food, clothing, school equipment and accessing health care. Almost three-quarters of participants claim that the programme enhances their children's school attendance at the primary level (MSD 2006a).

## Re-Traditionalizing Gender Roles in the Management of Poverty

The government justifies *Plan Familias* by suggesting that social exclusion encompasses a breakdown of the "work culture" as well as a weakening of the mechanisms of social reproduction that have traditionally given access to public or social goods and services to guarantee social integration (MSD 2005a). Following moral underclass theories on social exclusion developed in liberal welfare arrangements (Levitas 2005), gender-segmented trajectories are prescribed for people's integration into mainstream society: paid work and the ethics associated with it largely for men and responsible motherhood for women.

In its regulations *Plan Familias* is said to consider equal treatment and opportunities for all household members as well as guaranteeing the recognition and commitment of women and men to the education and development of their children (Resolution MSD 825/2005). However, the programme offers an inclusion strategy aimed at women, which strongly identifies them with caring roles and their reproductive capacities. The naturalization of care as an essentially female activity is evident in the way *Plan Familias* treats the few male beneficiaries of *Plan Jefas* who opt to transfer to the former. In such cases a thorough analysis of the characteristics of the male applicants is undertaken, their levels of vulnerability are assessed as well as the feasibility of passing the benefit to a female member of the household.[39] Extra scrutiny of these "suspicious" participants and their families often follows through an added home interview by programme representatives prior to their enrolment (Joint Resolution of MTESS and MSD 143 and 264/2005). The MSD then recommends that those men who are eligible should reassign the subsidy to a woman member of the household who can fulfil the programme's requirements, making her responsible for the contractual bidding stipulated in programme regulations (MSD 2005b). Men are not the ones who are meant to sign the contract with state institutions. Only in cases where the male applicant is a single parent, or when he has a partner who is a foreigner, disabled, imprisoned or below 18 years of age, is he allowed to act as the main participant in the programme (MSD 2006d: *Formulario C solicitud de aceptación de titulares varones por excepción*).

The targeting of mothers to contribute to human capital formation of future citizen-workers shows the maternalistic assumptions that underpin human development CCTs where women are positioned as "conduits of policy" since they acquire a visible role in poverty alleviation but their needs are not the ultimate policy objective (Molyneux 2006). *Plan Familias* is thus grounded in what Ann Whitehead (1991) labelled "the ideology of maternal altruism" and promotes a virtuous model of the "empowered" woman based on her alleged altruism and commitment to family welfare, willing to perform unpaid community and family work (Sabates-Wheeler and Kabeer 2003). The next sections consider the conjunction of contextual variables that serve to explain the motives and particular shapes acquired by the re-traditionalization of gender roles in the Argentine scenario.

### The Unmet Needs of Jefas Beneficiaries

There were specific social needs of a particular group of *Jefas'* beneficiaries that were not being addressed by the labour-related initiative. Women with large families and mounting care responsibilities may not necessarily have the opportunity to derive extra earnings (from formal or informal paid work). These women do have a real need for further income support, without the co-responsibility requirements imposed by *Plan Jefas* (MTESS 2004b). The latter, due to the direct link it constructed between poverty and unemployment, effectively overlooked the unpaid forms of work and caring that some women have to provide, which renders their participation in paid work difficult (without some kind of support for their caring duties).

Gender analysts suggest that with *Plan Familias*, state authorities seem to be partly acknowledging the difficulties that women with a low level of skill and education and intense domestic responsibilities face in accessing paid work (Rodriguez Enriquez 2006). Preliminary reports show that the reasons women cited for transferring to *Plan Familias* were the larger cash stipend it provided and the less demanding conditionalities (MSD 2005b). Therefore, these changes partially respond to a real and unmet need for further income support on the part of a certain beneficiary group of *Plan Jefas*.

But like other social programmes which identify women solely as mothers, the programme effectively overlooks their simultaneous contributions as workers and carers (Razavi and Hassim 2006), and makes it difficult for them to re-enter paid work (Rodriguez Enriquez 2006). The distinction made between *Plan Familias* and *Seguro*, social vulnerability and lack of work respectively, and the dissociation between them, overlooks women's links to labour markets. The reality of beneficiaries' lives is at variance with this abstract distinction. Almost half of *Plan Familias'* beneficiaries (48 per cent) claim to perform informal labour activities to gain an income, through domestic work, street vending and care of the elderly (MSD 2006a). The view of mother-carers being de-linked from paid labour is questioned by these preliminary findings, and has been partially acknowledged by subsequent changes in programme regulations that allow women receiving the cash stipend to work in the formal sector—only if the salary they earn is less than the minimum wage.

### Deactivating Women

In 2004, *Plan Jefas* reached a paradoxical situation: while it aims to provide a link with productive activities for all beneficiaries, there are not enough employment opportunities to absorb the large numbers turning to the programme, especially those with particular difficulties in accessing formal labour markets. This, together with the political necessity of reducing unemployment, seems to have increased the attraction to transfer women to *Plan Familias*. As documented by programme evaluations, women beneficiaries of *Plan Jefas* face greater barriers in accessing formal work opportunities. In addition, they are also less likely to become politically problematic for the state. Therefore, instead of providing them with further support in reaching their productive potential, *Plan Familias* deactivates them. This situation is reminiscent of the argument made by some feminist economists of the benefits (for capital) of having a female "reserve army" of labour that can be absorbed in times of economic expansion and relegated "not merely out of work but out of the labour force, back into dependency within the home" (Mackintosh 1991:5) when needed. Additionally, in the Argentine case, by encouraging female beneficiaries to enter *Plan Familias,* statistically they are classified as economically inactive, which reduces unemployment figures. *Plan Jefas* had a similar statistical effect on unemployment rates, but in this case workers who declared the programme conditionality as their main occupation (mostly women) were considered to be employed. Yet in the case of *Plan Familias,* beneficiaries are altogether removed from the economically active population.

Despite these governmental prerogatives, sociological studies suggest that given the positive evaluation that female beneficiaries made (whether inactive or in low-skill occupations such as domestic service) of the labour conditionality in *Plan Jefas,* levels of economic activity among women beneficiaries of *Plan Familias* are likely to remain high, contradicting official expectations of a reduction in female unemployment (Calvi and Zibecchi 2006). Participation in the informal economy and the multiple survival strategies that characterized women in *Plan Jefas* reinforce this assertion. If these assertions turn out to be true, then the result may be higher female unemployment since their levels of economic activity will remain stable, but the work created by *Plan Jefas* is dismantled.

### Global Ideologies and National Machineries

International institutions have carried an important weight in the design of national poverty alleviation strategies. Initially *Plan Jefas* was nationally funded. In January 2003 the World Bank approved a US$600 million loan for *Plan Jefas* (World Bank 2002) and publicly endorsed and financed the transformation of this original programme into *Plan Familias* and *Seguro* (Clarín 2006a; La Nación 2006).

Currently close to 70 per cent of *Plan Familias* is funded by the IDB. With the funding has come the pressure from international financial institutions to adopt what is seen as a highly successful model for poverty alleviation provided by programmes such as the *Oportunidades*. Academics are sceptical of the results of duplicating anti-poverty strategies without consideration of national contexts and local dynamics (de la Briere and Rawlings 2006). For instance, attaching cash transfers to improvements in access to compulsory education and basic health care makes sense in the Mexican context that has state institutional capacity but falls short of universal health and education coverage. The Mexican programme therefore improved performance in these areas. The benefits of reproducing the same form of co-responsibility in contexts with almost universal health and education coverage, though with high variations in the quality of that provision, as is the case in Argentina, have yet to be shown. By contrast there is no consideration of educational and childcare facilities for children under five years old—an area in which state provision in Argentina is weak, but which has significant implications for the autonomy and labour market success of women with young children.

When the IDH programme was redesigned to become *Plan Familias* and cater to the *Jefas'* female beneficiaries, some modifications in its design were introduced that reinforced traditional gender roles rather than transforming them. For example, a critical requirement for women's economic security and the enhancement of their labour market prospects is the provision of work-related training. Among the numerous activities available in the previous IDH programme,[40] beneficiaries had shown the greatest interest and participation in labour-related training (MSD 2006b). In spite of this, when negotiating the IDB loan, this institution showed little interest in this second component of the programme related to community activities; job training was cut down as one of the options available to women, and a rigid set of requirements for the implementation of community projects impeded the functioning of activities related to health and education of children. The views of key international players on gender relations thereby contributed to a more conservative interpretation of gender roles. Whereas before there was some form of training provision for women, this has now been curtailed. The conservative family ideologies of those heading the MSD in charge of the programme have further reinforced such traditionalist tendencies.

In sum, the transition from a labour-based to a human development CCT seems to have "feminized" poverty alleviation in a variety of ways. The current targeting of women brings their efforts into centre stage and intensifies the presence of women in CCT strategies. Second, the activities attached as conditionalities to *Plan Familias* naturalize traditional female roles within the family around motherhood and care.

The influence of international donors notwithstanding, national bureaucracies reproduce historical practices in social protection that impact programme development. The administrative structures and the employees of the programme's predecessor survived the transformations to *Plan Familias*. So there is significant continuity in terms of programme personnel. Short-term thinking, an emergency approach to social protection, assistential practices, lack of transparency and accountability towards beneficiaries and a general atmosphere of secretism surround the workings of the ministry. Historical legacies were also evident during the design phase when proposals were made to call the current *Familias* programme "Plan Evita", making reference to the social work of Eva Perón.

The cash entitlements provided by the *Familias* programme still correspond to the idea of minimal social rights; these have even been in fact slightly increased, are now proportional to family size and additionally provide support for a more extended time-span (since they continue to operate until all dependants reach 19 years of age). However, the entitlement provided by the stipend while an improvement on *Plan Jefas* is still below the income needed to lift families out of poverty.[41] Secondly, the contract signed between the programme and the key beneficiary includes a clause in which the latter relinquishes the right to make any claims or complaints (CELS 2007).[42] Furthermore, municipal workers note that beneficiaries' grievances have to be centrally channelled to the national ministry; but these concerns generally go unanswered.

Old habits die hard—as the saying goes—in the form relations between state institutions and the poor take. As one programme beneficiary elaborated:

> I am waiting for their promise, social inclusion, I want that . . . For me it is all a deceit to maintain the poor quiet, still, so that they do not rebel against the state, so that they do not do trouble . . . I don't see they do much to include people, for example, I could work in an office, and they give me 300 pesos but they don't give me the job that would strengthen me as a person, as an individual. They are feeding me like a little dog. If you have an animal in your house, you have to feed it or it will die of hunger. If you don't feed him he will get angry. What do you do with people who don't work? You give them money, for what? So that they will stay quiet, so they will continue being lazy, do you get it? There are some that like it. But they don't educate you, they don't strengthen you as a person.[43]

## CONCLUSION

As this chapter has shown, Argentina follows the regional trends towards new ways of thinking and addressing poverty and social polarization, labelled "inclusive liberalism". The Argentine experience shares many of the characteristics of CCTs being implemented in other countries of the region as well as the general understanding of managing social risks that emphasizes the administration, rather than the eradication, of poverty. The reinterpretation of social rights to sets of minimal conditions narrows the welfare entitlements attached to broader conceptions of social citizenship (Serrano 2005a). So, "while 'inclusive' liberalism may deliver palliative services to the poor, it is not any kind of immediate challenge to the basic disposition of global or local assets" (Porter and Craig 2004:412–413). Yet, despite the emphasis on the provision of minimal standards, a common theme across these efforts is the use of a citizenship-based rhetoric and the claims to enhance individual rights to social inclusion.

This chapter has considered some of the ways in which the citizenship claims of two Argentine CCT programmes have been, in turn, gendered, and how, through a diverse set of obligations and entitlements opened for men and women, the programmes construct gender-differentiated roles and identities in the process of tackling poverty. The first Argentine experiment—the *Plan Jefas*—does not solely target women as cash recipients, and provides a labour-based form of inclusion. On the basis of this initial phase as well as shifts in public opinion regarding the programme, and given the increasing stake of international financial institutions in funding and designing national measures, *Plan Familias* offers cash stipends to mothers in exchange for health checks and school attendance of their children, and provides integration through human capital formation.

This changing scenario provides a fruitful opportunity to analyse the distinct notions of membership to a given community structuring diverse paths for "integrating" women and men into mainstream society. To return to the guiding question of this chapter, table 11.5 provides a synthetic view of how these diverse approaches of "inclusive liberalism" articulate citizenship, gender and state mechanisms of providing social inclusion.

Gender-uniform citizenship based on women's equality with men is commonly associated with liberal feminism that emphasizes equal rights and obligations regardless of gender. The priority here is to enable women to compete on equal terms in the public spheres of politics and labour markets (Hobson and Lister 2002). As illustrated in table 11.5, *Plan Jefas* combines a gender-uniform understanding of citizenship with liberal notions that treat paid work as the priority avenue for exiting deprivation. This uniform vision leaves gender—and gender implications in access to resources—unproblematized.

*Table 11.5* Selected Features of Two Argentine CCT Initiatives

| CCT programme | Inclusion strategy | Gender citizenship | Claims and duties |
|---|---|---|---|
| *Plan Jefas* | Inclusion through paid work. Women and men as "workers". | Gender-uniform citizenship. | Equal in theory, but in practice it stimulates insecure paid work for men and provides minimal social reproduction for women. |
| *Plan Familias* | Inclusion by means of moral integration. Women as "mothers". | Gender-differentiated citizenship. | Different in theory and practice. Women have slightly more secure entitlements, but their duties naturalize conservative gender roles and could jeopardize their future livelihoods. |

In fact, as this chapter has shown, women's and men's claims to the programme were far from uniform; nor were their prospects of exiting the programme and entering paid work in the formal labour market. While the programme encourages women's participation in the workforce, and provides some opportunities for status enhancement through the labour conditionality, nevertheless female beneficiaries encounter more severe barriers in accessing formal labour markets. For many of these women, paid domestic work and other forms of informal work remain the most obvious destinations after exiting the programme. Men, on the other hand, especially those with pertinent skills and work experience have re-entered the workforce in sectors which have seen some modest growth in the post-crisis years. And yet despite such differences, it is also clear that *Plan Jefas* stimulated marginal jobs with significantly lower salaries and of a temporary nature, while features such as discretionary allocations, lack of monitoring of state performance and unclear complaints procedures diluted the rights-based rationale claimed by programme regulations.

*Plan Familias* offers a view of poverty as weak human capital formation, while providing gender-differentiated channels for social integration and citizenship, within which the strengthening of the family and the care of children are seen as women's main vocation and duty. A variety of factors have been identified behind the re-traditionalization of gender roles in Argentina, evident in the transition from *Plan Jefas* to *Plan Familias*. Some evaluations of *Plan Jefas* (MTESS 2004b) argued that female beneficiaries with many children and demanding care duties required more income support and less work conditionality. At the same time, the programme also serves a useful political aim of reducing the unemployment rate by counting women out of "economic activity." In addition, the increasing influence of donor agencies in the funding of poverty alleviation programmes has meant that "successful" regional formulas for fighting poverty are often prescribed, regardless of context.

In the US context, Mead (1997) referred to the trend towards growing governmental enforcement of personal responsibility as the "new paternalism" (Gerhard et al. 2002). Within Latin American this shift has been labelled as new forms of maternalism (Molyneux 2007, 2006). Maternalism here involves the devolution and individualization of this contractual citizenship to female members of the household, who are, in turn, required to conform to dominant stereotypes of "good wives" and mothers (Razavi and Hassim 2006). While the recognition of women's unpaid care responsibilities is to be welcomed, the one-dimensional association between care and women in *Plan Familias* has the unfortunate affect of naturalizing and reifying gender differences, while doing very little to improve women's labour market prospects and their economic security.

Even though the CCT programmes represent an important effort in providing social protection, one of their crucial flaws is "the failure, post-dependency theory, to adequately engage the causes and structural effects of peripherization, marginalization, and their relation to security and stability" (Porter and Craig 2004:415–416). With the unfolding of "liberal inclusion" and the passage from uniform to gender-differentiated citizenship, gender identities and relations are permeated by a strong moral rhetoric. The reified categories leave the dichotomy men/work and female/care unchallenged. Women then mostly remain the holders of a reproductive function, while care is essentialized as women's work regardless of their opportunities for seeking education, paid work and entrepreneurship. On the other hand, male participation is strictly associated with employment and related responsibilities to the detriment of their vulnerability in the market or their family relations.

The main developmental consequence of the progressive moralization of gender relations in CCT programmes is that, by encouraging family responses that are not adaptive for current forms of risk and vulnerability, these gender ideologies become an obstacle to positive policy outcomes (Jelin 2005). Thus, the way in which gender discourses are articulated obscures the necessities and pressing conditions of particularly vulnerable groups. The specific needs, for instance, of the residual group of men with lower incomes and difficulties in obtaining paid work still participating in *Plan Jefas*, as well as those of male beneficiaries attempting to transfer to *Plan Familias* that show high levels of social risk and weak and intermittent links with labour markets are made invisible. In addition, in spite of the increasing presence of women, CCT strategies do not consider their possible overburdening and time poverty, nor do they attend to their need for long-term exit strategies out of poverty through job training and the provision of affordable and accessible care services.

## NOTES

1. I would like to thank Shahra Razavi, Maxine Molyneux and Alessandra Dal Secco for comments, discussions and suggestions on earlier drafts of this chapter. Funding for this research was provided by the Institute for the Study of the Americas and the School of Advanced Study from the University of London. The author is grateful to both institutions for their support.
2. The concept of negotiating the reproductive bargain is taken from Pearson (1997).
3. Citizenship here is "more than simply the formal relationship between an individual and the state presented by an earlier liberal and political science literature". It understands "citizenship as a more total relationship, inflected by identity, social positioning, cultural assumptions, institutional practices and a sense of belonging" (Werbner and Yuval-Davis 1999:4, cited in Hobson and Lister 2002). The feminist literature locates gender within a broader analysis of diversity social divisions, and understands citizenship both as membership of a community, and as the patterns of inclusion and exclusion which shape that membership (Hobson and Lister 2002).
4. Programme for Unemployed Heads of Household: Family's Right to Social Inclusion.

5. Programme Families for Social Inclusion.
6. Employment and Training Insurance.
7. "Social funds were initially conceived to provide temporary low-wage employment on small-scale social and economic infrastructure projects under conditions of structural adjustment, such as building clinics, schools, roads and irrigation canals" (Sabates-Wheeler and Kabeer 2003:31).
8. In spite of these shortfalls, minor gains were made in terms of more flexible management styles that included social participation and that strengthened institutional capacity in the local public sector (Kessler and Roggi 2005).
9. There are two other programmes that will not be discussed here: *Programa Manos a la Obra* and *Programa Adulto Mayor Más*. For an analysis, see CELS (2007).
10. The Decree 565/2002 expanded and "universalized" the reach of the programme.
11. In particular, the decree establishes that, if beneficiaries' children are under 18, proof of school attendance and respective medical checks are to be provided while, if beneficiaries are above 60 years old, proof of unemployment and of not receiving any pension benefits are to be brought (Decree 565/2002).
12. Approximately US$49.
13. For a discussion of the ambiguities of the concept of household headship, see Budlender (1997).
14. The main exception is access through judicial rulings that, due to severe levels of social vulnerability, can dictate the inclusion of a particular family in the programme.
15. The programme provides ARS150. Poverty as measured by INDEC (*Instituto Nacional de Estadística y Censos*) was set in October 2002 at ARS764.84 covering nutritional and basic service needs of a nuclear family of two adults and two children; indigence was set at ARS346.07 for the same household. There is some disagreement about the extent of its effects. For the Ministry of Labour, poverty was reduced by 6.3 per cent and extreme poverty by 28 per cent (MTESS 2004b). World Bank evaluations argue that an extra 10 per cent of participants would have become extremely poor in the absence of the programme (Galasso and Ravallion 2003). Ronconi and others (2006) estimate the programme aided 3.5 per cent of households out of poverty and 6 per cent out of indigence, while one-third would have remained inactive or unemployed.
16. In 2003, the level of indigence was 20.5 per cent, considering the income provided by *Plan Jefas*, and 23.5 per cent without it. In contrast, in 2006, it was 9.95 per cent, considering the income provided by *Plan Jefas*, and 10.85 per cent without it.
17. Official documents note that their data on household structure and position of the beneficiary within the household might be incomplete; hence, we rely on studies based on the national household survey from the national statistic bureau.
18. As already stated, some gender analysts find problematic the notion of household headship. If we assume that the concept refers to the individual, that is, the main income earner of the household, we encounter the awkward fact that most households in Latin America today have two main breadwinners. A distinction often made is between de facto and de jure headship, where the former is determined by the real contributions of different individuals to the household economy, while the latter refers to normative criteria often underpinning how respondents interviewed in household surveys designate different household members. These two measures do not always correspond,

and women's contributions to household income are often underreported (Arriagada 2004). The data presented here refers to de jure headship and might therefore underestimate de facto female headship.

19. The average of income earners is 1.6 for households with male beneficiaries, in contrast to the case of female participants, that is, two income earners per household (Pautassi 2004).

20. Most beneficiaries declared being engaged in the informal economy as a strategy to complement the cash provided by the programme, at an average wage of US$127 for 18 hours per week (MTESS 2004ba).

21. But it is worth noting that women seem to make more use of training opportunities than men (6.5 per cent and 2 per cent, respectively; Pautassi 2004).

22. A paradigmatic example is provided by women working in communal kitchens. One of the women interviewed indicated that after a year of working there, she and her co-workers were like family, and that those for whom she cooked gave her much care and affection.

23. Information provided by the monitoring section of the *Plan Jefas* at MTESS, May 2007.

24. With measures such as the Law 25.877 that establishes a year exemption on employers' social security contributions for each new employed worker.

25. Domestic workers who are employed for up to 30 hours per week earn ARS5.1 per hour, while those who work more than 150 hours per week earn only ARS1.6 per hour (MTESS 2005).

26. While during the 1990s the number of participants in Social Funds did not exceed 140,000 (Golbert 2004), the *Plan Jefas*, at its peak, reached two million households, and today slightly over one million.

27. Figures 11.1 and 11.6 show, on the one hand, the decline in the number of beneficiaries of *Plan Jefas* and, on the other, those beneficiaries who are being transferred to the *Plan Familias*.

28. Inspired by the experience of Job Centres in the United Kingdom, it encompasses a two-year insurance of ARS225 (approximately US$73) per month (after 18 months the stipend is reduced to ARS200), conditional on active job search and training through the provision of job search support, training and employment intermediation. Additionally, the time spent in the programme is recognized for pension purposes (Decree 336/2006). This initiative is directed to those beneficiaries that due to their educational background and work experience have higher prospects of finding paid work (MTESS 2004b), that is, young males from *Plan Jefas*.

29. 33.4 per cent of *Plan Familias* beneficiaries are above 45 years, while in the *Plan Jefas* the percentage above that age is lower (26.4 per cent).

30. Information provided by the monitoring of *Plan Familias* at the MSD, April 2007.

31. The *Plan Familias* existed prior to 2004, though on a smaller scale and with a slightly different design, in the form of the human development programme IDH "programa de atencion a grupos vulnerables, subprograma de ingreso para el desarrollo humano". In October 2004 it was renamed *Programa Familias para la inclusion social* (Resolution MSD 825/2005).

32. A smaller number of families can be included in the programme through extraordinary judicial ruling: families that face grave social risks or inhabit vulnerable areas. These cannot surpass the 10 per cent of beneficiaries transferred from the *Plan Jefas* (Resolution MSD 825/2005). This should amount to approximately 40,000 families, yet there might be no administrative capacity to fulfil this target. Finally, this stipulation also enables the inclusion of additional beneficiaries financed by national sources only. Some critics point to the plausible use of this last instrument within the electoral year for political purposes.

33. The health conditionality requires them to fulfil the national vaccination plan for children, and to perform bimonthly health checks in the case of pregnant women. In terms of education, mothers need to present certificates of enrolment and assistance of children aged between 5 and 19 years old (MSD 2006c).
34. Approximately US$60.
35. Approximately US$99.
36. The stipend has increased over time. Resolution 648/2006 established ARS175 for two children and up until ARS275 for families with six or more children. While welcome, this sudden change seems to respond again to political or electoral considerations. It was announced by President Kirchner and not by those coordinating the programme, and was not based on an impact assessment of the changes in the subsidy.
37. Set at ARS921 in February 2007.
38. Of the beneficiaries, 80.74 per cent are between 26 and 45 years of age; 47.18 per cent of beneficiaries have three or four children, and 18.36 per cent have more than five (information provided in April 2007 by the monitoring of the *Plan Familias* at the MSD, based on the database of beneficiaries of 16 May 2007).
39. Male beneficiaries that opted to transfer to the *Plan Familias* have some particular features compared to male participants of *Plan Jefas*. They are characterized by extreme poverty, high vulnerability, heading large households, with a strong presence of children and with little possibilities of labour insertion. So the fact that there is no work co-responsibility, that it is not limited in time and that the money provided is determined by the number of dependants seems to provide them with a better alternative (MSD 2005b).
40. Training in health, childcare, school support for children, training in an occupation or craft, discussion forums and recreational activities (MSD 2006b).
41. For the institute of national statistics (INDEC), a basic supply of food for a family of five costs ARS425.44 and this, added to basic needs in terms of services, mainly health and education, is estimated at ARS931.73. The cash provided by *Plan Familias* to a family with two dependents (ARS185) is way below this figure.
42. The letter to be signed by the beneficiary says: "I certify that once the period of the programme is over, or that by other circumstances I am not a programme beneficiary, I will stop receiving the stipend without right to any complaint" (MSD 2006d, author's translation). For a discussion of the programme from a human rights' perspective, see CELS (2007).
43. Interview with *Plan Familias's* beneficiary, Morón, Province of Buenos Aires, 8 May 2007.

## REFERENCES

Abel, C. and Lewis (eds.). 2002. *Exclusion and Engagement: A Diagnosis of Social Policy in Latin America in the Long Run*. Institute of Latin American Studies, London.

Adato, M., B. de la Briere, D. Mindek and A. Quisumbing. 2000. *The Impact of Progresa on Women's Status and Intra-Household Relations*. International Food Policy Research Institute, Washington, DC.

Arriagada, I. 2004. *Tendencias de las familias latinoamericanas en la última década*. Paper presented at La Familia y la Vida Privada. Transformaciones,

Tensiones, Resistencias y Nuevos Sentidos, Economic Commission for Latin America and the Caribbean (ECLAC), Santiago de Chile, 29–30 September.

Auyero, J. 2000. "The hyper-shantytown. Neo-liberal violence(s) in the Argentine slum." *Ethnography*, Vol. 1, pp. 93–116.

Barrientos, A. 2004. "Latin America: Towards a liberal-informal welfare regime." In I. Gough and G. Wood, with A. Barrientos (eds.), *Insecurity and Welfare Regimes in Asia, Africa, and Latin America: Social Policy in Development Contexts*. Cambridge University Press, Cambridge.

Barrientos, A. and J. DeJong. 2004. *Child Poverty and Cash Transfers*. CHIP Report No. 4, Child Poverty Research and Policy Centre, London.

Bradshaw, S. 2008. "From structural adjustment to social adjustment: A gendered analysis of conditional cash transfer programmes in Mexico and Nicaragua." *Global Social Policy*, Vol. 8, No. 2, pp. 188–207.

Bradshaw, S. and B. Linneker. 2003. *Desafiando la pobreza de las mujeres. Perspectivas de género y estrategias para la reducción de la pobreza en Nicaragua y Honduras*. Catholic Institute for International Relations, London.

Bradshaw, S. with A. Quirós Víquez. 2007. *Women Beneficiaries or Women Bearing the Cost? A Gendered Analysis of the Red de Protección Social (RPS) in Nicaragua*. Mimeo, London.

Budlender, D. 1997. *The Debate about Household Headship*. Central Statistical Service, Government of South Africa. www.statsonline.gov.za/publications/Discuss-HouseholdHead/DiscussHouseholdHead.pdf, accessed in September 2007.

Calvi, G. and C. Zibecchi. 2006. "¿El epitafio del Plan Jefes de Hogar o una nueva orientación de la política social? Evaluando algunos de los escenarios socio-laborales posibles ante la consolidación del Plan Familia." *Laboratorio*, Vol. 8, No. 19, pp. 21–28. http://lavboratorio.fsoc.uba.ar/textos/19_4.htm, accessed in August 2007.

Central de Trabajadores Argentinos (CTA). 2006. *Sin cambio de planes. Acerca de las medidas de reconversión del Programa Jefes y Jefas de Hogar*. Paper presented at Mesa de Políticas Sociales, Instituto de Estudios y Formación-CTA, Buenos Aires, March.

Centro de Estudios Legales y Sociales (CELS). 2007. *Programa Familias por la inclusión social, entre el discurso de derechos y la práctica asistencial*. Colección, Investigación y Análisis No. 4. CELS, Buenos Aires.

———. 2003. *Plan Jefes y Jefas. ¿Derecho social o beneficio sin derechos?* CELS, Buenos Aires.

Chant, S. 2008. "The 'feminisation of poverty' and the 'feminisation' of anti-poverty programmes: Room for revision?" *Journal of Development Studies*, Vol. 44, No. 2, pp. 165–197.

———. 2006. *Not Incomes but Inputs: Critiquing the "Feminisation of Poverty" and the "Feminisation" of Anti-Poverty Programmes*. Paper prepared for International Seminar Development and Vulnerability: Outlooks for Resuming Development in Southern Countries, Institute of Economics, Federal University of Rio de Janeiro, 4–6 September.

Clarín. 2006a. "El banco mundial aprobó un préstamo de 350 millones de dólares." Clarín, 23 March. www.golf.clarin.com.ar/diario/2006/03/23/um/m-01163970.htm, accessed in September 2007.

———. 2006b. "Reestructuran los planes sociales, con aumentos a partir de Abril." Clarín, 14 February. www.clarin.com/diario/2006/02/14/elpais/p-0071.htm, accessed in June 2007.

Colmegna, P. 2004. *Planes sociales: ¿Mecanismos de inclusión o perpetuadores de exclusión? Vivir de planes: Efectos de las políticas sociales en un municipio bonaerense*. Presented at VII Congreso Argentino de Antropología Social, Cordoba, 25–28 May.

Cortés, R., F. Groisman and A. Hoszowki. 2004. "Transiciones ocupacionales: El caso del Plan Jefes y Jefas." *Realidad Económica*, Vol. 202, pp. 11–28.

Daeren, L. 2004. *Mujeres pobres: ¿Prestadoras de servicios o sujetos de derecho? Los programas de superación de la pobreza en América Latina desde una mirada de género*. Presented at Políticas y Programas de Superación de la Pobreza desde la Perspectiva de la Gobernabilidad Democrática y el Género, Economic Commission for Latin America and the Caribbean (ECLAC), Quito, 25 March.

de la Briere, B. and L. Rawlings. 2006. *Examining Conditional Cash Transfer Programs: A Role for Increased Social Inclusion?* Social Protection Discussion Paper Series No. 0603, World Bank, Washington, DC.

Di Marco, G., A.L. Rodríguez Gustá, V. Llobett and A. Brener. 2006. *Ejercicio de derechos y capacidades institucionales en la implementación de un programa de inclusión social*. Presented at ALACIP, 3er Congreso Latinoamericano de Ciencia Política, Universidad de Campinas, SP, Brazil, 4–6 September.

Esping-Andersen, G. 2003. "Against social inheritance." In A. Giddens (ed.), *Progressive Futures, New Ideas for the Centre-Left*. Policy Network, London.

———. 1991. *The Three Worlds of Welfare Capitalism*. Princeton University Press, Princeton, NJ.

Filgueira, F. 2005. *Welfare and Democracy in Latin America: The Development, Crises and Aftermath of Universal, Dual and Exclusionary Social States*. Mimeo, Paper prepared for the UNRISD project on Social Policy and Democratization, UNRISD, Geneva.

Filgueira, F. and C. Filgueira. 2002. "Models of welfare and models of capitalism: The limits of transferability." In E. Huber (ed.), *Models of Capitalism, Lessons from Latin America*. Pennsylvania State University Press, University Park.

Galasso, E. and M. Ravallion. 2003. *Social Protection in a Crisis: Argentina's Plan Jefes y Jefas*. World Bank Policy Research Working Paper No. 3165, World Bank, Washington, DC.

Gerhard, U., T. Knijn and J. Lewis. 2002. "Contractualization." In B. Hobson, J. Lewis and B. Siim (eds.), *Contested Concepts in Gender and Social Politics*. Edward Elgar, Cheltenham.

Giovagnoli, P.I. 2005. *Poverty Alleviation or Political Networking? A Combined Quali-Quanti Analysis of the Implementation of Safety Nets in Post-Crisis Argentina*. Destin Working Paper No. 05–66, London School of Economics, London.

Golbert, L. 2004. *¿Derecho a la inclusión o paz social? Plan Jefes y Jefas de Hogar desocupados*. Serie Políticas Social No. 84, Economic Commission for Latin America and the Caribbean (ECLAC), Santiago de Chile.

González de la Rocha, M. 2005. "Familias y política social en México. El caso de Oportunidades." *Serie Seminarios y Conferencias*, Vol. 46, pp. 245–274.

———. 2003. *Oportunidades y Capital Social*. Presented at Capital Social y Programas de Superación de la Pobreza: Lineamientos para la Acción, Economic Commission for Latin America and the Caribbean (ECLAC), Santiago de Chile, 10–11 November.

Hobson, B. and R. Lister. 2002. "Citizenship." In Barbara Hobson, Jane Lewis and Birte Siim (eds.), *Contested Concepts in Gender and Social Politics*. Edward Elgar, Cheltenham.

International Labour Organization (ILO). 2005. *Fact Sheet. Equal Remuneration for Men and Women in Argentina: Basic Facts and Regulatory Framework*. ILO, Geneva.

International Poverty Centre (IPC). 2006. *Do CCTs Reduce Poverty?* One Pager IPC, No. 21, IPC, Brazil, September.

Jelin, E. 2005. *Family Life and Public Policy: A South American Reflection on the Swedish Trajectory*. CONICET-IDES Report prepared for the EGDI Gender Report, Buenos Aires.

Kessler, G. and M.C. Roggi. 2005. "Programas de superación de la pobreza y capital social: La experiencia Argentina." In I. Arriagada (ed.), *Aprender de la experiencia. El capital social en la superación de la pobreza.* Economic Commission for Latin America and the Caribbean (ECLAC), Santiago de Chile.

La Nación. 2006. "Fondos del banco mundial para empleos. Planes sociales: Préstamo de 350 millones de dólares." 30 May. www.lanacion.com.ar/archivo/Nota.asp?nota_id=810183, accessed in June 2007.

Levitas, R. 2005. *The Inclusive Society? Social Exclusion and New Labour.* Palgrave Macmillan, Basingstoke.

Lister, R. 2003. "Investing in the citizen-worker of the future: Transformations in citizenship and the state under new labour." *Social Policy and Administration,* Vol. 37, No. 5, pp. 427–443.

Lo Vuolo, R., A. Barbeito and C. Rodriguez Enriquez. 2002. *La inseguridad socioeconómica como política pública: Transformación del sistema de protección social y financiamiento social en Argentina.* Working Paper 33, Centro Interdisciplinario para el Estudio de Politícas Públicas (CIEPP), Buenos Aires.

Mackintosh, M. 1991. "Gender and economics: The sexual division of labour and the subordination of women." In K. Young, C. Wolkowitz and R. McCullagh (eds.), *Of Marriage and the Market: Women's Subordination Internationally and Its Lessons.* Routledge & Kegan Paul, London.

Mead, L. (ed.). 1997. *The New Paternalism.* Brookings Institution, Washington, DC.

Mesa-Lago, C. 1991. "Social security in Latin America." In Inter-American Development Bank (ed.), *Economic and Social Progress in Latin America: 1991 Report.* IADB, Washington, DC.

Módolo, C. 2004. *Los peligros institucionales del Plan Jefes y Jefas de Hogar.* Paper presented at Novenas Jornadas de Investigación en la Facultad de Ciencias Económicas y Estadísticas, Universidad Nacional de Rosario, Rosario, November.

Molyneux, M. 2007. *Change and Continuity in Social Policy in Latin America: Mothers at the Service of the State?* Programme on Gender and Development, Paper No. 1, UNRISD, Geneva.

———. 2006. "Mothers at the service of the new poverty agenda: Progresa/Opportunidades, Mexico's conditional transfer programme." *Social Policy and Administration,* Vol. 40, No. 4, pp. 425–449.

Pautassi, L. 2006. "Política social en Argentina ¿Sustancia o procedimiento?" *Revista Escenarios* (La Plata), No. 10, March, pp. 1–20.

———. 2004. "Beneficiarios y beneficiarias: Análisis del Programa Jefes y Jefas de Hogar desocupados de Argentina." In M.E. Valenzuela (ed.), *Políticas de Empleo para Superar la Pobreza: Argentina.* International Labour Organization (ILO), Santiago de Chile.

Pearson, R. 1997. "Renegotiating the reproductive bargain: Gender analysis of economic transition in Cuba in the 1990s." *Development and Change,* Vol. 28, pp. 671–705.

Porter, D. and D. Craig. 2004. "The third way and the third world: Poverty reduction and social inclusion in the rise of 'inclusive' liberalism." *Review of International Political Economy,* Vol. 11, No. 2, pp. 388–424.

Rawlings, L. 2004. *A New Approach to Social Assistance: Latin America's Experience with CCT Programs.* Social Protection Discussion Paper Series No. 0416, World Bank, Washington, DC.

Rawlings, L. and G. Rubio. 2003. *Evaluating the Impact of Conditional Cash Transfer Programs: Lessons from Latin America.* Policy Research Working Paper No. 3119, World Bank, Washington, DC.

Razavi, S. and S. Hassim (eds.). 2006. *Gender and Social Policy in a Global Context: Uncovering the Gendered Structure of "the Social."* UNRISD/Palgrave and Macmillan, Basingstoke.

Resolution MTESS and MSD 336. 2005. *Programa Jefes de Hogar.* 28 February. MTESS and MSD, Buenos Aires.

Rodriguez Enriquez, C. 2006. *Gender Aspect of Social Policy in Argentina: The Case of Money Transfer Policy.* Paper presented at the 6th International Conference: Engendering Macroeconomics and International Economics, University of Utah, Salt Lake City, 2–3 July.

Ronconi, L., J. Sanguinetti, S. Fachelli, V. Casazza and I. Franceschelli. 2006. *Poverty and Employability Effects of Workfare Programs in Argentina.* PMMA Working Paper 14, Poverty and Economic Policy Research Network, Montreal.

Sabates-Wheeler, R. and N. Kabeer. 2003. *Gender Equality and the Extension of Social Protection.* Extension of Social Security Paper No. 16, International Labour Organization (ILO), Geneva.

Serrano, C. 2005a. "Familia como unidad de intervención de políticas sociales. Notas sobre el Programa Puente—Chile Solidario." *CEPAL Serie Seminarios y Conferencias,* Vol. 46, pp. 231–243.

———. 2005b. *La política social en la globalización. Programas de protección en América Latina.* Serie Mujer y Desarrollo No. 70, Economic Commission for Latin America and the Caribbean (ECLAC), Santiago de Chile.

Villatoro, P. 2004. *Programas de reducción de la pobreza en América Latina. Un análisis de cinco experiencias.* Serie Políticas Sociales No. 87, Economic Commission for Latin America and the Caribbean (ECLAC), Santiago de Chile.

Vinocur, P. and L. Halperin. 2004. *Pobreza y políticas sociales en Argentina de los años noventa.* Serie Políticas Sociales No. 85, Economic Commission for Latin America and the Caribbean (ECLAC), Santiago de Chile.

Werbner, P. and N. Yuval-Davis. 1999. "Introduction: Women and the new discourse of citizenship." In N. Yuval-Davis and P. Werbner (eds.), *Women, Citizenship and Difference.* Zed Books, London.

Whitehead, A. 1991. "'I'm hungry mum': The politics of domestic budgeting." In K. Young, C. Wolkowitz and R. McCullagh (eds.), *Of Marriage and the Market: Women's Subordination Internationally and its Lessons.* Routledge & Kegan Paul, London.

World Bank. 2006. *Argentina Country Brief.* World Bank, Washington, DC.

———. 2002. *Project Appraisal Document on a Proposed Loan in the Amount of US$600 million to the Argentine Republic for the Jefes de Hogar (Heads of Household) Program Project.* Report No. 23710–AR, World Bank, Washington, DC, 22 October.

## OFFICIAL DOCUMENTS

Decree 336. 2006. *Seguro de capacitación y empleo.* 29 March 2006. Poder Ejecutivo Nacional (National Executive Power), Buenos Aires.

Decree 1506. 2004. *Emergencia ocupacional nacional.* 28 October 2004. Poder Ejecutivo Nacional (National Executive Power), Buenos Aires.

Decree 565. 2002. *Programa Jefes de Hogar.* 3 April 2002. Poder Ejecutivo Nacional (National Executive Power), Buenos Aires.

Joint Resolution MTESS and MSD 143 and 264. 2005. *Programa Jefes de Hogar.* 28 February. MTESS and MSD, Buenos Aires.

Ministerio de Trabajo, Empleo y Seguridad Social (MTESS). 2007. *Inserción laboral de los beneficiarios del PJH en el empleo registrado.* Dirección General de Estudios y Formulación de Políticas de Empleo, Subsecretaría de Empleo, MTESS, Buenos Aires.

## 326  Constanza Tabbush

———. 2006a. *Encuesta de indicadores laborales. August 2006.* www.trabajo. gov.ar/left/estadisticas/eil/files/2006/eil_anual_2006.pdf, accessed in September 2007.

———. 2006b. *Presentación EIL octubre 2007: Otro mes de esta gestión que el empleo crece sin interrupción.* www.trabajo.gov.ar/prensa/historicos/2006/ gacetillas/12/05eil.doc, accessed in October 2007.

———. 2005. *Situación laboral del servicio doméstico en la Argentina.* Subsecretaría de Programación Técnica y Estudios Laborales, MTESS, Buenos Aires.

———. 2004a. *Inserción laboral de los beneficiarios del Programa Jefes de Hogar.* MTESS, Buenos Aires.

———. 2004b. *Segunda evaluación del Programa Jefes de Hogar. Resultados de la encuesta a beneficiarios.* MTESS, Buenos Aires.

Ministry of Social Development (MSD). 2006a. *Análisis de una encuesta a beneficiarios del Plan Familias.* Programa Familias para la Inclusión Social, MSD, Buenos Aires.

———. 2006b. *Encuesta de percepción y participación de actividades del Programa Familias.* Programa Familias para la Inclusión Social, MSD, Buenos Aires.

———. 2006c. *Reglamento operativo.* Programa Familias para la Inclusión Social, MSD, Buenos Aires, June.

———. 2006d. *Unidad de gestión operativa: Proceso de traspaso.* Programa Familias para la Inclusión Social, Área de Capacitación, MSD, Buenos Aires.

———. 2005a. *Documento conceptual sobre el Plan Familias II.* MSD, Buenos Aires.

———. 2005b. *Programa Familias II. Documento preparatorio a la misión del BID.* MSD, Buenos Aires, May.

Resolution MSD 693. 2007. Ministry of Social Development, Buenos Aires, 5 March.

Resolution MSD 648. 2006. Ministry of Social Development, Buenos Aires, 28 February.

Resolution MSD 825. 2005. Ministry of Social Development, Buenos Aires, 12 May.

Resolution MTESS 406. 2003. *Programa Jefes de Hogar.* MTESS, Buenos Aires, 29 December.

Resolution MTESS 256. 2003. *Promoción del empleo, creación del plan holístico para la promoción del empleo.* MTESS, Buenos Aires, 23 October.

# 12 Women in India's National Rural Employment Guarantee Scheme

*Smita Gupta*

## INTRODUCTION: THE IMPACT OF ECONOMIC LIBERALIZATION ON FEMALE WORKERS

The last decade in India has been marked by the dominance of deflationary macroeconomic policies and falling public development expenditure (Sawant et al. 2002; Gupta 2005). Because of this, an unparalleled and comprehensive crisis has taken firm root in rural India, resulting in growing unemployment, underemployment, peasant suicides, starvation deaths, impoverishment and hunger. The per capita availability of foodgrains has dropped due to a fall in production and purchasing power (Patnaik 2004). Public works programmes and employment-generation activities of the state have contracted. Farm incomes too have contracted due to rising input costs and a simultaneous fall in prices, as well as the withdrawal of the state from the provision of credit, extension services, procurement, price support and infrastructure (Sen 2002). Indebtedness and land alienation have grown, particularly among small and marginal farmers. Workforce participation rates in rural areas have declined, more so for rural women than men (Ghosh 1999a, 1999b). There is a growing feminization of lowly paid menial and arduous work, accompanied by a faster overall decline in women's employment in the post-reform 1990s (compared to the decline in men's employment). The rate of growth in employment fell in the 1990s, while the unemployment rate grew since the labour force increased at a faster pace than employment. After 2000, the increase in poorly paid self-employment, particularly for women, accounts for the recovery in workforce participation rates (Himanshu 2007).

This was the context of parliamentary elections in 2004, which witnessed a huge upset for the National Democratic Alliance (NDA), a right-wing coalition that aggressively pursued orthodox fiscal macroeconomic policies. Despite their commitment to fiscal conservatism, it became clear to their successors, the Congress-led United Progressive Alliance (UPA) that the National Rural Employment Guarantee Act (NREGA) and the revival of agriculture are political necessities. The central government promised to enact an employment guarantee scheme, which has the potential of turning around the agrarian distress to some extent. In September 2004, the National Advisory Council, headed by UPA Chairperson Sonia Gandhi,[1] issued a draft for rural areas that was in keeping with the commitment in the Common Minimum Programme (CMP).[2]

## THE STRUGGLE FOR THE RIGHT TO WORK

The passage of the historic NREGA by the Indian Parliament is of immense significance, especially in the context in which it has been enacted. It is a recognition that the state cannot retreat from pro-poor development and is responsible to ensure livelihood security and employment. It undermines to some extent the economic policies that restrict the state's pre-eminent role to "good governance" and the creation of a "conducive environment" for foreign capital.

Employment guarantee as part of a constitutional right to work has been a long-standing demand of the Left movement in India, and the present act is an outcome of their efforts. The process has by no means been an easy one. Its enactment generated a fierce debate, spurred in part by the government itself producing consistently inadequate versions of the draft legislation. It is perhaps not an exaggeration to state that the biggest opposition to the bill came from within the government itself, forcing the Left to ensure last-minute correctives in its design, scope and coverage.

### Approaches to the Employment Guarantee Scheme (EGS)

The initial euphoria over the inclusion of the NREGA in the CMP was replaced by growing scepticism as powerful forces worked to dilute the provisions. The paradox is that the same underlying factors that provided the compelling reasons to enact such legislation also fuelled opposition to the act. These arise from the policies of economic liberalization that serve the interests of finance capital and are pursued with equal vigour by the NDA and UPA governments.

Broadly speaking, three different positions were taken on this issue. One regarded universal employment guarantee as both a desirable and feasible engine of broad-based equitable growth that would revive agriculture and the rural economy through the creation of productive assets and the multiplier effects of demand expansion.[3] A second position opposed the act as neither desirable nor feasible on the grounds of its non-affordability, corruption and preference for infrastructure-led growth models. Some of these opponents, however, conceded its political necessity for a stable democratic system.[4]

Yet another position, which lies somewhere between these two, was taken by liberals who regarded employment guarantee as a means for giving a "human face" to globalization, or a kind of "social safety net" which is desirable but feasible only under very restricted conditions (Sen 2005; various press statements by Dr. Montek Singh Ahluwalia, Deputy Chairperson, Planning Commission and the Finance Minister). Though they advocated the need for an act, they were ambivalent about conservative macroeconomic policies. Their disagreement with finance capital was over the "social exclusion" of some from the "benefits" of globalization, while the dubious "benefits" in terms of growth and good governance, as well as the treatise of "scarcity of financial resources", were never questioned. Like the neoliberal opponents of the NREGA, they too viewed globalization as an opportunity and a challenge, and fiscal discipline as a virtue; where they differed was over the degree of "humanization" that is politically essential.[5]

Fiscal policy lies at the heart of these differences. The main plank of the Left-Keynesian argument for an EGS is the formation of the home market for non-inflationary growth through the multiplier effects of employment generation and utilization of idle resources (labour and installed capacity). Pre-Keynesian fiscal orthodoxy guides both the liberal support and neoliberal opposition, which claims a scarcity of rupee resources and the inherent superiority of zero or low fiscal deficits.[6] Since the urge to attain low deficits is accompanied by pro-rich tax concessions, prospects of mobilizing resources through debt recovery and tax effort too seem bleak to them. The mainstream media and those sections that directly benefited from the orthodox fiscal policies played upon the insecurities of the middle class by stating that a universal rural employment guarantee will pose an inordinate tax burden on the middle classes, already burdened by high consumer price inflation.

The decisive political verdict of the Indian voters against economic liberalization produced a brief period of consensus on the need for an Employment Guarantee Act (EGA), which, by its very nature, was fragile, breaking under the weight of its own contradictions. While advocates fought for a substantive and effective legislation, the neoliberals were willing to agree to cosmetic and superficial measures only. Financial interests are extremely wary of inflation and the EGA stands in direct conflict with their interests, with the result that they opposed it vigorously. There was strong opposition from the corporate media and other privileged interests as well.

## THE DILUTION: NATIONAL RURAL
## EMPLOYMENT GUARANTEE BILL (NREGB)

Political compulsions did not, however, allow the opponents of the EGA to prevent the introduction of the bill in Parliament. But they tried to dilute it by raising objections acceptable even to well-meaning advocates for whom the guarantee is a social security measure. The bill tabled in Parliament was not national, nor at minimum wages and violated the very notion of a guarantee. The lacunae fell into three categories: (i) access and entitlements; (ii) nature of permissible works; and (iii) institutional and financial structure.

## Access and Entitlements

Among the most crucial deficiencies in entitlements were the absence of a time-bound extension to the entire country and no commitment of the minimum number of districts to be covered. It also had a "switch-off" clause, which allowed the guarantee to be withdrawn at any time, effectively undermining the legal guarantee. It did not universally empower all rural households, targeting only those officially identified as poor or "below poverty line (BPL)",[7] roughly 27 per cent of the population in 2002. This it did for the poorest districts of the country. Individual entitlements were not given. It had a broad and all-encompassing definition of the household which would imply low entitlements per worker, with a limited guarantee for 100 days of work per year. It did not have a watertight provision for unemployment allowance. There were no safeguards for women's access to the guarantee given at the household level. Nor did it guarantee the payment of the statutory minimum wages for unskilled agricultural workers or provide any floor to the wages that were to be paid. The bill permitted productivity-linked wages (as opposed to time-rated wages), where wages would be paid in accordance with the quantity of work performed by each worker or work-team. Besides quantity of work, there was an attempt to introduce the additional measure of quality of work. This was done through the linking of the minimum wage payment to "diligent" work,[8] leaving the implementation of the criterion of diligence to the discretion of work supervisors, making it a vague and subjective measure that would tend to curb wages (Karat 2004).

## Permissible Works

The bill also had a rigid and restrictive overspecification of permissible works (focusing on durable assets) and conditions for commencement of new works instead of a flexible, inclusive and location-specific definition, with greater scope for decentralized local area planning (Gopal 2005).

## Institutional and Financial Structure

The NREGB also by-passed *Panchayati Raj* Institutions (PRIs)[9] since there was no mandatory devolution of funds to *Gram Panchayats*.[10] The principle of subsidiarity was ignored and district- and block[11]-level implementation officers were not made accountable to the *Panchayats* at the corresponding level (Jain 2005). The *Gram Sabhas*[12] were not empowered to implement, monitor and audit. The bill also placed an unaffordable and unjustifiable financial burden on the bankrupt state governments since it was not fully funded by the central government (Vaidyanathan 2005a, 2005b).

These shortcomings were a deliberate attempt to legislate a superficial bill with minimal financial commitment to address political compulsions without deviating from the pursuit of fiscally "prudent" macroeconomic policies. Had these proposals been accepted, they would have inevitably resulted in a narrow, exclusive and limited guarantee that does not address the basic problems it is meant to tackle (Drèze 2004, 2005a, 2005b; Joshi 2005; Roy and Dey 2005; Shah 2005; Vijayshankar and Reddy 2004). Many of the lacunae were ultimately corrected due to intense pressure from the Left parties.

## THE ENACTMENT: NATIONAL RURAL
## EMPLOYMENT GUARANTEE ACT (NREGA)

The main official amendments to the NREGB arrived at after intense negotiations with the Left parties remained elusive for a very long time. The act now has the following features: universal eligibility (all households are entitled to apply for work, and not just those below the official poverty line); irreversible guarantee, without "switch-off"; time-bound extension to all of rural India in five years; principal role and 50 per cent cost of works to PRIs; permissible works to be determined in consultation with states; more beneficiaries whose private land can be included for improvement under the scheme. In addition, women's organizations were successful in securing a clear definition of household as "nuclear" in the National Operational Guidelines (NOG) that would be used while implementing the act.[13]

The act guarantees each rural household 100 days of manual work on a casual basis each year. The household and those of the adult members who are willing to perform casual manual labour are required to register with the relevant authority, and are required to apply for work, each time specifying the period and timing of work. Though for the moment they will be paid the minimum wage fixed by the state governments for unskilled agricultural labourers, the centre has the power to notify wages under the act, provided these are no lower than 60 Rupees (Rs.).[14] A failure to provide work within 15 days of application would require the state governments to pay an unemployment allowance to the worker, which is at least one-fourth of the wage rate for the first 30 days and not less than one-half of the wage rate for the remaining period.

Priority will be given to women in such a way that at least one-third of the beneficiaries shall be women. Some minimal worksite and social security facilities will be provided by way of childcare if there are five or more children under the age of six at a worksite, safe drinking-water, shade during rest periods, first-aid, hospitalization in case of injury, ex gratia payment of Rs.25,000 and so on.

Clearly, this falls short of a full-fledged right to work. At least five basic features of a meaningful "right to work" are missing, which include full coverage of all urban and rural areas; individual entitlements; unlimited days for which work is guaranteed; an assured decent living wage; and the inclusion of non-manual work to address the needs of the elderly, the disabled and, in many instances, women. The act, however, is far more than what the government planned to enact. Thus, even as the present act is by no means a full-fledged employment guarantee, it is an indisputable defeat of fiscal orthodoxy.

## CHALLENGES IN IMPLEMENTATION

Previously, all employment-generation programmes were supply driven and the administration would "open" worksites and call workers to them. Under the National Rural Employment Guarantee Scheme (NREGS), the process of accessing employment in public works has been put the right way up and now the onus is on the workers to apply for work, marking a transition from a supply-driven programme to a demand-driven one. The most crucial aspect of the NREGA is this provision for demanding work according to workers' requirements which the government has to make available within 15 days or pay the unemployment allowance. However, the biggest challenge is the institutionalization of the demand-driven aspect through an efficient, transparent, simple and smooth mechanism. This requires registration of those demanding work and procedures for application; the mobilization of workers to assess the full demand for work and its timing around the year and thus plan works and projects to absorb the entire labour force seeking work at the time they want it (subject to their entitlements); the planning process, design and estimation of projects and work generation. The second challenge is to ensure that workers receive their four entitlements of wage, workdays, worksite facilities and unemployment allowance by legally enforcing the guarantee.

From a gender perspective, the NREGS holds great promise especially with its clause for protecting women's access to the scheme through proactive inclusion. Apart from employment, the programme can generate works that address gender needs. The NREGS has the potential of addressing women's "practical interests" (Molyneux 1985) through generation of income by way of wage employment and the creation of assets that address basic needs of food, water, fuel, fodder and so on. It can also address their "strategic interests" (Molyneux 1985) by improving their status and structured involvement in local area development and better intrafamily division of work. To meet women's interests, both practical and strategic, however, it is essential to have space and forums where women workers can meet, exchange views and formulate their demands.

Addressing gender concerns at the ground level, however, poses a great challenge, especially in a scheme that has the following four features: productivity-linked wages, household-based entitlements, permitting only casual manual work and the restrictions placed on permissible works. This is the subject matter of the next section. Since the society in which the scheme is to be implemented is patriarchal, unequal and hierarchical, the scheme needs to evolve mechanisms that ensure that women and other subaltern social groups can interact, find voice and mobilize to demand their rights.

## WOMEN'S ISSUES IN THE EMPLOYMENT GUARANTEE SCHEME

Some of the provisions in the act have particularly negative implications for women. These are the focus on manual work, the emphasis on productivity-linked wages, the specification of entitlements at the household (rather than individual) level, the limited worksite facilities (especially the provision of childcare services) and the emphasis on durable physical assets. These could produce a scheme that either excludes or exploits women's labour, both of which are dangerous in the context of abysmally high levels of malnutrition among women and poorly paid employment in rural areas.

### Exploiting Women's Labour

The gender-based division of labour, because of which women bear the triple burden of unpaid work for family reproduction, income generation and customary social responsibilities, gives rise to the compulsion for female workers to remain close to the homestead and family farm even though men may migrate in search of relatively higher income work. This reduces women's mobility and narrows down their work options considerably. Women's labour at government worksites too is exploited using the compulsions of proximity to homestead imposed by this gender division of labour. The past five to six decades of public works in India have demonstrated that women's entitlements have been curtailed in at least four interconnected ways: unequal access to paid work at government worksites; unpaid work due to the non-recognition of those tasks in the labour process that are typically performed by women (such as lifting and throwing the dug soil); low wages due to impossibly high productivity norms[15] that are established under piece-rate payments; and little say in the selection and prioritization of works. This is not an innocent oversight. The urge to save costs and make additional assets by exploiting existing gender biases that subsume women's labour under their husband's and that pay women less/nothing for their labour is the most important underlying factor behind the continued clubbing together of easily divisible tasks. In a sense, women's labour at public worksites gets treated almost in the same way as women's unpaid work for household reproduction and care. Unfortunately, administrative inertia has exacerbated this situation further, whereby difficulty in computing women's work has resulted in it not being recognized as independent work. This experience informed the interventions by women's and other mass organizations throughout the debate over successive drafts of the bill, amendments in Parliament and formulation of the NOG. Perhaps the biggest gain for women's social rights is that this debate forcefully placed women's rights to decent work and fair/equal wages on the national agenda.

## Access and Childcare

The absence of universal coverage and the original proposal to target only those households that are "below poverty line" would have excluded the majority of rural households. Women's groups opposed these proposals and argued that the identification of the poor is far from satisfactory; both in terms of the criteria being applied and as far as procedures were concerned. The problem of wrong exclusion (in this case, excluding the poor) is rampant in targeted schemes and has far more serious consequences than wrong inclusion (that is, including the non-poor). The livelihoods of vast sections of the near poor are also extremely precarious and fragile. No matter what measure is used for "measuring" hunger and malnutrition, there is no doubt that the vast majority of the rural population in most Indian states suffer pervasive and persistent food insufficiency, with women and young girls often bearing the brunt of this. In its original form, the bill would have converted most of the existing universally accessible rural employment programmes into targeted ones, as it would eventually replace those existing employment programmes.

Women's organizations also opposed the proposed upper limit of 100 days of work per household,[16] considering it to be inadequate for poverty alleviation and for obtaining food security. The use of the household as a unit for targeting welfare programmes or employment schemes also raises the vexed issue of how a fixed entitlement is to be distributed among household members. Given the power asymmetries based on gender (and seniority), it can very easily lead to either conflicts within the household over the division of that entitlement, or the exclusion or marginalization of women from the scheme. Experience has shown that women tend to get pushed to lower paid and arduous work when the men in the household are given the choice—not surprising in view of their greater power to control "family labour" and determine its allocation (Ghosh 1999a).

The women's movement argued in favour of individual entitlements instead of the proposed household-based ones. Individual entitlements would be simple, more gender-just and effective in tackling rural distress. The three provisions—limiting the scheme's coverage to those BPL, providing entitlements to households and limiting the guarantee to work to 100 days a year—would together prove insufficient to address women's basic food security and livelihood needs. Individual entitlements were, however, strongly opposed by the government on the grounds of their serious cost implications.

In the absence of individual entitlements, obviously the definition of household that is used becomes all-important. The household is often defined as a group of persons who live together and take their meals from a common kitchen unless the exigencies of work prevent any one of them from doing so. A second way of defining the household would be to equate it with a nuclear family comprising mother, father and their minor children, which may also include any other person who is wholly or substantially dependent on them. Households are defined for different purposes, including statistical, administrative and legal. A lot of data collection is done at the household level and the main criteria for defining households has been convenience and ease in data collection; comparability across regions and over time and consistency within the sample are additional considerations. Traditionally, self-identification was done on the basis of the "common pot" definition in India, which has been retained by the Census and by the National Sample Survey (NSS).

While this "common pot" definition is useful for some types of data management (for example, household consumption), it is problematic when it is carried into development schemes to determine entitlements. Any policy instrument that aims to transfer income, assets or purchasing power to alleviate poverty and generate demand would need to specify a viable and effective unit. If an asset (such as land) or a cash transfer (such as a pension) are to meet the needs of both women and men, then it cannot be assumed that a benevolent household "head" will distribute the benefits justly and equally to other household members; some mechanisms need to be put in place to guarantee fair distribution and to obstruct discretion on the part of the designated "head".

In the context of the work guarantee scheme under discussion, the NREGA, the problem with the "common pot" definition was that in order to reduce costs the entitlement was effectively divided among all adult members of the household, thereby reducing the beneficial effects of the intervention. The "common pot" definition also subsumes within the larger joint family household those female-headed households (formed when women are divorced, abandoned or widowed and including their dependents) which are forced to become part of the larger joint family of their natal or marital homes, effectively depriving them of their own entitlements to public work provision. It was therefore argued that all female-headed households, including those within marital/natal "common kitchens", should be treated as separate households with their own full (presently 100 days) entitlement. Household entitlements also work against the poor because lack of homestead space often compels joint families to live together. Despite the persistent demand made by women's organizations that if individual entitlements are not provided the household should be defined as a nuclear family, both the bill and the act had a wide and all-inclusive definition in terms of shared dwelling or a common ration card so that one household could include several nuclear families. The NOG, on the other hand, have adopted the more inclusive definition of nuclear family, as well as explicitly recognizing single-member households.

Another demand raised by women's organizations was that individual cards should be issued to all eligible workers since it gives women a sense of citizenship and independence, adding to their self-confidence in accessing paid work and other livelihood options, as well as their intrahousehold position. Individual cards also reduce the scope for exclusion or invisibilization of female-headed households in natal/marital homes. This was not acceded in the act. However, this was, to some extent, addressed by the NOG.[17]

Guaranteed employment is of great importance for women, especially for those who work in the unorganized sector, where work is irregular, badly paid and without any form of social protection. This demand was integrated in the NREGA through the provision that at least one-third of the beneficiaries will be women. This was opposed by several supporters of the NREGA on the grounds that in the bid to maintain the ratio, the total quantum of work generated may suffer. There was also an apprehension that this "quota" might undermine the demand-driven character of the scheme. The view was that a quota is unnecessary since there are already over 37 per cent women in rural employment programmes. However, women's groups argued that this is only because the wages that are offered in these programmes are low, and that if minimum wages are actually paid, women are likely to be displaced by men.

Some minimal worksite facilities were also demanded by women's groups. Due to the absence of any childcare, supplementary nutrition or crèche facilities, women often have no choice but to carry young children along with them to the worksites, especially those under school age and being breast-fed. The demand was for proper crèches and day-care centres to be provided with some nutritional provision, through dovetailing with the Integrated Child Development Services (ICDS) (which targets children less than six years of age with health, nutrition and education provision).[18]

## Labour Process and Wages

Since low availability of remunerative work results in distress wage rates and underemployment, or disguised unemployment besides open unemployment, the levels of both real wages and employment should be high to make any significant dent on poverty. Yet, workers earn no more than half or even a fourth of the minimum wage in most government public works programmes. The underpayment is a direct outcome of the prevalence of what are called "productivity-linked wages" with very high out-turn requirements, which workers often fail to meet.

Women's groups were particularly concerned about the nature of the labour process in public employment programmes. The employment is typically in manual labour for loosening, digging, lifting and throwing soil in what has come to be known as "earth works". Obviously, heavy and arduous earth work cannot, and should not, be the only type of work on offer, given the high levels of malnourishment among the working-class rural population who require the work most, especially women.

The entire edifice of such earth works rests on family-based couples or *jodis*, usually a husband and a wife, working as a team. Single women find it very difficult to find a partner and are therefore not included in groups. The norms are also fixed on this basis. Even though work is measured on a *jodi* or pair basis in most places, it is averaged for the entire worksite and everybody earns equal wages. For this reason, there is a lot of resistance from other workers to the elderly and pairs of women (sometimes, a mother and daughter) working on these sites since their productivity is likely to be less, which will pull down the average wage. While one regressive solution to this problem is to measure the output of each pair separately and paying them accordingly so that the able-bodied do not directly "subsidize" the elderly and the women, an alternative that is simple, fair and more capable of ensuring that all workers earn the minimum wage is to shift to wages on the basis of time-rates or to provide separate norms for women and the elderly.

Apart from unrealistically high productivity norms, there are other administrative causes for low wages under piece-rated earth works. The tasks may not be clearly defined or specified, with different components of the labour process such as digging and throwing clubbed together as one activity instead of being broken up into distinct tasks, with different rates of payment. Tasks performed by women, which are usually lifting and throwing earth after it has been loosened and dug by men, remain invisible, unaccounted and unpaid. Closely linked to this is the fact that work specification and productivity norms do not follow ecological conditions like soil, terrain and season. One of the most crucial but neglected aspects is the selection of qualified and trained persons to administer the worksites, who will identify soil conditions, specify tasks and productivity norms, and make lift and lead allowances, undertake timely measurement of the out-turn, maintain the muster-rolls[19] and pay wages. The role of contractors or middlemen in underpaying workers and other types of corruption in other schemes led to the successful insistence on banning them in the NREGS. The moment machinery and high material costs are permitted, contractors will follow. There was therefore opposition to the use of machinery and high material costs in NREGS works to avoid both the displacement of labour and leakages. The government acceded to these demands.

Liberals sometimes only see the low wages as a governance failure due to faulty implementation rather than anything intrinsic to task rates for manual work. According to them, the only corrective required is appropriate delineation of work and rate, accurate and timely measurement and stronger social audit provisions. From a gender perspective, though very important, these will not by themselves resolve the problem of low wages when payment is linked to the output of hard manual labour. It is for this reason that time-rates were advocated.

However, not all supporters of the NREGA opposed productivity-linked wages and supported a shift to work on a time-rate basis. Those in favour of piece-rate argued that it had the advantage of ensuring "self-selection", thereby targeting the scheme to the neediest. For them, the lower the wages, the more effectively self-selection will work as only the most desperate would want to avail of the employment opportunity. Furthermore, the incentive for corruption and leakages through non-serious applications and misuse of the unemployment allowance by the rural elite will come down with low wages. If the wages offered on public worksites are higher than the prevalent market wages, an upward pressure would be exerted on the latter which would be adverse for agriculture. It was also argued that piece-rate will ensure productive use of scarce fiscal resources and create a fixed quantum of durable assets per unit expenditure. The fact that a decent wage is as important as employment to pull people out of perpetual poverty was opposed by these advocates, who argued that asset creation and self-selection could only be ensured through productivity-linked wages. The financial motive behind low productivity norms was that the payment of lower wages will keep public spending very low under the scheme, since wages constitute 60 per cent of the total cost of the scheme and have to be fully borne by the central government.

In the face of opposition from all quarters, the women's groups argued that state governments must revise their productivity norms to establish rates that ensure that seven hours of work would earn the minimum wage across genders, age-groups and climatic and ecological conditions.

Ultimately, the act compromises on the wage issue in two ways: by permitting productivity-linked wages (though with a safeguard) and by de-linking wages from statutory cost indexation.[20] Even though it permits piece-rates, it adds two very important riders: That workers shall not receive less than the minimum wage; and that the state government shall set productivity norms and rates in such a way that seven hours of manual labour earns the minimum wage.[21]

The mode of wage payment—cash, grain or both—also has important gender consequences. Food security has always been the propelling force behind public works and famine relief programmes in India, with a significant grain component included as part of the wage. One of the main arguments in favour of the NREGA was that it would provide sustainable food security. This was to be achieved through the generation of purchasing power, as well as the spurt to food production from the creation of rural infrastructure like irrigation and roads, and by paying a part of the wage in food-grain. At present in India, the Food for Work Programme and the Sampoorna Grameen Rozgar Yojana meet the food security requirements of, at best, only a section of the rural population. The shift to cash payment only in the NREGS on account of administrative simplicity could become detrimental for food security, especially in the absence of an effective universal Public Distribution System for essential food items. Women, as those with the primary responsibility for feeding the family, often voice a preference for receiving at least part of the wage in essential food items, the poor quality of the grain and leakages notwithstanding. Payments in kind (such as grain), as opposed to only cash, also have the added advantage of not being fungible, that is, spent on personal items (for example, alcohol) by those who are handed the wage or control it.

## Works

There are a few concerns with regard to the type of permissible works under the NREGS and the procedure of their selection. The government was keen to have an all-inclusive list of public works that focused on durable assets, water management and connectivity. The women's organizations wanted flexibility and location specificity in the permissible list of works under the scheme, leaving identification and prioritization to the village assemblies and local initiatives. Such flexibility could allow different kinds of work to be included, such as the creation of social infrastructure, which is at least as important as physical infrastructure, and would improve the quality of life in rural areas for everybody. Health care, literacy programmes, nutrition and sanitation are just some of the possible activities which could be, but are not, permitted under the scheme. Another concern was the importance of thinking of works when employment is needed most, in the food-deficit months, after sowing and before harvesting in the rainy season when distress outmigration is most intense. At this time, heavy rain does not permit large-scale earth works. Another reason why flexibility in works is important is that the labour process is linked to the types of works, which in turn determines the wages earned. Despite such convincing arguments for flexibility in defining works and greater initiative with local bodies in this regard, rigidity is rooted in the dread of waste of scarce resources, and a belief in the inherent superiority of durable "hard" assets and infrastructure in promoting sustained growth. It was with a great deal of difficulty that an amendment was moved so that the states are given at least a consultative role in adding works.

## IMPLEMENTATION OF NREGS[22]

Contrary to what the scheme's critics claim, expenditure on the scheme remains extremely low, even below the paltry budgetary allocation that was made. Fiscal conservatism and the lack of official will to transform from a supply-driven public works programme to a demand-driven employment guarantee combine to keep spending low. Not surprisingly, women bear a disproportionately higher burden of this through three interrelated processes: disenfranchisement through non-recognition as right holders; inability to make claims due to the excessive bureaucratization of procedures and the imposition of a host of arbitrary and discretionary eligibility criteria; and non-fulfilment of entitlements guaranteed under the act. These issues are elaborated in the following.

## Recognition as Right Holders

Many women were forced to accept lower annual entitlements to public works due to their inclusion on the job cards of the extended joint family. Most states have issued job cards on the basis of a pre-existing household listing using the "common kitchen" definition of the household, previously used for the census and the ration cards. The relevant state officials were either unaware of the provision for nuclear family and single-member households in the Guidelines, or simply continued with the existing lists out of sheer inertia. This was particularly adverse for female-headed households nested within natal or marital homes (widows, separated/abandoned women) who were denied their rightful status as independent households under the act. Many older widows have also been refused cards on the grounds of their age, even though they worked under the National Food for Work Programme. The pressure to exclude older persons is due to the prevalence of piece-rate work with uniform productivity norms, and the arbitrary restriction on the number of eligible workers per household. In the absence of a universal and adequate pension scheme, the exclusion of the elderly purely on the basis of their physical strength is a cause for concern.

Women in migrant families (and, in fact, all migrants) have faced a severe problem of exclusion since registration was not a continuous process, as provided in the act, but took place at a time of high seasonal outmigration. If entire families had migrated, they were told on their return that they have to now wait till the registration "opens" again. If only husbands had migrated, the women who remained in their villages were turned back because they were not the "heads of the household", which is itself a violation of the law.

Local bureaucrats have evolved all kinds of completely illegal and unsound eligibility conditions resulting in workers not being recognized as right holders under the act. According to the act the only criteria that need verification are family, local residence and age. Neither the act nor the Guidelines call for any documentary proof. However, local bureaucrats administering the scheme have often demanded documentary evidence, such as ration cards, voter identity cards, census lists and so on. This echoes research findings from Bangladesh, which analysed the implementation of gender and development policies by government functionaries and development non-governmental organizations. Local workers and officials were found to reflect their own biases against progressive policy aims, like gender equity, through discretionary practices and unnecessary paperwork, which effectively undermined these very policies (Goetz 1996). In India, too, bureaucratic biases against gender equity have meant that despite the act having a clear provision for ensuring women's inclusion in the scheme, women, especially if elderly, migrant, physically challenged or members of a female-headed household, tend to be disproportionately excluded due to all kinds of documentary and eligibility conditions imposed during the implementation process, which act as barriers to access.

## Claiming Rights

After verification, registered households are issued job cards with the names of the eligible workers from the household marked on them. This job card is required when one household member applies for work through the scheme, and a record of the days worked and the wages received are also entered on this card.

Most reports and my own field-work (see appendix 12.1 for details) find that besides the delay in the distribution of job cards, often the cards are taken from the workers by contractors, *panchayat* officials and so on. Except in a few pockets, there is little awareness among the rural population that the onus is on them to apply for work, let alone any knowledge of how to do so. Workers are under the impression that the onus is on the administration to provide them 100 days of work and that the possession of the job card automatically ensures this. Most field surveys did not find worksites where the demand-driven aspect of the act was being put into practice. As a result, only those who are present in the village, have not migrated elsewhere and come to know about the work being provided through the scheme, are able to access it. Moreover, if the availability of work is less than the demand, many workers have to return empty-handed. The lack of awareness about the procedures in the scheme stems partly from the fact that it is still early days, and there is bound to be some amount of confusion and delay in the dissemination of information and awareness. With time, more people are likely to be informed about the scheme and its procedures.

Where workers are organized through grass-roots organizations, agricultural labour unions, peasant organizations, women's organizations and trade unions, and are aware that they have to apply for work, other impediments come in the way, especially where women apply on their own. In the latter case they are either dispossessed of their job card or are asked to get the approval of the male head of household. Dated acknowledgment of applications are not issued to claimants, with the result that they cannot hold the government accountable to the unemployment allowance if work is not provided within 15 days.

The complicated procedures for application and hurdles created in the process have resulted in several claimants giving up and not pursuing their claims. Claimants are, for example, informed that photographs are compulsory, even though this is not the case, and that they must arrange for it themselves, even though the Guidelines clearly put the responsibility on the officials and exhort them not to insist on photographs. The village functionaries claim that the applicant must approach the block (see glossary) officials. They are often required unnecessarily to travel to the block headquarters to pursue their applications, only to be told on arrival after a difficult journey that their papers are not in order, or that they have come to the wrong place. This has given rise to a system of informal intermediaries, the erstwhile private contractors,

| Glossary | |
|---|---|
| Anganwadi | A centre under the Integrated Child Development Services Scheme for childcare and supplementary nutrition for pre and post natal mothers and pre-school children. |
| Block | An intermediate administrative unit that is between the village and District. |
| Gram Sabha | Village assembly of all adults on the lectoral rolls |
| Gram Panchayat | Elected representatives at the village level |
| mate | An assistant at the worksite whose wages come from the Scheme who posseses minimal technical skills and has the responsibility of supervision, maintenance of attendance and wage records, measurement of output, etc. |
| muster roll | A proforma on which the record of attendance, output and work of each worker is maintained at each worksite with the thumb impression/signature of the worker, mate and engineer |
| Panchayati Raj institutions (PRIs) | In 1993, the Government of India enacted the Seventy third Amendment to the constitution which created decentralized institutions of local self-government called Panchayati Raj Institutions. PRIs comprised village assemblies (all adult voters) and a three tier structure of elected members at the village(Gram Panchayat), intermediate (Janpad Panchayat) and district level (Zila Parishad) nwith 1/3 reservation for women and proportionate reservation for SCs and STs. |
| productivity norms | The output that each worker (or pair of workers) is expected to produce in order to earn the statutory minimum wage |
| Sarpanch | Elected President of the Gram Panchayat |
| Scheduled Castes and Scheduled Tribes | a socially/economically marginalized Hindu caste/tribe, given special privileges by the government. Article 341 of the Indian Constitution provides that the President may, with respect to any State or Union territory, specify the castes, races or tribes or parts of or groups within castes, races or tribes which shall for the purposes of the Constitution be deemed to be Scheduled Castes in relation to that State or Union territory. Article 342 similarly provides for specification of tribes or tribal communities or parts of or groups within tribes or tribal communities which are to be deemed for the purposes of the Constitution to be Scheduled Tribes in relation to the various States and territories. In pursuance of these provisions, the list of Scheduled Castes and / or Scheduled Tribes are notified for each State and Union territory and are valid only within the jurisdiction of that State or Union territory and not outside. |

who step in as the middlemen and extract a share of the wages to smoothen the process. The addition of conditions and paperwork not in the original legislation prevents women from making claims. Research on women's access to welfare grants in South Africa documents similar impediments being set in the way of women applicants by local officials, "[s]uch misapplication of the rules that burden applicants or prevent them from getting grants are shaped in large part by negative perceptions held by officials at various levels of government and across departments. They view welfare recipients, particularly the poorest . . . youngest . . . and most vulnerable . . . as least deserving of assistance" (Goldblatt 2005:249).

The greatest strength of the Indian scheme is the provision that workers can apply and get work when they need it most. This demand-driven aspect of the scheme, which is its cornerstone, is not in place, resulting in the persistence of the bureaucracy-led supply-driven approach. This is because there is a vested interest in keeping control over the timing and amount of employment available across seasons in rural areas. This permits the local elite and landlords to continue their hold and discipline over local labour, and prevent an upward pressure on market wages. In the final analysis, barriers to fair and simple claim-making under the scheme curtail overall expenditure and sustain the local power equations and dismally low wages.

## Receiving Entitlements

### Wages

In gross violation of the act, workers at NREGS worksites are earning no more than 50 to 60 per cent of the minimum wage, sometimes even a mere quarter of it. This is the single most important problem in the scheme. Moreover, it is a problem that no one denies.[23] This problem has little to do with corruption, an issue raised repeatedly by opponents of NREGS. It is an outcome of deliberate state policy to keep wages low and curtail expenditure.

Wages are less than statutory minimum wages for two interrelated reasons. The first is structural in that the amount of production/out-turn expected from workers is humanly impossible in the prescribed time. The second is the governance or administration of the productivity-linked wage system, since it involves judgment, discretion and measurement.[24] From this follows the two-pronged solution adopted by some state governments. The first is the revision of the Schedules of Rates after time and motion studies under different conditions of ecology, worker age and gender and climate. The second is reform in administration through fair tasking as well as timely and accurate measurement by an expanded cadre of skilled village-level staff.

However, state government officials complained that the Finance Ministry at the centre is trying to thwart these attempts, seeing them as an upward revision of wages, through the backdoor. The motive behind this is that the payment of lower productivity-linked wages is one of the principal mechanisms by which spending remains very low under the scheme.[25]

Workers complained of delayed payment of wages—delays of up to four weeks. Maharashtra has a system of advances (which amounted to anything between Rs.50 and Rs.100 per worker, without any proper record of the payments made to each worker) that remained unsettled for well over the prescribed fortnight. On many sites workers received wages in their houses from the group leader, without public payment to the actual worker as prescribed by the act. As noted earlier, despite the poor quality of grain and leakages, food security considerations make women want at least part payment in kind. Interestingly, they wanted the men of their household to receive wages only in kind since, whatever the quality, whatever the quantity, it would at least reach home and fill empty stomachs. Over four-fifths of the sample preferred payment to be made partly in grain and partly in cash. Almost all female respondents and half of the male respondents wanted the wage partly to be paid in grain. This view is held all over the country, which once again underlines the primary importance of food security.[26]

## Working Conditions

Some households do not own the implements required for earth works as they are expensive. This was a serious problem for single women, Scheduled Caste[27] and landless and marginal farmer households. Workers also reported high wear and tear of the implements and thus an impending replacement cost. However the administration was unwilling to include implements under the material component.

The act provides for four minimal worksite facilities: childcare, shade, drinking-water and first aid. These are more conspicuous by their absence, except perhaps for drinking-water, without which it would be impossible for workers to sustain themselves in the heat. The provision of childcare is clearly not a priority in the implementation of the scheme. For one thing, such provision is to be made if there are at least five children at the worksite. But the lack of information itself means that some women leave children behind at home, so this becomes an excuse for the administration not to provide childcare facilities. Often the greatest stumbling block is the attitude of the officials, as exemplified by an officer in Maharashtra. When asked about the provision of crèches, he scoffed at them as elitist and alien concepts. Most women prefer permanent day-care centres located in the village and not at worksites, unless they are breast-feeding the child. Women also felt that if migration was reduced, they could send their children to school. One way of integrating childcare, food security and employment for women workers is through dovetailing the ICDS with NREGS. The *Anganwadis*[28] can double up as a day-care centre or crèche for children of NREGS workers and be treated as a NREGS worksite.

As far as provision of drinking-water at worksites is concerned, although many sites had employed women to fetch water, it was pitifully inadequate, particularly in view of the hard work and the intense heat in which it was being done. In many caste-ridden areas, there was a shockingly discriminatory practice to provide separate vessels for Scheduled Caste on grounds of "untouchability" and "purity".

## Preponderance of Women Workers

Close to 70 per cent of the workers at NREGS worksites were women in the age-group of 30–50 years, largely from landless, small and marginal farmer households, belonging to Scheduled Caste (SC) and Scheduled Tribe (ST) communities. The high percentage of poor SC and ST women at EGS worksites is because men are unwilling to work at such low wages. At these abysmal wages, men would prefer to migrate or find alternative employment to increase family income while women need to remain closer to home to fulfil their household responsibilities. A majority of them got work for between four to 10 days, which was inadequate. They earned far less than promised, due to the shortfall in measurement.

In fact, the lower than minimum wages have become a mechanism for targeting and exploiting the poorest and most vulnerable women, and even though persons from all sections registered, mostly women from low/no asset households availed of the work. Ironically, this has made it a self-defeating exercise as far as poverty alleviation is concerned. It has also promoted child labour as young female children (7–13 years of age) worked with their parents on the worksite to increase out-turn and the family's meagre earnings.

## Works: Durable Assets Through Manual Work

There are many deficiencies in the types of works selected and the methods followed. In many places, the *Gram Sabha* (see glossary) was held for the selection of works, but very few women attended it and none participated in the discussion. Despite their numerical predominance as workers under the scheme, women have had very little voice in the selection of works on which they labour. Where women were organized into collectives, it added to their self-confidence in articulating their priorities. Apart from not having a say in the selection of works, many of the activities women are keen to undertake under the scheme are not permitted in the rigidly defined list. Women's main concerns are food security, domestic water security, health, education, fuel, fodder and income generation. They also want the inclusion of infrastructure and personnel for social and human development, such as *Anganwadis*, crèches, ration shops and primary health-care centres in the list of selected works.

The other activities that women are keen to undertake in NREGS are home-based and small-scale industries. At the moment, individual benefi-ciary schemes for livelihood generation are not permitted under the NREGS. There are several suggestions for women-friendly economic activities and projects, such as civic services, sericulture, horticulture, floriculture, food processing, pisciculture and rearing livestock. However, such works are not permissible under the NREGS unless the labour-to-material cost ratio and the list of permissible works are changed. There are also several requests for convergence of training and literacy programmes with the NREGS. This is a good idea and, given the very high illiteracy rates among women workers, an important opportunity for not only imparting skills but also basic lit-eracy. There could be dovetailing with adult literacy programmes. One very useful suggestion from the All India Democratic Women's Association in Orissa was that a land improvement package, including land levelling, farm bunding and a farm pond, should be permitted and encouraged on farms of female-headed households as well as farms of migrant workers where women predominantly do the farming. At the moment this provision is allowed for in the case of SCs, STs, BPL families and beneficiaries of Indira Awaas Yojana and land reforms, who mostly remain unaware of it.

The scheme only permits arduous manual work, which militates against frail, undernourished and elderly people as well as some women. Single women or even pairs of women are turned back from worksites since they would bring down the average productivity. This focus on durable physical asset creation through manual work not only denies women full wages, but also promotes child labour, and makes it difficult for women to suggest key development activities to address needs. Furthermore, since large earth works are not possible during the rains—a time of food insecurity—this effectively suspends the guarantee in the rainy season. The desire to mini-mize waste and leakage through "unproductive" works ends up undermin-ing gender concerns.

## CHANGING RURAL EQUATIONS?

Despite all the restrictions within the scheme and denial of entitlements, the NREGS has a rich potential of redefining rural politics by empowering those low-income social groups ("the poor") who have had few avenues for bringing their interests into the policy-making process. In fact, an important source of opposition to a substantive guarantee is from the entrenched rural elite who fear erosion of their power base. The political equations are already begin-ning to change at the block and local level because the NREGS is disturbing the local power equations. In villages with a high degree of inequality, both along caste and class lines, the EGA is unleashing a new political dynamic.

The big farmers are very worried that workers will now become more "independent" or "demand higher wages" or not work against loan advances (since high interest is an important form of underpayment). Reacting in one (or all) of the following ways, they have ensured no works during the agricultural season, restricted the number of eligible workers per household, diverted workers to their own fields while showing them on NREGS muster-rolls and prevented registration of farm labour households.[29] The rural power elites succeeded because their interests on this issue coalesce with the aim of other interest groups such as central and state bureaucrats and others preaching fiscal restraint.

In many places where workers were more organized or had greater bargaining power, they refused to come to NREGA worksites after the first measurement cycle, if wage deductions on account of inability to achieve the unrealistically high productivity norms persisted. In a bargaining exercise resembling the market, workers were persuaded to settle for an *a priori* wage higher than their productivity-linked wage but below the minimum wage, which is typically close to the prevalent market wage. The paperwork to justify this wage involves fudged measurement and fabricated muster-rolls.

There is thus a clear sociopolitical dimension in determining the wages that workers earn, with a high positive correlation between the bargaining power of workers (a product of their political organization, equity, socioeconomic status and alternative livelihood opportunities) and the level of wages earned by them. Where there are strong movements and mass organizations, the balance tips in favour of the workers. There is also a fear among big farmers, landlords and others hiring labour that they will lose the labour, tied for generations through debt advances, working for a pittance. Obviously, the NREGS is not being implemented in a vacuum and social and political factors play a very important role in its success.

For a more gender-sensitive implementation, mass organizations of women as well as community-based women's groups can play a very important role. A formal assembly of registered workers, where issues such as work selection, working conditions, wages and worksite facilities may be discussed, is also capable of eliciting and articulating women's concerns. Such organizations can help subaltern women to articulate with more confidence their needs and preferences, and the selection of works. The greater status brought about through earning an income can combine with the self-confidence brought about through collective action to weaken, and ultimately undermine, social barriers. There are several examples of this in West Bengal and Tamil Nadu. In West Bengal, Self-Help Groups (SHGs) collectively applied for work and even put up project proposals for sanction under the NREGS. In Tamil Nadu, association through SHGs gave landless SC women the confidence to stand up to the might of upper-caste landed *Sarpanches*[30] on the issue of wages. SHGs often took the initiative—be it in application for work, or implementation of projects. However, they often had a bitter experience because the SHGs had spent their own money and the state government had not yet reimbursed them.

The one-third reservation for women in *Panchayats* too is an important (albeit with varying degrees of effectiveness) mechanism for empowering and addressing women's needs through decentralized development. The experience across the country is uneven, and while in some places elected women representatives have made a serious contribution to women's interests, in others their presence has remained a mere formality. The male family members of these elected representative (or *pati panches*[31] as they are known locally) have often subverted the mandated women's quota by usurping the powers of elected women representatives. There is substantial scope for elected women representatives to provide leadership in the selection and design of works as well as provision of basic worksite facilities through capacity-building and awareness-generation camps.

There are larger issues of gender equity through changing intrafamily and intravillage equations. Will more time spent doing wage work on NREGS worksites result in a greater burden on women, or will there be a consequent sharing of domestic responsibilities? It is early days yet, and whether the scheme will impact core areas like the division of labour within the family and society, and women's effective participation in village affairs like planning and development, all remain to be seen. Much will depend on the extent to which women's organizational capacities, at different levels of governance and within different institutional arenas, are developed to occupy the spaces created by policy and law and to shape them in transformative ways.

## CONCLUSIONS

The overall climate within which the NREGS was introduced in India has been one of fiscal orthodoxy, where low public expenditure and near-zero fiscal deficits are considered ends in themselves. This formed the ideological basis for the opposition to the act in the first place. Those opposed to the act believe that expenditure on the scheme is a waste of scarce resources, and that the money would be better spent on large infrastructure projects and human capital formation. Frustrated by Parliament's passage of a more pro-worker act than acceptable to fiscal conservatives, opponents have now changed tacks to narrow down the scheme during its implementation. This is through low coverage and unwarranted exclusion of the eligible population in notified districts; unfulfilled entitlements even for those fortunate enough to be registered; impermissible restrictions on eligibility, verification and works; inadequate administrative capabilities and little effort to overcome deficiencies in manpower, skills and training. The 100 days of work per rural household may not be adequate to address poverty and migration, nor reverse the rural crisis without individual entitlements or a more inclusive definition of the household.

## Restricting Access

Access to guaranteed work is restricted in many different ways across the states. Women are not registered if their husbands who are considered the "head of the household" have migrated outside of the village or locality. Though the act has a simple and non-bureaucratic procedure, in practice there is an insistence on documentary proof for verification (for example, ration cards, voter identity cards and so on). Individual cards are not issued in most states, and female-headed households are not recognized as independent households. All kinds of arbitrary and unjustifiable criteria are used for eligibility. Apart from women, the elderly and migrants face disproportionately high exclusion. However, getting registered is no guarantee that the household would manage to get a job card, and there is a large gap between registration and job card distribution. Finally, even after workers are issued job cards, they are sometimes unable to retain possession of these cards.

## Unfulfilled Entitlements

Workers are denied their due entitlements of work, wage, worksite facilities and unemployment allowance. "Common kitchen" is the operational definition of household instead of nuclear family and, consequently, there is a very high reduction in per capita entitlements. This is accompanied by very low wages (close to market wages) and non-payment of minimum wages due to unrealistically high productivity norms and no reduction in norms for women and the elderly. Inadequate identification of separate tasks in the labour process and imprecise task specification and decomposition, along with sketchy soil identification, stingy lift and lead provision and faulty measurement of out-turn at worksites combine to result in low wages.

The amount of work generated is very low. Wage payment is often delayed, with delays ranging from two to four weeks. Payment in cash only in most places is not in keeping with workers' preferences for part payment of wage in food-grain. Unemployment allowance or compensation is usually not paid and there is no attempt to encourage applications for work. The worksite facilities are highly inadequate, especially in the provision of childcare and drinking-water. Many workers are too poor to purchase implements, and implementing agencies are unwilling to provide such implements as part of the material cost.

## Administrative and Financial Shortcomings

There is gross underutilization of EGS funds due to fiscal conservatism. The lack of official will to transform from a supply-driven public works programme to a demand-driven employment guarantee is facilitated by low awareness about details of the scheme on the part of potential beneficiaries, *panchayat* members and officials. Shortage of staff, especially technical staff, and a hesitation to hire block-level programme officers on a contract or permanent basis reduces administrative capacities. The pace of estimate preparation of the works selected by the *Gram Sabha* is very slow. Inappropriate persons are appointed as mates[32] without adequate skills or training. Even once estimates are prepared, there are delays in the commencement of works due to non-issuance of work orders despite sanctions.

The focus on manual labour in earth works for durable assets has many adverse implications for women. The rigidities around works have meant that women's preferences and needs are not addressed in terms of (i) the labour process and working conditions; (ii) entitlements; and (iii) works created. There is an absence of creative thinking on works in the most food-deficit rainy months when there is greatest need for wage employment and lowest possibility of large-scale earth works. Even at other times, there is a non-innovative approach in the selection of works with an overemphasis on roads and ponds. The unwillingness to provide necessary means of production or material costs even to the extent permitted under the act introduces further rigidities in the scheme.

## APPENDIX 12.1

### List of Field Reports on NREGA

The following reports are available at: www.righttofoodindia.org/rtowork/ega_latest_activities.html

*NREGA Vigilance by Local Groups* (Amitabh Mukhopadhyay and Ramit Basu, Lok Sabha Secretariat and Social Watch, New Delhi; United Nations Country Team [India] Solution Exchange: issued 3 April 2006).
*Status Report on Implementation of NREGA in Gujarat* (Janpath and Sabar Ekta Manch, May 2006).
*Implementation of NREGA—Experience So Far* (Participatory Research and Action [PRIA], June 2006).
*Report of Workshop on NREGA in Bhawanipatna, Orissa* (TRUTH, Rupaayan, Khadya Adhikar Abhijan and Loak Adhikar Samukhiya Kalahandi, June 2006).
*Struggles to Ensure Employment and Minimum Wages in Barwani* (Jan Jagrit Adivasi Dalit Sangathan [JADS], June 2006).
*Employment Guarantee Act: Tall Claims and Ground Realities; Soaring Prices, Crumbling Public Distribution System, and the UPA Government* (Report of a public hearing organized by the All India Agrarian Labourers' Association [AIALA], 17 August 2006, Jantar Mantar, New Delhi).
*Political Economy of Pre-Launch Preparedness of NREGA in Kerala* (Jos Chathukulam and K Gireesan, Centre for Rural Management, Kerala, 19–20 August).
*Survey to Monitor Implementation of the NREGA: Andhra Pradesh, Chhattisgarh, Jharkhand, Madhya Pradesh* (Presented by Jayati Ghosh to Ministry of Rural Development on a Survey by the Centre for Budget and Governance Accountability, 30 August 2006).
*Fact Finding Report on the Status of Implementation of Scheme under NREGA in Bengabad Block of Giridih District, Jharkhand* (Mazdoor Kisan Samiti and Nari Shakti Sangathan, Jharkhand, September 2006).

*Irregularities Found during NREGA Survey in Jashpur (Chattisgarh): Summary of "Action Taken Report"* (Commissioners to the Supreme Court, September 2006).

*Status of NREGA in Dindugul District, Tamil Nadu* (Right to Food Campaign, Tamil Nadu, September 2006).

*Fact Finding Report on the National Rural Employment Guarantee Scheme in Tamil Nadu* (TN-FORCES, 8 September 2006).

*Madhya Pradesh Employment Guarantee Scheme: Inclusion of the Differently Abled* (Report prepared by Tanushre Sood of a workshop by Ashagram Trust, Bhopal, 15 September 2006).

*Follow-up of the Fact Finding Report on the National Rural Employment Guarantee Scheme in Tamil Nadu* (TN-FORCES, 25 September 2006).

*Monitoring and Evaluation of National Rural Employment Guarantee Scheme with Special Focus on Gender Issues* (Indian School of Women's Studies Development, New Delhi, October 2006).


# NOTES

1. Sonia Gandhi steered the Congress-led UPA alliance to victory through a rigorous campaign across the length and breadth of the country. In a dramatic turn of events, she turned down the Prime Minister's post, presumably to pre-empt civil disturbances spear-headed by right-wing forces against her Italian origins. She installed the present Prime Minister, Dr. Manmohan Singh, instead. He was the chief architect of India's neoliberal reforms initiated in the late 1980s when her husband Rajiv Gandhi was the Prime Minister. He, in turn, appointed well-known votaries of fiscal conservatism, P.C. Chidambaram and Montek Singh Ahluwalia, as Finance Minister and Deputy Chairperson (chief executive) of the Planning Commission, respectively. This hijacked the poll verdict against neoliberal reforms except that the sizeable presence of the Left parties in Parliament (with their highest ever tally since independence) acted as a countervailing force, with a higher degree of success in law-making than in policy.

2. "The UPA government will immediately enact a National Employment Guarantee Act. This will provide a legal guarantee for at least 100 days of employment to begin with on asset-creating public works programmes every year at minimum wages for at least one able-bodied person in every rural, urban poor and lower middle class household" (United Progressive Alliance 2004).

3. Communist Party of India (Marxist) in its various documents on www.cpim. org and articles in its journal *People's Democracy*; Bhaduri (2004, 2005); Dhavan (2005); Ghosh (2004); Karat (2005); Papola (2005); P. Patnaik (2005).

4. Acharya 2004a, 2004b; Aiyar 2005; Bhalla 2004, 2005; Debroy 2004, 2005.

5. Thus they argued that the EGS should replace other government spending and subsidies on rural development and agricultural so that overall expenditure could be reduced with this self-targeted programme (Roy 2005; I. Patnaik 2005).

6. Economists refuted claims that this act was unaffordable. The different estimates range between 0.7 and 1.4 per cent of gross domestic product (GDP). Economists pointed to the "gift" of Rs.5000 crores to a handful of traders at the stock exchange as a result of the dilution of the turn-over tax, which was a simple measure for raising revenue. Removal of the capital gains tax was

justified on the basis of the higher turn-over tax, but even after retracting on the turn-over tax front, the capital gains tax was not reintroduced. So the issue of finding resources is a political one. If the tax–GDP ratio was restored to the 1991 level, there would be more than enough money for a universal urban and rural EGS. The Fiscal Responsibility and Budget Management Bill was a dangerous act that tied the hands of the government. There was no harm in printing money to finance development schemes, since this is not inflationary in the current context, with wage goods and excess foreign exchange reserves available in the system.

7. The Planning Commission estimates the number of poor in the country based on the definition of poverty in terms of per capita monthly expenditure corresponding to per capita daily requirement of 2,400 calories in rural areas and 2,100 calories in urban areas from the consumer expenditure survey data of the National Sample Survey Organisation, which covers expenditure on food and certain non-food items by updating 1993 estimates using a regional specific price index and the consumption basket of 1973. Economists have criticized the methodology on several points: an outdated consumption basket, choice of price index and, most of all, the easy availability of far higher direct poverty estimates from the National Sample Survey (NSS) data in terms of the actual calorific consumption. Utsa Patnaik showed that the calculations based on indirect estimates actually lowered the minimum calorie content in the consumption basket, and that using the actual calorie consumption alone would yield much higher estimates of poverty (Patnaik 2004). Since 1992 the Ministry of Rural Development (MoRD) has conducted a BPL survey to actually identify the poor, timed with the five-year plans. The ministry funds the census conducted through field surveys by each state government. Unlike the Sample Surveys used by the Planning Commission to estimate poverty, the MoRD census to identify poor households is a house-to-house census of all households. The methodology and questionnaire is decided by the ministry. This has no absolute and uniform cut-off across states and even districts but is linked to the Planning Commission estimates in such a way that each state has to adhere to the percentage set by the Planning Commission.

8. "The schedule of rates of unskilled labourers shall be so fixed that a person working diligently for seven hours would normally earn a wage equal to the wage rate".

9. In 1993, the Government of India enacted the 73rd Amendment to the constitution, which created decentralized institutions of local self-government called PRIs. PRIs comprised village assemblies (all adult voters) and a three-tier structure of elected members at the village (*Gram Panchayat*), intermediate (*Janpad Panchayat*) and district levels (*Zila Parishad*), with one-third reservation for women and proportionate reservation for Scheduled Castes (SCs) and Scheduled Tribes (STs).

10. The body of elected representatives at the village level.

11. An intermediate administrative unit that is between the village and district.

12. Village assembly of all adults on the electoral rolls.

13. The preceding official definition of households on the basis of "common kitchen" would tend to reduce per capita entitlements as it includes more working adults per unit.

14. This allows the centre (if it so chooses) to pay less than minimum wages in those states where the relevant minimum wage is above Rs.60.

15. The output that each worker (or pair of workers) is expected to produce in order to earn the statutory minimum wage.

16. The upper limit of 100 days of work per year per household is from the CMP, despite mass organizations and Left parties asking for an open-ended

need-based scheme, or a minimum of at least 200 days of work per year per household.

17. The Guidelines state: "Individual identity slips may be given to each registered applicant of the family, if so desired."

18. A fully centrally sponsored scheme, the ICDS is an excellent programme aimed at enhancing the health, nutrition and learning opportunities for preschool children under six years of age, and expectant and nursing mothers, by simultaneously providing all the requisite services at the grass-roots/village level. It provides supplementary meals, health check-ups, immunization, referral services and non-formal preschool education at the *Anganwadi* centres. The services provided under the scheme are delivered to the *Anganwadi* centres through the *Anganwadi* workers and helpers appointed from among the locality. Suggestions and areas for intervention are universalization of ICDS, construction of more *Anganwadi* centres, compulsory admission and regularization of *Anganwadi* workers.

19. A proforma, on which the record of attendance, output and work of each worker is maintained at each worksite with the thumb impression/signature of the worker, mate and engineer.

20. This introduces the unprecedented possibility of superseding statutory minimum wages. At the moment, most centrally sponsored programmes, like the Food For Work Programme, entail payment at the rate of the statutory minimum wages fixed by the respective state governments for unskilled agricultural labourers in accordance with the Minimum Wages Act (1948) (an important victory of the working-class movement in India). The NREGA has an overriding clause that supersedes the Minimum Wages Act in which wages are not linked to any statutory or "cost of living" norms, and can be notified by the central government, provided the notified wage was above Rs.60.

21. This is also backed up by very detailed instructions in Section Three of the Guidelines.

22. This section is based on several field reports on the NREGA, available at www.righttofoodindia.org/rtowork/ega_latest_activities.html. See appendix 12.1 for details.

23. All government officials who were interviewed by different researchers always admitted it.

24. The procedure for calculating wages has four components: (i) task specification; (ii) soil identification; (iii) out-turn, lift and lead provision; and (iv) measurement. Typically men do the loosening and digging, while women lift the earth on their heads, carry it to some distance (10 metres, 20 metres or even more), lift it to some height (four feet, six feet or even more) and throw it, to return and repeat the process. When work is specified, the labour process is not broken up into the distinct tasks, with earth loosening, digging, carrying, lifting and throwing clubbed as one activity. Similarly, rarely are correct "lift and lead" allowances made. A single productivity norm is specified, unmindful of determinants of ability like weather, age, gender and soil. Work is rarely measured on a weekly basis, which leads to inaccuracies in measurement, since rain and wind can very easily distort the quantum.

25. That this was anticipated is indicated by the very low allocation for the scheme in the Union Budget.

26. It also reflects the inability of the Public Distribution System to successfully address this vital concern.

27. A socially/economically marginalized Hindu caste/tribe, given special privileges by the government. Article 341 of the Indian Constitution provides that the president may, with respect to any state or union territory, specify

the castes, races or tribes, or parts of, or groups within castes, races or tribes which shall for the purposes of the constitution be deemed to be SCs in relation to that state or union territory. Article 342 similarly provides for specification of tribes or tribal communities, or parts of, or groups within tribes or tribal communities which are deemed for the purposes of the constitution to be STs in relation to the various states and territories. In pursuance of these provisions, the list of SCs and/or STs are notified for each state and union territory and are valid only within the jurisdiction of that state or union territory and not outside.

28. A centre under the ICDS Scheme for childcare and supplementary nutrition for pre- and post-natal mothers and preschool children.
29. SCs in Tamil Nadu complained that the upper-caste *Sarpanch* did not inform them when the registration started and the photographs were taken. They only found out when they saw the women from upper-caste landed households dressed in their fineries go out together towards the school building, which is in the heart of the main village. They then demanded to be photographed too, but had to wait till the upper-caste households were photographed. After the upper castes were photographed, however, the photographer left! Not once had these upper-caste and landed persons worked in earth works under the Food for Work Programme (FFWP) or the Jawahar Rozgar Yojana (JRY).
30. Elected president of the *Gram Panchayat*.
31. The term can be literally translated as "husband-member" and implies that the husband usurps the powers of his wife (who is the elected representative), acting by proxy on her behalf.
32. An assistant at the worksite, whose wages come from the scheme, and who possesses minimal technical skills and has the responsibility of supervision, maintenance of attendance and wage records, measurement of output and so on.

# REFERENCES

Acharya, S. 2004a. "Bad ideas are winning." *Business Standard*, Kolkata, 28 December. www.business-standard.com, accessed in December 2007.
———. 2004b. "Guaranteeing jobs or fiscal crisis?" *Business Standard*, Kolkata, 30 November. www.businesstandard.com, accessed in December 2007.
Aiyar, S. Swaminathan. 2005. "Poverty reduction by helicopter." *Times of India*, New Delhi, 14 February. www.timesofindia.indiatimes.com/articleshow, accessed in December 2007.
Bhaduri, A. 2005. "First priority: Guarantee employment and the right to information." *Economic and Political Weekly*, Mumbai, 22 January, Vol. 40, No. 4, pp. 267–268.
———. 2004. "Guaranteeing employment." *The Hindu*, New Delhi, 27 December. www.hindu.com, accessed in December 2007.
Bhalla, S. Surjit. 2005. "Ten lies and an act: III." *Business Standard*, Kolkata, 8 January, p. 6.
———. 2004. "Ten lies and an act: I & II." *Business Standard*, Kolkata, 25–26 December, p. 6.
Debroy, B. 2005. "Jobs, not the government's job." *The Indian Express*, New Delhi, 13 October. www.indianexpress.com, accessed in December 2007.
———. 2004. "The Rs. 208,000 crore riddle." *The Indian Express*, New Delhi, 23 October. www.indianexpress.com, accessed in December 2007.

Dhavan, R. 2005. "The case for employment guarantee." *The Hindu*, New Delhi, 21 January. www.hinduonnet.com, accessed in December 2007.

Drèze, J. 2005a. "Time to clean up." *Times of India*, New Delhi, 13 August. http:// timesofindia.indiatimes.com/articleshow/1199545.cms, accessed in December 2007.

———. 2005b. "Totally off target." *Times of India*, New Delhi, 12 August. www. righttofoodindia.org/data/dreze12aug-discontents.doc, accessed in December 2007.

———. 2004. *Financial Implications of an Employment Guarantee Act: Preliminary Estimates*. Note prepared for the National Advisory Council, Government of India, New Delhi, 15 August. http://nac.nic.in/communication/Financial-REGA.pdf, accessed in December 2007.

Ghosh, J. 2004. *How to Pay for the Employment Guarantee*. 15 October. www. macroscan.com, accessed in December 2007.

———. 1999a. "Macroeconomic trends and female employment: India in the Asian context." In T.S Papola and A.N. Sharma (eds.), *Gender and Employment in India*. Vikas Publishing House, New Delhi.

———. 1999b. *Trends in Economic Participation and Poverty of Women in the Asia-Pacific Region*. Paper written for the United Nations Economic and Social Commission for Asia and the Pacific (ESCAP), Bangkok.

Goetz, A. 1996. *Local Heroes: Patterns of Field Worker Discretion in Implementing GAD Policy in Bangladesh*. IDS Discussion Paper 358, Institute of Development Studies, Brighton.

Goldblatt, B. 2005. "Gender and social assistance in the first decade of democracy: A case study of South Africa's child support grant." *Politikon*, Vol. 32, No. 2, pp. 239–257.

Gopal, K.S. 2005. *Moving to Substance on the Employment Guarantee Bill*. Note prepared for a Seminar at the Centre for Environmental Concerns, Hyderabad.

Gupta, S. 2005. *Indian Agriculture and Rural Areas in Crises under Neo-Liberal Policy*. Working Paper, Institute for Human Development, New Delhi.

Himanshu. 2007. "Wages and work in rural India: Sources, trends and comparability." *Indian Journal of Labour Economics*, April, New Delhi, pp. 110–121.

Jain, L.C. 2005. "Grassroots guarantee for employment." *The Hindu*, New Delhi, 24 February. www.hinduonnet.com, accessed in December 2007.

Joshi, A. 2005. "For effective employment guarantee." *The Hindu*, New Delhi, 8 February. www.hinduonnet.com, accessed in December 2007.

Karat, B. 2005. "Towards implementing the Rural Employment Guarantee Act." *People's Democracy*, New Delhi, Vol. XXIX, No. 42, 16 October. http://pd.cpim.org/2005/1016/10162005_brinda.htm, accessed in December 2007.

———. 2004. *No Jobs Ahead: Dilution in Employment Guarantee*. 10 December. www.timesofindia.indiatimes.com, accessed in December 2007.

Molyneux, M. 1985. "Mobilization without emancipation? Women's interests, the state, and revolution in Nicaragua." Feminist Studies, Vol. 11, No. 2, pp. 227–254.

Papola, T.S. 2005. "A universal programme is feasible." *Economic and Political Weekly*, Mumbai, 12 February, Vol. 40, No. 7, pp. 594–598.

Patnaik, Ila. 2005. "Sincere about job guarantee? Give up subsidies you milk." *Indian Express*, New Delhi, 9 December. www.indianexpress.com, accessed in December 2007.

Patnaik, Prabhat. 2005. *On the Need for Providing Employment Guarantee*. www.macroscan.com, accessed in December 2007.

Patnaik, Utsa. 2004. *The Republic of Hunger*. Safdar Hashmi Memorial Trust, New Delhi.

Roy, A. and N. Dey. 2005. "Guaranteeing action for employment." *The Hindu*, New Delhi, 15 August. www.hindu.com/2005/08/15/stories/2005081501721000. htm, accessed in December 2007.

Roy, B. 2005. "100 days that will change India." *The Indian Express*, New Delhi, 5 January. www.indianexpress.com, accessed in December 2007.

Sawant, S.D., V. Daptardar and S. Mhatre. 2002. "Capital formation and growth in agriculture: Neglected aspects and dimensions." *Economic and Political Weekly*, Mumbai, Vol. 37, No. 11, pp. 1068–1072.

Sen, Abhijit. 2002. "Agriculture, employment and poverty: Recent trends in rural India." In V.K. Ramachandran and M. Swaminathan (eds.), *Agrarian Studies: Essays on Agrarian Relations in Less Developed Countries*. Tulika, New Delhi.

Sen, Amartya. 2005. *India: Large and Small*. www.planningcommission.nic.in, accessed in December 2007.

Shah, M. 2005. "Saving the Employment Guarantee Act." *Economic and Political Weekly*, Mumbai, 12 February, Vol. 40, No. 7, pp. 599–602.

United Progressive Alliance. 2004. *Common Minimum Programme of the Government of India*. United Progressive Alliance, New Delhi.

Vaidyanathan, A. 2005a. "Need for involvement of states." *Economic and Political Weekly*, Mumbai, 13 August, pp. 1735–1741.

———. 2005b. "Panchayats and employment guarantee." *The Hindu*, New Delhi, 15 February. www.hindu.com/2005/02/15/stories/2005021505211000.htm, accessed in December 2007.

Vijayshankar, P. and C. Rammanohar Reddy. 2004. "Making employment guarantee a reality." In *Seminar, No. 541, New Priorities: A Symposium on a Social Agenda for India*, September. http://www.righttofoodindia.org/rtowork/ega_articles.html, accessed in December 2007.

# Contributors

**Martha Alter Chen** is a Lecturer in Public Policy at the Harvard Kennedy School and International Coordinator of the global research-policy-action network Women in Informal Employment: Globalizing and Organizing (WIEGO). An experienced development practitioner and scholar, her areas of specialization are employment, gender and poverty. Dr. Chen is the author of many books including *Perpetual Mourning: Widowhood in Rural India* and *Progress of the World's Women 2005: Women, Work, and Poverty*. Before joining Harvard University in 1987, she had two decades of resident experience in Bangladesh working with the large NGO BRAC and in India where she served as field representative of Oxfam America for India and Bangladesh. Dr. Chen received a PhD in South Asia Regional Studies from the University of Pennsylvania.

**Carmen Diana Deere** is Director of the Center for Latin American Studies and Professor of Food and Resource Economics and Latin American Studies at the University of Florida. She is a past President of the Latin American Studies Association (LASA) and of the New England Council of Latin American Studies (NECLAS) and serves on numerous editorial boards, including *World Development* and *Feminist Economics*. Her primary areas of research are land policy and agrarian reform, rural social movements and gender issues in Latin American agricultural development. She is the co-author of *Empowering Women: Land and Property Rights in Latin America* (University of Pittsburgh Press, 2001), winner of LASA's Bryce Wood Book Award and NECLAS's Best Book Award. She is the co-editor of a special issue of *Feminist Economics* (2006) on Women and the Distribution of Wealth, and is currently co-editing a volume on the rural social movements in Latin America.

**Jayati Ghosh** is Professor of Economics at the Centre for Economic Studies and Planning, School of Social Sciences, Jawaharlal Nehru University, New Delhi. She was born in 1955 and educated at Delhi University, Jawaharlal Nehru University and the University of Cambridge, England, where she obtained her PhD in 1983. In addition to authoring numerous academic books and articles, she is a regular columnist for several newspapers in India. Since 2002 she has been the Executive Secretary of International Development Economics Associates (IDEAS), an international network of heterodox development economists (www. networkideas.org). Her current research interests include globalization, international trade and finance, employment patterns in developing countries, macroeconomic policy and issues related to gender and development. Recent books include *Work and Well Being in the Age of Finance* (Tulika Books, New Delhi); *The Market That Failed: Neoliberal Economic Reforms in India* (Leftword Books, New Delhi); *Tracking the Macroeconomy* (ICFAI University Press, Hyderabad) and the forthcoming *A Decade After: Recovery and Adjustment After the Asian Crisis* (Tulika Books, New Delhi).

**Mercedes González de la Rocha** is a Mexican social anthropologist who studied in Mexico (BA, Universidad Iberoamericana) and the United Kingdom (MA and PhD, University of Manchester). She combines research and teaching activities in her work at CIESAS (*Centro de Investigaciones y Estudios Superiores en Antropología Social*). She has been a visiting scholar and professor at various universities in the United States, England, Colombia and Nicaragua. She has instructed undergraduates and graduate students. Her research interests, besides household economy and dynamics, include labour markets and social policy programmes. From 1999 to 2005, she co-directed (with Agustín Escobar) the yearly qualitative evaluations of *Oportunidades* (the former PROGRESA), a human development programme implemented in Mexico to reduce the reproduction of poverty. Since 2005, she acts as Director of the qualitative evaluation of *Oportunidades*. Her most recent book is precisely the result of her ethnographic research on changes produced at the household level by the action of the programme (*Procesos domésticos y vulnerabilidad: perspectives antropológicas de los hogares con Oportunidades*, Publicaciones de la Casa Chata, Mexico, 2006).

**Smita Gupta** is an Economist at the Institute for Human Development since 2000. Her main areas of research are rural employment, public finance, decentralization, agriculture, natural resource economics and tribal issues. She worked on a comparative study of seven states on Empowering Local Governments for UNICEF and has completed a Study on Gender Issues in the People's Plan Campaign in Kerala. She undertook two studies for the Planning Commission on Water Policy in Chhattisgarh and the Manipur State Development Report. She has a number of articles on the nature of Federalism and Fiscal Policy, the Agrarian Crisis, etc. She has worked on pro-people legislations with mass organizations and Parliamentarians. She is a part of the campaign for an effective National Rural Employment Guarantee Scheme and is working with the

All India Democratic Women's Association in several states to monitor and evaluate the NREGS with special focus on gender issues.

**Cecile Jackson** is a Professor in Development Studies at the School of Development Studies, University of East Anglia. Her past research has focused on gender analysis of environmental change, poverty and well-being, and reproduction, as well as embodiment and gender divisions of labour. Her recent research is centred on epistemologies and methods for multidisciplinary gendered research, and on conjugality, and she has conducted a study of marriage and well-being in eastern Uganda using multiple methods, including experimental economics.

**Agustín Escobar Latapí** is Professor at CIESAS Occidente. He holds a PhD in Sociology from the University of Manchester. He acted as regional director (2001–2003). He is a member of the National System of Researchers (SNI, level III); winner of the National Award for Scientific Research of the Mexican Academy of Sciences, in 1994, together with Mercedes González de la Rocha; member of the Academy since 1991. His main interests include international migration and Mexican social policy. He has directed the external qualitative evaluation of the PROGRESA–*Oportunidades* programme, and his current interest in migration focuses on the migration of the poor, and the impact of migration on poverty and inequality in Mexico. He has advised the Mexican Social Development Ministry on the design of qualitative evaluations in general. In February, 2006, he was elected to the National Social Policy Evaluation Council.

**Ching Kwan Lee** is Associate Professor of Sociology at the University of Michigan. She is author of *Against the Law: Labor Protests in China's Rustbelt and Sunbelt* (California, 2007) and *Gender and the South China Miracle: Two Worlds of Factory Women* (California, 1998). Her edited books include *Working in China: Ethnographies of Labor and Workplace Transformation* (Routledge, 2007) and *Reenvisioning the Chinese Revolution: Politics and Poetics of Collective Memories in Reform China* (Woodrow Wilson Center Press and Stanford University Press, 2007). She is currently working on two projects: the politics of citizenship rights in China and Chinese investments in Africa.

**Nitya Rao** is Senior Lecturer at the School of Development Studies, University of East Anglia, United Kingdom. She has worked extensively in the field of women's organization, livelihoods and literacy for over two decades, as a practitioner, trainer, researcher and policy advocate. Her current research interests include gendered changes in land and agrarian relations, food security and livelihood strategies, equity issues in education policies and people's movements. She has published in several international and national journals.

**Shahra Razavi** is Research Coordinator at the United Nations Research Institute for Social Development (UNRISD), where she oversees the Institute's Programme on Gender and Development. She has conceptualized and coordinated global research projects in a number of areas, including on Agrarian Change, Gender and Land Rights; Gender and Social Policy; and The Political and Social Economy of Care. Her recent books include *Gender and Social Policy in a Global Context: Uncovering the Gendered Structure of "the Social"*, edited with Shireen Hassim (Palgrave, 2006); *Agrarian Change, Gender and Land Rights*, special issue of *Journal of Agrarian Change* (Blackwell, 2003); *Gender Justice, Development and Rights*, edited with Maxine Molyneux (Oxford University Press, 2002). In 2004–2005, she coordinated the preparation of an UNRISD flagship report, *Gender Equality: Striving for Justice in an Unequal World*, which was the Institute's contribution to the "Beijing+10" process.

**Constanza Tabbush** is a PhD student at the Institute for the Study of the Americas at the University of London. She has worked in London, Geneva and Buenos Aires on migrant women in the United Kingdom; gender and development; and violence and public policy issues. Her research interests are: gender, social policy, violence and development, and Latin America, especially Argentina and Chile. She has authored *Civil Society and UN Conferences: A Literature Review*, UNRISD Programme on Civil Society and Social Movements, Paper No. 17 (UNRISD, Geneva, 2005).

**Dzodzi Tsikata** is a Senior Research Fellow at the Institute of Statistical, Social and Economic Research (ISSER) and the Deputy Head of the Centre for Gender Studies and Advocacy (CEGENSA) at the University of Ghana. Her research interests are in the areas of gender and livelihoods, gender and development policy and practice and the politics of land tenure reforms. She is currently involved in research on intergenerational change in women's everyday lives, with special reference to work under the auspices of the Pathways to Women's Empowerment Research Consortium. She is also the principal researcher in a study on women in domestic work and the banking sector in Ghana supported by the IDRC. She is the author of the book *Living in the Shadow of the Large Dams: Long Term Responses of Downstream and Lakeside Communities of Ghana's Volta River Project* (Brill, 2006).

**Ann Whitehead** is Professor of Anthropology at the University of Sussex and a contributor to foundational debates on feminist engagement with development and on theorizing gender. Building on ethnographic research on agrarian transformation and changes in rural social and gender relations in Northern Ghana, much of her work centres on the impact of economic processes on gender relations and analysing development policy discourses on gender and economic change.

**Nicola Yeates** is Senior Lecturer in Social Policy at The Open University, Milton Keynes. Her research focuses on the intersections between social policy, international migration and globalization processes and she has published widely on these issues, including *Globalisation and Social Policy* (Sage, 2001); "Globalization and social policy: From global neoliberal hegemony to global political pluralism", *Global Social Policy*, Vol. 2, No. 1 (Sage, 2002); "Global Care Chains: Critical reflections and lines of enquiry", *International Feminist Journal of Politics*, Vol. 6, No. 3 (2004); "Changing places: Ireland in the international division of labour", *Translocations: The Irish Migration, Race and Social Transformation Review*, Vol. 1, No. 1 (2006). Her forthcoming publications include *Globalising Care Economies, Migrating Workers: Explorations in Global Care Chains* (Palgrave, 2008); *Understanding Global Social Policy* (The Policy Press, 2008); and *Social Justice: Welfare, Crime and Society* (with J. Newman, Open University Press, 2008). She is co-editor of *Global Social Policy* (Sage).

# Index

Page numbers in *italics* denote a table/illustration